Contributions to Financial Econometrics

Contributions to Financial Econometrics
Theoretical and Practical Issues

EDITED BY

Michael McAleer and Les Oxley

Blackwell
Publishing

© 2002 by Blackwell Publishing Ltd
a Blackwell Publishing company

First published as a special issue of *Journal of Economic Surveys*, 2002

Editorial Offices:
9600 Garsington Road, Oxford OX4 2DQ, UK
Tel: +44 (0)1865 776868
350 Main Street, Malden, MA 02148-5018, USA
Tel: +1 781 388 8250
Iowa State University Press, a Blackwell Publishing company, 2121 S. State Avenue, Ames, Iowa
50014-8300, USA
Tel: +1 515 292 0140
Blackwell Munksgaard, Nørre Søgade 35, PO Box 2148, Copenhagen, DK-1016, Denmark
Tel: +45 77 33 33 33
Blackwell Publishing Asia, 54 University Street, Carlton, Victoria 3053, Australia
Tel: +61 (0)3 347 0300
Blackwell Verlag, Kurfürstendamm 57, 10707 Berlin, Germany
Tel: +49 (0)30 32 79 060
Blackwell Publishing, 10, rue Casimir Delavigne, 75006 Paris, France
Tel: +331 5310 3310

First published 2002 by Blackwell Publishing Ltd
Reprinted 2004

Library of Congress Cataloging-in-Publication Data has been applied for

ISBN 1-405-10743-X

A catalogue record for this title is available from the British Library.

Typeset by Mathematical Composition Setters Ltd, Salisbury, Wiltshire

For further information on
Blackwell Publishing visit our website:
www.blackwellpublishing.com

CONTENTS

Chapter 1

THE ECONOMETRICS
OF FINANCIAL TIME SERIES

Michael McAleer

University of Western Australia

Les Oxley

University of Canterbury

1. Introduction

The publication in 1982 of 'Autoregressive Conditional Heteroskedasticity, with Estimates of the Variance of United Kingdom Inflation' by Rob Engle contributed substantially to the birth of the new field of 'financial econometrics'. Few papers before or since have surpassed this seminal article in terms of measured citations, with references to Durbin and Watson's DW test possibly being one instance that actually surpasses citations to Engle's paper. Understandably, Engle's development of ARCH is widely regarded as one of the five most important papers in econometrics over the last three decades (see Oxley (2000).

Interestingly, Engle's (1995, p. xi) original intention in developing ARCH was to 'breathe new life into the macroeconometrics of rational expectations'. In particular, taking the traditional approach of mapping uncertainty into variance, he sought to model the response of agents to uncertain outcomes. A constant variance assumption created an identification problem which was solved by specifying the variance to change over time. This time-varying specification allowed the likelihood function to be decomposed into its conditional densities and gave birth to the ARCH family of conditionally heteroscedastic processes.

The original ARCH paper spawned an enormous family of direct descendants, including generalised ARCH (GARCH), GARCH-M, log-ARCH, EGARCH, GJR-GARCH, GQ-ARCH, general GARCH, asymmetric power GARCH, IGARCH, FIGARCH, HYGARCH, FIEGARCH, FIAPARCH, NARCH, TARCH, TGARCH, STAR-GARCH, STAR-STGARCH, VS-GARCH, BEKK-GARCH, MGARCH, CC-MGARCH, and VC-MGARCH, as well as the more computationally demanding new generation of stochastic volatility siblings. These models might not have been so easily estimated, and subsequently popularised, without the creative simplicity inherent in the ARCH model.

It is worth noting the point raised by Bera and Higgins (1993, p. 305), that 'applications (typically) lag theoretical developments, but Engle's original ARCH model and its various generalisations have been applied to numerous economic and financial data, while it has seen relatively fewer theoretical advancements'. This is possibly a more important issue today than previously, given the rate of proliferation of ARCH-based offsprings. The recent theoretical results established by, among others, Ling and McAleer (2002a,b) and Li, Ling and McAleer (chapter 2 in this volume), regarding the structural conditions for stationarity and the existence of moments, and the statistical conditions for consistency and asymptotic normality of the (quasi) maximum likelihood estimators, for the ARMA-GARCH and asymmetric GARCH models, could be viewed as a cautionary tale of the 'empirical tail wagging the theoretical dog'. In particular, the huge proliferation of *empirically-driven* extensions of the original ARCH model has generally not been followed by carefully derived theoretical foundations.

In *Contributions to Financial Econometrics: Theoretical and Practical Issues*, we are most fortunate to be able to present five state-of-the-art survey papers on time series econometrics, and a recent financial econometrics software package that is able to estimate many of the models reviewed in the surveys. The papers are not only surveys of recent developments in the field, they are also scholarly contributions to the literature. Commencing with a survey of recent theoretical developments for time series models with GARCH errors (Li, Ling and McAleer), the contributions examine the bootstrapping of financial time series (Ruiz and Pascual), recent developments in futures hedging (Lien and Tse), measures of fit for rational expectations models (Engsted), asset pricing with observable stochastic discount factors (Smith and Wickens), and a financial time series econometric software package for estimating and forecasting ARCH models (Laurent and Peters). Each of these papers has made a concerted attempt to blend theoretical and empirical issues to enable theoreticians and practitioners alike to appreciate the most recent developments in these fields.

Given Engle's motivation for writing his original paper, it is particularly fitting that this volume should include a contribution on the current state of research in rational expectations models. It is also entirely fitting that investigating the theoretical properties of the ARCH and GARCH family of conditional volatility models is specifically mentioned and discussed in each of the other five contributions to the volume. A more detailed introduction and overview to these contributions is given below.

2. Overview

The first survey paper by W. K. Li (University of Hong Kong), Shiqing Ling (Hong Kong University of Science and Technology) and Michael McAleer (University of Western Australia) is 'Some Recent Theoretical Results for Time Series Models with GARCH Errors'. Following the pathbreaking work on developing the autoregressive conditional heteroscedasticity (ARCH) model by Engle (1982), which is clearly one of the most widely-cited papers in econometrics over the last few decades, the area of time-varying conditional volatility has had many theoretical contributions in recent years. There have been many extensions of ARCH, including: the highly popular symmetric and asymmetric (namely, GJR) GARCH; logarithmic, exponential, quadratic, power and other non-linear representations; fractional, threshold and smooth transition variants; and multivariate versions, including constant and variable dynamic correlation GARCH models, among many others. Some of these models, particularly ARCH and GARCH, have beeen analysed in detail with respect to the regularity (or structural) conditions underlying the strict stationarity and ergodicity of the process, the necessary and sufficient conditions for the existence of moments, and the sufficient conditions for the (typically) least squares, quasi-maximum likelihood or adaptive estimators to be consistent and asymptotic normal. The authors review some of the more recent and important theoretical results for time-varying conditional volatility models with (symmetric) GARCH errors. In view of the straightforward analytical conditions that have been derived, the survey is directed towards practitioners. Starting with the simple univariate ARCH model and proceeding to the multivariate GARCH model, some structural and statistical results for stationary and non-stationary ARMA-GARCH models are summarised. Various new ARCH-type models, including double threshold ARCH and GARCH, fractional ARIMA, CHARMA, and a class of symmetric vector ARMA-GARCH, are also reviewed. Some new and powerful unit root tests based on quasi-maximum likelihood estimators are also discussed and compared with existing procedures.

Esther Ruiz (Universidad Carlos III de Madrid) and Lorenzo Pascual (Universidad Carlos III de Madrid) follow a theoretical contribution by considering 'Bootstrapping Financial Time Series'. As time series of high frequency financial returns are often characterized by fat-tailed non-Gaussian distributions (that is, volatility clustering and excess kurtosis), usually of unknown form, bootstrap techniques are especially suited for empirical analysis in such cases. However, when bootstrap procedures are applied to financial data, it must be realised that, although returns are usually serially uncorrelated, they are not independent. The volatility of returns evolves over time, so that squared returns are dependent. There are two main types of bootstrap methods designed to replicate this dynamic dependence: (i) it is possible to use parametric bootstrap procedures, based on resampling from the estimated residuals of a conditionally heterocedastic model; (ii) non-parametric bootstrapping can be performed without assuming a particular model for returns. This paper critically reviews the application of both bootstrap methods for the empirical analysis of financial time series data, with an emphasis on inference and prediction. Several empirical and simulated examples are presented to illustrate these methods. The main applications can be classified into methods that try to estimate the sample distribution of a given statistic and methods to estimate the density of returns. In the first group, the main application analyzes the predictive power of technical trading rules. Within the second class, the main application obtains measures of the Value at Risk (VaR) of a given asset. One of the main problems encountered in the surveyed papers is that quite a few apply the bootstrap procedure incorrectly by resampling directly from the raw returns. Finally, the authors note that there are very few results regarding the theoretical properties of bootstrap methods in the context of non-linear models and, in particular, for heterocedastic models, which are of particular relevance in the analysis of financial returns.

'Some Recent Developments in Futures Hedging' by Donald Lien (University of Texas at San Antonio) and Y. K. Tse (Singapore Management University) reviews some recent developments in the literature of futures hedging. It is assumed that hedgers are faced with a given spot position to hedge, so that the problem of hedging quantity uncertainty is not discussed. Various theories of futures hedging are discussed. An optimal hedge strategy is traditionally based on the expected-utility maximization paradigm, a simplification of which leads to the minimum-variance criterion. Although this paradigm is quite well accepted, alternative approaches have been proposed, particularly the questionable use of variance as a measure of risk. It is argued that as far as hedging is concerned, a one-sided measure such as the downside risk is more relevant, which leads to the use of lower partial moments as an alternative criterion to variance. In addition, the application of the theories of stochastic dominance has resolved some of the restrictions in the expected-utility maximization framework. Given the parallel developments in the stochastic dominance literature, the mean-Gini approach also facilitates the implementation of a hedge strategy. All of these alternative theories are discussed and compared. At the empirical level, research on futures hedging has benefited from developments in the econometrics literature. As more has become known about the statistical properties of financial time series, more sophisticated estimation methods have been proposed. For example, the classical regression method, which assumes a time-invariant hedge ratio, has been replaced by time-varying estimates. The cointegration literature suggests that futures and spot prices are cointegrated and that better estimates can be obtained by exploring this relationship. Moreover, the conditional volatility literature has provided many models to capture the time-varying variance and covariance of the spot and futures prices. Finally, the use of nonparametric methods has freed researchers from making assumptions that may not be justifiable, such as normality in asset returns.

Tom Engsted (Aarhus School of Business) surveys the literature on econometric time series methods and approaches for evaluating the fit of rational expectations models in 'Measures of Fit for Rational Expectations Models'. Since the inception of rational expectations econometrics in the 1970s, the standard approach to estimate and formally test rational expectations models has been either: (i) the Generalized Method of Moments (GMM) and its associated J-test; or (ii) the full-information methodology with explicit specification of stochastic processes for the forcing variables and derivation and testing of the implied cross-equation restrictions. However, this approach has been criticized because formal statistical tests of over identifying restrictions are not very informative about the accuracy of the underlying model. A model that is statistically rejected at a 5% level may be able to explain important aspects of the data, just as a model that is not statistically rejected may not have much economic content. The author describes and illustrates three alternatives for evaluating rational expectations models that have been suggested in the literature as a response to this criticism: the Campbell-Shiller, Durlauf-Hall, and Hansen-Jagannathan approaches. A characteristic feature of these methods is that they are much less focused on formal statistical testing, but examine the degree to which a particular model provides a useful approximation to reality. All three methods have become very popular and widely used in empirical research. The author summarizes the many empirical studies that have used these methods in areas such as stock price determination and asset pricing, interest rates and the term structure, exchange rate determination, consumption and saving, the balance of payments, tax-smoothing, hyperinflation, and linear quadratic adjustment cost models of inventories, labour demand, and money demand. An illustration of the methods using data from the Danish stock market is also provided. The survey pays particular attention to the mean-nonstationarity that characterizes many financial and macroeconomic time series.

Asset pricing is analysed by P. N. Smith (University of York) and M. R. Wickens (University of York) in 'Asset Pricing With Observable Stochastic Discount Factors'. The stochastic discount factor (SDF) model is rapidly emerging as the most general and convenient way to price assets. By a suitable specification of the discount factor, the SDF model can be shown to encompass most of the theories currently in use, including the capital asset pricing model (CAPM), the general equilibrium consumption-based intertemporal CAPM, and the Black-Scholes theorem for pricing options. The SDF model has been based on the use of single and multiple factors, and on latent and observed factors. In most situations, and particularly for the term structure, single factor models are inappropriate, while latent variables require the somewhat arbitrary specification of generating processes, which can also be difficult to interpret. Focusing primarily on the absolute rather than relative approach to asset pricing, the authors survey the principal different implementations of the SDF model for FOREX, equity and bonds. They propose a new approach, which is based on the use of multiple factors that are observable, and on modelling the joint distribution of excess returns and the factors using a multivariate GARCH-in-mean process. In comparison, much of the research to date that has made explicit use of the SDF model has been based on latent factors. The authors argue that, in general, single equation and VAR models, although widely used in empirical finance, are inappropriate as they do not satisfy the no-arbitrage condition. As risk premia arise from conditional covariation between the returns and factors, both a multivariate context and the use of conditional covariances in the conditional mean are essential. The authors explain how apparent exceptions, such as the CIR and Vasicek models, meet these requirements, but at a price. The new approach is explained, its implementation is discussed, and some empirical evidence is presented. For purposes of comparison, the paper also includes recent evidence using more traditional approaches.

In the final contribution, which is not a standard survey paper, 'G@RCH 2.2: An Ox Package for Estimating and Forecasting Various ARCH Models', Sebastien Laurent (Universite de Liege, Universite Catholique de Louvain and Maastricht University) and Jean-Philippe Peters (Universite de Liege) discuss and document G@RCH 2.2, an Ox package for estimating and forecasting various univariate ARCH-type models. There is a focus on asymmetric and long-memory models as the package provides GARCH, EGARCH, GJR, APARCH, IGARCH, FIGARCH, HYGARCH, FIEGARCH and FIAPARCH specifications of the conditional variance, and an AR(FI)MA specification of the conditional mean. Two versions of this package are available, namely a menu-driven interface for OxPack users (the 'Full' version) and a simple code version for Ox console users (the 'Light' version). These models can be estimated by an approximate (quasi) maximum likelihood method under four different assumptions: normal, Student-t, GED, or skewed Student-t errors. In addition, estimated parameters can be bounded between or fixed at some predefined values, while positivity constraints and conditions for the existence of moments can be checked for several of the models. Explanatory variables can enter both the conditional mean and the conditional variance equations. Moreover, h-step-ahead forecasts of both the conditional mean and the conditional variance are available, as well as a number of mispecification tests and various graphical possibilities. The authors propose an overview of the features of the package, with a presentation of the different specifications of the conditional mean and conditional variance. Further explanations are given about the estimation methods. Measures of the accuracy of the procedures are presented for both short and long memory models. The GARCH features provided by the G@RCH package are compared with those of nine other well-known econometric software packages. Finally, a practical application of G@RCH 2.2 using the CAC40 stock index is provided and presented as a short, accessible and helpful user guide.

3. Epilogue

For researchers who are intending to undertake applied research in financial econometrics, it is important to reflect upon a number of questions: (i) Which theoretical model is to be chosen, and why? (ii) What restrictions are to be imposed or tested? (iii) Which hypotheses are to be tested, and why? (iv) What method of estimation is to be used? (v) What are the theoretical properties of the estimation method used? and (vi) Which statistical and econometric softwares are to be used, and how accurate and efficient are they? If the intending researcher does not know the answers to some or all of these questions, the papers presented in this volume will provide state-of-the-art guidance as to how to proceed. A failure to address these issues seriously will lead to the presentation of unconvincing empirical results, as well as to the criticism of 'measurement without (structural, statistical and econometric) theory'.

Acknowledgements

The first author wishes to acknowledge the financial support of an Australian Research Council Discovery Grant, and the second author the Royal Society of New Zealand, Marsden Fund.

References

Bera, A. L. and Higgins, M. L. (1993) On ARCH models: Properties, estimation and testing, *Journal of Economic Surveys*, 7, 305–66. Reprinted as chapter 8 in Oxley, L., *et al.* (eds) (1995), *Surveys in Econometrics*, Blackwell: Oxford, 215–272.

Engle, R. F. (1982) Autoregressive conditional heteroskedasticity with estimates of the variance of United Kingdom inflation, *Econometrica*, 50, 987–1007.

Engle, R. F. (ed.) (1995) *ARCH: Selected Readings*, Oxford University Press: Oxford.

Ling, S. and McAleer, M. (2002a), Stationarity and the existence of moments of a family of GARCH processes, *Journal of Econometrics*, 106, 109–117.

Ling, S. and McAleer, M. (2002b), Necessary and sufficient moment conditions for the GARCH(r,s) and asymmetric power GARCH(r,s) models, *Econometric Theory*, 18, 722–729.

Oxley, L. (2000) The top 10 papers in econometrics: 1980–2000, Invited Paper to the *New Zealand Statistical Society*, Christchurch, September.

Chapter 2

RECENT THEORETICAL RESULTS
FOR TIME SERIES MODELS
WITH GARCH ERRORS

W. K. Li

University of Hong Kong

Shiqing Ling

Hong Kong University of Science and Technology

Michael McAleer

University of Western Australia

1. Introduction

A primary feature of the autoregressive conditional heteroscedasticity (ARCH) model, as developed by Engle (1982), is that the conditional variances change over time. Following the seminal idea, numerous models incorporating this feature have been proposed. Among these models, Bollerslev's (1986) generalized ARCH (GARCH) model is certainly the most popular and successful because it is easy to estimate and interpret by analogy with the autoregressive moving average (ARMA) time series model. Analyzing financial and economic time series data with ARCH and GARCH models has become very common in empirical research, with a huge literature having been established. Several excellent surveys on ARCH/GARCH models are available, such as Bollerslev, Chou and Kroner (1992), Bollerslev, Engle and Nelson (1994), and Bera and Higgins (1993). More recently, the Stochastic Volatility model of Taylor (1986) offers an alternative to GARCH. Stochastic Volatility models will not be discussed in this paper and interested readers are referred to the excellent review by Shephard (1996). In a series of papers, Nelson has made important contributions to the filtering theory of ARCH processes. His work has been nicely summarized by Ross (1996), and hence will not be the focus of attention in this paper. Gourieroux (1997) provides a summary of some earlier results on GARCH models.

The aim of this paper is to provide a review of some recent theoretical results for time series models with ARCH/GARCH errors, and is directed towards practitioners. The plan of the paper is as follows. We begin with the simple ARCH model in Section 2 and proceed to the GARCH model in Section 3. The stationary ARMA-GARCH model is considered in Section 4, and its nonstationary counterpart in Section 5. Finally, we review some results for other ARCH-type models, including double threshold ARCH, ARFIMA-GARCH, CHARMA, and vector ARMA-GARCH, in Section 6. Concluding marks are given in Section 7.

2. ARCH models

Engle's (1982) ARCH (r) model can be defined as follows:

$$\varepsilon_t = \eta_t h_t^{1/2}, \qquad h_t = \alpha_0 + \alpha_1 \varepsilon_{t-1}^2 + \cdots + \alpha_r \varepsilon_{t-r}^2, \tag{2.1}$$

where $\alpha_0 > 0$, $\alpha_i \geqslant 0$ ($i = 1, ..., r$) are sufficient for $h_t > 0$ and the η_t are a sequence of independently and identically distributed (i.i.d.) random variables with zero mean and unit variance. Denote by $\mathcal{F}_t$ the σ-field generated by $\{\eta_t, \eta_{t-1}, ...\}$. Then $E(\varepsilon_t^2 \mid \mathcal{F}_{t-1}) = h_t$, that is, the conditional variance of the process ε_t varies over time instead of being constant, as in traditional time series analysis.

2.1. *Basic properties*

When a new time series model is proposed, a basic question concerns the conditions under which the model will be stationary. Engle (1982) showed that ε_t is second-order stationary (i.e. $E\varepsilon_t^2 < \infty$) if and only if all the roots of

$$z^r - \sum_{i=1}^{r} \alpha_i z^{r-1} = 0 \tag{2.2}$$

are outside the unit circle. To prove this result, Engle (1982) assumed that ε_t starts infinitely far in the past with finite variance, which is impossible to verify in practice. Using a different method, Milhøj (1985) avoided Engle's (1982) assumption and showed that ε_t is second-order stationary if and only if

$$\alpha_1 + \cdots + \alpha_r < 1. \tag{2.3}$$

In particular, Milhøj (1985) showed that (2.3) is also a sufficient condition for strict stationarity and ergodicity of ε_t. Since α_i is nonnegative for $i = 1, ..., r$, conditions (2.2) and (2.3) are equivalent by Lemma 2.1 in Ling (1999b).

For the first-order ARCH model, Engle (1982) showed that, if η_t is normal, the $2m$th moment of ε_t exists if and only if

$$\alpha_1^m \prod_{j=1}^{m} (2j - 1) < 1, \tag{2.4}$$

under the assumption that ε_t starts infinitely far in the past with finite $2m$th moment. Without this assumption, Milhøj (1985) obtained the necessary and sufficient condition for the existence of the $2m$th moment of ε_t. When η_t is normal and $r = 1$, Milhøj's condition is the same as (2.4). A unique drawback is that Milhøj's (1985) condition cannot be given an explicit form when $r > 1$ and $m > 2$.

It should be noted that (2.3) is not necessary for the strict stationarity of model (2.1). The necessary and sufficient condition for the strict stationarity of model (2.1) was established by Bougerol and Picard (1992) in terms of the top Lyapunov exponent (see Section 3.1). The regions of strict stationarity are, in general, much larger than those of second-order stationarity. As an illustration, for the first-order ARCH model, ARCH(1), the various conditions under normality are summarized as follows:

			Moments		
Variable	ε_t	Strict stationarity	2nd	4th	8th
Coefficient	α_1	$(0, 3.56214)$	$(0, 1)$	$(0, 0.57735)$	$(0, 0.31239)$

Non-normality reduces the permissible range of the ARCH(1) parameter for the 4th and higher moments. It seems difficult to obtain a closed form expression of strict stationarity in terms of the ARCH(r) parameters for any $r > 1$.

2.2. Sample ACVF and ACF

In time series analysis, the autocovariance function (ACVF) and autocorrelation function (ACF) are important because they usually provide meaningful information about the series. Define the sample ACVF and sample ACF, respectively, by

$$\gamma_{n\varepsilon}(k) = \frac{1}{n} \sum_{t=k+1}^{n} \varepsilon_t \varepsilon_{t-k},$$

$$\rho_{n\varepsilon}(k) = \frac{\gamma_{n,\varepsilon}(k)}{\gamma_{n,\varepsilon}(0)},$$

where n is the sample size and $k \geqslant 0$. Correspondingly, the true values are given by:

$$\gamma_\varepsilon(k) = E(\varepsilon_0 \varepsilon_k),$$

$$\rho_\varepsilon(k) = \frac{\gamma_\varepsilon(k)}{\gamma_\varepsilon(0)}.$$

As the ARCH process ε_t is an uncorrelated white noise sequence, $\gamma_\varepsilon(k) = \rho_\varepsilon(k) = 0$ if $k > 0$. Under the fourth moment condition, Milhøj (1985) showed that $\gamma_{n\varepsilon}(k)$ and $\rho_{n\varepsilon}(k)$ are consistent estimators of $\gamma_\varepsilon(k)$ and $\rho_\varepsilon(k)$, respectively, and $\sqrt{n}\,[\gamma_{n\varepsilon}(k) - \gamma_\varepsilon(k)]$ and $\sqrt{n}\,[\rho_{n\varepsilon}(k) - \rho_\varepsilon(k)]$ are asymptotically normal.

It is natural to ask if Milhøj's results still hold if the fourth moment condition is not satisfied. This is a difficult problem because ARCH processes exhibit a strong heavy-tailed feature when $E\varepsilon_t^4 = \infty$. Using the point process technique, Davis and Mikosch (1998) showed that, if $E\varepsilon_t^2 < \infty$ but $E\varepsilon_t^4 = \infty$, then

$$n^{1-2/q}L(n)^{-2}\gamma_{n\varepsilon}(k) \to_d V_q(k),$$

$$n^{1-2/q}L(n)^{-2}\rho_{n\varepsilon}(k) \to_d \frac{V_q(k)}{E\varepsilon_t^2},$$

where $q \in (2, 4)$ is the unique solution to $E(\alpha_1\eta_t^2)^{q/2} = 1$, $V_q(k)$ is $q/2$-stable in R, and $L(n)$ is some slowly-varying function. From the above results, $\gamma_{n\varepsilon}(k)$ and $\rho_{n\varepsilon}(k)$ are consistent estimators of $\gamma_\varepsilon(k)$ and $\rho_\varepsilon(k)$, respectively, but the convergence rate is slower than the usual $n^{1/2}$. This result is different from those for linear processes with i.i.d. regularly varying noise. Davis and Resnick (1985, 1986) showed that the sample ACF is still asymptotically normal with scaling $n^{1/2}$ if the i.i.d. noise has finite variance but infinite fourth moment.

Furthermore, Davis and Mikosch (1998) showed that, if $E|\varepsilon|^p < \infty$ for $0 < p < 2$ but $E\varepsilon_t^2 = \infty$, then

$$n^{1-2/q}L(n)^{-2}\gamma_{n\varepsilon}(k) \to_d V_q(k),$$

$$\rho_{n\varepsilon}(k) \to_d \frac{V_q(k)}{V_q(0)},$$

where $q \in (0, 2)$. In this case, the estimator of the ACF is inconsistent. This result is quite different from that for linear processes with i.i.d. regularly varying noise, in which the sample ACF converges to the true ACF with a convergence rate greater than $n^{1/2}$ (see Davis and Resnick 1985, 1986).

The sample ACVF and ACF of ε_t^2 have also been investigated by Davis and Mikosch (1998). Although they considered only the first-order ARCH model, their results can be extended to higher-order ARCH models. de Vries (1991) demonstrated that, under certain conditions, GARCH processes can generate realizations that have a stable distribution unconditionally.

2.3. Parameter estimation

The parameters of model (2.1) can be estimated by several methods. The simplest method is the least squares estimator (LSE). First, write model (2.1) as

$$\varepsilon_t^2 = \alpha_0 + \alpha_1\varepsilon_{t-1}^2 + \cdots + \alpha_r\varepsilon_{t-r}^2 + \xi_t, \tag{2.5}$$

where $\xi_t = \varepsilon_t^2 - h_t$ and ξ_t can now be considered as a martingale difference. Let $\delta = (\alpha_0, \alpha_1, ..., \alpha_r)'$ and $\tilde{\varepsilon}_t = (1, \varepsilon_t^2, ..., \varepsilon_{t-r+1}^2)'$. Then the LSE of δ is

$$\hat{\delta} = \left(\sum_{t=2}^n \tilde{\varepsilon}_{t-1}\tilde{\varepsilon}_{t-1}'\right)^{-1}\left(\sum_{t=2}^n \tilde{\varepsilon}_{t-1}\tilde{\varepsilon}_t\right).$$

Weiss (1986) and Pantula (1989) showed that $\hat{\delta}$ is consistent and asymptotically normal. However, their results assume that the 8th moment of ε_t exists, which is a strong condition.

In general, maximum likelihood estimation (MLE) is used to estimate the parameter δ. Given observations ε_t, $t = 1, ..., n$, the conditional log-likelihood can be written as

$$L(\delta) = \sum_{t=1}^{n} l_t, \qquad l_t = -\frac{1}{2}\ln h_t - \frac{1}{2}\frac{\varepsilon_t^2}{h_t}, \tag{2.6}$$

where h_t is treated as a function of ε_t. Assume that $\delta \in \Theta$, a compact subset of R^{r+1}, and that the true value of δ is δ_0. Define

$$\hat{\delta} = \text{argmax}_{\delta \in \Theta} \, L(\delta). \tag{2.7}$$

Since the conditional error η_t is not assumed to be normal, $\hat{\delta}$ is called the quasi-maximum likelihood estimator (QMLE). Under the fourth moment condition, Weiss (1986) and Pantula (1989) showed that the QMLE $\hat{\lambda}$ is consistent and asymptotically normal. Ling and McAleer (2002b) proved that the QMLE of δ is consistent and asymptotically normal under only the second moment condition. It is expected that, when ε_t is strictly stationary but $E\varepsilon_t^2 = \infty$, the QMLE will still be consistent and asymptotically normal. The BHHH algorithm is often used to determine $\hat{\delta}$. However, Mak, Wong and Li (1997) suggested that the BHHH algorithm has a convergence problem if the starting values are not sufficiently close to the solutions and that a full Newton–Raphson procedure should instead be used.

When η_t is not normal, the QMLE is not efficient, that is, its asymptotic covariance matrix is not minimal in the class of asymptotically normal estimators. In order to obtain an efficient estimator, one needs to know or estimate the density function of η_t and use an adaptive estimation procedure. This was considered by Linton (1993) and Drost, Klaassen and Werker (1995), who proved that the ARCH model belongs to the locally asymptotically normal (LAN) family. After suitable re-parameterisation, they also constructed adaptive estimators for the parameters of interest.

3. GARCH models

Bollerslev (1986) extended the ARCH model to the generalized autoregressive conditional heteroscedasticity (GARCH(r, s)) model:

$$\varepsilon_t = \eta_t \sqrt{h_t}, \tag{3.1}$$

$$h_t = \alpha_0 + \sum_{i=1}^{r} \alpha_i \varepsilon_{t-i}^2 + \sum_{i=1}^{s} \beta_i h_{t-i} \tag{3.2}$$

where $\alpha_0 > 0$, $\alpha_i \geqslant 0$, $\beta_i \geqslant 0$ are sufficient for $h_t > 0$ and η_t is defined as in (2.1).

3.1. *Basic properties*

Bollerslev (1986) showed that the necessary and sufficient condition for the second-order stationarity of models (3.1)–(3.2) is:

$$\sum_{i=1}^{r} \alpha_i + \sum_{i=1}^{s} \beta_i < 1. \tag{3.3}$$

For the GARCH(1,1) model, Nelson (1990) obtained the necessary and sufficient condition for strict stationarity and ergodicity as follows:

$$E(\ln(\alpha_1 \eta_t^2 + \beta_1)) < 0. \tag{3.4}$$

Condition (3.4) allows $\alpha_1 + \beta_1$ to be 1, or slightly larger than 1, in which case $E\varepsilon_t^2 = \infty$. For the general model (3.1)–(3.2), the necessary and sufficient condition for strict stationarity and ergodicity was established by Bougerol and Picard (1992) and Nelson (1990). Ling and Li (1997c) proved that, under (3.3), there exists a unique $\mathcal{F}_t$-measurable and second-order stationary solution to model (3.1)–(3.2), and that the solution is strictly stationary and ergodic, with the following causal representation:

$$h_t = \alpha_0 + \sum_{j=1}^{\infty} c' \left(\prod_{i=1}^{j} A_{t-i} \right) \xi_{t-j} \quad a.s., \tag{3.5}$$

where $\xi_t = (\alpha_0 \eta_t, 0, ..., 0, \alpha_0, 0, ..., 0)_{(r+s) \times 1}$, with the first component $\alpha_0 \eta_t$ and $(r+1)$-th component α_0, $c = (\alpha_1, ..., \alpha_r, \beta_1, ..., \beta_s)'$, and

$$A_t = \left(\begin{array}{ccc|ccc} \alpha_1 \eta_t & \cdots & \alpha_r \eta_t & \beta_1 \eta_t & \cdots & \beta_s \eta_t \\ I_{(r-1) \times (r-1)} & O_{(r-1) \times 1} & & O_{(r-1 \times s} & \\ \hline \alpha_1 & \cdots & \alpha_r & \beta_1 & \cdots & \beta_s \\ O_{(s-1) \times r} & & & I_{(s-1) \times (s-1)} & O_{(s-1) \times 1} \end{array} \right). \tag{3.6}$$

Bollerslev (1986) provided the necessary and sufficient condition for the existence of the $2m$th moment of the GARCH(1,1) model, and the necessary and sufficient condition for the fourth-order moments of the GARCH(1,2) and GARCH(2,1) models. Using a similar method as in Bollerslev (1986), He and Teräsvirta (1999a) provided the moment conditions for a family of GARCH(1,1) models. Ling and McAleer (2002d) derived the sufficient condition for the existence of the stationary solution for this family of GARCH(1,1) models, showed that He and Terävirta's (1999a) condition is necessary but not sufficient, and provided the sufficient moment condition. He and Teräsvirta (1999b) and Karanasos (1999) examined the fourth moment structure of the GARCH(r, s) process. From the proof in Karanasos (1999), it can be seen that the condition is necessary but not sufficient. He and Teräsvirta (1999b) stated that their condition is necessary and sufficient. Ling and McAleer (2002c) showed that the necessary condition for the existence of the fourth moment is incomplete, that the condition is not sufficient for the existence of the fourth moment, and also derived the necessary and sufficient conditions for the existence of all the moments.

Based on Theorem 2.1 in Ling and Li (1997c) and Theorem 2 in Tweedie (1988), Ling (1999b) showed that a sufficient condition for the existence of the $2m$th moment of model (3.1)–(3.2) is

$$\rho[E(A_t^{\otimes m})] < 1, \tag{3.7}$$

where $\rho(A) = \max\{\text{eigenvalues of a matrix } A\}$. Ling's result does not need to assume that the GARCH(r, s) process starts infinitely far in the past with finite $2m$th moment, as is required in Bollerslev (1986) and He and Teräsvirta (1999a,b), and has a far simpler form as compared with that of Milhøj (1985). Ling and McAleer (2002c) further showed that condition (3.7) is also necessary for the existence of the $2m$th moment. Thus, the moment structure of the GARCH(r, s) model in (3.1)–(3.2) has now been established completely. Bera, Higgins and Lee (1996) considered a random coefficient formulation of GARCH processes. An asymptotic theory for the sample autocorrelations and extremes of a GARCH$(1,1)$ process is provided in Mikosch and Stărică (2000). As an extension of the GARCH(r, s) process, Ling and McAleer (2002c) also derived the necessary and sufficient moment conditions of the asymmetric power GARCH(r, s) model of Ding *et al.* (1993).

3.2. *Quasi-maximum likelihood estimation*

The GARCH model is usually estimated by the quasi-maximum likelihood method. However, the properties of the QMLE are not completely clear. Consider the simple but important GARCH$(1,1)$ model. In this case, the likelihood can be written as

$$L(\delta) = \sum_{t=1}^{n} l_t, \qquad l_t = -\frac{1}{2} \ln h_t - \frac{1}{2} \frac{\varepsilon_t^2}{h_t}, \tag{3.8}$$

where h_t is treated as a function of ε_t, and the parameter $\delta = (\alpha_0, \alpha_1 \, \beta_1)'$ and h_t are calculated through the following recursion:

$$h_t = \alpha_0 + \alpha_1 \varepsilon_{t-1}^2 + \beta_1 h_{t-1}, \qquad h_0 = \text{a positive constant.} \tag{3.9}$$

Lee and Hansen (1994) and Lumsdaine (1996) proved that the local QMLE is consistent and asymptotically normal, assuming that $E(\ln(\alpha_1 \eta_t^2 + \beta_1)) < 0$, which is the necessary and sufficient condition for strict stationarity. However, Lee and Hansen (1994) required that all the conditional expectations of $\eta_t^{2+\kappa} < \infty$ uniformly with $\kappa > 0$, while Lumsdaine (1996) required that $E\eta_t^{32} < \infty$. In addition, Lee and Hansen (1994) showed that the global QMLE is consistent if ε_t is second-order stationary. Lee and Hansen (1994) and Lumsdaine (1996) stated that their methods are valid only for the simple GARCH$(1,1)$ model and cannot be extended to more general cases.

For the general order GARCH(r, s) model, Ling and Li (1997b) proved that the local QMLE is consistent and asymptotically normal if $E\varepsilon_t^4 < \infty$. Based on uniform convergence as a modification of a theorem in Amemiya (1985, page 116), Ling and McAleer (2002b) proved the consistency of the global QMLE under only the second- order moment condition. They also derived the asymptotic normality of the global QMLE under the 6th moment condition.

When η_t is not normal, the QMLE is inefficient. Drost and Klaassen (1997) investigated adaptive estimation of the GARCH(1,1) model. This method was extended to nonstationary ARMA models with higher-order GARCH(r,s) errors by Ling and McAleer (2002a). Francq and Zakoïan (2000) consider the estimation of weak GARCH representations (Drost and Nijman, 1993) characterized by an ARMA structure for the squared error terms.

4. Stationary ARMA-GARCH models

The ARCH process is a non-independent white noise sequence, which first appeared in the regression model of Engle (1982). Engle's original motivation seems to have been that an ARCH structure provides improved statistical inference for the mean of the regression model, such as confidence intervals and forecasting. Over the last decade, there has been a tendency to employ the ARCH/GARCH model to analyze the volatilities of financial and economic data, while ignoring the specification and estimation of the conditional mean. However, if the conditional mean is not specified adequately, then it may not be possible to construct consistent estimates of the true ARCH process, for which statistical inference and empirical analysis regarding the ARCH component might be misleading. Thus, even though the primary interest might be on the volatilities in the data, the specification and estimation of the conditional mean are still important.

The conditional mean is typically given as an AR or ARMA model. However, since the conditional variances of the white noise are not constant, the generating mechanism of the AR or ARMA model is quite different from the traditional AR or ARMA model with i.i.d. errors, or martingale differences with a constant conditional variance. As a number of statistical properties of the traditional AR or ARMA model cannot be extended to the present case, it is necessary to have a thorough investigation of these types of models.

We define the ARMA-GARCH model by the following equations:

$$y_t = \sum_{i=1}^{p} \varphi_i y_{t-i} + \sum_{i=1}^{q} \psi_i \varepsilon_{t-1} + \varepsilon_t, \tag{4.1}$$

$$\varepsilon_t = \eta_t \sqrt{h_t}, \qquad h_t = \alpha_0 + \sum_{i=1}^{r} \alpha_i \varepsilon_{t-i}^2 + \sum_{i=1}^{s} \beta_i h_{t-i}. \tag{4.2}$$

There is no paper which is especially devoted to the ARMA-GARCH model, although it is a special case of Ling and Li (1997c, 1998) and Ling and McAleer

(2002b). When $s = 0$, the ARMA-GARCH model reduces to the ARMA-ARCH model, which is a special case of the ARMA-ARCH model of Weiss (1986). When $q = 0$, $s = 0$ and $r = 1$, the AR-ARCH(1) model was investigated by Pantula (1988). The properties of the ARMA-GARCH model appear in Ling and Li (1997c). When all the roots of $\phi(z) = z^p - \sum_{i=1}^{p} \varphi_i z^{p-i}$ lie outside the unit circle, y_t is strictly stationary if ε_t is strictly stationary, and y_t is $2m$th order stationary if ε_t is $2m$th stationary. Thus, in this section, we consider estimation of only the ARMA-GARCH model.

The parameters in (4.1)–(4.2) consist of two sets: one set includes the parameters of the conditional mean, denoted by m, and another set includes the parameters of the conditional variance h_t, denoted by δ. In practice, m is first estimated and then the residuals from the estimated conditional mean are calculated. When the residuals have been obtained, δ can be estimated using the methods in Sections 2–3. Furthermore, the estimated h_t is used to obtain a more efficient estimator of m. If the density function of η_t is symmetric, the MLE of m and δ can be obtained through a separate iteration procedure without loss of asymptotic efficiency. The following section examines the estimation of m when δ is assumed to be known.

4.1 Least squares estimation

Denote the true value of m by m_0. Given observations $y_1, ..., y_n$, the LSE of m_0, $\hat{m}$, is defined as the values in Θ which minimize

$$S_n = \sum_{t=1}^{n} \varepsilon_t^2. \tag{4.3}$$

For the ARMA-ARCH model, Weiss (1986) showed that $\hat{m}$ is consistent for m_0 and

$$\sqrt{n}(\hat{m} - m_0) \to_{\mathscr{L}} N(0, A), \tag{4.4}$$

with

$$A = E^{-1}\left[\frac{\partial \varepsilon_t}{\partial m} \frac{\partial \varepsilon_t}{\partial m'}\right] E\left[\varepsilon_t^2 \frac{\partial \varepsilon_t}{\partial m} \frac{\partial \varepsilon_t}{\partial m'}\right] E^{-1}\left[\frac{\partial \varepsilon_t}{\partial m} \frac{\partial \varepsilon_t}{\partial m'}\right]_{m = m_0}$$

Pantula (1989) also obtained the asymptotic distribution of the LSE for the AR model with ARCH(1) errors, and gave an explicit form for A. The results in Weiss (1986) and Pantula (1989) require that y_t has finite fourth moment. As yet, no one seems to have considered the LSE of m_0 for the ARMA-GARCH model. However, the result in Weiss (1986) for the LSE can be easily extended to the ARMA-GARCH model. When GARCH reduces to an i.i.d. white noise process, the LSE is equivalent to the MLE of m_0.

There is presently no asymptotic theory for the LSE of the ARMA-GARCH model when the fourth moment condition is not satisfied. From the results of

Davis and Mikosch (1998), it would be expected that the LSE is inconsistent if the variance of ε_t is infinite, but is consistent but with a slower convergence rate than $\sqrt{n}$ if ε_t has finite variance and infinite fourth moment. In such cases, the results would be different from those in Davis and Resnick (1985, 1986).

4.2. Quasi-maximum likelihood estimation

Although the LSE is consistent and asymptotically normal if the fourth moment is finite, it is inefficient for ARMA-ARCH/GARCH models. In such cases, it is standard to use MLE. The maximum likelihood method was first used by Engle (1982) for both the AR-ARCH model and a fixed design regression with ARCH errors. First, the log-likelihood function can be written as

$$L(m) = \sum_{t=1}^{n} l_t, \qquad l_t = -\frac{1}{2} \ln h_t - \frac{1}{2} \frac{\varepsilon_t^2}{h_t}, \tag{4.5}$$

where h_t is treated as a function of y_t and m, and is calculated through the following recursion:

$$h_t = \alpha_0 + \sum_{i=1}^{r} \alpha_i \varepsilon_{t-i}^2 + \sum_{i=1}^{s} \beta_i h_{t-i}, \qquad h_0 = \text{a positive constant.} \tag{4.6}$$

Define $\hat{m} = \max_{m \in \Theta} L(m)$. Since η_t is not assumed to be normal, $\hat{m}$ is referred to as the QMLE of m. For the ARMA-ARCH model, Weiss (1986) showed that the QMLE is consistent and asymptotically normal under a finite fourth moment condition. From Ling and Li (1997c), there exists a locally consistent and asymptotically normal QMLE for the ARMA-GARCH model if it has finite fourth moment. When η_t is normal, the asymptotic covariance matrix of $\sqrt{n}(\hat{m} - m_0)$ is

$$B = E\left[\frac{1}{h_t} \frac{\partial \varepsilon_t}{\partial m} \frac{\partial \varepsilon_t}{\partial m'} + \frac{1}{2h_t^2} \frac{\partial h_t}{\partial m} \frac{\partial h_t}{\partial m'} \right]_{m=m_0}^{-1} \tag{4.7}$$

Engle (1982) demonstrated that the MLE is more efficient than the LSE through a simple fixed design regression model and a first-order ARCH process. Pantula (1989) also showed that the MLE is more efficient than the LSE for the AR model with ARCH(1) errors. In fact, it can be shown that $A \geq B$ for the general ARMA-GARCH case.

Under the existence of the second moment, Ling and McAleer (2002b) showed that the global QMLE is consistent. However, in order to derive the asymptotic normality of the global QMLE, the model must satisfy the sixth moment condition. For the ARMA-GARCH$(1, q)$ model, it is possible to show that the global QMLE of m_0 is consistent and asymptotically normal, even if the fourth moment condition is not satisfied.

4.3. *Adaptive estimation*

The QMLE of m_0 in the stationary ARMA-GARCH model is efficient only if η_t is normal. When η_t is not normal, adaptive estimation is useful for obtaining efficient estimators. A comprehensive account of the theory and method of adaptive estimation can be found in Bickel (1982) and Bickel, Klaassen, Ritov and Wellner (1993), with valuable surveys available in Robinson (1988) and Stoker (1991).

In the time series context, Kreiss (1987a) investigated the stationary ARMA model with i.i.d. errors. He proved the local asymptotic normality (LAN) property of the model and constructed adaptive estimators of m_0. Unlike Bickel (1982), Kreiss' adaptive procedure avoids the split sample technique, and hence is quite useful for practical applications. Jeganathan (1995) and Koul and Schick (1996) constructed adaptive estimators without splitting the sample for some nonlinear AR time series with i.i.d. noise. Koul and Schick (1996) also showed through simulation that the adaptive estimator without splitting the sample is superior to those based on the split sample technique.

Lee and Tse (1991) and Engle and González-Rivera (1991) are among the first to have used a semiparametric approach for models (4.1)–(4.2), but they did not obtain any theoretical results. Koul and Schick (1996) investigated adaptive estimation for a random coefficient AR model, which is an ARCH-type time series model. Jeganathan (1995) and Drost, Klaassen and Werker (1997) developed general frameworks suitable for stationary ARCH-type times series. The results in Ling and McAleer (2002a) include the development of the adaptive method for stationary ARMA-GARCH models and the conditions required for adaptive estimation.

5. Nonstationary ARMA-GARCH models

Nonstationary time series have now been extensively investigated for the last two decades. Some important results for nonstationary AR models can be found in Fuller (1976), Dickey and Fuller (1979), Phillips (1987), Chan and Wei (1987, 1988), Tsay and Tiao (1990) and Jeganathan (1995), among many others. However, research on nonstationary time series is almost always limited to innovations with constant conditional variances. Under the framework of Phillips and Durlauf (1986) and Phillips (1987), the long-run variance and the innovation variances are equal in the presence of heteroscedasticity, but it does not include conditional heteroscedastic processes as defined in (3.1)–(3.2).

The ARMA-GARCH model is called nonstationary if the characteristic polynomial $\phi(z)$ has a root on the unit circle. Consider the simple AR(1) case:

$$y_t = \phi y_{t-1} + \varepsilon_t \tag{5.1}$$

where $\phi = 1$, and ε_t follows the GARCH(1,1) process, that is,

$$\varepsilon_t = \eta_t \sqrt{h_t}, \qquad h_t = \alpha_0 + \alpha_1 \varepsilon_{t-1}^2 + \beta_1 h_{t-1}. \tag{5.2}$$

When $\beta_1 = 0$, in which case ε_t follows a first-order ARCH process, Pantula (1989) derived the asymptotic distribution of the LSE of the unit root under the fourth moment condition. Ling and Li (1997b) obtained the same result under the second moment condition, namely $\alpha_1 + \beta_1 < 1$. The asymptotic distribution is

$$n(\hat{\phi}_{LS} - 1) \xrightarrow{\mathscr{L}} \frac{\int_0^1 B(t)\, dB(t)}{\int_0^1 B^2(t)\, dt},$$

where $\hat{\phi}_{LS} = (\sum_{t=2}^n y_{t-1}^2)^{-1}(\sum_{t=2}^n y_t y_{t-1})$ and $B(t)$ is a standard Brownian motion. Thus, the Dickey–Fuller test statistic can still be used. However, Peters and Veloce (1988) and Kim and Schmidt (1993) provided simulation results showing that Dickey–Fuller tests based on the LSE are generally not robust.

It should be noted that, for stationary ARMA-GARCH models, the QMLE is more efficient than the LSE. It seems natural to expect this advantage to extend to nonstationary time series, in which case unit root tests based on the MLE in the presence of ARCH/GARCH innovations should be useful. According to standard statistical theory, an efficient estimator will often provide locally most powerful tests [e.g. see Rao (1973; Chapter 7)]. For this reason, unit root tests based on QMLE would be expected to be more powerful than those based on LSE.

Note that Leybourne, McCabe and Tremayne (1996) observed that heteroscedasticity will be present automatically if ϕ is actually a random variable fluctuating about 1. They developed a score test for such a randomized unit root.

5.1. *Quasi-maximum likelihood estimation*

In this section, we assume that the characteristic polynomial $\phi(z)$ has only a unit root of $+1$. The general case was investigated in Ling and Li (1998). Since $\varphi(z)$ has a unit root, it can be decomposed as $(1 - z)\phi(z)$, where $\phi(z) = 1 - \sum_{i=1}^{p-1} \phi_i z^i$. Let $w_t = (1 - B)y_t$, where B is the backshift operator. Model (4.1) can be rewritten as

$$y_t = \gamma y_{t-1} + w_t, \qquad w_t = \sum_{i=1}^{p-1} \phi_i w_{t-i} + \sum_{i=1}^q \psi_i \varepsilon_{t-i}, \qquad (5.3)$$

where $\gamma = 1$ and ε_t is defined by (4.2). The parameters in model (5.3) are γ and $m = (\phi', \psi')'$, where $\phi = (\phi_1, ..., \phi_{p-1})'$ and $\psi = (\psi_1, ..., \psi_q)'$. As in the stationary case, we assume that the parameters in (4.2) are known or can be estimated consistently.

Given the observations $y_1, ..., y_n$, with initial values $y_i = 0$, or some constants, for $i \leqslant 0$, the log-likelihood function can be written as

$$L(\lambda) = \sum_{t=1}^n l_t, \qquad l_t = -\frac{1}{2}\ln h_t - \frac{1}{2}\frac{\varepsilon_t^2}{h_t}, \qquad (5.4)$$

where $\lambda = (\gamma, m')'$, and h_t is treated as a function of y_t and λ. Ling and Li (1998) showed that there exists a locally consistent QMLE such that

$$G_n^{-1}(\hat{\lambda} - \lambda) \to_{\mathscr{L}} (\xi_{ML}, N')',$$ (5.5)

where

$$\xi_{ML} = \frac{c \int_0^1 w_1(t) \, dw_2(t)}{F \int_0^1 w_1^2(t) \, dt},$$ (5.6)

$c = [1 - \phi(1)]^{-1}$, N is a normal random vector independent of ξ_{ML}, F is a constant depending on the GARCH parameters, $\kappa = E\eta_t^4 - 1$, and $(w_1(t), w_2(t))$ is a bivariate Brownian motion with covariance $t\Omega$. When $r = s = 1$,

$$\Omega = \begin{pmatrix} Eh_t & 1 \\ 1 & E(1/h_t) + \kappa\alpha^2 \sum_{k=1}^{\infty} \beta^{2(k-1)} E(\varepsilon_{t-k}^2/h_t^2) \end{pmatrix},$$ (5.7)

and when η_t is normal, $\kappa = 2$ and $F = E(1/h_t) + 2\alpha^2 \sum_{k=1}^{\infty} \beta^{2(k-1)} E(\varepsilon_{t-k}^2/h_t^2)$. For higher-order GARCH models, the structure of Ω can be found in Ling and Li (1998). Note also that, unlike the least squares case, the moving average parameters do not appear in (5.6) and (5.7).

The above results were derived under the fourth moment condition in Ling and Li (1998). Furthermore, under the second moment condition, Ling and Li (1997b) derived the same result for models (5.1)–(5.2) when $c = 1$. If the second moment condition is not satisfied, the asymptotic distribution for the LSE or QMLE of the unit root is as yet unknown. For the unit root process with i.i.d. errors having infinite variance and in the domain of attraction of an α-stable law, Chan and Tran (1989) and Chan (1990) showed that $n^{-1}(\hat{\phi}_{LS} - 1)$ converges to a functional of a Levy process with $\alpha \in (0, 2)$. It is conjectured that there is a similar asymptotic distribution for the LSE or QMLE of the unit root when the GARCH noise has an infinite variance.

5.2. *Unit root tests based on QMLE*

The asymptotic distribution for the QMLE of the unit root can be used to construct a unit root test. For simplicity, we consider only models (5.1)–(5.2). Denote $\tilde{\phi}_{ML}$ as the QMLE of ϕ, and let

$$B_1(t) = \frac{1}{\sigma} w_1(t) \quad \text{and} \quad B_2(t) = -\frac{1}{\sigma^2} \sqrt{\frac{\sigma^2}{\sigma^2 K - 1}} w_1(t) + \sqrt{\frac{\sigma^2}{\sigma^2 K - 1}} w_2(t),$$

where $\sigma^2 = Eh_t$ and K is the $(2,2)$th element of Ω. Then $B_1(t)$ and $B_2(t)$ are two independent standard Brownian motions. As shown in Ling and Li (1998),

$$n(\tilde{\phi}_{ML} - 1) \xrightarrow{\mathscr{L}} \frac{\int_0^1 B_1(t) \, dB_1(t)}{\sigma^2 F \int_0^1 B_1^2(t) \, dt} + \frac{\sqrt{\sigma^2 K - 1}}{\sigma^2 F} \frac{\int_0^1 B_1(t) \, dB_2(t)}{\int_0^1 B_1^2(t) \, dt}.$$ (5.8)

The second term in (5.8) can be simplified to $[\sqrt{\sigma^2 K - 1}/F\sigma^2](\int_0^1 B_1^2(t)\, dt)^{-1/2}\xi$, where ξ is a standard normal random variable independent of $\int_0^1 B_1^2(t)\, dt$ (see Phillips, 1989). Thus,

$$n(\hat{\phi}_{ML} - 1) \xrightarrow{\mathscr{L}} \frac{\int_0^1 B_1(t)\, dB_1(t)}{\sigma^2 F \int_0^1 B_1^2(t)\, dt} + \frac{\sqrt{\sigma^2 K - 1}}{\sigma^2 F} \left(\int_0^1 B_1^2(t)\, dt \right)^{-1/2} \xi. \quad (5.9)$$

From (5.8)–(5.9), we see that the asymptotic distribution of $\hat{\phi}_{ML}$ can be represented as a combination of the asymptotic distribution of $\hat{\phi}_{LS}$ and a scale mixture of normals. This property is similar to that of the least absolute deviation estimator of unit roots given in Herce (1996). Ling and Li (1998) showed that the QMLE of ϕ is more efficient than the LSE.

As the asymptotic distribution in (5.9) includes nuisance parameters, we cannot use it directly to test for a unit root. There are two methods to overcome this difficulty. The first is to combine the LSE and QMLE to construct a unit root test, as in Ling and Li (1997b). Let

$$L_\phi = n(\hat{\phi}_{LS} - 1), \qquad L_t = \left(\frac{1}{n^2} \sum_{t=1}^n y_{t-1}^2 \right)^{1/2} L_\phi,$$

where $\bar{y} = n^{-1} \sum_{t=1}^n y_{t-1}$. Furthermore, define

$$M_\phi = \frac{\hat{\sigma}^2 \hat{F}}{\sqrt{\hat{\sigma}^2 \hat{K} - 1}} \{ n(\hat{\phi}_{ML} - 1) - (\hat{F}\hat{\sigma}^2)^{-1} [n(\hat{\phi}_{LS} - 1)] \},$$

$$M_t = \left(\frac{1}{n^2} \sum_{t=1}^n y_{t-1}^2 \right)^{1/2} M_\phi.$$

Ling and Li (1997b) showed that

$$M_\phi \xrightarrow{\mathscr{L}} \left[\int_0^1 B_1^2(t)\, dt \right]^{-1/2} \xi \qquad \text{and} \qquad M_t \xrightarrow{\mathscr{L}} \xi,$$

where ξ is a standard normal random variable independent of $\int_0^1 B_1^2(t)\, dt$.

The limiting distributions of M_ϕ and M_t are the same as those based on the least absolute deviations estimators of Herce (1996). However, the test statistics themselves are quite different. Empirical critical values of these distributions were reported in Ling, Li and McAleer (2002), who showed that M_ϕ and M_t can overcome the excessive sizes, as reported in Peters and Veloce (1988) and Kim and Schmidt (1993), and have power comparable to that of the Dickey–Fuller test.

Another method of overcoming the presence of nuisance parameters is to construct a unit root test without using the LSE, as used in Seo (1999). First, rewrite (5.9) as

$$nc_1(\tilde{\phi}_{ML} - 1) \xrightarrow{\mathscr{L}} \frac{\rho \int_0^1 B_1(t)\, dB_1(t)}{\int_0^1 B_1^2(t)\, dt} + \sqrt{1 - \rho^2} \frac{\int_0^1 B_1(t)\, dB_2(t)}{\int_0^1 B_1^2(t)\, dt}, \quad (5.10)$$

where $c_1 = \sigma F / \sqrt{K}$ and $\rho^2 = 1/(\sigma^2 K) \in (0, 1)$. The t-statistic is then given by

$$nc_2 \left(\frac{1}{n^2} \sum_{t=1}^{n} y_{t-1}^2 \right)^{1/2} (\tilde{\phi}_{ML} - 1) \xrightarrow{\mathscr{L}}$$

$$\frac{\rho \int_0^1 B_1(t)\, dB_1(t)}{(\int_0^1 B_1^2(t)\, dt)^{-1/2}} + \sqrt{1 - \rho^2} \frac{\int_0^1 B_1(t)\, dB_2(t)}{(\int_0^1 B_1^2(t)\, dt)^{-1/2}}, \quad (5.11)$$

where $c_2 = c_1/\sigma$. Seo (1999) tabulated the limiting distribution in (5.11) for different values of ρ. The simulation results in Seo (1999) showed that the unit root test based on (5.11) not only overcomes the size distortion problem, but is also consistently more powerful than tests based on the LSE. These results confirm the expectation that more efficient estimates of unit roots yield more powerful unit root tests.

When the conditional errors η_t are not normal, the estimator of the unit root is not efficient. Ling and McAleer (2002c) investigated adaptive estimation of the non-stationary ARMA model with GARCH errors. They obtained the locally asymptotic quadratic form of the log-likelihood ratio, and showed that it was neither locally asymptotic normal nor locally asymptotic mixed normal. A new efficiency criterion was given for a class of defined M-estimators. When the conditional error density is known, Ling and McAleer (2002c) showed that efficient estimators can be constructed using the kernel estimator for the score function. It is also shown that the adaptive procedure for the parameters in the conditional mean part uses the full sample.

6. Other ARCH-type models

In this section, some other ARCH-type models are considered, namely double threshold ARCH, ARFIMA-GARCH, CHARMA, and vector ARMA-GARCH.

6.1. Double threshold ARCH models

Given the success of Tong's (1978, 1980) threshold model in nonlinear time series, it is natural to consider threshold structures for the conditional variance specification. The use of thresholds to model asymmetries is supported by well known empirical characteristics as to the likely asymmetric behaviour of volatility in the stock market (see, for example, French *et al.* (1987)).

Li and Li (1996) proposed the double threshold AR conditional heteroskedastic (DTARCH) time series model:

$$y_t = \phi_0^{(j)} + \sum_{i=1}^{p_i} \phi_i^{(j)} y_{t-i} + \varepsilon_t, \qquad a_{j-1} < y_{t-b} \leq a_j, \tag{6.1}$$

$$\varepsilon_t = \eta_t h_t^{1/2}, \tag{6.2}$$

$$h_t = \alpha_0^{(k)} + \sum_{i=1}^{r_k} \alpha_i^{(k)} \varepsilon_{t-i}^2, \qquad c_{k-1} < y_{t-d} \leq c_k, \tag{6.3}$$

where $j = 1, ..., \nu_1$; $k = 1, ..., \nu_2$; and b and $d \geq 1$ are the delay parameters. In (6.1)–(6.3), the threshold parameters satisfy $-\infty = a_0 < a_1 < \cdots < a_{\nu_1} = \infty$ and $-\infty < c_0 < c_1 < \cdots < c_{\nu_2} = \infty$, $\phi_i^{(j)}$ and $\alpha_i^{(k)}$ are constants, $\alpha_0^{(k)} > 0$ and $\alpha_i^{(k)} \geq 0$. The model generalizes the threshold AR model of Tong (1978, 1980) to include a threshold ARCH component. Tong (1990) referred to this type of hybrid model as a second generation model. Note that other indicator variables may be used in place of y_{t-b} and y_{t-d}. The threshold variables are typically defined as a linear combination of the lagged values of the observed process, but van Dijk, Teräsvirta and Franses (2000) relaxed this definition of threshold variables to include non-linear combinations of the lags of the observed process as well as of other variables. Li and Lam (1995) combined the threshold autoregressive model with a fixed ARCH specification in studying the asymmetry of a stock index. Extension to a double-threshold GARCH model was considered by Brooks (2001).

Ling (1999b) showed that, if $\sum_{i=1}^{p} \max_j |\phi_i^{(j)}| < 1$ and $\sum_{i=1}^{r} \max_k \alpha_i^{(k)} < 1$, then there exists a strictly stationary solution $\{y_t, \varepsilon_t\}$ satisfying models (6.1)–(6.3), and $E_{\pi_1}(|y_t|)$ and $E_{\pi_2}(\varepsilon_t^2)$ are finite, where π_1 and π_2 are the stationary distributions of $\{y_t\}$ and $\{\varepsilon_t\}$, respectively. However, the uniqueness and ergodicity conditions are as yet unknown. If the second threshold, $c_{k-1} < y_{t-d} \leq c_k$, is replaced by $c_{k-1} < \varepsilon_{t-d} \leq c_k$, the strict stationarity and ergodicity condition has been obtained by Liu, Li and Li (1997).

Under the assumption that y_t is strictly stationary and ergodic, and the threshold parameters a_i and c_i are known, Li and Li (1996) proved that the MLE is consistent and asymptotically normal. In practice, the threshold parameters a_i and c_i are unknown and can be estimated by the maximum likelihood method. However, the asymptotic distributions of the estimators are as yet unknown. For the threshold AR model with i.i.d. errors, Chan (1993) showed that the estimator of the threshold parameter has a convergence rate of n and an asymptotic distribution associated with the compound Poisson process. This method could possibly be used for the DTARCH model.

Pesaran and Potter (1997) considered a floor and ceiling model of US output which may be interpreted as a double threshold ARCH model. Rabemanjara and Zakoïan (1993) examined an asymmetric ARCH model which may be regarded as a special case of the DTARCH model. Fornari and Mele (1997) considered a similar formulation to handle asymmetry in volatility. Lee and Li (1998) developed a smooth transition double threshold model. Lundbergh and Teräsvirta (1998a) used a double smooth AR-GARCH model to analyse some high-frequency exchange rate data. Wong and Li (1997) considered tests for the presence of autoregression under ARCH, while Wong and Li (1999) examined tests for the null of AR-ARCH against the double threshold ARCH model.

In the spirit of threshold nonlinear models Wong and Li (2000), Wong and Li (2001a,b) considered mixtures of autoregressive models and mixtures of autoregressive models with ARCH. Some interesting features of these types of models are that some components of the mixture can be non-stationary while the entire series can be stationary, the predictive distributions can be multimodal, and it is fairly easy to derive the conditions for stationarity and expressions for the autocorrelations.

6.2. Fractional ARIMA models

Let $\{y_t\}$ satisfy

$$\phi(B)(1 - B)^d(y_t - \mu) = \theta(B)\varepsilon_t, \tag{6.4}$$

$$\varepsilon_t \mid F_{t-1} \sim N(0, h_t), \qquad h_t = \alpha_0 + \sum_{i=1}^{r} \alpha_i \varepsilon_{t-i}^2 + \sum_{i=1}^{s} \beta_i h_{t-i}, \tag{6.5}$$

where $(1 - B)^d$ is defined by the binomial series:

$$(1 - B)^d = \sum_{k=0}^{\infty} \frac{(k + d - 1)!}{k!(d - 1)!} B^k. \tag{6.6}$$

The specifications in (6.4)–(6.5) are referred to as the fractional ARIMA-GARCH or equivalently the ARFIMA-GARCH model, which was investigated by Ling and Li (1997c). Baillie, Chung and Tieslau (1995) considered a fractional ARIMA$(0, d, 1)$-GARCH$(1,1)$ model for the CPI series of 10 different countries. Note that exact maximum likelihood estimation of (6.4) with $h_t = $ a constant was considered as early as 1981 in the University of Western Ontario Ph.D. Thesis by W. K. Li.

Sufficient conditions for stationarity, ergodicity and the existence of higher-order moments of the fractional ARIMA model were derived by Ling and Li (1997c). Under some mild conditions, it is shown that the MLE is locally consistent and asymptotically normal. It is well known that, when $p = q = 0$ so that $(1 - B)^d y_t = \varepsilon_t$, the MLE of d converges to $N(0, 6/\pi^2)$ in distribution if ε_t is i.i.d. (see Li and McLeod, 1986). However, when ε_t is a GARCH process, Ling and Li (1997c) showed that the asymptotic variance is

$$\Omega_\gamma = E\left[\frac{1}{h_t}\left(\frac{\partial \varepsilon_t}{\partial d}\right)^2 + \frac{1}{2h_t^2}\left(\frac{\partial h_t}{\partial d}\right)^2\right],$$

which is no longer independent of d and is less than $6/\pi^2$. Ling and Li (1997c) also examined the large sample distributions of the residual autocorrelations and the squared-residual autocorrelations, and two portmanteau test statistics. Robinson (1991) considered tests for conditional heteroskedasticity in long memory processes. More recently, Beran and Feng (1999) considered local polynomial estimation of a fractional ARIMA model similar to the above.

6.3. *CHARMA models*

Tsay (1987) proposed the conditional heteroskedastic autoregressive moving average (CHARMA) model, given by:

$$y_t - \mu = \sum_{i=1}^{p} \psi_i(y_{t-i} - \mu) + \sum_{i=1}^{q} \theta_i \varepsilon_{t-i} + \varepsilon_t, \tag{6.7}$$

$$\varepsilon_t = \sum_{i=1}^{r} \delta_{it}\varepsilon_{t-i} + \sum_{i=1}^{s} w_{it}(y_{t-i} - \mu) + w_{0t}(\hat{y}_{t-1}(1) - \mu) + \varepsilon_t, \tag{6.8}$$

where the orders p, q, r and s are finite and non-negative integers; μ, ψ_i and θ_i are constant; δ_{it}, w_{it} and e_t are random variables; and $\hat{y}_{t-1}(1) = E(y_t \mid \mathscr{F}_{t-1})$, where $\mathscr{F}_{t-1}$ is the σ-field generated by $\{e_{t-i}, w_{t-i}, \delta_{t-i} \mid i = 1, 2, ...\}$, $w_t = (w_{0t}, w_{1t}, ..., w_{st})'$, and $\delta_t = (\delta_{1t}, ..., \delta_{rt})'$.

The LSE method can be used to estimate the parameters in (6.7). Tsay (1987) proved that the LSE is consistent if $E\varepsilon_t^4 < \infty$, and is asymptotically normal if $E\varepsilon_t^8 < \infty$. Since the model is an extension of the random coefficient AR model, the asymptotic MLE results can be obtained using the method in Nicholls and Quinn (1982). Basic properties such as strict stationarity, ergodicity and the moment structure are given in Ling (1999a).

The CHARMA model has been extended to the multivariate case. Wong and Li (1997) considered a stationary multivariate CHARMA model, and Li, Ling and Wong (1999) investigated a partially nonstationary AR model with conditional heteroscedasticity, as follows:

$$Y_t = \Phi_1 Y_{t-1} + \cdots + \Phi_p Y_{t-p} + \varepsilon_t \tag{6.9}$$

and

$$\varepsilon_t = \alpha_{1t}\varepsilon_{t-1} + \cdots + \alpha_{qt}\varepsilon_{t-q} + e_t, \tag{6.10}$$

where the Φ_i are constant matrices; $\det\{\Phi(z)\} = |I - \Phi_1 z - \cdots - \Phi_p z^p| = 0$ has $d \leqslant m$ unit roots and other roots outside the unit circle; $\text{rank}[\Phi(1)] = m - d$; $\delta_t = (\alpha_{1t}, ..., \alpha_{qt})$ is a sequence of i.i.d. matrices with mean zero and nonnegative covariance $E[vec(\delta_t)vec'(\delta_t)] = \Omega$; and e_t is an i.i.d. random vector with mean zero and positive covariance $E(e_t e_t') = G$.

Under the condition for the finite fourth moment, Li, Ling and Wong (1998) derived the asymptotic distributions of the LSE, a full rank MLE, and a reduced rank MLE. When the multivariate ARCH process reduces to the innovation with a constant covariance matrix, these asymptotic distributions are the same as in Ahn and Reinsel (1990). However, in the presence of multivariate ARCH innovations, the asymptotic distributions of the full rank MLE and the reduced rank MLE involve two correlated multivariate Brownian motions, which are different from those given in Ahn and Reinsel (1990). The asymptotic results in Li, Ling and Wong (1998) can be used to construct cointegration tests based on the MLE.

6.4. *Vector ARMA-GARCH models*

Ling and McAleer (2002b) proposed the vector ARMA-GARCH model:

$$\Phi(B)(Y_t - \mu) = \Psi(B)\varepsilon_t \tag{6.11}$$

$$\varepsilon_t = D_t^{1/2}\eta_t, \qquad H_t = W + \sum_{i=1}^{r} A_i\tilde{\varepsilon}_{t-i} + \sum_{i=1}^{s} B_i H_{t-i}, \tag{6.12}$$

where $D_t = diag(h_{1t}, ..., h_{mt})'$, $H_t = (h_{1t}, ..., h_{mt})'$, $\Phi(B) = I - \Phi_1 B - \cdots - \Phi_p B^p$ and $\Psi(B) = I + \Psi_1 B + \cdots + \Psi_q B^q$ are polynomials in B, $\tilde{\varepsilon}_t = (\varepsilon_{1t}^2, ..., \varepsilon_{mt}^2)'$, and $\eta_t = (\eta_{1t}, ..., \eta_{mt})'$ is a sequence of i.i.d. random vectors with mean zero and covariance Γ. The constant correlation multivariate GARCH (CC-MGARCH) model of Bollerslev (1990) is a special case of (6.11)–(6.12). There are as yet no asymptotic results available for the extension of the constant correlation model to its dynamic counterpart, VC-MGARCH, namely the variable correlation multivariate GARCH model.

Ling and McAleer (2002b) obtained the conditions for strict stationarity and ergodicity, and the higher-order moments of the model. The consistency of the global QMLE is proved under the existence of only the second-order moment. In order to derive the asymptotic normality of the global QMLE, the results require the second moment condition for the vector ARCH model, the fourth moment condition for the vector ARMA-ARCH model, and the sixth moment condition for the vector ARMA-GARCH model.

7. Conclusion

Most of the theoretical results for GARCH-type processes require that the fourth- or higher-order moments exist. In practice, this condition may not be satisfied. When the fourth moment of the GARCH process is infinite, it exhibits the feature of heavy tails. At present, a theory is lacking for ARMA models derived from this type of GARCH specification, even for ARMA models with i.i.d. heavy-tailed noise (see Resnick (1997)). Since heavy-tailed phenomena are often encountered in finance and economics, an analysis of data exhibiting heavy tails would seem to be an important direction for future research.

Although there have been many contributions to the ARCH/GARCH literature, it seems that until recently very little attention has been paid to model selection. Apart from the diagnostic checking method of Li and Mak (1994) and its extension by Ling and Li (1997a), there would seem to be few formal tools for checking model adequacy. Tse and Zuo (1997) provided a simulation study of the Li–Mak test. More recently, Lundbergh and Teräsvirta (1998b) showed that the Li–Mak test is equivalent to a Lagrange multiplier test of no residual ARCH. Tse (1999) provides a recent review of this literature. A generalization of Li and Mak (1994) is obtained by Horvath and Kokoszka (2001). A robustified version of Li and Mak (1994) against outliers is developed by Jiang, Shao and Hui (2001). All order selection methods for ARMA models, such as those in Hannan (1980), Potscher (1983, 1989), Tsay (1984), and Wei (1992), require that the error processes are i.i.d. or martingale differences with $\sup_t E(\varepsilon_t^2 \mid \mathscr{F}_{t-1}) \leqslant$ a constant. However, ARCH-type models generally do not satisfy these conditions. It is important to develop a theory for order selection of ARCH, GARCH and ARMA-GARCH models, with Wong and Li (1996) and An, Fong and Li (1999) being two useful attempts in this direction.

Acknowledgements

The authors are most grateful for the helpful comments and suggestions of a referee and seminar participants at the Institute for Monetary and Economic Studies, Bank of Japan, Bocconi University, Milan, Chinese University of Hong Kong, Curtin University of Technology, Edith Cowan University, Erasmus University Rotterdam, Griffith University, Hiroshima University, Hitotsubashi University, International Foundation for Artificial Intelligence, Tokyo, Kyoto University, Monash University, Murdoch University, Centre for Financial Engineering, National University of Singapore, Osaka School of International Public Policy, Osaka University, Queensland University of Technology, Yokohama National University, and University of Waikato. For financial support, the first author would like to thank the Hong Kong Research Grants Council, the second author wishes to acknowledge the Australian Research Council, and the third author is grateful to the Australian Research Council and the Institute of Social and Economic Research, Osaka University.

References

Ahn, S. K. and Reinsel, G. C. (1990) Estimation for partially nonstationary multivariate models. *Journal of the American Statistical Association*, 85, 813–823.

Amemiya, T. (1985) Advanced Econometrics. Cambridge, Harvard University Press.

An, H. Z., Fong, P. W. and Li, W. K. (1999) An approach to modelling subset multivariate ARCH model via the AIC principle. Technical Report 223, Department of Statistics and Actuarial Science, The University of Hong Kong.

Baillie, R. T., Chung, C. F. and Tieslau, M. A. (1995) Analyzing inflation by the fractionally integrated ARFIMA-GARCH model. *Journal of Applied Econometrics*, 11, 23–40.

Bera, A. K. and Higgins, M. L. (1993) ARCH models: Properties, estimation and testing. *Journal of Economic Surveys*, 7, 305–366; reprinted in L. Oxley *et al.* (eds), *Surveys in Econometrics*, Oxford: Blackwell, 1995, pp. 215–272.

Bera, A. K., Higgins, M. L. and Lee, S. (1996) Random coefficient formulation of conditional heteroskedasticity and augmented ARCH models. *Sankhyā B*, 58, 199–220.

Beran, J. and Feng, Y. (1999) Local polynomial estimation with a FARIMA-GARCH error process. Manuscript, University of Konstanz.

Bickel, P. J. (1982) On adaptive estimation. *Annals of Statistics*, 10, 647–671.

Bickel, P. J., Klaassen, C. A. J., Ritov, Y. and Wellner, J. A. (1993) *Efficient and Adaptive Estimation for Semiparametric Models*. Baltimore: Johns Hopkins University Press.

Bollerslev, T. (1986) Generalized autoregressive conditional heteroskedasticity. *Journal of Econometrics*, 31, 307–327.

Bollerslev, T. (1990) Modelling the coherence in short-run nominal exchange rates: A multivariate generalized ARCH approach. *Review of Economics and Statistics*, 72, 498–505.

Bollerslev, T., Chou, R. Y. and Kroner, K. F. (1992) ARCH modeling in finance: A review of the theory and empirical evidence. *Journal of Econometrics*, 52, 5–59.

Bollerslev, T., Engle, R. F. and Nelson, D. B. (1994) ARCH models. In R. F. Engle and D. L. McFadden (eds), *Handbook of Econometrics*, 4, Amsterdam: North-Holland, pp. 2961–3038.

Bougerol, P. and Picard, N. M. (1992) Stationarity of GARCH processes and of some nonnegative time series. *Journal of Econometrics*, 52, 115–127.

Brooks, C. (2001) A double-threshold GARCH model for the French France/Deutschmark exchange rate. *Journal of Forecasting*, 20 135–143.

Chan, K. S. (1993) Consistency and limiting distribution of the least squares estimator of a threshold autoregressive model. *Annals of Statistics*, 21, 520–533.

Chan, N. H. (1990) Inference for near-integrated time series with infinite variance. *Journal of the American Statistical Association*, 85, 1069–1074.

Chan, N. H. and Tran, L. T. (1989) On the first order autoregressive processes with infinite variance. *Econometric Theory*, 5, 354–362.

Chan, N. H. and Wei, C. Z. (1987) Asymptotic inference for nearly nonstationary AR(1) processes. *Annals of Statistics*, 15, 1050–1063.

Chan, N. H. and Wei, C. Z. (1988) Limiting distributions of least squares estimates of unstable autoregressive processes. *Annals of Statistics*, 16, 367–401.

Davis, R. A. and Mikosch, M. (1998) The sample autocorrelations of heavy-tailed process with applications to ARCH. *Annals of Statistics*, 26, 2049–2080.

Davis, R. A. and Resnick, S. (1985) More limit theory for the sample correlation function of moving averages. *Stochastic Processes and Applications*, 20, 257– 279.

Davis, R. A. and Resnick, S. (1986) Limit theory for the sample covariance and correlation functions of moving averages. *Annals of Statistics*, 14, 533–558.

de Vries, C. G. (1991) On the relation between GARCH and stable processes. *Journal of Econometrics*, 48, 313–324.

Dickey, D. A. and Fuller, W. A. (1979) Distribution of the estimators for autoregressive time series with a unit root. *Journal of the American Statistical Association*, 74, 427–431.

van Dijk, D., Teräsvirta, T. and Franses, P. H. (2000) Smooth transition autoregressive models – a survey of recent developments. To appear in *Econometric Reviews*.

Ding, Z., Granger, C. W. J. and Engle, R. F. (1973) A long memory property of stock market returns and a new model. *Journal of Empirical Finance*, 1, 83–106.

Drost, F. C. and Klaassen, C. A. J. (1997) Efficient estimation in semiparametric GARCH models. *Journal of Econometrics*, 81, 193–221.

Drost, F. C., Klaassen, C. A. J. and Werker, B. J. M. (1997) Adaptive estimation in time series models. *Annals of Statistics*, 25, 786–817.

Drost, F. C. and Nijman, T. (1993) Temporal aggregation of GARCH processes. *Econometrica*, 61, 909–927.

Engle, R. F. (1982) Autoregressive conditional heteroskedasticity with estimates of the variance of United Kingdom inflation. *Econometrica*, 50, 987–1007.

Engle, R. F. and González-Rivera, G.-R. (1991) Semiparametric ARCH models. *Journal of Business & Economic Statistics*, 9, 345–359.

Engle, R. F. and Kroner, K. F. (1995) Multivariate simultaneous generalized ARCH. *Econometric Theory*, 11, 122–150.

Fornari, F. and Mele, A. (1997) Sign-and volatility-switching ARCH models: Theory and applications to international stock markets. *Journal of Applied Econometrics*, 12, 49–65.

Francq, C. and Zakoian, J.-M. (2000) Estimating weak GARCH representations. *Econometric Theory*, 16, 692–728.

French, K. R., Schwert, G. W. and Stambaugh, R. F. (1987) Expected stock returns and volatility. *Journal of Financial Economics*, 19, 3–30.

Fuller, W. A. (1976) *Introduction to Statistical Time Series*. New York: Wiley.

Gourieroux, C. (1997) *ARCH Models and Financial Applications*. Springer-Verlag: New York.

Hannan, E. J. (1980) The estimation of the order of an ARMA model. *Annals of Statistics*, 8, 1071–1081.

He, C. and Teräsvirta, T. (1999a) Properties of moments of a family of GARCH processes. *Journal of Econometrics*, 92, 173–192.

He, C. and Teräsvirta, T. (1999b) Fourth moment structure of the GARCH(p,q) process. *Econometric Theory*, 15, 824–846.

Herce, M. A. (1996) Asymptotic theory of LAD estimation in a unit root process with finite variance errors. *Econometric Theory* 12, 129–53.

Horvath, L. and Kokoszka, P. (2001) Large sample distribution of weighted sum of ARCH(p) squared residual correlation. *Econometric Theory*, 17, 283–295.

Jeganathan, P. (1995) Some aspects of asymptotic theory with applications to time series models. *Econometric Theory*, 11, 818–887.

Jeganathan, P. (1997) On asymptotic inference in linear cointegrated time series systems. *Econometric Theory* 13, 692–745.

Jiang, J., Zhao, Q. and Hui, Y. V. (2001) Robust modelling of ARCH models. *Journal of Forecasting*, 20, 111–133.

Karanasos, M. (1999) The second moment and the autocovariance function of the squared errors of the GARCH model. *Journal of Econometrics*, 90, 63–76.

Kim, K. and Schmidt, P. (1993) Unit root tests with conditional heteroskedasticity. *Journal of Econometrics*, 59, 287–300.

Koul, H. L. and Schick, A. (1996) Adaptive estimation in a random coefficient autoregressive model. *Annals of Statistics*, 24, 1025–1052.

Kreiss, J.-P. (1987) On adaptive estimation in stationary ARMA processes. *Annals of Statistics*, 15, 112–133.

Lee, S.-W. and Hansen, B. E. (1994) Asymptotic theory for the GARCH(1,1) quasi-maximum likelihood estimator. *Econometric Theory*, 10, 29–52.

Lee, T. K. Y. and Tse, Y. K. (1991) Term structure of interest rates in the Singapore Asian dollar market. *Journal of Applied Econometrics*, 6, 143–152.

Lee, Y. N. and Li, W. K. (1998) On smooth transition double threshold models. In *Statistics and Finance: An Interface* (editors, W. S. Chan, W. K. Li and H. Tong) pp. 205–225. London: Imperial College Press.

Leybourne, S. J., McCabe, B. P. M. and Tremayne, A. R. (1996) Can economic time series be differenced to stationarity? *Journal of Business and Economic Statistics*, 14, 435–446.

Li, C. W. and Li, W. K. (1996) On a double threshold autoregressive heteroskedasticity time series model. *Journal of Applied Econometrics*, 11, 253–74.

Li, W. K. and Lam, K. (1995) Modelling asymmetry in stock returns by a threshold autoregressive conditional heteroscedastic model. *The Statistician* 44, 333–341.

Li, W. K., Ling, S. and Wong, H. (1998) Estimation for partially nonstationary multivariate autoregressive models with conditional heteroskedasticity. Technical report, Department of Statistics and Actuarial Science, The University of Hong Kong.

Li, W. K. and Mak, T. K. (1994) On the squared residual autocorrelations in non-linear time series with conditional heteroscedasticity. *Journal of Time Series Analysis*, 15, 627–636.

Li, W. K. and McLeod, A. I. (1986) Fractional time series modelling. *Biometrika*, 73, 217–21.

Ling, S. (1999a) On the stationarity and the existence of moments of conditional heteroskedastic ARMA models. *Statistica Sinica*, 9, 1119–1130.

Ling, S. (1999b) On the probabilistic properties of a double threshold ARMA conditional heteroskedasticity model. *Journal of Applied Probability*, 36, 1–18.

Ling, S. and Li, W. K. (1997a) Diagnostic checking nonlinear multivariate time series with multivariate ARCH errors. *Journal of Time Series Analysis*, 18, 447–464.

Ling, S. and Li, W. K. (1997b) Estimating and testing for unit root processes with GARCH(1,1) errors. Technical report, Department of Statistics, The University of Hong Kong, Hong Kong.

Ling, S. and Li, W. K. (1997c) On fractionally integrated autoregressive moving-average time series models with conditional heteroskedasticity. *Journal of the American Statistical Association*, 92, 1184–1194.

Ling, S. and Li, W. K. (1998) Limiting distributions of maximum likelihood estimators for unstable ARMA models with GARCH errors. *Annals of Statistics*, 26, 84–125.

Ling, S., Li, W. K. and McAleer, M. (2002) Efficient estimation and testing for unit root processes with GARCH(1,1) errors: Theory and Monte Carlo evidence. To appear in *Econometric Reviews*.

Ling, S. and McAleer, M. (2002a) On adaptive estimation in nonstationary ARMA models with GARCH errors. To appear in *Annals of Statistics*.

Ling, S. and McAleer, M. (2002b) Asymptotic theory for a vector ARMA-GARCH model. To appear in *Econometric Theory*.

Ling, S. and McAleer, M. (2002c) Necessary and sufficient moment conditions for the GARCH(r, s) and asymmetric power GARCH(r, s) models. *Econometric Theory*, 18, 722–729.

Ling, S. and McAleer, M. (2002d) Stationarity and the existence of moments of a family of GARCH processes. *Journal of Econometrics*, 106, 109–117.

Linton, O. (1993) Adaptive estimation in ARCH models. *Econometric Theory*, 9, 535–569.

Liu, J., Li, W. K. and Li, C. W. (1997) On a threshold autoregression with conditional heteroscedastic variances. *Journal of Statistical Planning and Inference*, 62, 279–300.

Lumsdaine, R. L. (1996) Consistency and asymptotic normality of the quasi-maximum likelihood estimator in IGARCH(1,1) and covariance stationary GARCH(1,1). models. *Econometrica*, 64, 575–596.

Lundbergh, S. and Teräsvirta T. (1998a) Modelling economic high-frequency time series with STAR-STGARCH models. Working paper 291, Stockholm School of Economics, Stockholm, Sweden.

Lundbergh, S. and Teräsvirta T. (1998b) Evaluating GARCH models. Working paper 292, Stockholm School of Economics, Stockholm, Sweden.

Mak, T. K., Wong, H. and Li, W. K. (1997) Estimation of nonlinear time series with conditional heteroscedastic variances by iteratively weighted least squares. *Computational Statistics & Data Analysis*, 24, 169–178.

Mikosch, T. and Stărică C. (2000) Limit theory for the sample autocorrelations and extremes of a GARCH(1,1) process. *Annals of Statistics*, 28, 1427–1451.

Milhøj, A.(1985) The moment structure of ARCH processes. *Scandinavian Journal of Statistics*, 12, 281–292.

Nelson, D. B. (1990) Stationarity and persistence in the GARCH(1, 1) model. *Econometric Theory*, 6, 318–334.

Nicholls, D. F. and Quinn, B. G. (1982) *Random Coefficient Autoregressive Model: An Introduction*. New York: Springer-Verlag.

Pantula, S. G. (1989) Estimation of autoregressive models with ARCH errors. *Sankhya B*, 50, 119–38.

Pesaran, M. H. and Potter, S. M. (1997) A floor and ceiling model of US output. *Journal of Economic Dynamics and Control*, 21, 661–695.

Peters, T. A. and Veloce, W. (1988) Robustness of unit root tests in ARMA models with generalized ARCH errors. Manuscript, Brock University, St. Catherine, Canada.

Phillips, P. C. B. (1987) Time series regression with a unit root. *Econometrica*, 55, 277–301.

Phillips, P. C. B. and Durlauf, S. N. (1986) Multiple time series regression with integrated processes. *Review of Economic Studies*, LIII, 473–495.

Potscher, B. M. (1983) Order estimation in ARMA-models by Lagrangian multiplier tests. *Annals of Statistics*, 11, 872–885.

Potscher, B. M. (1989) Model selection under nonstationarity: Autoregression models and stochastic linear regression models. *Annals of Statistics*, 17, 1257–1274.

Rabemanjara, R. and Zakoian, J.-M. (1993) Threshold ARCH model and asymmetrics in volatility. *Journal of Applied Econometrics*, 8, 31–49.

Rao, C. R. (1978) *Linear Models and Statistical Inference*. New York: Wiley.

Resnick, S. I. (1997) Heavy tail modeling and teletraffic data. *Annals of Statistics*, 25, 1805–1869.

Robinson, P. M. (1988) Semiparametric econometrics: A survey. *Journal of Applied Econometrics*, 3, 35–51.

Robinson, P. M. (1991) Testing for strong serial correlation and dynamic conditional heteroskedasticity in multiple regression. *Journal of Econometrics*, 47, 67–84.

Ross, P. E. (1996) *Modelling Stock Market Volatility: Bridging the Gap to Continuous Time*. New York: Academic Press.

Seo, B. (1999) Distribution theory for unit root tests with conditional heteroskedasticity. *Journal of Econometrics*, 91, 113–144.

Shephard, N. (1996) Statistical aspects of ARCH and stochastic volatility. In *Time Series Models: In Econometrics, Finance and Other Fields*, D. R. Cox, D. V. Hinkley and O. Barndorff-Nielsen (eds), London: Chapman and Hall, pp. 1–67.

Stoker, T. M. (1991) *Lectures on Semiparametric Econometrics*. Louvain-la-Neuve, Belgium: CORE.

Taylor, S. J. (1986) *Modelling Financial Time Series*. New York: Wiley.

Tong, H. (1978) On a threshold model. In *Pattern Recognition and Signal Processing*. (editor C. H. Chan) pp. 575–586. Amsterdam: Sijthoff and Noordhoff.

Tong, H. (1990) *Non-linear Time Series: A Dynamical System Approach*. Oxford: Oxford University Press.

Tong, H. and Lim, K. S. (1980) Threshold autoregression, limit cycles and cyclical data. *Journal of the Royal Statistical Association*, B 42, 245–292.

Tsay, R. S. (1984) Order section in nonstationary autoregression models. *Annals of Statistics*, 12, 1425–1433.

Tsay, R. S. (1987) Conditional heteroscedastic time series models. *Journal of the American Statistical Association*, 82, 590–604.

Tsay, R. S. and Tiao, G. C. (1990) Asymptotic properties of multivariate nonstationary processes with applications to autoregressions. *Annals of Statistics*, 18, 220–250.

Tse, Y. K. (1999) Residual-based diagnostics for conditional heteroscedasticity models. Manuscript, Department of Economics, National University of Singapore.

Tse, Y. K. and Zuo, X. L. (1997) Testing for conditional heteroscedasticity: Some Monte Carlo results. *Journal of Statistical Computation and Simulation*, 58, 237–253.

Tweedie, R. L. (1988) Invariant measure for Markov chains with no irreducibility assumptions. *Journal of Applied Probability*, 25A, 275–85.

Wei, C. Z. (1992) On predictive least squares principles. *Annals of Statistics*, 20, 1–42.

Weiss, A. A. (1986) Asymptotic theory for ARCH models: Estimation and testing. *Econometric Theory*, 2, 107–131.

Wong, C. S. and Li, W. K. (1996) On the use of the predictive least squares criterion in time series with changing conditional variance. Technical Report 117, The Department of Statistics and Actuarial Science, The University of Hong Kong.

Wong, C. S. and Li, W. K. (1997) Testing for threshold autoregression with conditional heteroscedasticity. *Biometrika*, 84, 407–418.

Wong, C. S. and Li, W. K. (1999) Testing for double threshold autoregressive conditional heteroscedasticity model. To appear in *Statistica Sinica*.

Wong, C. S. and Li, W. K. (2000) On a mixture autoregressive model. *Journal of the Royal Statistical Association*, B 62, 95–115.

Wong, C. S. and Li, W. K. (2001a) On a mixture autoregressive conditional heteroscedastic model. To appear in *Journal of the American Statistical Association*.

Wong, C. S. and Li, W. K. (2001b) On a logistic mixture autoregressive model. To appear in *Biometrika*.

Wong, H. and Li, W. K. (1997) On a multivariate conditional heteroscedasticity model. *Biometrika*, 4, 111–123.

Yap, S. F. and Reinsel, G. C. (1995) Estimation and testing for unit roots in a partially nonstationary vector autoregressive moving average model. *Journal of the American Statistical Association*, 90, 253–267.

Chapter 3

BOOTSTRAPPING FINANCIAL TIME SERIES

Esther Ruiz

Lorenzo Pascual

Universidad Carlos III de Madrid

1. Introduction

High frequency time series of returns are often characterized by having excess kurtosis and autocorrelated squared observations. These stylized facts can be explained by the presence of conditional heteroscedasticity, i.e. the volatility of returns evolves over time. Given that the marginal distribution of returns is usually non-Gaussian, the inference and prediction of models fitted to returns should not rely on methods based on Gaussianity assumptions. However, bootstrap methods can be adequate in this context; see Korajczyk (1985) for one of the earliest applications of bootstrap methods to analyze financial problems. Many of the earlier papers using bootstrap methods in finance, use procedures based on resampling directly from observed returns without taking into account that returns are sometimes correlated and often not independent. Given that the basic bootstrap techniques were originally developed for independent observations, the bootstrap inference has not the desired properties when applied to raw returns; see, for example, Bookstaber and McDonald (1987), Chatterjee and Pari (1990), Hsieh and Miller (1990) and Levich and Thomas (1993) for some applications where returns are directly bootstrapped.

The application of bootstrap methods in finance has been previously reviewed by Maddala and Li (1996) who pointed out these shortcomings in some of the applications. To take into account the dynamic dependence of returns and, in particular, the conditional heteroscedasticity, there are two possible bootstrap alternatives. First, it is possible to assume a particular model for the volatility and to resample from the returns standardized using the estimated conditional standard deviations. If the volatility is correctly specified, these standardized returns are asymptotically independent and, consequently, the bootstrap procedure has the usual asymptotic properties. Alternatively, the bootstrap procedure can be adapted to take into account that the observations are dependent without assuming a particular model as, for example, in the block bootstrap method.

The objective of this paper is to review the use of bootstrap methods in the analysis of financial time series. In general, these techniques can be used for two objectives. First of all, it is possible to estimate the distribution of an estimator or test statistic. Secondly, it is possible to estimate directly the probability distribution of returns. The paper is organized as follows. In Section 2, we briefly describe the main bootstrap procedures for time series. Section 3 reviews the application of bootstrap procedures for inference in financial models. The main application of bootstrap techniques in this context is to analyze the predictive ability of technical trading rules. In Section 4, we describe several studies that apply bootstrap methods to obtain the distribution function of returns that is fundamental in prediction and Value at Risk (VaR) models. Finally, Section 5 contains the conclusions.

2. Bootstrap techniques for time series

The bootstrap, introduced by Efron (1979), appeared originally as a procedure to measure the accuracy of an estimator. Its main attraction relies on the fact that it can approximate the sampling distribution of the estimator of interest even when this is very difficult or impossible to obtain analytically and only an asymptotic approximation is available. Even more, the bootstrap has the advantage that is very easy to apply independently of the complexity of the statistic of interest.

To illustrate the bootstrap methodology, let us consider one of the most common situations found in statistics. Let $\mathbf{x} = (x_1, x_2, ..., x_n)$ be a set of n independent and identically distributed (*iid*) observations with distribution function F, and let $\theta = s(F)$ be the unknown parameter to be estimated. Given that the empirical distribution function $\mathbf{F}_n$ is a good approximation of the true but unknown distribution F, a natural estimator for θ is $\hat{\theta} = s(\mathbf{F}_n)$. However, knowledge of the sampling distribution of the estimator or at least its mean and variance is only possible in very simple situations and, usually, the asymptotic distribution is used to approximate it. Furthermore, the standard errors are useful for summarizing the precision of estimates when the distribution is symmetric. However, when the estimator has a severely skewed finite sample distribution, bootstrap interval estimates summarize better the distribution. The bootstrap methodology allows an approximation of the distribution of $\hat{\theta}$ under very general conditions and it is based on obtaining a bootstrap replicate, $x_1^*, x_2^*, ..., x_n^*$, of the available data set $x_1, x_2, ..., x_n$, by drawing with replacement random samples from $\mathbf{F}_n$. Once B bootstrap replicates of the original data set, with the corresponding B bootstrap realizations of the parameter of interest $\hat{\theta}_i^*$, $i = 1, ..., B$, have been obtained, the resampling distribution of the bootstrap statistic θ^* is used to approximate the distribution of $\hat{\theta}$. Obviously, the bigger the value of B, the better is the Monte Carlo approximation of θ^*, with the only price of larger computational cost; see Efron and Tibshirany (1993) and Shao and Tu (1995).

With respect to the asymptotic validity of the bootstrap procedure, it is usual to prove that some distance, usually the Mallows distance, between the bootstrap distribution of θ^* and the sampling distribution of $\hat{\theta}$ goes to zero as the sample size increases to infinity. Under some circumstances, the bootstrap distribution enables us to make more accurate inferences than the asymptotic approximation.

The bootstrap method just described is the simplest version and is only valid in the case of *iid* observations. If the standard bootstrap is applied directly to dependent observations, the resampled data will not preserve the properties of the original data set, providing inconsistent statistical results. In particular, the standard bootstrap procedure is neither consistent nor asymptotically unbiased under heteroscedasticity; see Wu (1986) in the context of regression models. Recently, several parametric and nonparametric bootstrap methods have been developed for time series data. The parametric methods are based on assuming a specific model for the data. After estimating the model by a consistent method, the residuals are bootstrapped; see Freedman and Peters (1984) and Efron and Tibshirani (1986). If the serial dependence of the data is misspecified, the parametric bootstrap could be inconsistent. Consequently, alternative approaches that do not require fitting a parametric model have been developed to deal with dependent time series data. Kunsch (1989) proposed the moving block bootstrap method that divide the data into overlapping blocks of fixed length and resample with replacement from these blocks. The bootstrap replicates generated by the moving block method are not stationary even if the original series is stationary. For this reason, Politis and Romano (1994) suggest the stationary bootstrap method that resamples from blocks of data with random lengths. In the context of heteroscedastic time series, Wu (1986) proposed a weighted or wild bootstrap method that provides a consistent estimate of the variance of a test statistic in the presence of heteroscedasticity. The wild bootstrap is based on weighting each original observation with random draws with replacement from a standard normal distribution. Malliaropulos and Priestley (1999) propose a nonparametric implementation of this method that does not rely on the normal distribution. Hafner and Herwartz (2000) also use another alternative version of this procedure.

Li and Maddala (1996) and Berkowitz and Kilian (2000) review the most relevant developments in bootstrapping time series models, and show that the bootstrap algorithms that make use of some parametric assumptions about the model appropriate for the data, are preferable in many applications in time series econometrics.

With respect to testing a given null hypothesis, H_0, it is fundamental to bootstrap from the correct model. In the case of time series data, it is usually not recommended to bootstrap from the raw data but from the residuals from a given model. However, it is necessary to decide which are the residuals to be bootstrapped. Consider, for example, the following AR(1) model:

$$y_t = \phi y_{t-1} + u_t$$

and the null hypothesis $H_0: \phi = \phi_0$. In this case, we have mainly two alternative series of residuals from the following models:

$$a) \ y_t = \hat{\phi} y_{t-1} + \hat{u}_t$$

$$b) \ y_t = \phi_0 y_{t-1} + \tilde{u}_t$$

Denote by $\hat{u}_t^*$ the residuals resampled from $\hat{u}_t$ and by $\tilde{u}_t^*$, the residuals resampled from $\tilde{u}_t$. Then, it is possible to obtain bootstrap replicates of the variable y_t by one of the following schemes:

$$i) \ y_t^* = \hat{\phi} y_{t-1}^* + \hat{u}_t^*$$

$$ii) \ y_t^* = \phi_0 y_{t-1}^* + \hat{u}_t^*$$

$$iii) \ y_t^* = \phi_0 y_{t-1}^* + \tilde{u}_t^*$$

Although, the third scheme is the most appropriate for hypothesis testing, the other two alternatives have also been used in practice. For example, Hall and Wilson (1991) provide guidelines for hypothesis testing using the first alternative while Ferreti and Romo (1996) consider the second one to test for unit roots.

Bootstrap based methods can also be used to obtain prediction densities and intervals for future values of a given variable without making distributional assumptions on the innovations and, at the same time, allowing the introduction, into the estimated prediction densities, of the variability due to parameter estimation. The most influential bootstrap procedure to construct prediction intervals for future values of time series generated by linear AR(p) models, is due to Thombs and Schucany (1990). This method needs the backward representation of the autoregressive model to generate bootstrap series that mimic the structure of the original data, keeping fixed the last p observations in all bootstrap replicates. The use of the backward representation to generate bootstrap series makes the method computationally expensive and, what is more important, restricts its applicability exclusively to those models having a backward representation, excluding, for example, the Generalized Autoregressive Conditional Heteroscedasticity (GARCH) class of models. Furthermore, the prediction in models with a moving average component is not possible with this methodology since, at least theoretically, the whole sample should be kept fixed when generating bootstrap replicates because of the infinite order of the corresponding autoregressive representation. Cao *et al.* (1997) present an alternative bootstrap method that does no require the backward representation. However, the corresponding prediction intervals do not incorporate the uncertainty due to parameter estimation as they are conditional on parameter estimates.

To overcome these drawbacks, Pascual *et al.* (1998) propose a new bootstrap strategy to obtain prediction densities for general ARIMA models. With this new methodology it is possible to incorporate the variability due to parameter estimation into the prediction densities without requiring the backward representation of the process. Therefore, the procedure is very flexible and easy to use, and what is more important, can be extended and adapted easily to processes without a backward representation and, in particular, to GARCH processes. Finally, Gospodinov (2002) analyses the prediction accuracy of another bootstrap procedure to compute the median unbiased forecast of near-integrated autoregressive processes. He illustrates the properties of this procedure analyzing one-month U.S. T-bill yields which are highly persistent although the presence of an exact unit root is inconsistent with the bond pricing theory. This procedure is also based on the use of the backward representation and could be modified along the lines of the procedure suggested by Pascual *et al.* (1998).

In a recent essay on bootstrap techniques, Horowitz (2001) points out that bootstrap methods for time series data are less well developed than methods for *iid* observations and that important research remains to be done. This fact is even more clear when looking at applications of bootstrap procedures to data generated by non-linear models and, in particular, by GARCH and Stochastic Volatility (SV) models.

3. Inference

In this section, we describe several applications of bootstrap procedures to analyze the dynamic properties of financial returns that appear after the review of Maddala and Li (1996). First, we consider tests related with the dynamic behavior of the conditional mean of returns. Then we review the papers where bootstrap procedures have been applied to test for dynamics in the conditional variance. One of the areas where bootstrap techniques have been widely applied is to test for the superiority of technical trading rules and we dedicate one separate subsection to inference on trading rules. Finally, we present other applications of bootstrap procedures to financial time series.

3.1. *Testing for dynamics in the conditional mean of returns*

In this subsection, we review the papers using bootstrap procedures to test for the dynamic components in the conditional mean of returns. Numerous studies have found that daily stock market returns exhibit positive low-serial correlation that is often attributed to non-synchronous trading effects. Consequently, there is great interest in testing for the presence of such autoregressive dynamics in returns. For example, Malliaropulos (1996) apply the variance ratio test, proposed by Cochrane (1988), to monthly observations of the FT-A All Share index and Pan *et al.* (1997) to currency futures prices. The latter authors use both the asymptotic standard errors and bootstrap p-values for the test and conclude that the results are similar. However, it is important to notice that both Malliaropulos (1996) and Pan *et al.* (1997) bootstrap directly from the raw returns that, as mentioned in the introduction, are not independent, although they are uncorrelated under the null hypothesis. Therefore, the bootstrap p-values may be inappropriate. To solve this problem, Malliaropulos and Priestley (1999) obtain the finite sample distribution of the variance ratio test using the weighted bootstrap method. They apply the variance ratio test to unexpected excess returns of several South Asian stock markets after accounting for time-varying risk and potential partial integration of the local stock market into the world stock market. It is concluded that, although excess returns exhibit mean reversion in a number of markets, the failure to reject the random walk hypothesis is related to mean-reversion of expected returns rather than to market inefficiency. Alternatively, Politis, *et al.* (1997) propose a subsampling method to test the null hypothesis of uncorrelated returns by means of the variance ratio test. This method has the advantage that it works for dependent and heteroscedastic returns.

To illustrate the effect of the presence of conditional heteroscedasticity on the bootstrap densities of the variance ratio test, 1000 series have been simulated by the following GARCH(1, 1) model

$$y_t = \varepsilon_t \sigma_t, \qquad t = 1, ..., T$$
$$\sigma_t^2 = 0.05 + 0.1 y_{t-1}^2 + 0.85 \sigma_{t-1}^2 \tag{1}$$

where y_t represents the series of returns, i.e. $y_t = \log(p_t/p_{t-1})$, p_t is the stock price at time t, σ_t is the volatility and ε_t is a white noise that has been generated by both a Gaussian distribution and a standardized Student-t distribution with 5 degrees of freedom. Notice that the Student-t distribution has been proposed by many authors as the conditional distribution of returns; see, for example, Baillie and Bollerslev (1989). Table 1 reports the Monte Carlo results on the average p-values of the variance ratio statistic given by

$$VR(q) = \frac{\sum_{t=q+1}^{T} (p_t - p_{t-q})^2}{\sum_{t=2}^{T} (p_t - p_{t-1})^2} \tag{2}$$

for $T = 300$ and $T = 1000$ and $q = 2, 5, 10$ and 20 when series are generated by model (1) with ε_t being Gaussian. To make the comparisons simpler, the statistic

Table 1. Monte Carlo results on p-values of $VR(q)$ statistic. GARCH $(1, 1)$ returns with Gaussian errors

		Average p-values			
q	T	Empirical	Asymptotic	Bootstrap 1	Bootstrap 2
2	300	0.4858	0.5183	0.5105	0.4965
	1000	0.4994	0.5250	0.5120	0.5035
5	300	0.4769	0.5246	0.5195	0.4872
	1000	0.4976	0.5158	0.5105	0.4935
10	300	0.4858	0.5568	0.5417	0.4958
	1000	0.5026	0.5299	0.5240	0.4966
20	300	0.4881	0.5941	0.5650	0.5026
	1000	0.5043	0.5468	0.5372	0.4987

has been standardized using its asymptotic standard deviation, as given by Lo and McKinlay (1989) so that all the statistics are asymptotically $N(0,1)$. In this table, it is possible to observe that when the bootstrap is based on resampling from the raw returns (Bootstrap 1), the asymptotic and bootstrap p-values are similar, a result that was also reported by Pan *et al.* (1997). Furthermore, both the asymptotic and bootstrap p-values exceed the corresponding empirical p-values. However, when the bootstrap is based on the standardized returns (Bootstrap 2), the sampling and the bootstrap distributions of the VR(q) statistic are closer.

Figures 1 and 2 represent the empirical density of the VR(q) statistic for series generated by model (1) with ε_t having a Student-t distribution for $T = 300$ and 1000, respectively. These figures also represent the bootstrap densities obtained by resampling from the raw returns (bootstrap 1) and from the returns standardized using the estimated GARCH conditional standard deviations (bootstrap 2) for two particular series generated by the same model. It is clear that, in the latter case, the estimated sampling density is closer to the empirical density. Furthermore, notice that the performance of bootstrapping without taking into account the conditional heteroscedasticity deteriorates as the sample size increases. Consequently, the p-values based on bootstrapping directly from the raw returns may have important distortions. For example, for a series generated with $T = 1000$, the statistic VR(2) is 0.838. In this case, the asymptotic p-value and the bootstrap p-value obtained by resampling from the raw returns are nearly the same, 0.201 and 0.209, respectively. However, bootstrap p-values obtained from the heteroscedastic model is 0.249 that is closer to the empirical p-value of 0.271. Notice that, once more, it is possible to observe that the asymptotic and the bootstrap p-values based on raw returns are similar.

We now consider the empirical application of the VR statistic to test for the presence of autoregressive components in the exchange rate of the British Pound against the Dollar observed daily from the 1 January 1990 to 31 December 2001, with $T = 3040$. The series of returns, $y_t = 100 \log(p_t/p_{t-1})$, where p_t is the

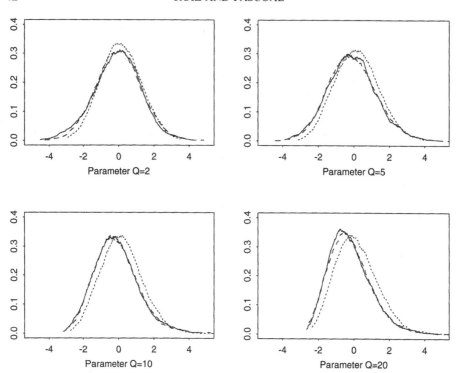

Figure 1. Empirical (−) and bootstrap densities of variance ratio statistic for a series generated by a GARCH(1, 1) model with conditional Student-t distribution with 5 degrees of freedom. $T = 300$.

exchange rate at time t, has been plotted in Figure 3. Table 2 reports the values of the VR(q) statistic for $q = 2, 5, 10$ and 20, together with the corresponding asymptotic p-values and the bootstrap p-values obtained from the raw returns. Notice that both p-values are very similar for all values of q considered. However, the returns are not independent. Fitting a GARCH(1, 1) model, the following estimates are obtained:

$$\hat{\sigma}_t^2 = \underset{(0.0001)}{0.0007} + \underset{(0.0047)}{0.0444} \ y_{t-1}^2 + \underset{(0.0058)}{0.9443} \ \hat{\sigma}_{t-1}^2 \qquad (3)$$

The p-values obtained by resampling from the corresponding standardized returns are also reported in Table 3. Observe that, these p-values are always greater than the corresponding asymptotic p-values. Furthermore, the results of the test can be reversed depending on which p-value is used. For example, when $q = 10$, the null of no autocorrelation is rejected using both the asymptotic and the bootstrap p-values based on raw returns. However, the null hypothesis is not rejected when bootstrapping from the standardized returns.

Summarizing, we have shown with both simulated and real data that bootstrapping raw returns in order to obtain p-values of the VR statistic when

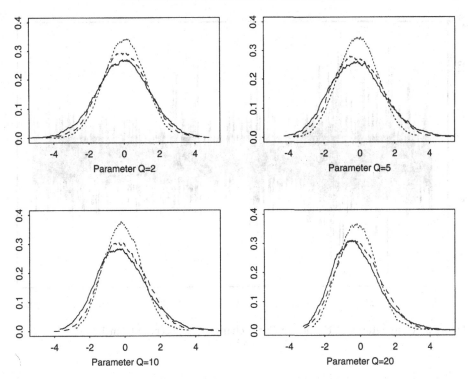

Figure 2. Empirical (−) and bootstrap densities of variance ratio statistic for a series generated by a GARCH(1, 1) model with conditional Student-t distribution with 5 degrees of freedom. $T = 1000$.

there is conditional heteroscedasticity, could seriously distort the results of the test. Furthermore, it could be expected that the corresponding bootstrap p-values are not very different from the asymptotic p-values. Using bootstrap procedures appropriate for the characteristics of returns, yields p-values remarkably close to the empirical p-values.

The variance ratio test is not the only statistic used in finance to test for autoregressive components in the conditional mean of returns. In a very interesting paper, Hafner and Herwartz (2000) consider two Wald tests based on Quasi-Maximum Likelihood (QML) estimation assuming a GARCH(1, 1) model for the conditional variance. As QML inference depends on the specification of the variance process, they also consider tests based on Ordinary Least Squares (OLS) estimation and a bootstrapped version of the OLS based statistics using the wild bootstrap. The asymptotic convergence of the distribution of the bootstrapped statistics to the asymptotic distribution of the original statistic is proven. By means of Monte Carlo experiments, they show that the wild bootstrap inference shows superior size properties relative to all the other tests considered. However, the power of the bootstrap tests is low in the cases were the volatility is highly persistent. Finally, they apply the alternative tests considered to

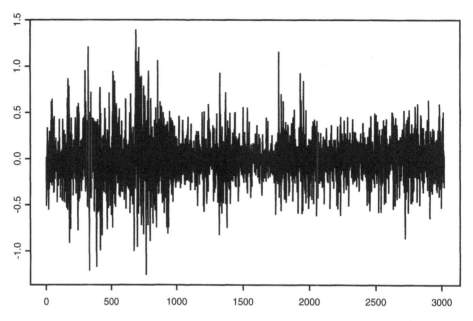

Figure 3. Daily returns of Pound–Dollar exchange rate observed from 1 January 1990 to 31 December 2001.

Table 2. $VR(q)$ statistic and p-values for British Pound–Dollar exchange rate.

		p-values		
q	Statistic	Asymptotic	Bootstrap 1	Bootstrap 2
2	3.0438	0.0012	0.0020	0.0070
5	2.5821	0.0049	0.009	0.0360
10	1.9790	0.0239	0.0270	0.0510
20	1.3291	0.0919	0.0960	0.1310

German stock returns, giving in many cases different decisions about acceptance or rejection of the null hypothesis of no autocorrelation.

White and Racine (2001) also test for predictable components in returns by applying bootstrap techniques for inference in artificial neural networks (ANN). They conclude that exchange rates do appear to contain information that is exploitable for enhanced point prediction, but the nature of the predictive relation evolves over time. However, they do not take into account the evolution of the conditional variance.

In relation to testing for the presence of unit roots in exchange rates, Kanas (1998) investigates whether the Dickey-Fuller (DF) test is affected by the presence

Table 3. Summary of recent bootstrap applications testing for dynamics of returns.

Author	Test for	Boot. procedure	Results
Conditional mean			
Malliaropulos (1996)	Autocor. of returns	Raw returns	Not take into account heteros.
Pan et al. (1997)	Autocor. of returns	Raw returns	Not take into account heteros.
Kanas (1998)	Unit root in prices		
Mallia. and Priest. (1999)	Autocor. of returns	Weighted boot.	Mean reversion is due to time-varying expected returns and partial integration
Politis et al. (1999)	Autocor. of returns	Subsampling	Asymptotic properties
Gospodinov (2000)	Non-linearities	Standard. returns	Finite sample properties
		Wild Bootstrap	Specifies a TAR model with GARCH errors
		Feasible GLS Boot	
Hafner and Herwa. (2000)	Autocor. of returns	Wild bootstrap	Boots. test have good size and power properties
White and Racine (2001)	Predictable regularities in exchange rates	Raw returns	Not take into account heteros.
Conditional variance			
Tauchen et al. (1996)	Persistence	Sampling from fitted conditional density	Dynamic impulse response analysis
	Asymmetry		
	Relation vol.-prices		
Brock. and Chow. (1997)	Chaos	Raw returns	Not take into account heteros.
Bollers. and Mikk. (1999)	Fractional integration	Standard. returns	Best model: FIEGARCH
Blake and Kapet. (2000)	ARCH	Raw returns	Artificial neural network
			Under the null is appropriate
Eftekhari et al. (2000)	Measures of risk	Raw returns	Monthly data (homoscedastic)

(continued)

Table 3. *Continued.*

Author	Test for	Boot. procedure	Results
Technical trading rules			
Brock *et al.* (1992)	Performance of TTR	Standard. returns	TTR are profitable
Kho (1996)	Performance of TTR	Standard. returns	Different conclusions with standard and bootstrap tests
Mills (1997)	Performance of TTR	Standard. returns	Predictability dissapears after 1980
Besse. and Chan (1998)	Performance of TTR	Raw returns	Not take into account heteros.
Ito (1999)	Performance of TTR	Standard. returns	Importance of time-varying expected returns
LeBaron (1999)	Performance of TTR	Raw returns	Effect of Federal Reserve
			Not take into account heteros.
White (1999)	Performance of TTR	Stationary boot.	Avoid data snooping
Sullivan *et al.* (1999)	Performance of TTR	Stationary boot.	Outperformance disappears out of sample
Chang and Osler (1999)	Performance of TTR	Raw returns	Not take into account heteros
Millet and Michel (2000)	Performance of TTR	Raw returns	Not take into account heteros
Taylor (2000)	Performance of TTR	Standard. returns	Test based on TTR have less power than standard uncorrelation tests
Other applications			
Ikenberry *et al.* (1995)	Event study		Long-run returns are not zero
Kothari and Warner (1997)	Event study		Parametric long-horizon tests can be missleading
Stanton (1997)	Term structure	Block boot.	Continuous time
Garrant *et al.* (2001)	Target-zone nonlinearities	Block boot.	Nonlinearities in specific subsamples
Carriere (2000)	Forward rates	Block boot.	Uses splines
Groene. and Fraser (2001a)	Asset Pricing model	Block boot.	Monthly data (homosced.)
Groene. and Fraser (2001b)	Asset Pricing model	Block boot.	Monthly data (homosced.)

of structural breaks due to realignments in the central parities. Bootstrap simulations are used to generate critical values of the DF test in the presence of multiple dummy variables. He concludes that, once you take into account the realignments, there is no evidence of the presence of unit roots in exchange rates.

Although most of the previous authors conclude that stock returns are not predictable in the short run, there is an interest for long horizon regressions that usually take the following expression:

$$\sum_{i=1}^{k} y_{t+i} = \alpha_k + \beta_k x_k + u_{tk} \tag{4}$$

where x_t is some variable measuring fundamental values, usually dividend yield. Maddala and Li (1996) review extensively several papers using bootstrap techniques in this context. Ikenberry et al. (1995) also analyze the long-run behavior of returns by means of an event study analysis. They conclude that long-run abnormal returns are systematically nonzero. They defined the sample buy-and-hold abnormal return as the difference between the buy-and-hold return and the corresponding return on a portfolio of securities matched by book-to-market, size and event date. To assess the statistical significance, this difference is compared to a bootstrap distribution of buy-and-hold abnormal returns. However, Kothari and Warner (1997) point out several potential shortcoming of bootstrap techniques for long-horizon event studies.

In relation to testing for non-linearities in the conditional mean of a series in the presence of high persistence and conditional heteroscedasticity, Gospodinov (2000) proposes to use a Threshold Autoregressive of order one (TAR(1)) model with GARCH(1, 1) errors which is applied to the analysis of the term structure of interest rates. He uses bootstrap approximations to ensure the validity of the statistical inference. In particular, he proposes three alternative bootstrap procedures. The first one is based on bootstrapping the standardized residuals, the second is a wild bootstrap procedure and, finally, he considers a feasible GLS bootstrap. The size and power properties of these approximations are evaluated by simulation and the conclusion is that all of the bootstrap tests have excellent size properties.

Garrant et al. (2001) also test for the presence of target-zone nonlinearities in the Pound/Deutschmark exchange rate using the block bootstrap to compute the corresponding p-values.

3.2. Testing for dynamics in the conditional variance of returns

There are also hypothesis related to the dynamics of volatility that have been tested using bootstrap procedures. Lamoureux and Lastrapes (1990) were the first to use bootstrap procedures to test if the Integrated GARCH (IGARCH) models, often found in empirical applications, can be the result of structural changes in otherwise stationary GARCH models. However, Maddala and Li (1996) point out that they do not formulate correctly the null hypothesis to be tested and show how the test should be carried out properly.

Tauchen *et al.* (1996) investigate multi-step nonlinear dynamics of daily price and volume movements. Their objective is to examine the persistence properties of stochastic volatility, the asymmetric responses of conditional variances to positive and negative movements in prices and the nonlinear relation between volume and prices. They construct confidence bands for the corresponding impulse response functions by resampling from the fitted conditional densities. The bootstrap method they used is described in Gallant *et al.* (1993).

Later, Brockman and Chowdhury (1997) applied bootstrap techniques to distinguish whether the intra-day implied volatility of the S&P100 index call option is stochastic or has a chaotic deterministic behavior. However, they are bootstrapping from the raw returns series that are not independent. Therefore, the properties of the bootstrap procedure can be seriously affected.

Bollerslev and Mikkelsen (1999) analyze whether the long-run dependence in U.S. stock market volatility is best described by a slowly mean-reverting fractionally integrated process by inferring the degree of mean-reversion implicit in a panel data set of transaction prices on the S&P500 composite stock price index. They compare the observed prices with risk-neutralized prices boot-strapped from the residuals standardized with standard deviations estimated by different heteroscedastic models. They conclude that the Fractionally Integrated EGARCH (FIEGARCH) model of Bollerslev and Mikkelsen (1996) results in the lowest average absolute and relative pricing errors.

Also, in relation to testing the dynamics of volatility, Blake and Kapetanios (2000) propose a test for ARCH based on a neural network specification. As the test suffers from size distortions, they use bootstrap procedures to correct them.

Finally, Eftekhari *et al.* (2000) compare different measures of risk, namely the semi-variance, the lower partial moment, the Gini and the absolute deviation using both simulated and real series of monthly returns. They draw, with replacement, returns from each of the samples of real data and the alternative measures of risk are calculated for each of the bootstrapped samples.

3.3. *Technical trading rules*

One of the most popular methods to analyze the hypothesis that equity markets are efficient is based on technical analysis. Trading rules are used to classify each day t as either Buy, Sell or Neutral, using information available up to day t. Technical trading rules are rather important in practice given that they are almost universally used by practitioners; see the references in Chang and Osler (1999). A trading rule is said to uncover evidence of price predictability if expected returns depend on the Buy/Sell information. To assess this dependency, it is natural to test for the difference between the average returns for Buy and Sell days. The obvious test of the null hypothesis that there is no predictability is based on the following statistic

$$z = \frac{\bar{r}_I - \bar{r}_J}{\left(\dfrac{s_I^2}{n_I} + \dfrac{s_J^2}{n_J}\right)^{0.5}}$$

where $\bar{r}_I$, s_I^2 and n_I are, respectively, the sample mean, variance and number of returns for Buy days, and $\bar{r}_J$, s_J^2 and n_J are the corresponding measures for Sell days. The asymptotic distribution of the z statistic is standard normal when the returns process is a strictly stationary, martingale difference with finite second moments.

When several trading rules are considered, another interesting hypothesis is whether there exists a superior technical trading rule that significantly outperforms a benchmark of holding cash. The null hypothesis, in this case, is that the expected return of the best trading rule is no better than the expected return of the benchmark.

Due to the non-normality of returns, it is sensible to use bootstrap procedures to estimate the distribution of these statistics. In a seminal paper in this area, Brock *et al.* (1992) propose to combine technical analysis and bootstrap procedures. They proposed a bootstrap procedure to obtain a better approximation of these statistics and to decide if some specific statistical model can explain the observed trading rules results. A statistic z is calculated from a trading rule applied to the observed series. Then a particular statistical model is fitted to the observed returns and artificial price series are generated by sampling from the corresponding residuals together with the estimated parameters. The same statistic z is computed for each of the artificial price series, obtaining a sequence of bootstrap statistics, $z_1^*, z_2^*, ..., z_B^*$. The proportion of statistics z_i^* that are more extreme than z, is the p-value for the test of the null hypothesis that the particular model generates observed prices. They apply this bootstrap method to analyze the properties of the Dow Jones Index observed daily from 1897 to 1986, bootstrapping the p-values for the difference between Buy and Sell average returns by applying 26 technical trading rules, and conclude that they significantly outperform the benchmark. However, they explicitly mention that the asymptotic properties of the bootstrap procedure proposed are not known for some models of the GARCH family as, for example, EGARCH and GARCH-M. Furthermore, they suggest that the results of the test are not qualitatively altered whether the asymptotic or the bootstrapped standard errors are used. Finally, they note the dangers of data-snooping when testing the profitability of a large number of trading rules on the same sample of returns. Data-snooping occurs when a given data set is used more than once for inference or data selection. In this case, there is the possibility that positive results can be due simply to chance. As they are testing 26 trading rules one by one, there is a reasonable possibility that data-snooping could be occurring. Therefore, the evidence in favor of a superior performance of trading rules can be tempered. Finally, it should be mentioned that the

combination of bootstrap methods with trading rules has been more fruitful as an
instrument to check the adequacy of several commonly used models like Random
Walks, GARCH and the Markov switching regression models. For this purpose,
Brock *et al.* (1992) propose to bootstrap the residuals from a fitted model and the
estimated parameters to obtain bootstrap replicates of the original data. They
compute the trading rule profits for each bootstrap replicate and compare the
corresponding bootstrap distribution with the trading rule profits derived from
the actual data.

The application of the procedures proposed by Brock *et al.* (1992) is very
extensive in the literature. For example, Mills (1997) applies their methodology to
data on the London Stock Exchange FT30 index for the period 1935–1994.
Although he found that trading rules outperform the benchmark when using data
up to 1980, the predictive ability of the trading rules after this date disappears.
Later, LeBaron (1999) tests whether the predictive ability of trading rules over
future movements of foreign exchange rates changes after removing periods in
which the Federal Reserve is active. Maillet and Michel (2000) apply the test
proposed by LeBaron (1999) to twelve exchange rates. They also use bootstrap
methods to estimate the distribution of both trading rule returns and raw returns
to analyze whether filtering the raw exchange series with some trading rule
significantly changes their characteristics. Finally, Taylor (2000) studies the
predictability of several U.K. financial prices by fitting ARMA-ARCH models to
the corresponding returns.

As noted by Brock *et al.* (1992), there is a danger of data-snooping when testing
one by one the performance of a high number of trading rules. To avoid it, White
(2000) applies the stationary bootstrap to test whether the performance of the best
trading rule is no better than the benchmark. Later, Sullivan *et al.* (1999) apply
White's (2000) bootstrap methodology to present a comprehensive test of
performance across several technical rules. They show that, even after adjustments
for data-snooping, some of the trading rules considered by Brock *et al.* (1992)
outperform the benchmark. However, their results do not hold out-of-sample.

However, even after Maddala and Li (1996) highlighted the dangers of
bootstrapping from raw returns, there are some authors who still do not take into
account the presence of conditional heteroscedasticity when using bootstrap
procedures to analyze the profitability of technical trading rules; see, for example,
Bessembinder and Chan (1998) and Chang and Osler (1999).

Kho (1996) analyses the performance of trading rules on currency futures
markets using an alternative procedure to the one proposed by Brock *et al.* (1992).
He applies a bootstrap procedure based on observations standardized assuming
a GARCH-M specification, to some versions of the conditional international
Capital Asset Pricing Model (CAPM) for time-varying expected returns and risk.
Subsequently, Ito (1999) evaluates the profitability of technical trading rules by
using equilibrium asset pricing models. He found that using standard or bootstrap
p-values, the conclusions can be reversed.

Finally, the Contrarian Hypothesis, also related to trading rules, states that
stocks that consistently underperform (outperform) the market will outperform

(underperform) over subsequent periods, those stocks that have previously outperformed (underperformed) the market. In two closely related papers, Mum *et al.* (1999, 2000), use exactly the same methodology to test this hypothesis for French and German stock markets in the first paper, and for US and Canadian stock markets in the second. The bootstrap procedure they use, however, is not appropriate, in the main because they are not resampling under the null hypothesis, but also because it is hard to believe that it is really a bootstrap procedure.

3.4. *Other tests*

There are other applications of bootstrap procedures to hypothesis testing related to financial data. For example, Stanton (1997) estimates non-parametrically the parameters of continuous time diffusion processes that are observed at discrete times using kernel estimators of the corresponding conditional expectations. He uses the block bootstrap to calculate confidence bands for the estimated densities.

Later, Carriere (2000) constructs confidence intervals for forward rates estimated with spline models that take into account the heteroscedasticity and correlation in the data. They resample from the residuals standardized to have constant variance and no autocorrelation.

Finally, in two very closely related papers, Groenewold and Fraser (2001a,b) analyze the sensitivity of tests of asset-pricing models to violations of the Gaussianity hypothesis. In the former paper, they use Australian data and in the latter, US and UK data, to compare the standard test with those based on GMM estimators and on bootstrap procedures. They conclude that standard methods are robust to Gaussianity. However, their results have two limitations. First, although they mention three alternative bootstrap procedures, the standard procedure based on resampling directly from the returns, a block bootstrap and a parametric bootstrap based on fitting a model for the conditional variance, the first is inappropriate and they do not implement the third. Therefore, only the block bootstrap may have the desired properties. The second limitation is concerned with the properties of the data they analyze, namely the observations are monthly and the presence of conditional heteroscedasticity is very weak. Therefore, it is not surprising that the results based on the bootstrap or on standard asymptotic distributions are similar.

Table 3 summarizes the main contributions described in this section.

4. Distribution of returns and volatilities

Bootstrap procedures can be used not only to estimate the sample distribution of a given statistic but also to obtain estimates of the density of the variable being analyzed. In this section, we review the papers that apply bootstrap procedures to obtain prediction densities of future returns and their volatilities and to estimate the VaR.

4.1. *Prediction*

Prediction is one of the main goals when a dynamic model is fitted to returns. In that sense, GARCH and SV models have the attraction that they can provide dynamic prediction intervals that are narrow in tranquil times and wide in volatile periods. Furthermore, there is an increasing interest in interval forecasts as measures of uncertainty; see, for example, Bollerslev (2001) and Engle (2001). On the other hand, the volatility of returns is a key factor in many models of option valuation and portfolio allocation problems. Therefore, accurate predictions of volatilities are critical for the implementation and evaluation of asset and derivative pricing theories, as well as trading and hedging strategies. Bootstrap-based methods lead to prediction intervals that incorporate the uncertainty due to parameter estimation without distributional assumptions on the sequence of innovations. As described in Section 2, these methods have proved to be very useful for obtaining prediction intervals for future values of series generated by linear ARIMA models. However, if the presence of conditional heteroscedasticity is not taken into account, the coverage properties of bootstrap intervals for high frequency returns can be distorted; see, for example, Kim (2001) in the context of VAR(1) models. Consequently, Miguel and Olave (1999a) extend the procedure of Cao *et al.* (1997) to stationary ARMA processes with GARCH(1, 1) innovations and prove the asymptotic validity of the corresponding bootstrap procedure to obtain prediction intervals for future returns. These prediction intervals are conditional on the parameter estimates and, consequently, do not incorporate the uncertainty due to parameter estimation. As volatility is specified as a function of past observations in GARCH models, future volatilities are known given the parameters and past observations. As a consequence, the bootstrap procedure proposed by Miguel and Olave (1999a) cannot be used to obtain prediction intervals for future volatilities. Miguel and Olave (1999b) carry out a Monte Carlo experiment to compare the performance of the conditional bootstrap intervals with the Cornish-Fisher approximation proposed by Baillie and Bollerslev (1992). They show that when the prediction horizon is longer than one period, the bootstrap prediction intervals have coverages closer to the nominal than the intervals based on Cornish-Fisher approximations. Gospodinov (2002) also proposes an alternative bootstrap procedure conditional on parameter estimates to forecast future returns modeled by a TAR(1) model with GARCH(1, 1) errors.

Pascual *et al.* (2000) generalize the bootstrap procedure of Pascual *et al.* (1998) to obtain prediction densities of both returns and volatilities of series generated by GARCH processes. The main advantage of their proposal is that the procedure incorporates the variability due to parameter estimation and, therefore, it is possible to obtain bootstrap prediction densities for the volatility process. The asymptotic properties of the procedure are derived and the finite sample properties are analyzed by means of Monte Carlo experiments which show that the properties of intervals for future returns are adequate. They also show that incorporating the uncertainty due to parameter estimation makes no difference when generating prediction intervals for returns if the error distribution is symmetric. However, when constructing prediction intervals for future volatilities, it is necessary to introduce this uncertainty to have coverage close to the nominal values. However, the length of intervals for future volatilities is well above the empirical values. Finally, they apply their bootstrap procedure to obtain prediction densities of future values and volatilities of the IBEX35 index of the Madrid Stock Exchange.

To illustrate the use of the bootstrap to obtain prediction densities for future returns and volatilities, the procedure proposed by Pascual *et al.* (2000) has been applied to the series of returns of the Pound–Dollar exchange rate described in Section 3. Although the series consists of $T = 3039$ observations, only 3019 have been used for estimation purposes, leaving the last 20 observations for out-of-sample forecast evaluation. Recall that the VR(q) test detects autoregressive components in the returns series for q = 2 and 5. Therefore, we fit an AR(1) model with GARCH(1, 1) errors. The estimated model is given by

$$y_t = \underset{(0.0181)}{0.0652}\, y_{t-1} + a_t$$

$$a_t = \varepsilon_t \sigma_t \tag{5}$$

$$\hat{\sigma}_t^2 = \underset{(0.0001)}{0.0007} + \underset{(0.0047)}{0.0443}\, a_{t-1}^2 + \underset{(0.0058)}{0.9447}\, \hat{\sigma}_{t-1}^2$$

Figure 4 represents a kernel estimate of the density of the standardized residuals, $\hat{\varepsilon}_t = a_t/\hat{\sigma}_t$, together with the standard normal density. Notice that the density of $\hat{\varepsilon}_t$ has fat tails. In particular, the kurtosis is 4.6711. Therefore, the conditional

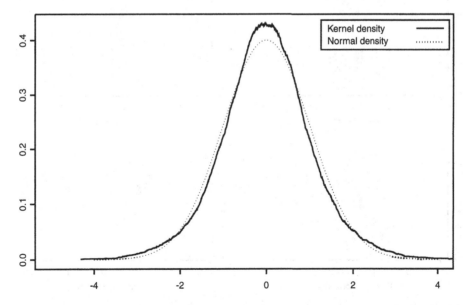

Figure 4. Kernel density of Pound–Dollar exchange rate returns standardized with GARCH(1, 1) standard deviations.

Gaussianity of returns is rejected when a GARCH(1, 1) model is fitted. Figure 5 represents the bootstrap densities estimated for 1, 5, 10 and 20 steps-ahead predictions of returns. Using these bootstrap densities, it is possible to construct the corresponding prediction intervals for future returns. Figure 6 represents the 80% and 95% intervals for y_{T+k}, $k = 1, ..., 20$, together with the intervals obtained using the Box-Jenkins methodology. We also plot the point predictions that, in this case, are equal to zero and the actual values of y_{T+k}. Notice that approximately 4 of 20 observations are supposed to lie out the 80% prediction interval. However, the Box-Jenkins intervals are unnecessarily wide leaving only one outside. While the bootstrap intervals are thinner, they leave 4 observations outside. On the other hand, looking at the 95% intervals, they are supposed to leave one observation out.

With respect to the prediction of future volatilities, Figure 7 represents the bootstrap densities for different prediction horizons. The corresponding bootstrap prediction intervals for future volatilities have been plotted in Figure 8, together with the point predictions obtained from the estimated GARCH(1, 1) model in equation (5).

The extension of these bootstrap procedures to estimate prediction densities of returns and volatilities of series generated by SV models seems rather promising in the context of predicting future volatilities. Remember that while in GARCH models the volatility is known one-step-ahead, SV models introduce an

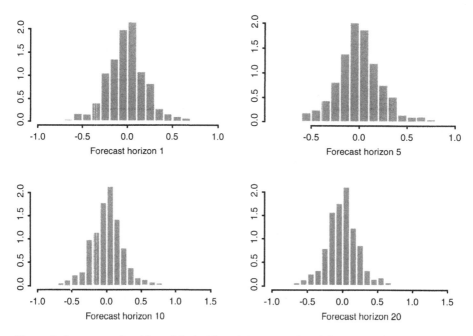

Figure 5. Bootstrap densities of 1, 5, 10 and 20 steps ahead forecasts of Pound–Dollar exchange rate returns.

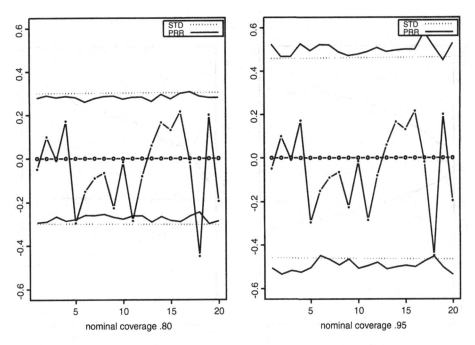

Figure 6. Box-Jenkins and bootstrap 80% and 95% prediction intervals for Pound–Dollar exchange rate returns together with point predictions (O) and actual values (□).

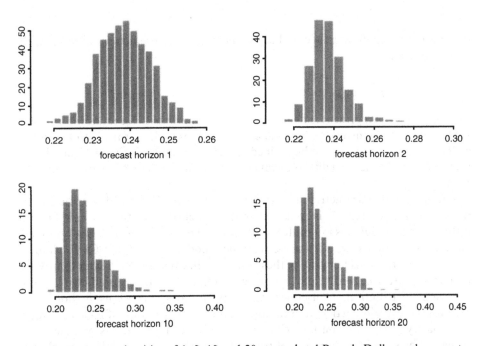

Figure 7. Bootstrap densities of 1, 2, 10 and 20 steps ahead Pound–Dollar exchange rate volatilities.

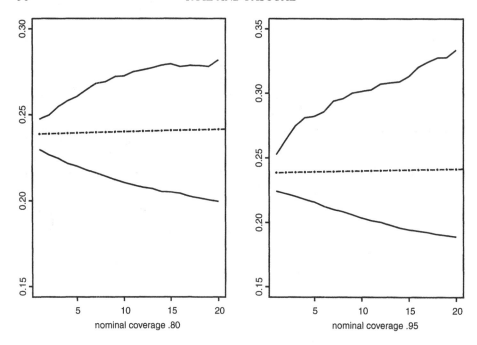

Figure 8. Bootstrap prediction intervals for future Pound–Dollar exchange rates volatilities together with their GARCH point predictions (□).

unexpected component that could allow more realistic prediction intervals with better coverage.

4.2. Value-at-Risk (VaR)

Financial risk management is dedicated to providing density forecasts of portfolio values and to tracking certain aspects of the densities such as, for example, Value-at-Risk (VaR). The VaR can be defined as the expected loss of a portfolio after a given period of time (usually 10 days) corresponding to the $\alpha\%$ quantile (usually 1%).

The early VaR parametric models impose a known theoretical distribution to price changes. Usually it is assumed that the density function of risk factors influencing asset returns is a multivariate normal distribution. The most popular parametric methods are variance-covariance models and Monte Carlo simulation. However, excess kurtosis of these factors will cause losses greater than VaR to occur more frequently and be more extreme than those predicted by the Gaussian distribution. Consequently, many authors suggest using bootstrap techniques to avoid particular assumptions on the distribution of factors beyond stationarity of the distribution of returns. The procedure consists of generating scenarios by sampling observed returns associated with each risk factor included in the portfolio. The aggregate value of all linear and derivative positions produces a simulated portfolio value. Vlaar (2000) investigates the accuracy of various VaR models on Dutch interest rate-based portfolios and concludes that bootstrap techniques produce satisfactory results when long periods of data are available.

Early bootstrap procedures to compute the VaR of a portfolio assumed constant volatility of returns. However, the ability of bootstrap techniques to predict future losses can be undermined when the volatility evolves over time and, therefore the distribution of risk factors is not i.i.d.. In this case, the probability of having a large loss is not equal across different days. Barone-Adesi et al. (1999) propose a bootstrap procedure to obtain VaR estimates based on resampling from returns standardized using GARCH estimates of the volatility. The bootstrapping is done conditional on the parameter estimates and, therefore, is similar to the one proposed by Miguel and Olave (1999a) for obtaining prediction intervals. They illustrate the procedure with a very informative numerical example of a portfolio of three assets. Later, Barone-Adesi et al. (2001) compare this method with traditional bootstrapping estimates using three hypothetical portfolios on the S&P500 index and show that the advantages of the standardized bootstrap is magnified by the presence of options in the portfolio.

To illustrate the different alternatives to estimate the VaR, we perform the following experiment. We simulate 1000 series by the GARCH(1, 1) model in (1) and compute the empirical VaR for $\alpha = 0.01$, 0.05 and 0.1. Then for each simulated series, we estimate the VaR by each of the following procedures:

  (i) Assuming that returns are $N(0, \hat{s}^2)$, where $\hat{s}^2$ is the sample variance.
 (ii) Assuming that returns are a conditionally Gaussian GARCH(1, 1) process.
(iii) Resampling from the raw returns and estimating their density under conditional homoscedasticity.
 (iv) Resampling from the returns standardized with the GARCH estimates of the conditional standard deviation and estimating the density conditional on parameter estimates, as proposed by Barone-Adessi et al. (1999).
  (v) Resampling from the returns standardized with the GARCH estimates of the conditional standard deviation and estimating the density incorporating parameter uncertainty. Notice that, in this case, the procedure used to obtain the density is the one proposed by Pascual et al. (2000).

Tables 4 and 5 report the average VaR values across all the replicates when ε_t in (1) is a Student-t distribution with 5 degrees of freedom and a minus χ^2 distribution with 4 degrees of freedom, respectively. In these tables we do not report the average VaR values for the bootstrap procedure based on resampling the standardized returns conditional on parameter estimates because they are very similar to those obtained by incorporating the parameter uncertainty. Pascual et al. (2000) show that whether or not the parameter uncertainty is incorporated in intervals for returns does not have any significant effect. With respect to the Student-t distribution, Table 4 shows that, assuming marginal Gaussianity of returns, the VaR values obtained are well under the empirical

Table 4. Monte Carlo results on VaR values using conditionally Gaussian GARCH(1, 1) model and bootstrap methods. Student-5 distribution

Forecast horizon	Sample size		Average VaR values				
			Empirical	Normal	GARCH	Bootstrap 1	Bootstrap 2
1	T	Probability	—	—	—	—	—
	300	10%	−1.094	−1.253	−1.212	−1.090	−1.084
		5%	−1.497	−1.616	−1.563	−1.534	−1.499
		1%	−2.538	−2.272	−2.197	−2.746	−2.548
	1000	10%	−1.081	−1.264	−1.202	−1.073	−1.079
		5%	−1.478	−1.630	−1.549	−1.504	−1.477
		1%	−2.504	−2.291	−2.178	−2.747	−2.505
5	T	Probability	—	—	—	—	—
	300	10%	−1.086	−1.253	−1.238	−1.088	−1.080
		5%	−1.499	−1.616	−1.596	−1.533	−1.506
		1%	−2.588	−2.272	−2.244	−2.751	−2.637
	1000	10%	−1.075	−1.264	−1.224	−1.079	−1.073
		5%	−1.485	−1.630	−1.578	−1.513	−1.483
		1%	−2.565	−2.291	−2.218	−2.755	−2.592
10	T	Probability	—	—	—	—	—
	300	10%	−1.083	−1.253	−1.257	−1.085	−1.078
		5%	−1.508	−1.616	−1.621	−1.530	−1.509
		1%	−2.656	−2.272	−2.278	−2.768	−2.673
	1000	10%	−1.074	−1.264	−1.242	−1.075	−1.072
		5%	−1.495	−1.630	−1.601	−1.513	−1.496
		1%	−2.630	−2.291	−2.251	−2.769	−2.654
20	T	Probability	—	—	—	—	—
	300	10%	−1.079	−1.253	−1.278	−1.086	−1.074
		5%	−1.510	−1.616	−1.648	−1.528	−1.509
		1%	−2.695	−2.272	−2.318	−2.744	−2.734
	1000	10%	−1.074	−1.264	−1.264	−1.078	−1.069
		5%	−1.503	−1.630	−1.629	−1.518	−1.497
		1%	−2.682	−2.291	−2.291	−2.767	−2.692

values at the 0.05 and 0.1 probabilities, implying more expected losses than actual. However, at the most common 0.01 probability, the estimated VaR is larger than the empirical value. Therefore, the estimated loss is smaller than the actual. The same conclusions are reached for all horizons and the problem is not solved by increasing the sample size. Although the expected losses are slightly closer to the empirical values, the same results are observed when a conditionally Gaussian GARCH(1, 1) model is assumed. The estimated VaR values are clearly improved when they are computed using bootstrap

Table 5. Monte Carlo results on VaR values using conditionally Gaussian GARCH(1, 1) model and bootstrap methods. $-\chi^2$ distribution with 4 degrees of freedom

Forecast horizon	Sample size		Average VaR values				
			Empirical	Normal	GARCH	Bootstrap 1	Bootstrap 2
1	T	Probability	—	—	—	—	—
	300	10%	−1.284	−1.254	−1.220	−1.271	−1.280
		5%	−1.869	−1.616	−1.572	−1.881	−1.863
		1%	−3.178	−2.272	−2.211	−3.323	−3.140
	1000	10%	−1.292	−1.263	−1.238	−1.259	−1.296
		5%	−1.879	−1.628	−1.597	−1.867	−1.882
		1%	−3.195	−2.289	−2.245	−3.375	−3.200
5	T	Probability	—	—	—	—	—
	300	10%	−1.278	−1.254	−1.242	−1.272	−1.272
		5%	−1.873	−1.616	−1.601	−1.887	−1.860
		1%	−3.247	−2.273	−2.251	−3.321	−3.204
	1000	10%	−1.283	−1.263	−1.255	−1.260	−1.282
		5%	−1.881	−1.628	−1.617	−1.863	−1.884
		1%	−3.256	−2.289	−2.274	−3.368	−3.278
10	T	Probability	—	—	—	—	—
	300	10%	−1.276	−1.254	−1.257	−1.275	−1.265
		5%	−1.881	−1.616	−1.620	−1.884	−1.862
		1%	−3.332	−2.273	−2.278	−3.305	−3.260
	1000	10%	−1.281	−1.263	−1.267	−1.259	−1.270
		5%	−1.888	−1.628	−1.634	−1.863	−1.869
		1%	−3.341	−2.289	−2.297	−3.376	−3.330
20	T	Probability	—	—	—	—	—
	300	10%	−1.252	−1.254	−1.274	−1.275	−1.253
		5%	−1.869	−1.616	−1.642	−1.886	−1.855
		1%	−3.365	−2.273	−2.309	−3.285	−3.296
	1000	10%	−1.265	−1.262	−1.281	−1.256	−1.257
		5%	−1.874	−1.628	−1.651	−1.860	−1.860
		1%	−3.376	−2.289	−2.321	−3.383	−3.348

procedures. The expected losses when bootstrapping from the raw returns are generally bigger than the actual losses. However, when the bootstrap is done by resampling from the standardized returns, i.e. the presence of conditional heteroscedasticity is taken into account, the estimated VaR's are remarkably close to the actual values. The bootstrap procedure performs well in estimating the VaR.

With respect to the results for the asymmetric minus χ^2 distribution, Table 5 shows that the VaR values computed assuming a marginal Gaussian distribution of returns are systematically bigger than the actual values. Even larger or similar estimates are obtained when a conditionally Gaussian GARCH(1,1) model is assumed. Therefore, the actual losses will be, on average, bigger than the losses predicted by both models. This problem is observed for all probabilities, forecast horizons and sample sizes considered. On the other hand, when the bootstrap procedures are applied, the estimated VaR's are closer to the empirical values. Once more, the estimated bootstrap VaR values are more accurate, specially for the shorter horizons, when resampling from the standardized returns.

Finally, we have obtained the VaR of the Pound–Dollar exchange rate using the normality assumption and by the procedure proposed by Pascual *et al.* (2000). For $\alpha = 0.05$ and three steps ahead, the expected loss assuming normality is -0.3865 while the bootstrap VaR is bigger at -0.3724. On the other hand, when $\alpha = 0.01$, under normality the VaR is -0.5435 and the bootstrap is smaller at -0.6108. Notice that the more important differences between both values of the VaR appear when looking at the tails of the distribution that are the focus of interest from the empirical point of view.

Table 6 summarizes the main contributions in this area.

Table 6. Summary of recent bootstrap applications to estimate the distribution of returns.

Author	Model	Boot. proced.	Results
Prediction of returns			
Mig. and Olav. (1999a)	ARMA-GARCH(1,1)	Stand. returns	Conditional on parameter estimates Asymptotic validity
Mig. and Olav. (1999b)	ARMA-GARCH(1,1)	Stand. returns	Conditional on parameter estimates Monte Carlo results
Pascual *et al.* (2000)	GARCH(1,1)	Stand. returns	Parameter uncertainty. Asympt. and finite samp properties
Gospodinov (2002)	Highly persistent AR	Raw returns	Finite sample properties
		Backward repr.	Forecast interest rates
Prediction of volatilities			
Pascual *et al.* (2000)	GARCH(1,1)	Stand. returns	Parameter uncertainty. Asympt. and finite samp properties
Value at Risk			
Baro.-Ad. *et al.* (1999)	GARCH(1,1)	Stand. returns	Conditional on parameter estimates
Vlaar (2001)	GARCH(1,1)	Raw returns	Boot. satisfactory for long series
Baro.-Ad. *et al.* (2001)	GARCH(1,1)	Raw returns Stand. returns	Advantages of Stand. boot. when there are options in portfolio

5. Conclusions

In this paper, we reviewed the literature on the application of bootstrap procedures to the analysis of financial time series. We focused mainly on the papers that have appeared after the review of Maddala and Li (1996). High frequency financial returns are often characterized by a leptokurtic marginal distribution of unknown form. Consequently, bootstrap methods are especially well suited for their analysis. However, when applying these methods to the empirical analysis of financial returns, it should be kept in mind that they were originally designed for *i.i.d.* observations. Although financial returns are usually uncorrelated, they are not independent. Volatility clustering generates correlations between squared observations. Therefore, the bootstrap procedures should be adapted to take into account this dependence. There are two main alternatives. The first is to assume a parametric model for the dynamic evolution of the volatility and to bootstrap from the returns standardized with the estimated standard deviations. Alternatively, it is possible to adopt nonparametric bootstrap methods designed for dependent observations as, for example, the block bootstrap.

There are many empirical applications where bootstrap methods have been adopted to test a great variety of null hypothesis related with financial returns as, for example, the presence of predictable components in the conditional mean, the long-memory property of the conditional variance, or the predictive ability of trading rules. Bootstrap procedures have also been used to obtain the predictive densities of future returns and volatilities, which are fundamental, for example, for VaR models. However, there are very few analytical results on the finite sample and asymptotic properties of the bootstrap procedures when applied to heteroscedastic time series.

Although we focused on the application of bootstrap techniques to the analysis of univariate financial time series, there are also multivariate applications. For example, Engsted and Tanggaard (2001) use bootstrap procedures to compute the bias, standard errors and confidence intervals for the parameters of VAR models fitted to model the Danish stock and bond markets. Kim (2001) also uses bootstrap procedures in the context of VAR models applied to financial series.

Acknowledgements

We are very grateful to E. Ferreira and to the editors, M. McAleer and L. Oxley for useful comments. Financial support from project PB98-0026 from the Spanish Government is gratefully acknowledged by the first author.

References

Baillie, R. T. and Bollerslev, T. (1989) The message in daily exchange rates: a conditional variance tale. *Journal of Business and Economic Statistics*, 7, 297–305.
Baillie, R. T. and Bollerslev, T. (1992) Prediction in dynamic models with time-dependent conditional variances. *Journal of Econometrics*, 52, 91–113.

Barone-Adesi, G., Giannopoulos, K. and Vosper, L. (1999) VaR without correlations for non-linear portfolios. *Journal of Futures Markets*, 19, 583–602.

Barone-Adesi, G. and Giannopoulos, K. (2001) Non-parametric VaR techniques. Myths and Realities. *Economic Notes*, 30, 167–181.

Berkowitz, J. and Kilian, L. (2000) Recent developments in bootstrapping time series. *Econometric Reviews*, 19, 1–48.

Bessembinder, H. and Chan, K. (1998) Market efficiency and the returns to technical analysis. *Financial Management*, 27, 5–17.

Blake, A. P. and Kapetanios, G. (2000) A radial basis function artificial neural network test for ARCH. *Economics Letters*, 69, 15–23.

Bollerslev, T. (2001) Financial econometrics: Past developments and future challenges. *Journal of Econometrics*, 100, 41–51.

Bollerslev, T. and Mikkelsen, H. O. (1996) Modelling and pricing long memory in stock market volatility. *Journal of Econometrics*, 92, 151–184.

Bollerslev, T. and Mikkelsen, H. O. (1999) Long-Term equity anticipation securities and stock market volatility dynamics. *Journal of Econometrics*, 92, 75–99.

Bookstaber, R. M. and McDonald, J. B. (1987) A general distribution for describing security price returns. *Journal of Business*, 60, 401–24.

Brock, W., Lakonishok, J. and LeBaron, B. (1992) Simple technical trading rules and the stochastic properties of stock returns. *Journal of Finance*, 47, 1731–1764.

Brockman, P. and Chowdhury, M. (1997) Deterministic versus stochastic volatility: implications for option pricing models. *Applied Financial Economics*, 7, 499–505.

Cao, R., Febrero-Bande, M., González-Manteiga, W., Prada-Sánchez, J. M. and García-jurado, I. (1997) Saving computing time in constructing consistent bootstrap prediction intervals for autoregressive processes. *Communications in Statistics, Simulation and Computation*, 26, 961–978.

Carriere, J. F. (2000) Non-parametric confidence intervals of instantaneous forward rates. *Insurance: Mathematics and Economics*, 26, 193–202.

Chang, P. H. K. and Osler, C. L. (1999) Methodical madness: Technical analysis and the irrationality of exchange-rate forecasts. *Economic Journal*, 109, 636–661.

Chatterjee, S. and Pari, R. A. (1990) Bootstrapping the number of factors in the arbitrage pricing theory. *J. Financ. Res.*, 13, 15–21.

Cochrane, J. (1988) How big is the random walk in GNP? *Journal of Political Economy*, 96, 893–920.

Efron, B. (1979) Bootstrap methods: another look at the jackknife. *Annals of Statistics*, 7, 1–26.

Efron, B. and Tibshirani, R. (1993) *An Introduction to the Bootstrap*, Chapman & Hall, New York.

Eftekhari, B., Pedersen, C. S. and Satchell, S. E. (2000) On the volatility of measures of financial risk: an investigation using returns from European markets. *European Journal of Finance*, 6, 18–38.

Engle, R. (2001) Financial econometrics. A new discipline with new methods. *Journal of Econometrics*, 100, 53–56.

Engsted, T. and Tanggaard, C. (2001) The Danish stock and bond markets: Comovement, return predictability and variance decomposition. *Journal of Empirical Finance*, 8, 243–271.

Ferreti, N. and Romo, J. (1996) Bootstrap tests for unit root AR(1) models. *Biometrika*.

Freedman, D. A. and Peters, S. F. (1984) Bootstrapping a regression equation: Some empirical results. *Journal of the American Statistical Association*, 79, 97–106.

Gallant, A. R., Rossi, P. E. and Tauchen, G. (1993) Nonlinear dynamic structures. *Econometrica*, 61, 871–907.

Garrant, A., Psaradakis, Z. and Sola, M. (2001) An empirical reassessment of target-zone nonlinearities. *Journal of International Money and Finance*, 20, 533–548.

Gospodinov, N. (2000) Nonlinearities in short-term interest rates, manuscript, Concordia University, Montreal.

Gospodinov, N. (2002) Median unbiased forecasts for highly persistent autoregressive processes. *Journal of Econometrics*, forthcoming.

Groenewold, N. and Fraser, P. (2001a) Test of asset-pricing models: how important is the iid-normal assumption? *Journal of Empirical Finance*, 8, 427–449.

Groenewold, N. and Fraser, P. (2001b) The sensitivity of tests of asset pricing models to the iid-normal assumption: Contemporaneous evidence from the US and UK stock markets. *Journal of Business Finance & Accounting*, 28, 771–798.

Hafner, C. M. and Herwartz, H. (2000) Testing for linear autoregressive dynamics under heteroskedasticity. *Econometrics Journal*, 3, 177–197.

Hall, P. and Wilson, S. R. (1991) Two guidelines for bootstrap hypothesis testing. *Biometrics*, 47, 757–762.

Horowitz, J. L. (2001) The bootstrap and hypothesis tests in Econometrics. *Journal of Econometrics*, 100, 37–40.

Hsie, D. A. and Miller, M. H. (1990) Margin regulation and stock market volatility. *Journal of Finance*, 45, 3–29.

Ikenberry, D., Lakonishok, J. and Vermaelen, T. (1995) Market underreaction to open share repurchases. *Journal of Financial Economics*, 39, 181–208.

Ito, A. (1999) Profits on technical trading rules and time-varying expected returns: Evidence from Pacific-Basin equity markets. *Pacific-Basin Finance Journal*, 7, 283–330.

Kanas, A. (1998) Testing for a unit root in ERM exchange rates in the presence of structural breaks: evidence from the bootstrap. *Applied Economics Letters*, 5, 407–410.

Kho, B. (1996) Time-varying risk premia, volatility and technical trading rule profits: Evidence from foreign currency futures markets. *Journal of Financial Economics*, 41, 249–290.

Kim, J. H. (2001) Bootstrap-after-bootstrap prediction intervals for autoregressive models. *Journal of Business & Economic Statistics*, 19, 117–128.

Korajczyk, R. A. (1985) The pricing of forward contracts for foreign exchange. *Journal of Political Economy*, 93, 346–368.

Kothari, S. P. and Warner, J. B. (1997) Measuring long-horizon security price performance. *Journal of Financial Economics*, 43, 301–339.

Künsch, H. R. (1989) The jackknife and the bootstrap for general stationary observations. *Annals of Statistics*, 17, 1217–1241.

Lamoureux, C. G. and Lastrapes, W. D. (1990) Persistence in variance, structural change and the GARCH models. *Journal of Business and Economic Statistics*, 8, 225–34.

LeBaron, B. (1999) Technical trading rule profitability and foreign exchange intervention. *Journal of International Economics*, 49, 125–143.

Levich, R. M. and Thomas, L. R. (1993) The significance of technical trading-rule profits in the foreign exchange market: a bootstrap approach. *Journal of International Money and Finance*, 12, 451–474.

Li, H. and Maddala, G. S. (1996) Bootstrapping time series models. *Econometric Reviews*, 15, 115–158.

Lo, A. and McKinlay, A. C. (1989) The size and power of the variance ratio test in finite samples: A Monte Carlo investigation. *Journal of Econometrics*, 40, 203–238.

Maddala, G. S. and Li, H. (1996) Bootstrap based tests in financial models. In Maddala, G. S. and Rao, C. R. (eds). *Handbook of Statistics*, vol. 14, Elsevier, Amsterdam, 463–488.

Maillet, B. and Michel, T. (2000) Further insights on the puzzle of technical analysis profitability, *European Journal of Finance*, 6, 196–224.

Malliaropulos, D. (1996) Are long-horizon stock returns predictable? A bootstrap analysis. *Journal of Business Finance and Accounting*, 23, 93–105.

Malliaropulos, D. and Priestley, R. (1999) Mean reversion in Southeast Asian stock markets. *Journal of Empirical Finance*, 6, 355–384.

Miguel, J. A. and Olave, P. (1999a) Bootstrapping forecast intervals in ARCH models. *TEST*, 8, 345–364.

Miguel, J. A. and Olave, P. (1999b) Forecast intervals in ARCH models: Bootstrap versus parametric methods. *Applied Economics Letters*, 6, 323–27.

Mills, T. (1997) Technical analysis and the London Stock Exchange: Testing trading rules using the FT30. *International Journal of Finance and Economics*, 2, 319–31.

Mun, J. C., Vasconcellos, G. M. and Kish, R. (1999) Test of the contrarian investment strategy. Evidence from the French and German Stock Markets. *International Review of Financial Analysis*, 83, 215–234.

Mun, J. C., Vasconcellos, G. M. and Kish, R. (2000) The contrarian/overreaction hypothesis. An analysis of the US and Canadian Stock Markets. *Global Finance Journal*, 11, 53–72.

Pan, M., Chan, K. C. and Fok, R. C. W. (1997) Do currency futures prices follow random walks? *Journal of Empirical Finance*, 4, 1–15.

Pascual, L., Romo, J. and Ruiz, E. (1998) Bootstrap predictive inference for ARIMA processes, Working paper 98–86, Universidad Carlos III de Madrid, Spain.

Pascual, L., Romo, J. and Ruiz, E. (2000) Forecasting returns and volatilities in GARCH processes using the bootstrap, Working paper 00–68(31), Universidad Carlos III de Madrid, Spain.

Politis, D. N. and Romano, J. P. (1994) The stationary bootstrap. *Journal of the American Statistical Association*, 89, 1303–1313.

Politis, D. N., Romano, J. P., and Wolf, M. (1997) Subsampling for heteroskedastic time series. *Journal of Econometrics*, 81, 281–317.

Shao, J. and Tu, D. (1995) *The jackknife and bootstrap*, Springer, New York.

Stanton, R. (1997) A nonparametric model of term structure dynamics and the market price of interest rate risk. *Journal of Finance*, 52, 1973–2002.

Sullivan, R., Timmermann, A. and White, H. (1999) Data-snooping, technical trading rule performance and the bootstrap, *Journal of Finance*, 46, 1647–1691.

Tauchen, G., Zhang, H. and Liu, M. (1996) Volume, volatility and leverage: A dynamic analysis. *Journal of Econometrics*, 74, 177–208.

Taylor, S. J. (2000) Stock index and price dynamics in the UK and the US: new evidence from a trading rule and statistical analysis. *European Journal of Finance*, 6, 39–69.

Thombs, L. A. and Schucany, W. R. (1990) Bootstrap prediction intervals for autoregressions. *Journal of the American Statistical Association*, 85, 486–492.

Vlaar, P. J. G. (2000) Value at risk models for Dutch bond portfolios. *Journal of Banking & Finance*, 24, 1131–1154.

White, H. (2000) A reality check for data snooping. *Econometrica*, 68, 1097–1126.

White, H. and Racine, J. (2001) Statistical Inference, the bootstrap and neural-network modeling with application to foreign exchange rates. *IEEE Transactions on Neural Networks*, 12, 657–673.

Wu, C. F. J. (1986) Jackknife, bootstrap and other resampling methods in regression analysis. *Annals of Statistics*, 14, 1261–1295.

Chapter 4

MEASURES OF FIT FOR RATIONAL EXPECTATIONS MODELS

Tom Engsted

Aarhus School of Business

1. Introduction

In the last 25 years the development and application of methods and techniques to estimate and evaluate rational expectations (RE) models using time series data have been very intense. As a result, important insights have been gained, not only in the theoretical RE econometrics literature but also on the actual behaviour of agents in the macro-economy and financial markets. First-generation RE econometrics started with Thomas Sargent's work in the 1970s (see the collection of papers in Lucas and Sargent, 1981), as a response to a general dissatisfaction among researchers about the ad hoc nature of most applied econometrics that was conducted at that time. The Lucas (1976) critique in particular was thought to completely undermine traditional econometric practice. RE econometricians argued that one should search for structurally stable 'deep' parameters characterizing preferences and technology in a dynamic optimizing framework. Hansen and Sargent (1980) developed a general framework for estimating and testing RE models in such an environment and they termed the often highly non-linear cross-equation restrictions characterizing the system to be estimated as the 'hallmark' of rational expectations models.

The *full-information* methodology of Hansen and Sargent was considered extremely powerful due to its explicit grounding in dynamic economic theory, and due to the specific and unique testable restrictions that it delivered. However, the main weaknesses of the approach were its non-robustness to misspecification of the processes governing the forcing (exogenous) variables, and the highly restrictive distributional assumptions that usually had to be made in order to estimate the models using maximum likelihood. The latter aspect, in particular, prevented serious application of the full-information methodology in empirical finance (asset pricing, etc.). As a result, estimation and testing of RE models in finance usually followed the *Generalized Method of Moments* (GMM) methodology developed by Hansen (1982) and Hansen and Singleton (1982) which does not require a detailed specification of the processes governing the forcing variables (thus it can be termed a *limited-information* methodology), and does allow variables to be non-normal and heteroscedastic.

Beginning in the mid 1980s RE econometrics (both the full-information and limited-information methodologies) was confronted with two major concerns which were quite different in nature. The first concern had to do with a general recognition among researchers that many financial and macro-economic time-series are probably not mean-stationary, but are driven by stochastic trends, i.e. they are *integrated*, I(1), processes. Since such I(1)'ness has profound implications for estimation and statistical inference, RE econometrics had to deal with it. Campbell and Shiller (1987) and Dolado *et al.* (1991), *inter alia*, proposed to combine the full-information and limited-information methodologies with the theory of *cointegration* (c.f. Engle and Granger, 1987) in order to deal with the non-stationarity issue.

The second concern that was raised as a sort of critique on the way RE econometrics had progressed, had to do with how to *interpret* formal statistical tests of the restrictions implied by RE models. Within the full-information methodology, the practice was to set up a dynamic economic theory (intertemporal optimization under certain constraints), estimate the empirical model derived from it (including assumed processes for the forcing variables), and finally test the particular overidentifying restrictions implied using a Likelihood Ratio- or Wald test. If the test did not reject the restrictions at conventional significance levels, the underlying economic theory was taken to be a valid theory describing the data. On the other hand, if the test did reject the restrictions the theory was refuted.

The problem with this approach is that it presumes that the economic model can be formulated within a complete *probability* model, whereby estimation and test procedures follow naturally from the *likelihood principle*. Thus, the economic model is thought to give a *complete* probability structure for the variables in the model, i.e. the model must describe *all* aspects of the observed data (in the sense that the difference between model and data is unsystematic and unpredictable white noise). If this is not the case, the classical statistical test procedure loses its basic foundation. However, in most cases dynamic RE models should not be considered the 'true' models of reality, but should rather be considered 'approximate' models that may be able to describe certain (but not all) aspects or dimensions of the data. In fact, *any* economic theory is an abstraction from reality so statistical tests should, if they are sufficiently powerful, reject the theory. But this does not necessarily say anything about how good the theory is as an *approximation* to reality. The problem with classical statistical tests is that they are uninformative about the *degree to which* a particular (inherently misspecified) economic model fits a particular dimension of the data.[1]

Within the limited-information (GMM) methodology, a complete probability model for the variables under study is not specified. However, the *J-test*, which within this methodology is usually computed as a formal test of the underlying theoretical model, still has as a basic premise that, under the null, the difference between model and data is unsystematic and unpredictable. In addition, as we shall see (Section 4.4), there is no unique relationship between the size of the *J*-test value and the magnitude of deviations from the model. For example, when applied to asset pricing models, the model with the highest (lowest) *J*-test value is not necessarily the one that produces the largest (smallest) pricing errors. This makes *economic* interpretation of the outcome of the *J*-test procedure difficult.

In light of the above, a number of researchers have expressed their dissatisfaction with the standard RE econometric methodology. Summers (1991), in particular, has made a forceful critique of the methodology, exemplified by the work of Hansen and Singleton (1982). Summers writes:

> Hansen and Singletons model, like any theory, is literally false ... . The interesting question is how accurate it is as an approximation to reality for the purpose of making different types of predictions or understanding different types of behavior. Their *J-statistic* sheds no light at all on this question (p. 134).

> Science proceeds by falsifying theories and constructing better ones. Falsification of hypotheses based on overidentifying restrictions of the kind provided by Hansen and Singleton are unenlightening in two senses. First, they provide little insight into whether the reason for the theory's failure is central to its logical structure or is instead a consequence of auxiliary assumptions made in testing it ... . Second, suppose the theory is rejected ... . The fact of rejection gives little insight into the direction in which the theory should be modified (p. 135).

> Without some idea of the power of statistical tests against interesting alternative hypotheses and/or some metric for evaluating the extent to which the data are inconsistent with a maintained hypothesis, formal statistical tests are uninformative (p. 135).

What is needed is a metric or explicit measure of *the degree to which* RE models fit — or do not fit — economic data. Although not recognized by Summers (1991), such measures have in fact been developed. Campbell and Shiller (1987, 1988b) and Durlauf and Hall (1989abc, 1994) have developed measures of fit not based on formal statistical tests, in the context of simple present value models. Similarly, non-parametric alternatives to the standard GMM methodology of Hansen and Singleton (1982) have been developed, starting with Hansen and Jagannathan (1991) and further developed by Hansen and Jagannathan (1997), who derive volatility bounds and deviation measures for stochastic discount factors in asset pricing models. The characterizing feature of these methods is that they are much less focused on formal statistical testing, and instead ask to which degree a particular model provides a useful approximation to reality. The methodologies have become very popular and widely used in recent empirical work.

In this survey I provide a detailed description of these methodologies. Excellent surveys of RE econometrics with *stationary* variables have previously been provided by e.g. Pesaran (1987) and Cuthbertson (1990). Similarly, Baillie (1989) and Wickens (1993) give useful surveys of RE econometrics when time series are *non-stationary*.[2] These surveys, however, discuss only the traditional statistical measures of fit. To my knowledge, there is no coherent description of the alternative measures of fit developed by Campbell and Shiller, Durlauf and Hall, and Hansen and Jagannathan. In the present survey I describe and illustrate these measures, and I provide an overview of the many results obtained recently using these measures in areas as diverse as asset pricing, the term structure of interest rates, exchange rates, consumption and saving, the balance of payments, tax-smoothing, hyperinflation, and linear quadratic adjustment cost models of inventories, labour demand, and money demand. Throughout the article, the present value model and a consumption based asset pricing model will be used to illustrate the methods using annual Danish stock market data from 1922 to 1996.

2. A simple rational expectations model

2.1. *The optimizing approach*

As economists we want to be able to predict how economic agents' behaviour changes when their environment changes, e.g. as a result of changes in government policy. For that purpose we need estimates of parameters describing agents' preferences and firms' technologies, i.e. *structural* parameters. Within the RE macroeconometric school these parameters are estimated based on dynamic equilibrium theories where agents solve constrained optimization problems.

The optimizing approach to economic modelling is powerful, not only because it explicitly addresses the Lucas-critique, but also because if we can explain a phenomenon as the result of rational behaviour, then we have an indication whether this phenomenon could occur systematically and not just by coincidence. In principle all types of phenomena can be explained by some sort of irrational or non-systematic behaviour, but such explanations are not robust and do not allow us to make predictions in new situations (see e.g. Andersen (1994, p. 7) and Lazear (2000, p. 100). In order to interpret in a consistent way the whole array of different (but not necessarily independent) phenomena that show up, we need some common basic principles. To most economists the principle of optimizing behaviour is the most fundamental of these, and the approach of basing economic analysis on optimizing behaviour and rational expectations has gained general support within the economics profession. It characterizes both modern classical and keynesian theory building (c.f. Andersen, 1994). The difference between these schools lies more in the *additional* assumptions that characterize the theories, for example whether prices are regarded rigid or fully flexible.

The school represented by e.g. Hansen, Sargent, Lucas, and Prescott can be said to take the consequence of the above point of view, i.e. that economic theorizing needs to be based on optimizing behaviour and rational expectations, by insisting that in that case econometric models must also be based on these features. However, this point of view remains quite controversial within the econometrics profession. For example, the very influential *General-to-Specific* (GTS) approach (also called the 'LSE approach' since it originates from the London School of Economics), represented in particular by David Hendry (see e.g. Hendry, 1995), generally rejects the idea of basing econometric modelling on an explicit optimizing setup.[3]

Following Kim and Pagan (1995), the difference between the various methodologies can be explained by reference to what characterize the *discrepancy* (ε_t, say) between model and data. The *modus operandi* of the GTS modellers is to make ε_t satisfy a set of desirable features like lack of serial correlation and lack of correlation with the variables of the model, and they obtain this by including enough variables and by conditioning on enough lags of these. However, the outcome of such modelling is often empirical models that are very hard to interpret economically. RE modellers, on the other hand, suggest to base empirical modelling on tightly specified optimizing theories which have clearcut economic interpretations. Under the null that the theories are true, ε_t will be serially uncorrelated and uncorrelated with the variables of the model. However, precisely due to the theories tightly specified nature, in *reality* the difference between model and data should not be expected to have these properties. Therefore, testing the null hypothesis that the model is 'true' by a formal statistical test loses some of its appeal. This is the reason why *Real Business Cycle* (RBC) modellers use calibration instead of testing to evaluate their models. Note that although the basic optimizing framework is common to the group of RE modellers, there is an important *econometric* methodological distinction within the group. Like the GTS approach, the traditional RE approach represented by Hansen and Sargent (1980) and Hansen and Singleton (1982), puts strong weight on statistical estimation and testing. The RBC approach (represented by Kydland and Prescott, 1996), on the contrary, totally rejects using statistical estimation and testing. (Hoover (1995) gives a detailed discussion of the relative merits of *estimation/testing* versus *calibration* in empirical RE macroeconomics).

In the present survey I will not discuss further the computable general equilibrium models, and the associated calibration techniques, that characterize the RBC approach (although see the concluding remarks in Section 6). Instead I will focus on simple dynamic rational expectations models that have been used to a great extent, and with varying success, in recent years to explain and interpret the development in central macroeconomic and financial time series variables. I illustrate the methods I am going to describe using financial data and a simple consumption based asset pricing model (including its risk-neutral version resulting in a constant discount rate present value model), c.f. e.g. Lucas (1978).

2.2. *A consumption based asset pricing model*

At time t the representative investor chooses consumption, C_t, and investment in a financial asset, Z_t, in order to maximize expected discounted utility over an infinite horizon, subject to a budget constraint which says that consumption plus new aquisition of the asset must not exceed the endowment, I_t (labour income), plus the dividends, D_t, paid from the asset:

$$\max E_t \sum_{i=0}^{\infty} \beta^i U(C_{t+i}) \tag{1}$$

$$s.t. \quad C_t + P_t(Z_{t+1} - Z_t) \leqslant I_t + D_t Z_t$$

P_t is the price of the asset; β is the constant discount factor following from the subjective rate of time-preference; and E_t denotes the mathematical expectations operator conditional on information at time t. All variables dated t and earlier are assumed to be in the information set. We further assume that there are no taxes, transactions costs, or other frictions, and financial markets are complete. The first-order condition to this maximization problem is the following Euler equation:

$$E_t\left(\beta\left(\frac{U'_{t+1}}{U'_t}\right)\left(\frac{P_{t+1} + D_{t+1}}{P_t}\right) - 1\right) = 0 \tag{2}$$

The above model is both extremely simplified and extremely general. Simplified due to the many strong assumptions made (representative agent living forever, no frictions, complete markets, etc.).[4] But at the same time general in the sense that within the class of models belonging to the frictionless market paradigm, financial market prices can always be represented by a *stochastic discount factor* (see e.g. Cochrane and Hansen, 1992), which in the present model is given by the *intertemporal marginal rate of substitution* (IMRS), $\beta U'_{t+1}/U'_t$. The model implies a direct and unique relationship between the variation in asset returns, $R_{t+1} \equiv (P_{t+1} + D_{t+1})/P_t$, and the variation in the IMRS, that is, there is a strong relationship between financial market prices and consumption.

The intuition behind the model is most easily seen by rewriting (2) as

$$E_t[\beta U'_{t+1}(P_{t+1} + D_{t+1})] = U'_t P_t \tag{3}$$

The right-hand side of (3) expresses the utility value of selling an asset today at price P_t and consume the proceeds. The left-hand side gives the expected utility (discounted back till today) of keeping the asset till tomorrow, receiving the dividends, D_{t+1}, and then selling it at price P_{t+1}. In equilibrium these two strategies should result in the same utility value.

The model can be simplified further by assuming that the representative investor is *risk-neutral*. This implies that $U'_{t+1}/U'_t = 1$, whereby (3) becomes the well-known (from any basic finance textbook, e.g. Brealey and Myers, 1996) simple arbitrage relationship in which consumption plays no role:

$$P_t = \beta E_t(P_{t+1} + D_{t+1}) \tag{4}$$

Equation (4) is an example of what Hansen and Sargent (1991) have termed an *exact linear rational expectations model*, i.e. there is an exact linear relationship between the price today and expected price and dividends tomorrow. The solution to this simple linear expectational difference equation is not unique, since (4) is consistent with more than one rational expectations equilibrium. However, only one of these is stable. The stable equilibrium solution is obtained by iterating (4) forward and imposing the no-bubble transversality condition $\lim_{n \to \infty} \beta^n E_t P_{t+n} = 0$.[5] This gives the following *present value model*:

$$P_t = \sum_{i=1}^{\infty} \beta^i E_t D_{t+i} \tag{5}$$

Thus, the price of the asset is basically determined as the present discounted value of expected future dividends.

Equation (4) is the risk-neutral special case of equation (3). If the representative investor is *risk-averse*, an often used utility function is the socalled *Constant Relative Risk-Aversion* (CRRA) specification, where α is the degree of relative risk-aversion (α measures the elasticity of marginal utility w.r.t. consumption):

$$U(C_t) = \begin{cases} \dfrac{C_t^{1-\alpha} - 1}{1 - \alpha} & \alpha \geqslant 0, \alpha \neq 1 \\[2mm] \log(C_t) & \alpha = 1 \end{cases} \tag{6}$$

With CRRA utility, the Euler equation (2) becomes

$$E_t \left[\beta \left(\frac{C_{t+1}}{C_t} \right)^{-\alpha} \left(\frac{P_{t+1} + D_{t+1}}{P_t} \right) - 1 \right] = 0 \tag{7}$$

i.e. the IMRS is given as β times the consumption growth rate raised to the power of $-\alpha$. The CRRA specification is attractive because under certain assumptions investors with CRRA utility and *different* wealth levels can be aggregated into a single representative investor (see e.g. Campbell *et al.*, 1997, ch. 8).

Finally, it is worth noting that in this section I have followed the tradition in the asset pricing literature and interpreted the Euler equation (2) (or (7)) as determining equilibrium expected returns, given the expected IMRS. However, as noted by Cochrane (2001), an equally valid interpretation is that the Euler equation determines the expected IMRS, given expected returns. For example, Hall's (1978) random walk model for consumption is obtained as the special case of (7) where utility is logarithmic ($\alpha = 1$) and where the expected return is constant and equal to the rate of time-preference. Of course, in reality both returns and consumption are endogenous variables, and a complete model requires stating them in terms of truly exogenous variables, i.e. a fully general equilibrium model. This is, however, a difficult task, and is usually not pursued in the empirical RE econometrics literature. Instead, estimation and testing are either based on moment conditions implied by the Euler equation in a GMM framework, or on joint modelling of returns and consumption growth (or P_t, D_t, and C_t) in a vector-autoregressive framework (see Sections 3 and 4).

3. Traditional statistical tests and evaluation of rational expectations models

The consumption based asset pricing model described in the previous section is one of the most thoroughly tested models in the empirical finance literature. The reason is that the model constitutes a consistent intertemporal framework for understanding variation in financial asset returns. The model supplies consistent equilibrium explanations for e.g. risk-premia and predictable asset returns, and it provides a link from the macro-economy (business cycle) to the financial markets, i.e. the direct relationship between returns and consumption.

Hansen and Singleton (1982) were the first to suggest a method for estimating and testing the consumption based model, and most of the subsequent literature has applied their methodology. The method builds on Hansen's (1982) GMM methodology (which in turn is a generalization of Sargan's (1958) instrumental variables methodology), and takes its starting point in the Euler equation (like equation (7)).[6] Let the $((l + 1) \times 1)$ vector x_{t+1} contain the gross returns, R_{t+1}, on l assets, and consumption growth rate $G_{t+1} = C_{t+1}/C_t$, i.e. $x'_{t+1} = (R'_{t+1}, G_{t+1})$. Similarly, let b be the (2×1) vector containing the unknown parameters β and α, i.e. $b' = (\beta, \alpha)$. According to (7) $h(x_{t+1}, b) \equiv \beta R_{t+1} G_{t+1}^{-\alpha} - 1$ is unpredictable given information at time t. Thus, if we let the $(k \times 1)$ vector z_t contain k variables known at time t, the following *orthogonality conditions* will hold:

$$E\{h(x_{t+1}, b) \otimes z_t\} = 0 \tag{8}$$

The empirical counterpart (based on a sample of size T) to the left-hand side of (8) is the following:

$$g(b) = \frac{1}{T} \sum_{t=1}^{T} h(x_{t+1}, b) \otimes z_t \tag{9}$$

The GMM estimator is the value of b that makes $g(b)$ as close to zero as possible, or more precisely, the value that minimizes the quadratic form $J(b) = g(b)'Wg(b)$, where W is a given weighting matrix. If the model is correctly specified, T times the minimized value of $J(b)$ will be asymptotically χ^2 distributed with degrees of freedom equal to the number of orthogonality conditions minus the number of estimated parameters, i.e. $kl-2$. This test of the overidentifying restrictions is known as the *J*-test.

Regarding the weighting matrix W, the most efficient estimate of b is obtained by setting W equal to the inverse of the asymptotic covariance matrix of $T^{1/2}g(b_o)$,

$$W = S^{-1}, \qquad S = avar(T^{1/2}g(b_o))$$

where b_o is the true value of the parameter vector. In practice it will be necessary to start with an arbitrary weighting matrix (typically the identity matrix), and then minimize $J(b)$ to get an initial estimate of b from which S (and thereby W) can be computed, giving a new estimate of b. This second-stage estimate of b is asymptotically efficient. The asymptotic covariance matrix of $\hat{b}$ is given as

$$avar(\hat{b}) = \frac{1}{T} \left[\frac{\partial g(\hat{b})'}{\partial b} S^{-1} \frac{\partial g(\hat{b})}{\partial b} \right]^{-1}$$

Finally, in estimating S typically the Newey and West (1987) estimator is applied.[7]

The GMM methodology has several quite favourable properties. First, it does not require a specification of the processes generating the variables. Second, provided the variables in x_t and z_t are stationary processes, the method gives consistent and asymptotically normal parameter estimates even when the data are heteroscedastic and non-normal. This in particular makes it favourable, compared to maximum likelihood, in the study of high-frequency financial data, which typically exhibit both heteroscedasticity and non-normality. Finally, the method supplies a simple chi-squared test of the underlying theory.

There exists a vast empirical literature using GMM to estimate and test the consumption based asset pricing model with CRRA utility, see e.g. Braun *et al.* (1993) and Lund and Engsted (1996) and their references. In many of these studies the J-test rejects the model, and in those studies where the model is not statistically rejected, the parameter estimates are typically very imprecise and implausible. These results indicate that there are statistically significant deviations from the simple consumption based model with CRRA utility, and in those cases where the J-test is insignificant, it may be due to low power of the test (as we shall see in Section 4.4, the J-test rewards sampling error associated with the orthogonality conditions).[8]

Similar results have been reported for dynamic rational expectations models in other areas of economics and finance. The models clearly do not give a perfect description of the data. The problem with this 'classical' statistical approach to empirical evaluation of economic theories, exemplified by GMM, is that the J-test is almost totally uninformative about how *economically* important the statistically significant deviations from the model are. In addition, the test says nothing about in which way the theory has to be modified in order to better fit the data.[9] Summers (1991) has expressed these problems very clearly (c.f. the quotations from Summers' article in the introduction of the present paper), and he calls for methods to measure the *extent to which* data are (in)consistent with a given (inherently misspecified) theoretical model.

In Section 4 I describe a number of alternative methods that have been developed since the late 1980s, and that have been widely used in the recent

Table 1. GMM estimation of the Euler equation.

$\hat{\beta}$	$\hat{\alpha}$	J-test
0.953	0.367	6.683
(0.025)	(0.711)	(0.245)

empirical rational expectations literature, but first I illustrate the GMM approach using data from the Danish stock market (the data are listed in the Appendix).

3.1. *Illustration of the traditional approach using Danish stock market data*

I use the annual Danish data from Lund and Engsted (1996) on the extended sample period 1922–1996. P_t is the real stock price at the end of year t, and D_t is real dividends paid during year t. C_t is real per capita consumption at year t. All nominal values are deflated with the consumption deflator. The stock index is a value weighted portfolio of individual stocks chosen to obtain maximum coverage of the 'market' index of the Copenhagen Stock Exchange. In constructing the data corrections were made for stock splits and new equity issues below market prices (the appendix of Lund and Engsted contains a more detailed description of the data). The yearly mean real stock return over the period 1922–1996 is 6.2%, and the mean growth rate of real consumption is 1.8%.

Table 1 reports the GMM estimates of the Euler equation (7). The instruments chosen are a constant and two lags of consumption growth, returns, and the dividend-price ratio, i.e. the vector z_t contains seven variables ($k = 7$). The discount factor β is fairly precisely estimated at 0.953 with a standard error of 0.025. The estimated value of the degree of relative risk-aversion, $\hat{\alpha} = 0.367$, is of the 'correct' sign but very close to zero and with a quite large standard error. The J-test of overidentifying restrictions does not reject the model at conventional significance levels (p-value equal to 0.245). Taken at face value these results imply that Danish stock returns behave in accordance with a very simple efficient markets model where investors are risk-neutral. Thus, the deviations from the model are not *statistically* significant, but that may be due to low power of the statistical test (in addition, other diagnostic tests may find significant deviations, c.f. footnote 9) We would also like to know how *economically* important the deviations are. The methodologies described in the next section are explicitly designed to address that question.[10]

4. Alternative methods for evaluating rational expectations models

4.1. *The Campbell-Shiller approach*

Campbell and Shiller (1987) were the first to suggest a method for evaluating the extent to which a given rational expectations model fits the observed data, as an alternative to the traditional method of testing overidentifying restrictions. The background for their development of this method is the following (which, as seen, is totally in line with what Summers' (1991) writes):

> ... a statistical rejection of the model ... may not have much economic significance. It is entirely possible that the model explains most of the variation in [P_t] even if it is rejected at a 5% level (Campbell and Shiller, 1987, p. 1063).

In addition to suggesting an alternative method of evaluating rational expectations models, Campbell and Shiller also address the problems that arise due to non-stationarity of the data involved. The idea of the Campbell-Shiller method is most easily seen by taking the constant discount rate present value model (5) to be the economic model that we want to evaluate empirically.

4.1.1. *The present value model with constant discount rate*

Since in many applications P_t and D_t will be non-stationary, integrated of order one, I(1), Campbell and Shiller suggest to define a new variable S_t (which they call the *spread*) as $P_t - [\beta/(1 - \beta)]D_t$, and then rewrite (5) by subtracting $[\beta/(1 - \beta)]D_t$ from both sides:

$$S_t \equiv P_t - \frac{\beta}{1 - \beta} D_t = \frac{1}{1 - \beta} \sum_{i=1}^{\infty} \beta^i E_t \Delta D_{t+i} \qquad (10)$$

When D_t is I(1), ΔD_t is stationary I(0), so the right-hand side of (10) is stationary. Thus, if the present value model is true, the left-hand side, S_t, must also be stationary, implying that P_t and D_t must *cointegrate* (in the sense of Engle and Granger, 1987) with cointegrating vector $(1, -\beta/(1 - \beta))$. This cointegrating property of the model is important and should be tested. At the same time cointegration analysis delivers an estimate of the parameter β which is quite robust compared to alternative estimates, in the sense that the cointegration estimate is *super-consistent* (c.f. Stock, 1987). This means that it converges to its true value at the rate T, where T is the sample size, instead of the usual rate $\sqrt{T}$ which characterizes a consistent estimator. However, the cointegrating property should be regarded a very general, and thus weak, implication of the model, since it remains unaltered under a range of important perturbations to the model. It would obtain if expectations are adaptive instead of rational, and the property would also hold if we allow β to vary, or if we add an error term ε_t to the right-hand side of (10), as long as the variation in β and ε_t is stationary. Thus, cointegration analysis is important and necessary, but it should be regarded a *preliminary* analysis, which does not give much information about the economically essential distinguishing features of the model at hand.[11]

Having tested the basic cointegrating property of the model, and obtained a super-consistent estimate of β,[12] the next step in the Campbell-Shiller analysis is to set up a *Vector-AutoRegressive* (VAR) model for the two stationary variables S_t

and ΔD_t (both in deviations from their means):[13]

$$\begin{bmatrix} S_t \\ \Delta D_t \end{bmatrix} = \begin{bmatrix} a_1 & a_2 \\ a_3 & a_4 \end{bmatrix} \begin{bmatrix} S_{t-1} \\ \Delta D_{t-1} \end{bmatrix} + \begin{bmatrix} u_{1t} \\ u_{2t} \end{bmatrix} \tag{11}$$

The relation (10) then has certain implications for this VAR system.

First, according to (10) the spread, S_t, is the optimal predictor of future changes in dividends. An increase (decrease) in the spread is due only to the market expecting future increases (decreases) in dividend growth. This has the testable implication that, if expectations of future dividends are formed rationally based on more information than just current and lagged dividends, then there should be positive *Granger causality* from S to ΔD, i.e. the parameter a_3 should be larger than zero.[14]

Second, equation (10) imposes a set of cross-equation restrictions on all the VAR parameters. These restrictions can be derived as follows: The VAR model can be written more comprehensively as $Z_t = AZ_{t-1} + u_t$, where $Z_t' = (S_t, \Delta D_t)$, $u_t' = (u_{1t}, u_{2t})$, and A is the matrix

$$\begin{bmatrix} a_1 & a_2 \\ a_3 & a_4 \end{bmatrix}$$

Next, define the limited information set $H_t = \{S_{t-i}, \Delta D_{t-i}, i \geqslant 0)$, and let g' and h' be vectors that pick out S_t and ΔD_t, respectively, from the vector Z_t, i.e. $g' = (1, 0)$ and $h' = (0, 1)$, such that $S_t = g'Z_t$ and $\Delta D_t = h'Z_t$. Then VAR forecasts of future ΔD's can be generated as $E(\Delta D_{t+i} \mid H_t) = h'A^iZ_t$. Since S_t is contained in H_t, projecting both sides of (10) onto H_t gives

$$S_t = g'Z_t = \frac{\beta}{1 - \beta} h'A(I - \beta A)^{-1}Z_t \tag{12}$$

From (12) it follows that $g'(I - \beta A) = \beta(1 - \beta)^{-1}h'A$, which is the compact form of the cross-equation restrictions. In terms of the individual parameters the restrictions are:

$$a_3 = (1 - \beta)(\beta^{-1} - a_1)$$
$$a_4 = -(1 - \beta)a_2 \tag{13}$$

The economic interpretation of these restrictions is that one-period excess returns are unpredictable. This can be seen by imposing the restrictions on the VAR model (11). This results in the variable $\zeta_{t+1} \equiv P_t - \beta(P_{t+1} + D_{t+1})$ which is (minus) the ex post one-period excess return multiplied by the time t stock price (c.f. equation (4)). This variable should be unpredictable given information available at time t. An easy way to test the restrictions (13) is therefore to regress ζ_{t+1} onto the variables in H_t; these variables should then be jointly insignificant. Since β can be treated as fixed, the restrictions in (13) are linear. However, an alternative non-linear expression for the restrictions is obtained from (12) as $g' = \beta(1 - \beta)^{-1}h'A(I - \beta A)^{-1}$, which is algebraically equivalent to the linear restrictions $g'(I - \beta A) = \beta(1 - \beta)^{-1}h'A$. The interpretation of the former is that *multi-period* excess returns are unpredictable. Thus, multi-period returns are unpredictable if and only if one-period returns are unpredictable. A likelihood ratio test or a non-linear Wald test can be used to test the restrictions $g' = \beta(1 - \beta)^{-1}h'A(I - \beta A)^{-1}$.[15] Note that in contrast to the former test, the latter is not invariant to non-linear transformations, c.f. Gregory and Veall (1985). The LR test is, however, computationally more cumbersome as it requires estimation of the VAR with the restrictions imposed.[16]

The cross-equation restrictions (13) are what Hansen and Sargent (1980) have termed the *hallmark* of rational expectations models, and in traditional rational expectations econometrics tests of such restrictions constitute the basic ground for accepting or rejecting the underlying economic model. Thus, in its heart the approach is very similar to the GMM approach described in Section 3. In both approaches judging the empirical performance of a given economic model is based on a formal statistical test.

The basic innovative aspect of the method of Campbell and Shiller (1987) is that they next suggest a specific alternative — or supplementary — approach to the evaluation of economic models. The idea is basically to make use of the optimal prediction property that characterizes S_t if the present value model (5) (or (10)) holds. This property implies that if we estimate the parameters in the VAR model (11), and use these to generate an unrestricted forecast of $(1 - \beta)^{-1} \sum \beta^i \Delta D_{t+i}$, then according to (10) this forecast should equal S_t. Campbell and Shiller term this VAR forecast the *theoretical spread* because it gives the spread that would be set in the market if the theoretical model (the present value model) is true. Thus, the differences between the actual spread and the theoretical spread measure the deviations in the data from the present value model. Plotting the actual and theoretical spread together in a diagram gives a visual picture of the magnitude of these deviations. From (12) the theoretical spread, S'_t, is computed as

$$S'_t = \frac{\beta}{1 - \beta} h'A(I - \beta A)^{-1}Z_t \tag{14}$$

where A contains the unrestricted VAR parameter estimates, and where β is set equal to the cointegrating estimate between P_t and D_t. If a formal statistical test rejects the restrictions (13), but at the same time there is a high degree of comovement of S_t and S'_t, it indicates that the *statistically* significant deviations from the model do not completely destroy the model as a useful *approximation* to reality. Similarly, if the test does not reject the model but there is a very low degree of comovement between S_t and S'_t, it indicates that the model does *not* approximate reality well and, hence, that the statistical test lacks power towards relevant alternatives to the model.

The inclusion of S_t in the VAR model effectively eliminates the problem that the econometrician does not know all the variables that agents use in forming expectations about future dividends. This is due to the optimal prediction property of S_t when the underlying theory is true. According to (10) S_t summarizes *all* the information that agents use in making forecasts. Thus, the degree of comovement of S_t and S'_t can be interpreted as measuring the degree of forward-looking behaviour in asset prices: a high (low) degree of comovement indicates that a large (small) part of the predictable variation in dividends is incorporated in the current price.

The approach of measuring the fit of a rational expectations model by comparing actual and theoretical spreads, can be given a more stringent theoretical justification within the framework of Durlauf and Hall (1989abc, 1994), to which we turn in Section 4.2. However, before we get there let us relax the strong assumption of a constant discount rate (i.e. risk-neutrality) and look at the consumption based asset pricing model with a CRRA utility specification.

4.1.2. *The present value model with time-varying discount rate*

Campbell and Shiller (1988b) have extended their (1987) approach so that it can handle present value models with a time-varying (stochastic) discount factor. The consumption based asset pricing model set out in Section 2.2 can be formulated as such a present value model, where the stochastic discount factor is given by the intertemporal marginal rate of substitution in consumption. Allowing the discount factor to vary complicates matters because then the relation between prices and dividends becomes non-linear. However, by log-linearizing the non-linear relationship between prices, dividends, and returns, an approximate present value model for the *logarithm* of prices, $p_t \equiv \log(P_t)$, can be derived as a function of the present value of expected future log dividends, $d_{t+i} \equiv \log(D_{t+i})$, and log gross returns, $r_{t+i} \equiv \log(R_{t+i})$. Stated in terms of the log dividend-price ratio, $\delta_t \equiv d_t - p_t$, instead of log prices, the approximate present value model can be written as:

$$\delta_t = \sum_{i=1}^{\infty} \rho^{i-1} E_t[r_{t+i} - \Delta d_{t+i}] + k_o \qquad (15)$$

The parameter ρ is equal to $1/(1 + \exp(\bar{\delta}))$, where $\bar{\delta}$ is the average of δ_t, and k_o is an inessential constant arising from the linearization. If we assume that stock returns and consumption growth are jointly homoscedastic and log normally distributed, then according to the consumption based asset pricing model with CRRA utility (see equations (6) and (7)), the expected log return $E_t r_t$ is given as $\alpha E_t \Delta c_t + k_1$, where c_t is log consumption, $c_t \equiv \log(C_t)$, and k_1 is a constant. Thus, equation (15) becomes:

$$\delta_t = \sum_{i=1}^{\infty} \rho^{i-1} E_t[\alpha \Delta c_{t+i} - \Delta d_{t+i}] + k_2 \qquad (16)$$

This equation is of the same form as the equation determining the spread, S_t, under the present value model with a constant discount factor, i.e. equation (10), but with S_t replaced by δ_t, and ΔD_t replaced by $(\alpha \Delta c_t - \Delta d_t)$. Thus, the VAR approach described in Section 4.1.1 can be applied to the consumption based model with only slight modification. The variables in the VAR are now δ_t and $(\alpha \Delta c_t - \Delta d_t)$ instead of S_t and ΔD_t, and instead of comparing actual and theoretical spreads, the comparison is now between actual and theoretical log dividend-price ratio's.[17] The cross-equation restrictions are:

$$a_3 = 1 - \rho a_1$$

$$a_4 = -\rho a_2$$

(17)

Under risk-neutrality $\alpha = 0$, and in that case (16) is essentially identical to (10) except that the variables are stated in logs rather than in levels. Usually dividends are better described as having a unit root in log-levels rather than in levels, so in evaluating the present value model with a constant discount factor, the log-linearized present value model with α set equal to zero may be preferred to the model in Section 4.1.1. According to (16) when log consumption and log dividends both are unit root processes, the log dividend-price ratio should be stationary, i.e. p_t and d_t should cointegrate with cointegrating vector $(1, -1)$.

4.2. *The Durlauf-Hall approach*

Durlauf and Hall (1989abc, 1994) have developed a method which in its origin is very similar to the method of Campbell and Shiller. However, the two approaches differ somewhat in their practical implementation.[18] Just like Campbell and Shiller, Durlauf and Hall express their dissatisfaction with the traditional statistical approach of evaluating economic models. They note that a model which is statistically rejected may still largely explain the time-series in question, and that the value of a model as a way of thinking about economic behaviour ought not to depend on the complete consistency of the model with all aspects of the data. Rather, it should depend on whether the model has substantial empirical relevance (Durlauf and Hall, 1989c, p. 2–3). Durlauf and Maccini (1995, p. 67) make the same kind of remarks when discussing the GMM methodology's *J*-test.

In order to describe the Durlauf-Hall approach, let us again focus on the simple present value model with a constant discount rate, i.e. (5).[19] This model is derived by solving the simple arbitrage relationship (4) recursively forward. Now, the idea is to add a stochastic variable, η_t, to the right-hand side of (4), such that η_t measures the deviations from the *exact* relationship between P_t and D_t given in (4). This implies that a stochastic variable, ε_t, must be added to equation (5),

$$P_t = \sum_{i=1}^{\infty} \beta^i E_t D_{t+i} + \varepsilon_t$$

(18)

where $\varepsilon_t = \sum_{i=0}^{\infty} \beta^i E_t \eta_{t+i}$. Thus, ε_t contains the variation in P_t that cannot be described by the expected present value of future dividends. Durlauf and Hall denote ε_t 'model noise', and the purpose is then to obtain an estimate of this unobservable noise component.

Define P_t^e and P_t^* as follows,

$$P_t^e = \sum_{i=1}^{\infty} \beta^i E_t D_{t+i} \qquad P_t^* = \sum_{i=1}^{\infty} \beta^i D_{t+i} \qquad (19)$$

and note that $P_t^e = E_t P_t^*$. P_t^e is the asset price according to the exact present value model, i.e. the model without noise, while P_t^* is the *perfect foresight* price, i.e. the price that would be set in a world with no uncertainty about future dividends. Thus,

$$P_t = P_t^e + \varepsilon_t \qquad P_t^* = P_t^e + v_t \qquad (20)$$

where v_t is a rational forecast error. The variables observable to the econometrician in the unobserved components model (20) are P_t and P_t^*, while P_t^e, ε_t, and v_t are unobservable. A time-series estimate of model noise can be obtained by treating ε_t as an unobserved component in the following signal extraction problem: Define the limited information set Φ_t, which is a subset of the full market information set, and let $M_\Phi(t)$ denote linear projections onto Φ_t. From (20) we have

$$P_t - P_t^* = \varepsilon_t - v_t \qquad (21)$$

Since v_t is a rational forecast error, it will be uncorrelated with information available at time t. Thus, the projection of $(P_t - P_t^*)$ onto Φ_t will be identical to the projection of ε_t onto Φ_t. Therefore, the fitted values from the regression of $(P_t - P_t^*)$ on the variables in Φ_t, i.e. $M_\Phi(t)(P_t - P_t^*)$, constitute an estimate of model noise, ε_t. Durlauf and Hall show that the variance of these fitted values is a lower bound on the variance of the true but unobservable noise term.

As we have seen, when P_t and D_t are nonstationary, I(1), a more convenient way of writing the present value model is as in (10) instead of (5). This means that instead of computing the perfect foresight price, P_t^*, one should compute the perfect foresight *spread* $S_t^* = (1 - \beta)^{-1} \sum_{i=1}^{\infty} \beta^i \Delta D_{t+i}$, and the estimate of model noise is then obtained from the linear projection $M_\Phi(t)(S_t - S_t^*)$, where the variables in Φ_t should all be stationary.

In practice the Durlauf-Hall approach faces the problem of how to construct the perfect foresight price, P_t^*, or spread, S_t^*, from a finite observable data series. They suggest, following Shiller (1981), to truncate the series at time T, with P_T^* set equal to the end-sample value, P_T, and then work backwards in time using the relation (c.f. equation (4)), $P_t^* = \beta(P_{t+1}^* + D_{t+1})$. Similarly, to obtain S_t^*, set S_T^* equal to S_T and use the relation $S_t^* = \beta(S_{t+1}^* + [1/(1 - \beta)]\Delta D_{t+1})$ to obtain the whole sequence of S_t^* values. However, this suggestion is not without problems. In the next subsection we compare the Durlauf-Hall approach with the Campbell-Shiller approach, and we discuss the various problems of the two approaches.

4.2.1. *Comparing the Durlauf-Hall approach with the Campbell-Shiller approach*

What exactly is it the difference between the actual and theoretical spread measures in the Campbell-Shiller analysis? Consider the non-exact present value model (18). Combining this expression with the analysis in Section 4.1.1, it follows that

$$S_t - S_t' = \sum_{i=0}^{\infty} \beta^i E(\eta_{t+i} \mid H_t) \equiv E(\varepsilon_t \mid H_t) \tag{22}$$

In the present context the economic interpretation of η_t is that it represents the one-period excess return on the asset from time t to $t + 1$,[20] and this excess return should be unpredictable given information at time t. Thus, in Campbell and Shiller's words: '... the difference between S_t and the theoretical spread ... is large if the present value of all future excess returns is predictable. By this measure, a large deviation from the model requires not only that movements in $[\eta]$ be predictable one period in advance but that they be predictable many periods in advance. Loosely speaking, predictable excess returns must be persistent as well as variable.' (Campbell and Shiller, 1987, p. 1069).

Since $E(\varepsilon_t \mid H_t)$ is by definition equal to $M_{\Phi}(t)\varepsilon_t$, projecting $(P_t - P_t^*)$ or $(S_t - S_t^*)$ onto H_t gives an estimate of model noise which is conceptually identical to the estimate given by $S_t - S_t'$ when the information sets H_t and Φ_t are identical. Thus, measuring model noise using Durlauf and Hall's approach is in principle equivalent to comparing actual and theoretical spreads using Campbell and Shiller's approach. However, in *practice* the two methodologies differ. The former approach is based on calculating perfect-foresight prices, which requires a truncation of the series at time T with an arbitrary end-sample value. It has been widely documented that such perfect-foresight calculations can be extremely problematic, especially when the discount factor β is close to unity. Alternatively, following Durlauf and Maccini (1995), a noise measure can be computed by focusing on the simple arbitrage relation $P_t = \beta E_t(P_{t+1} + D_{t+1}) + \eta_t$, from which we can define a new variable $\zeta_{t+1} \equiv P_t - \beta(P_{t+1} + D_{t+1}) = \eta_t - \beta\mu_{t+1}$, where μ_{t+1} is the rational expectations error $(P_{t+1} + D_{t+1}) - E_t(P_{t+1} + D_{t+1})$. (Note that ζ_{t+1} is just the ex post one-period excess return from Section 4.1.1). This expression is equivalent to (21) with $(P_t - P_t^*)$, ε_t, and ν_t replaced by ζ_{t+1}, η_t, and $\beta\mu_{t+1}$, respectively. Hence, an estimate of model noise can be constructed as the linear projection $M_{\Phi}(t)\zeta_{t+1}$. However, the drawback of this alternative measure is that since it builds on the one-period arbitrage relation rather than the multi-period present value model, essentially it measures 'short-horizon' noise rather than 'long-horizon' noise. Thus, it will have difficulties in capturing slow-moving noise, see Durlauf and Hall (1989a, Section 3).

The Campbell-Shiller approach has the clear advantage of measuring 'long-horizon' noise without the need to impose arbitrary terminal conditions as in the Durlauf-Hall approach. Instead, a VAR model is used to generate expected future values of dividends. This requires, of course, that the data can be represented statistically by a stable linear VAR. If this is not the case, e.g. due to regime-changes within the sample period, then the basic Campbell-Shiller approach becomes invalid.[21] Campbell and Shiller (1989) investigate the small-sample properties of the VAR approach. Although there is some evidence of size distortions in the Wald tests of the cross-equation restrictions, in general the finite-sample performance of the estimators and tests is found to be satisfactory. Bekaert *et al.* (1997) investigate the small-sample properties of the two statistics used to measure the degree of comovement of S_t and S'_t (the correlation-coefficient and standard-deviation ratio, see below) from a VAR model where they have also corrected the VAR parameter estimates for small-sample bias. Some bias is found for the standard-deviation ratio, but the correlation-coefficient displays surprisingly little bias.[22]

An issue remains of how exactly to measure the *degree of comovement* of actual and theoretical spreads, and the *relative amount* of model noise. Durlauf and Hall (1989b) suggest to normalize the 'long-horizon' noise variance measure by dividing the variance of noise either by the variance of $(P_t - P_t^*)$ or the variance of P_t. The latter noise ratio is particularly appealing because it measures the fraction of the movements of the actual price explained by noise. Similarly, Durlauf and Maccini (1995) suggest to construct the 'short-horizon' noise ratio $var[M_\Phi(t)\zeta_{t+1}]/var(\zeta_{t+1})$, which can be interpreted as a lower bound on the percentage of $var(\zeta_{t+1})$ which is attributable to noise. Note that this ratio is just the R^2-value from the excess return regression in Section 4.1.1 used to test the restrictions (13). Campbell and Shiller (1987) suggest to compute the correlation coefficient between S_t and S'_t, and the ratio of their standard deviations, in measuring the fit of the model. If there is no noise, both of these should be equal to unity. Alternatively, a 'long-horizon' noise ratio directly comparable to the Durlauf-Hall noise ratio's, can be computed as $var(S_t - S'_t)/var(S_t)$. This ratio gives a lower bound on the fraction of the movements in S_t that are explained by noise. Standard errors on these statistics and noise ratio's can be computed either using the *delta method*, see e.g. Campbell and Shiller (1988b, p. 209), or by bootstrap simulation, see e.g. Engsted and Tanggaard (2001).

4.3. *Illustration of the Campbell-Shiller and Durlauf-Hall approaches using Danish stock market data*

In this section we illustrate the methods from Sections 4.1 and 4.2 using the data described in Section 3.1. First, we test and evaluate the constant discount factor present value model from Section 4.1.1. Figure 1 shows Danish real stock prices and (scaled) dividends over the period 1922–1996. Dickey-Fuller tests for P_t and D_t give DF values of -2.29 and -2.20, respectively (no augmentation lags are significant). Compared to the 5% critical value of approximately -2.90, we cannot reject the unit root hypothesis for these two series. A cointegrating regression of P_t on D_t gives a Dickey-Fuller test value for the null of no cointegration of -2.97, which is not significant at a 5% level (MacKinnon, 1991).

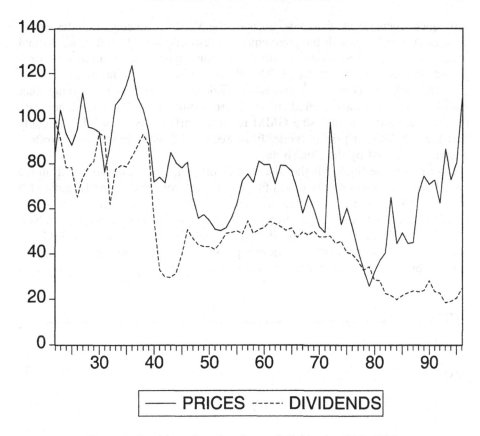

Figure 1. Danish real stock prices and dividends, 1922–1996.

Since cointegration is a quite weak implication of the present value model, the finding of no cointegration is clearly bad news for the model.

In order to analyze further the cointegration properties among prices and dividends, we also test for cointegration using Johansen's (1991) method. Based on a one-lag vector ECM (one lag is chosen by both the Schwarz and Hannan-Quinn criteria), the two Johansen tests (*maximal eigenvalue-* and *trace* tests) associated with the largest eigenvalue give the values 16.04 and 20.36 which clearly indicate, in contrast to the simple OLS regression, that P_t and D_t are cointegrated. The estimated cointegrating vector is $(1, -16.203)$. Thus, $\hat{\beta}/(1 - \hat{\beta}) = 16.203$, implying $\hat{\beta} = 0.942$ which is not an unreasonable estimate of the discount factor.

The results from the Johansen cointegration analysis suggest that the spread, $S_t = P_t - 16.203D_t$, is a stationary variable, so the first step in the Campbell-Shiller analysis is to estimate the VAR model (11). The result is reported in Table 2. First, we see that S significantly Granger-causes ΔD in the direction implied by the present value model (a_3 is significantly positive). Thus, an increase in the spread, e.g. due to increasing stock prices, is on average followed by a subsequent increase in dividends. Second, the VAR parameter estimates are in close correspondence with the cross-equation restrictions (13). In fact, the formal $\chi^2(2)$ test of these restrictions is not statistically significant, meaning that one-period returns are unpredictable. The *Wald* test of the non-linear restrictions $g' = \beta(1 - \beta)^{-1}h'A(I - \beta A)^{-1}$ is also statistically insignificant, meaning that multi-period returns are unpredictable. These results are in full accordance with the Euler-equation results using GMM reported earlier in Section 3.1, and imply that the simple asset pricing model from Section 2.2 with risk-neutral investors cannot be rejected by the Danish data.

In order to investigate whether the statistically *in*significant deviations from the model are also *economically* insignificant, we next compute, using formula (14) with $\beta = 0.942$ and the estimates of A from Table 2, the theoretical spread, S'_t, and compare it with the actual spread, S_t. Figure 2 plots the two spread variables. The two variables are highly positively correlated, meaning that a substantial part of the variation in future dividend growth is incorporated into the current spread, but S_t is somewhat more volatile compared to S'_t. The noise ratio

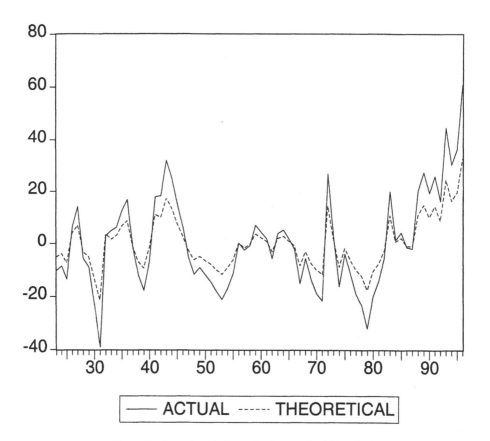

Figure 2. Actual and theoretical spread, 1923–1996.

Table 2. Summary statistics from the VAR model, and noise ratio's.

Estimated A matrix	$\begin{bmatrix} 0.767 & -6.356 \\ (0.118) & (2.391) \\ 0.010 & 0.144 \\ (0.003) & (0.203) \end{bmatrix}$	
$\bar{R}^2$, S-equation		0.52
$\bar{R}^2$, ΔD-equation		0.14
Test of linear restrictions		3.564
		(0.168)
Test of non-linear restrictions		3.058
		(0.217)
Correlation(S, S')		0.999
$\text{Var}(S')/\text{Var}(S)$		0.296
$\text{Var}(S - S')/\text{Var}(S)$		0.210
$\text{Var}[M_\Phi(t)(S - S^*)]/\text{Var}(S)$		0.0054
$\text{Var}[M_\Phi(t)\zeta_{t+1}]/\text{Var}(\zeta_{t+1})$		0.047

Notes: The numbers in parentheses in the A matrix are standard errors.
The tests of restrictions are chi-squared tests with 2 degrees of freedom.
The numbers in parentheses under test statistics are p-values.

$var(S_t - S'_t)/var(S_t)$ is equal to 0.21 which means that 21% of the variation in S_t is explained by noise. This means that despite of the statistical non-rejection of the simple present value model, there are economically important deviations from the model that cannot be neglected.

The noise measures obtained using the Durlauf-Hall approach do not point to the same amount of noise as the Campbell-Shiller analysis indicates. By calculating the perfect-foresight spread, S_t^*, and regressing $(S_t - S_t^*)$ onto S_t and ΔD_t, a noise ratio equal to 0.0054 is obtained, meaning that noise only accounts for 0.5% of the variation in S_t. The 'short-horizon' noise ratio obtained by regressing the ex post one-period excess return ζ_{t+1} on S_t and ΔD_t, indicates that 4.7% of the variation in excess returns is attributable to noise.

Finally, let us use the Campbell-Shiller methodology to investigate the empirical content of the consumption based asset pricing model with CRRA utility. As we saw in Section 4.1.2 this model can be formulated as a log-linearized present value model where the log dividend-price ratio is equal to the expected present value of future dividend growth and consumption growth. Table 3 reports the results of estimating first-order VAR models for δ_t and $(\alpha\Delta c_t - \Delta d_t)$ with various values of the risk-aversion parameter α imposed, i.e. $\alpha = 0, 1, 2, 3$. Under risk-neutrality ($\alpha = 0$) the model is not rejected statistically, and the degree of comovement of δ_t and δ'_t is quite high with a noise ratio indicating that only 7.6% of the variation in δ_t is due to noise. Since the results based on the model from Section 4.1.1 give a Campbell-Shiller noise ratio of 21% (c.f. Table 2), there is more support to the constant discount rate present value model when we base the analysis on the log-linearized setup instead of the non-linearized setup.

Table 3. Summary statistics from VAR model, and noise ratio's.

	$\alpha = 0$	$\alpha = 1$	$\alpha = 2$	$\alpha = 3$
$\bar{R}^2$, δ-equation	0.721	0.710	0.711	0.722
$\bar{R}^2$, $(\alpha\Delta c - \Delta d)$-equation	0.134	0.067	−0.004	−0.012
$\chi^2(2)$ test of restrictions	0.890	1.610	4.245	6.584
	(0.641)	(0.447)	(0.120)	(0.037)
Correlation(δ, δ')	0.999	0.998	0.996	−0.940
$\text{Var}(\delta')/\text{Var}(\delta)$	0.525	0.296	0.058	0.006
$\text{Var}(\delta - \delta')/\text{Var}(\delta)$	0.076	0.210	0.579	1.156

Notes: The numbers in parantheses are p-values.

It is interesting to observe that as we increase the value of the risk-aversion parameter, the model performs worse. With $\alpha = 3$ the cross-equation restrictions (17) are rejected at a 5% level, and δ_t and δ'_t become highly *negatively* correlated. Thus, according to this analysis the (small) deviations that are observed for the model under risk-neutrality, cannot be explained by risk-aversion in terms of a CRRA utility specification.

4.4. *The Hansen-Jagannathan approach*

The Hansen-Jagannathan (HJ) approach which I will describe and illustrate in this section, is in some ways quite different from the approaches described in Sections 4.1–4.3. However, the overall aim of the HJ methodology is the same as for the other methodologies. As Cochrane and Hansen (1992) point out in their description of the HJ methodology:

> ... statistical measures of fit such as a chi-square test statistic may not provide the most useful guide to the modifications that will reduce pricing or other specification errors ... Also, application of the minimum chi-square approach to estimation and inference sometimes focuses too much attention on whether a model is perfectly specified and not enough attention on assessing model performance (Cochrane and Hansen, 1992, p. 122).

Hansen and Jagannathan (1997), in their extension of the original 1991 methodology, note the similarity of their approach with the Durlauf-Hall approach. In both approaches the purpose is not to formally test economic models but to evaluate the performance of models that are inherently misspecified.

The HJ methodology is basically developed for evaluating asset pricing models, and the starting point for the approach is the fact (which we briefly noted in Section 2.2), that frictionless asset pricing models imply that prices can always be represented by a *stochastic discount factor*. In addition, if financial markets are complete this stochastic discount factor is unique. Thus, the observable implications of different asset pricing models are conveniently summarized in terms of their implied stochastic discount factors. As we saw in Section 2.2, for the *consumption based* asset pricing model, the stochastic discount factor is given by the intertemporal marginal rate of substitution in consumption (IMRS). The basic idea of the HJ methodology is now to derive a lower volatility bound for the IMRS, given the available set of asset return data. Next, various economic models can be evaluated by computing the implied volatility for the IMRS and comparing it with the lower volatility bound.

To be specific, denote by m_{t+1} the IMRS, let x_{t+1} be the vector of gross returns at date $t+1$, and i a vector of one's. The consumption based asset pricing model then implies the Euler equation $i = E_t(m_{t+1}x_{t+1})$. For the consumption based model with CRRA utility and only one asset return, $m_{t+1} = \beta(C_{t+1}/C_t)^{-\alpha}$ and $x_{t+1} = (P_{t+1} + D_{t+1})/P_t$, c.f. equation (7). In general, however, x_{t+1} may contain a whole set of returns on different assets, e.g. stocks, bonds, and bills. By taking unconditional expectations on both sides of the Euler equation, we obtain

$$i = E(m_{t+1}x_{t+1}) \tag{23}$$

Now consider the linear least squares projection of $(m_{t+1} - Em_{t+1})$ onto $(x_{t+1} - Ex_{t+1})$

$$(m - Em) = (x - Ex)'\gamma + \varepsilon \tag{24}$$

where γ and ε are the least squares parameters and errors, respectively, and where subscripts are dropped for notational simplicity. Using (23) and the fact that $E(m - Em) = 0$, we find that $E(x - Ex)(m - Em) = E[x(m - Em)] - E[Ex(m - Em)] = [E(mx) - EmEx] - ExE(m - Em) = i - EmEx$. Thus, γ is given as

$$\gamma = \Sigma_x^{-1}[E(x - Ex)(m - Em)] = \Sigma_x^{-1}[i - EmEx] \tag{25}$$

where Σ_x is the covariance matrix of asset returns. Since ε is by construction orthogonal to x, it follows from (24) and (25) that the variance of m is given as $V(m) = \gamma'\Sigma_x\gamma + V(\varepsilon) = [i - EmEx]'\Sigma_x^{-1}\Sigma_x\Sigma_x^{-1}[i - EmEx] + V(\varepsilon) = [i - EmEx]' \times \Sigma_x^{-1}[i - EmEx] + V(\varepsilon)$. Thus, if we denote by σ_m the standard deviation of the IMRS, m, we have the following lower volatility bound for m:

$$\sigma_m \geqslant ([i - EmEx]'\Sigma_x^{-1}[i - EmEx])^{1/2} \tag{26}$$

The interpretation of the HJ volatility bound (26) is straightforward: If investors are risk-neutral, m is just a constant ($= \beta$ in the consumption based/CRRA model), whereby $\sigma_m = 0$. Hence, the bound measures the deviations of the observed asset prices from the risk-neutral prices. The bound can be drawn as a parabola in a (Em, σ_m)-diagram, see Figure 3 below, where the population values Ex and Σ_x are estimated from the available asset return data.

Note that the bound is model-free in the sense that it is derived only from asset returns with no reference to a particular economic model. Thus, the bound can be used as a yardstick against which different economic models can be

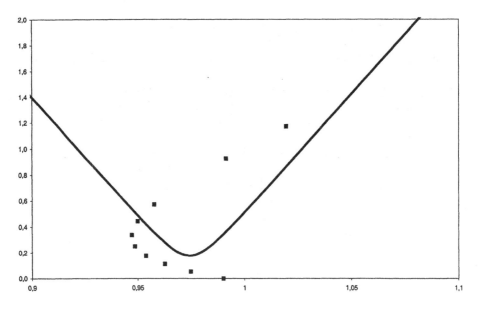

Figure 3. Hansen-Jagannathan bound (the horizontal axis displays *Em*, and the vertical axis displays σ_m).

compared. Each model implies a particular stochastic discount factor, the standard deviation of which can be computed using a particular set of data (consumption data in the case of the consumption based model), and it can be checked whether the standard deviation lies within the bound given by the right-hand side of (26). Different economic models can be compared by investigating whether or not the volatilities of their implied stochastic discount factors are consistent with (26).

A good asset pricing model is one which produces a 'high' correlation of its stochastic discount factor with asset returns. The lower volatility bound (26) gives the standard deviation of an *m* which is *perfectly* correlated with returns. However, as pointed out by Cochrane and Hansen (1992) and Cochrane (2001), it is easy to come up with a very volatile discount factor that satisfies the bound but which doesn't explain asset prices very well because it has a low correlation with returns. Cochrane (2001) therefore suggests to compute a minimum standard deviation of *m*, given the mean of *m*, *and* a maximum value for the correlation of *m* with returns. This can be done by dividing the HJ-bound by the square-root of R^2, where R^2 is the coefficient of determination in a regression of *m* onto a constant and the set of asset returns. Thus, the lower the value of R^2, the higher the bound for σ_m, thereby requiring a more volatile discount factor compared to the case where *m* is perfectly correlated with returns.

Cochrane's (2001) suggestion is a simple way to construct sharper volatility bounds by scaling returns with predictive variables in the information set. More sophisticated methods for using conditioning information in construction of the bounds have been developed by Gallant *et al.* (1990) and Bekaert and Liu (1999). Burnside (1994) and Cecchetti *et al.* (1994) develop statistical tests of the underlying asset pricing model based on the vertical distance between the stochastic discount factor implied by the model and the volatility bound. Otrok *et al.* (1999) conduct Monte Carlo experiments to examine the finite-sample properties of such tests. Finally, Luttmer (1996) shows how to incorporate transaction costs and short-sale constraints into the construction of the volatility bound. As seen, research investigating and extending the basic HJ volatility bound is currently very active.

The methodology from Hansen and Jagannathan (1991) does not give a direct measure of the degree of model misspecification. In their 1997 paper, however, Hansen and Jagannathan develop the methodology further, such that it supplies such a measure. The idea is to associate a stochastic discount factor proxy with an asset pricing model and then determine the magnitude of the specification error of that proxy. They propose the following distance measure

$$dist = [(E(yx) - i)' E(xx')^{-1}(E(yx) - i)]^{1/2} \qquad (27)$$

where, as before, x is the vector of asset returns and i is a vector of one's. y is the stochastic discount factor *proxy* (again, all time subscripts have been dropped for notational simplicity). In the case of the C-CAPM/CRRA model, y is given as β times the gross consumption growth rate raised to the power of $-\alpha$. Hansen and Jagannathan show that *dist* measures the minimum distance between y and the set of admissible stochastic discount factors. Furthermore, *dist* can be given an intuitively appealing pricing error interpretation in the sense that *dist* measures the maximum pricing error per unit norm induced by y. The right-hand sides of (26) and (27) look very similar, but they are in general not identical. In the special case of risk-neutral agents the two expressions coincide, and *dist* is just equal to the minimum value of the volatility bound, see Hansen and Jagannathan (1997, p. 578). Note that a less than perfect correlation between y and x is implicit in (27). Thus, in case that y is modified such that its volatility is sufficient to obey the volatility bound (26), if the modification does not make y more correlated with x, *dist* may not decrease. Therefore, it is possible to have two stochastic discount factor proxies, y_1 and y_2, where y_2 obeys (26) while y_1 does not, but where *dist* for y_2 is not smaller than *dist* for y_1.

In comparing the Hansen and Jagannathan (1997) methodology with the GMM methodology described in Section 3, note that whereas both methods involve a quadratic form in the pricing error vector $E(yx) - i$, the weighting matrices are different. In (27) the weighting matrix is $E(xx')^{-1}$ which is invariant to the choice of the stochastic discount factor. In the GMM methodology's J-test, however, the weighting matrix depends directly on the stochastic discount factor model. This implies that the test rewards sampling error associated with the sample moments of $yx - i$. The more sampling uncertainty associated with these moments, the less likely the J-test will reject the model. From this it also follows that the J-test cannot be used to compare different models since the weighting matrix changes as the model and its parameters change. By contrast, since the weighting matrix in (27) is invariant to the choice of model, *dist* can be used to compare models. The model with the lowest *dist* produces the smallest pricing errors, but that model may or may not have a lower *J*-test value compared to other models.

In calculating the associated asymptotic standard error of the *dist*-estimate, the method from Hansen *et al.* (1995) can be used: Construct the time-series

$$u \equiv (y)^2 - (y - \hat{\lambda}'x)^2 - 2i'\hat{\lambda}$$

where $\hat{\lambda}$ is the sample estimate of

$$\lambda = E(xx')^{-1}(E(yx) - i)).$$

The sample mean of u is equal to $\widehat{dist}^2$. Denote by s^2 the estimate of the variance of this sample mean; then the asymptotic standard error of $\widehat{dist}$ is given as $s/(2\widehat{dist})$. The asymptotic distribution of $\widehat{dist}$ is degenerate under the null hypothesis that $dist = 0$. Thus, using this approach, the hypothesis of no pricing errors cannot be tested based on asymptotic approximations. Instead, Engsted *et al.* (2000) develop a Markovian bootstrap approach which, among other things, can be used to test the hypothesis $dist = 0$.

4.4.1. *The equity premium puzzle*

One application of the HJ methodology, which in particular illustrates its usefulness, is in evaluating the famous *equity premium puzzle* of Mehra and Prescott (1985). The puzzle arises due to the very large premium on stocks over short-term risk-free bills or money market certificates, that has been observed in the US over the last century. Real stock returns have averaged approximately 7% while real risk-free assets have given only around 1% in annual return, and standard consumption based asset pricing models have had a very hard time explaining this large equity premium.

According to the consumption based model the expected return on asset j, x_j, is a function of the mean stochastic discount factor (the IMRS) and the covariance between the stochastic discount factor and the asset return. This can be seen by taking unconditional expectation of the Euler equation for asset j, $i = E_t(m_{t+1}x_{j,t+1})$, and using the fact that $E(m_{t+1}x_{j,t+1}) = E(m_{t+1})E(x_{j,t+1}) + cov(m_{t+1}, x_{j,t+1})$. This gives the following expression for the expected asset return:

$$E(x_{j,t+1}) = \frac{1 - cov(m_{t+1}, x_{j,t+1})}{E(m_{t+1})} \tag{28}$$

Assets whose returns have a high positive covariance with consumption growth (i.e. $cov(m_{t+1}, x_{j,t+1})$ is highly negative), are considered very risky and, hence, according to (28) demand a high return. Now the puzzle arises because consumption is very smooth so that the consumption growth rate is much less volatile compared to stock returns. This means that stock returns do not have a high covariation with consumption growth. Thus, with CRRA utility, $m_{t+1} = \beta(C_{t+1}/C_t)^{-\alpha}$, the only way we can make the IMRS sufficiently volatile, is to allow the risk-aversion parameter α to be very large, i.e. >10. Most economists consider such an extreme degree of risk-aversion to be counter-intuitive, (see Kocherlakota (1996) for an excellent survey of the equity premium puzzle literature).

Cochrane and Hansen (1992) use the HJ volatility bound (26) to illustrate the puzzle as follows: Define x to be the (scalar) *excess* return on stocks over the risk-free rate, and Σ_x its (scalar) variance. Thus, i is replaced by a vector of zero's, and the right-hand side of (26) becomes $(EmEx)/(std.dev(x))$. Thus, in the (Em, σ_m)-diagram the lower volatility bound is just a ray from the origin with slope equal to the mean excess return divided by the standard deviation of excess return.[23] The puzzle arises because a very large value of α is needed in order to push the (Em, σ_m) pair, calculated from the consumption based/CRRA model, above the ray.

Of course the puzzle is only a puzzle if the consumption based/CRRA model is the correct underlying equilibrium model of asset returns, and if we don't believe in high degrees of risk-aversion. Maybe people *are* extremely risk-averse. However, in that case another puzzle arises, namely that the model then generates an extremely high real risk-free rate (c.f. Weil, 1989). This can be explained as follows. The risk-free return has zero covariance with the stochastic discount factor. Thus, from (28) its expected return is $1/Em$, and since the (Em, σ_m) pair gets above the ray for a quite low value of Em, it implies a high risk-free rate. As seen, the HJ methodology illustrates nicely how the consumption based/CRRA asset prising theory fails in explaining the equity premium, and it points in directions to which the theory needs to be modified. It shows that we cannot 'save' the theory by allowing people to have a high and constant degree of risk-aversion, because then we get a risk-free rate puzzle. Instead we have to introduce more volatility in the IMRS without increasing risk-aversion.

4.4.2. *Illustration of the Hansen-Jagannathan approach using Danish data*

We illustrate the HJ methodology using the same Danish data for stock returns and consumption as in the previous sections, plus data representing a short-term riskless asset.[24] Over the period 1922–1996 the real average annual stock return is 6.2%, with the real risk-free rate averaging 2.5%. Thus, the Danish equity premium is not nearly as large as the US premium. Also, since the standard deviation of the mean consumption growth rate is 5.3%, which is somewhat higher compared to the volatility of US consumption growth, we do not expect the equity premium puzzle to show up to the same extent as for the US.

Figure 3 shows the HJ lower volatility bound for the Danish data. The minimum standard deviation of the stochastic discount factor is almost 20% and is reached with a mean stochastic discount factor equal to approximately 0.97. The 'squares' represent sample means and standard deviations of the stochastic discount factor $m_{t+1} = \beta(C_{t+1}/C_t)^{-\alpha}$ for values of α ranging from 0 to 10, and with β set equal to 0.99. We see that for $\alpha > 6$ the consumption based model with CRRA utility does generate a stochastic discount factor sufficiently volatile to fall within the admissible region implied by the observed asset returns.

Table 4. Hansen-Jagannathan specification error measure.

$\alpha = 0$	$\alpha = 1$	$\alpha = 2$	$\alpha = 4$	$\alpha = 8$	$\alpha = 12$	$\alpha = 16$
0.180	0.182	0.184	0.187	0.176	0.153	0.389
(0.090)	(0.090)	(0.091)	(0.091)	(0.097)	(0.084)	(0.436)

Notes: The table reports the estimates of 'dist' as in equation (27), with asymptotic standard errors in parantheses (computed as in Hansen, Heaton, and Luttmer, 1995). The time-discount factor β is set equal to 0.99.

Table 4 reports the distance measure *dist* given in (27). The lowest value (0.153) is obtained with α equal to 12 and indicates that pricing errors associated with that particular model account for 15.3%. Interestingly, the lowest pricing errors are obtained for more or less the same α values that make the C-CAPM/CRRA model satisfy the volatility bound (26), see Figure 3.

Note also that the results based on (26) are in contrast to the results reported in Section 4.3 (Table 3). Using the Campbell-Shiller analysis, the consumption based model performs worse when we increase the value of α, but using the HJ volatility bound methodology the model performs better by increasing α. This just reflect the fact that different versions of the model explain different dimensions of the data. The results in Section 4.3 show that a model with $\alpha = 0$ explains the *time-series behaviour of the dividend-price ratio* better than a model with $\alpha > 0$. Whereas the analysis based on (26) shows that the model can only make the *volatility of the stochastic discount factor* consistent with the data if $\alpha > 0$. Thus, in empirical work it is always a good idea to use a variety of different methods in order to see which dimensions of the data the model can fit, and which it cannot.

5. Overview of the recent empirical literature using the alternative measures of fit

In this section I summarize the recent empirical literature on rational expectations models where the measures of fit described in Section 4 have been applied. Table 5 lists all the papers (that I am aware of) using the Campbell-Shiller and Durlauf-Hall approaches, the specific topics examined (present value model, term structure, exchange rates, etc.), the data used, whether the overidentifying restrictions of the models are statistically rejected, and, finally, the implied noise ratio's computed using the methods described in Sections 4.1–4.3. In most of the papers using the Campbell-Shiller method a noise ratio is not explicitly calculated. Instead the correlation coefficient between the actual and theoretical spread is reported along with the ratio of their variances or standard deviations. However, from these two statistics the noise ratio $NR = var(S - S')/var(S)$ is easily obtained as

$$NR = 1 + \frac{var(S')}{var(S)} - 2corr(S, S')\sqrt{\frac{var(S')}{var(S)}} \tag{29}$$

Table 5. List of papers using the Campbell-Shiller and Durlauf-Hall approaches.

Area	Literature	Data	Restrictions rejected	Noise ratio
Present Value Model (constant discount rate)	Campbell and Shiller (1987)	US stock market 1871–1986	Yes and no	0.38–>1
	Campbell and Shiller (1988b)	US stock market 1871–1986	Yes	0.14–0.90
		US stock market 1926–1986	Yes	0.29–>1
	Durlauf and Hall (1989b)	US stock market 1871–1980	Yes	0.04–1.00
		US stock market 1928–1978	Yes	0.04–>1
	Durlauf and Hall (1994)	US stock market 1947–1992	Yes	0.12–0.42
	Mills (1993)	UK stock market 1965–1990	Yes	0.67–0.75
	Cuthbertson and Hayes (1994)	UK stock market 1965–1993	Yes	0.95
	Cuthbertson et al. (1997)	UK stock market 1918–1993	Yes	0.23–0.73
	Lund and Engsted (1996)	UK stock market 1919–1987	—	0.43–>1
		Danish stock market 1922–1990	—	0.18–0.24
		German stock market 1885–1913	—	0.12–0.17
		German stock market 1951–1990	—	0.002–0.27
		Swedish stock market 1919–1990		0.05–0.21
	Falk (1991)	US farmland prices 1921–1986	Yes	>1
	Falk (1992)	US farmland prices 1921–1986	Yes	>1
	Engsted (1998b)	US farmland prices 1921–1989	Yes	>1
Consumption-based Asset Pricing Model	Campbell and Shiller (1988b)	US stock market 1871–1986	Yes and no	Low degree of comovement of δ and δ'
		US stock market 1926–1986	Yes and no	Low degree of comovement of δ and δ'
	Cuthbertson and Hayes (1994)	UK stock market 1965–1993	Yes	>1
	Cuthbertson et al. (1997)	UK stock market 1965–1992	Yes	>1
	Lund and Engsted (1996)	UK stock market 1919–1987	No	0.11–>1
		Danish stock market 1922–1990	No	0.01–0.12
		German stock market 1885–1913	No	0.31–0.63
		German stock market 1951–1990	Yes and no	0.002–0.26
		Swedish stock market 1919–1990	No	0.08–0.24

(continued)

Table 5. *Continued.*

Area	Literature	Data	Restrictions rejected	Noise ratio
Term structure of Interest Rates	Campbell and Shiller (1987)	US 1959–1983	Yes	0.26
		US 1959–1978	Yes	0.06
	Campbell and Shiller (1991)	US 1952–1987	Yes and no	0.21→1
		US 1952–1978	Yes and no	0.08–0.70
	Shea (1992)	US 1952–1987	Yes	0.42–0.56
		US 1952–1978	Yes and no	0.29–0.42
		US 1952–1970	No	0.02
	MacDonald and Speight (1991)	US 1964–1986	Yes	0.41
	Hardouvelis (1994)	Belgium 1964–1986	Yes	0.30
		Canada 1964–1986	Yes	0.37
		Germany 1964–1986	Yes	0.16
		UK 1964–1986	No	0.23
		US 1953–1992	No	0.61
		Canada 1950–1992	No	0.03
		UK 1961–1992	No	0.04
		Germany 1967–1992	No	0.03
		Japan 1961–1992	No	0.15
		France 1968–1992	No	0.01
		Italy 1971–1992	No	0.08
	Mills (1991)	UK 1871–1913	Yes	Low degree of comovement of S and S'
		UK 1919–1939	Yes	Low degree of comovement of S and S'
		UK 1952–1988	No	High degree of comovement of S and S'

		Yes	Low degree of comovement of S and S'
Taylor (1992)	UK 1985–1989	Yes	Low degree of comovement of S and S'
Campbell and Hamao (1993)	Japan 1980–1985	Yes and no	0.43–>1
	Japan 1985–1990	Yes and no	0.08–>1
Hurn et al. (1995)	UK 1975–1991	No	0.03–0.09
Cuthbertson (1996)	UK 1981–1992	Yes and no	0.003–0.42
Cuthbertson et al. (1996)	UK 1975–1992	Yes and no	0.02–0.21
Cuthbertson et al. (2000)	Germany 1976–1993	Yes	0.09–0.60
Engsted (1993a)	Denmark 1982–1989	Yes and no	0.07–0.50
Engsted and Tanggaard (1995)	Denmark 1976–1985	Yes and no	0.01–0.84
	Denmark 1985–1991	Yes and no	0.41–>1
Engsted and Tanggaard (2001)	Denmark 1922–1996	Yes and no	0.02–>1
Engsted (1996a)	Denmark 1988–1992	Yes and no	0.13–0.53
	Denmark 1992–1993	Yes and no	0.01–0.06
Engsted and Nyholm (2000)	Denmark 1976–1991	Yes	>1
	Denmark 1985–1997	No	0.13
Warne (1990)	Sweden 1983–1989	Yes	High degree of comovement of S and S'
Blix (1997)	Sweden 1984–1997	Yes	0.08–0.14
	US 1982–1997	Yes	0.22–0.28
Johnson (1997)	US 1951–1987	Yes and no	0.02–0.51
	US 1951–1979	Yes and no	0.01–0.41
Fisher Hypothesis			
Johnson (1994)	US 1953–1979	Yes and no	0.01–0.38
	US 1979–1982	Yes and no	0.06–0.96
	US 1982–1987	Yes and no	0.06–0.89
Engsted (1995)	US 1962–1993	Yes	0.47–0.86
	UK 1962–1993	No	0.01–0.02
	Canada 1962–1993	Yes	0.44–0.70
	Japan 1974–1992	No	0.01–0.12
	Australia 1969–1993	Yes	0.37–0.41
	Belgium 1962–1993	Yes	0.11–0.21
	Denmark 1962–1993	Yes	0.03–0.06

(continued)

Table 5. *Continued.*

Area	Literature	Data	Restrictions rejected	Noise ratio
		France 1962–1993	Yes	0.37–0.91
		Germany 1962–1993	Yes	0.12–0.24
		Ireland 1971–1993	Yes	0.20–0.23
		Italy 1962–1992	Yes	0.26–0.31
		Sweden 1962–1993	Yes	0.05–0.10
		Switzerland 1962–1993	Yes	0.05–0.05
	Engsted (1996b)	Denmark 1948–1988	No	High degree of comovement of S and S'
	Garcia (1993)	Brazil 1973–1990	Yes	0.01
Monetary Model of Exchange Rates	MacDonald and Taylor (1993)	\$-DM 1976–1990	Yes	Low degree of comovement of S and S'
	MacDonald and Taylor (1993)	\$-Franc 1976–1990	Yes	Low degree of comovement of S and S'
	Engsted (1996c)	£-DM 1921–1923	No	0.02
	Konuki (1999)	\$ rates 1976–1994	No	0.12–0.26
Consumption and Saving	Campbell (1987)	US 1953–1984	Yes	0.11–>1
	Campbell and Clarida (1988)	UK 1955–1984	Yes	>1
		Canada 1955–1984	Yes	0.01
	Engsted (1992)	Denmark 1971–1988	Yes	(High) degree of comovement of S and S'
	Kim (1996)	US	Yes	0.04–0.10

The Balance of Payments	Sheffrin and Woo (1990)	Belgium 1955–1985	No	Low degree of comovement of S and S'
		Denmark 1955–1985	Yes	High degree of comovement of S and S'
		Canada 1955–1985	Yes	Low degree of comovement of S and S'
		UK 1955–1985	Yes	Low degree of comovement of S and S'
	Otto (1992)	US 1950–1988	Yes	0.18
		Canada 1950–1987	Yes	0.80
	Ghosh (1995a)	US 1960–1988	No	0.14
		Japan 1960–1988	Yes	0.10
		Germany 1962–1988	Yes	0.52
		UK 1960–1988	Yes	0.58
		Canada 1960–1988	Yes	0.39
	Agenor et al. (1999)	France 1970–1996	No	High degree of comovement of S and S'
	Ghosh and Ostry (1995)	45 developing countries 1948–1991	Yes and No	High degree of comovement of S and S'
	Obstfeld and Rogoff (1996)	Belgium 1954–1990	—	(High) degree of comovement of S and S'
		Canada 1952–1990	—	Low degree of comovement of S and S'
		Denmark 1951–1990	—	(High) degree of comovement of S and S'
		Sweden 1951–1990	—	High degree of comovement of S and S'

(*continued*)

Table 5. *Continued.*

Area	Literature	Data	Restrictions rejected	Noise ratio
	Bergin and Sheffrin (2000)	UK 1949–1990	—	Low degree of comovement of S and S'
		Australia 1961–1996	No	High degree of comovement of S and S'
		Canada 1961–1996	Yes	(High) degree of comovement of S and S'
		UK	Yes	(High) degree of comovement of S and S'
Tax-Smoothing	Huang and Lin (1993)	US 1929–1988	Yes and no	0.09
	Ghosh (1995b)	US 1961–1988	No	High degree of comovement of S and S'
		Canada 1962–1988	No	(High) degree of comovement of S and S'
Hyperinflation	Engsted (1993b)	Germany 1920–1923	Yes	0.28
	Engsted (1994)	Germany 1921–1923	Yes	High degree of comovement of S and S'
		Austria 1921–1922	Yes	High degree of comovement of S and S'
		Hungary 1922–1924	No	High degree of comovement of S and S'
		Poland 1922–1923	No	Low degree of comovement of S and S'

			(High) degree of comovement of S and S'
Engsted(1996c)	Russia 1921–1924	Yes	(High) degree of comovement of S and S'
Petrovic and Vujocevic (1996)	Greece 1943–1944	Yes	High degree of comovement of S and S'
Engsted (1998c)	Germany 1921–1923	No	0.02
	Yugoslavia 1990–1993	Yes	0.57
	Yugoslavia 1990–1993	Yes	0.18–0.78
	China 1946–1949	Yes	0.32–0.65
LQAC Model			(High) degree of comovement of S and S'
Cuthbertson and Taylor (1990)	UK Money Demand 1965–1986	No	
Engsted and Haldrup (1997)	UK Money Demand 1963–1989	Yes	0.62–>1
Engsted and Haldrup (1999)	UK Money Demand 1963–1989	Yes	0.92–>1
Engsted and Haldrup (1994)	Danish Labour Demand, 1974–1990	Yes	0.89–>1
Amano and Wirjanto (1997)	Canadian Labour Demand, 1967–1993	No	0.62
Durlauf and Maccini (1995)	US Inventories 1959–1990	Yes and no	0.02–0.59
Petursson (1996)	Icelandic Prices 1962–1993	Yes	0.44–0.57

In some of the papers $corr(S, S')$ and the slope-coefficient, β, in a regression of S' on S are reported. In that case the noise ratio is

$$NR = 1 + \left(\frac{\beta}{corr(S, S')} \right)^2 - 2\beta \qquad (30)$$

Finally, some papers only report one of either $corr(S, S')$ or $var(S')/var(S)$, or report none of them and only show graphs of S and S'. In those cases I cannot compute a noise ratio and, instead, I just indicate whether the degree of comovement of S and S' seems to be high or low.

In Table 6 I summarize the results for the consumption based asset pricing model with CRRA utility obtained using the Hansen and Jagannathan (1991) methodology. Here a noise ratio is not directly obtainable; instead I report the value of the degree of relative risk-aversion, in the CRRA utility specification, for which the volatility of the stochastic discount factor is consistent with the HJ volatility bound. At the end of Section 5.1, I briefly note the empirical results obtained using the Hansen and Jagannathan (1997) methodology.

5.1. *Asset pricing and the stock market*

The simple present value model with a constant discount rate that I described in detail in Section 4.1.1, has been much applied when examining stock price movements.[25] Most recent literature using this model has applied either the *spread* formulation in Equation (10) or the *log dividend-price ratio* formulation in Equation (15) where $E_t r_{t+i} = $ constant. On US data Campbell and Shiller (1987, 1988b) in general find the model to be statistically rejected and with high noise ratios, see Table 5. Durlauf and Hall (1989b) also report high noise ratios as long

Table 6. List of papers using the Hansen-Jagannathan (1991) approach.

Area	Literature	Data	Degree of risk-aversion
Consumption-based Asset Pricing	Hansen and Jagannathan (1991)	US 1871–1986	25
		US 1959–1986	⩾100
	Ferson and Harvey (1992)	US 1946–1987	48
	Cochrane and Hansen (1992)	US 1947–1990	40–210
	Burnside (1994)	US 1888–1978	22
	Cecchetti *et al.* (1994)	US 1890–1987	25
		US 1964–1988	⩾30
	Campbell *et al.* (1997)	US 1889–1994	25
	Engsted (1998a)	UK 1919–1987	7–12
	Engsted *et al.* (2000)	US 1889–1985	>20
		Denmark 1922–1996	4–8

as the information set Φ_t contains current and lagged stock prices (the low noise ratio of 4% is for the (uninteresting) case where Φ_t only contains dividends). Mills (1993), Cuthbertson and Hayes (1994), Cuthbertson et al. (1997), and Lund and Engsted (1996) also report high noise ratios using UK stock market data. However, using data from Denmark, Germany, and Sweden, Lund and Engsted (1996) report much lower noise ratios (from 0.2 to 27%). Thus for the US and the UK, the constant discount rate present value model is decisively rejected, whereas for Denmark, Germany, and Sweden the evidence against the model is less substantial. As seen from Table 5, attempts to model time-variation in the discount rate in terms of the consumption based asset pricing model with CRRA utility, has not been successful for the US and the UK, and for the other countries the noise ratios hardly change compared to the case with a constant discount rate (except for Pre World War I Germany where the noise ratio actually *increases*).

In many of the studies that try to estimate the degree of relative risk-aversion, α, in the consumption-based/CRRA model, the estimates are often very imprecise and of the 'wrong' sign. This implies that standard parametric statistical techniques in general are unable to provide solid information about stochastic discount factors in financial markets. The Hansen and Jagannathan (1991) methodology, on the other hand, attempts to provide such information non-parametrically without explicitly estimating the degree of risk-aversion. Using the methodology described in Section 4.4 on annual US stock and bond returns beginning in 1871, and monthly returns beginning in 1959, Hansen and Jagannathan (1991) find that the degree of relative risk-aversion has to be higher than 25 in the annual data, and much higher than 100 in the monthly data, in order for the volatility of the stochastic discount factor to be inside the volatility bound dictated by the observed asset return data (c.f. Table 6). All subsequent studies using this methodology on US data find results essentially similar to those of Hansen and Jagannathan (1991). The reason that the required value of α tend to be lower in the annual data covering the pre World War II period, is that consumption growth is much less volatile in the Post War period compared to the Pre War period; therefore the value of α has to be much higher in order to generate enough variation in the stochastic discount factor. However, values of α around 25 also represent an extreme degree of risk-aversion. On UK asset returns, Engsted (1998a) finds that a high degree of risk-aversion is also needed in order to fit the data, although not as high as for the US.

On monthly US returns from 1959–1990, Hansen and Jagannathan (1997) report estimates of *dist* (see equation (27)) indicating that pricing errors associated with the C-CAPM/CRRA model amount to around 33% irrespective of the value of α. Similar results are reported by Engsted et al. (2000) for yearly returns over the longer period 1889–1985.

5.2. *Interest rates and the term structure*

One of the most active and voluminous areas within the empirical rational expectations literature is the term structure of interest rates. There exists a vast number of studies that test and evaluate the *Expectations Hypothesis of the Term Structure* (EHTS). The term structure is important because it is related both to the notion of market efficiency in the bond market and to the transmission mechanism of monetary policy. In addition, the term structure has proven to be a very useful predictor of future interest rates, inflation, and real economic activity.

In linearized form the EHTS can be stated as

$$R_t^{(n)} = \frac{1}{k} \sum_{i=0}^{k-1} E_t R_{t+i}^{(m)} + c, \quad k = \frac{n}{m}, \quad n > m$$

where $R_t^{(n)}$ and $R_t^{(m)}$ are n-period and m-period pure discount yields on bonds or money market instruments, and c is a time-invarying term premium. This relation can be rewritten into the following expression, which relates the interest rate spread, $S_t^{(n,m)} \equiv R_t^{(n)} - R_t^{(m)}$, to a weighted average of expected future changes in the m-period rate:

$$S_t^{(n,m)} = \sum_{i=1}^{k-1} \left(1 - \frac{i}{k}\right)(R_{t+mi}^{(m)} - R_{t+m(i-1)}^{(m)}) + c$$

It says that under rational expectations and a constant term premium, the EHTS implies that the spread between a long (n-period) and short (m-period) interest rate, is the optimal predictor of a weighted average of the changes in short rates over the life of the long-term bond. This expression is of the same basic form as Equation (10) from Section 4.1.1. Thus, the VAR approach described in that section is readily applicable in testing/evaluating the EHTS, including a comparison of actual and 'theoretical' spreads, and by now there exists a vast amount of evidence across many different countries and time periods using this methodology to analyze the term structure, see Table 5.

The evidence is not at all clearcut. The results are highly dependent on country, sample period, and whether it is the long or short end of the term structure that is being analyzed. Perhaps the study by Hardouvelis (1994) summarizes in the best possible manner the overall conclusion that can be drawn from these analyzes. He finds that for the US the EHTS does not describe the term structure very accurately. Noise accounts for 61% of the variation in the interest rate spread. However, for most of the remaining countries (Canada, Germany, France, Italy, and the UK) the hypothesis actually provides a quite good description of the term structure, since noise only amounts to between 1 and 8%. Another quite robust finding in several of the studies listed in Table 5 is that the EHTS seems to work better in periods of relatively volatile interest rates, such as periods of monetary targeting by the monetary authorities, and less well in periods of relatively smooth interest rates, such as periods of interest rate targeting.

Many studies find interest rates to be well approximated as non-stationary, I(1), processes that cointegrate such that interest rate spreads are stationary, I(0). This is in full accordance with the EHTS. In fact, since according to the EHTS all bivariate spreads are stationary, in a system of $p > 2$ interest rates there should be p-1 independent cointegrating vectors, corresponding to one common stochastic trend driving the term structure. Using the Johansen (1991) cointegration methodology, Hall *et al.* (1992), Shea (1992), and Engsted and Tanggaard (1994a), *inter alia*, overall find this basic cointegration implication of the EHTS to be supported by the data.

The next natural question to ask is then what this common stochastic trend represents. An obvious answer comes from the *Fisher hypothesis*, according to which the nominal interest rate is determined as the sum of a constant real rate and the expected inflation rate. Many studies find *price-levels* to be I(2) processes, c.f. e.g. Haldrup (1998), such that inflation rates are I(1). Thus, according to the Fisher hypothesis the inflation rate constitutes the common stochastic trend driving the overall *level* of I(1) interest rates. Engsted (1995) analyzes the relationship between inflation and long-term interest rates in 13 OECD countries, and finds that in countries like Denmark, Japan, Sweden, Switzerland, and the UK, the Fisher hypothesis under rational expectations and a constant *ex ante* real rate provides a good description of the interest rate-inflation relationship. In those countries the noise ratio lies between 1 and 12%. However, in other countries (US, Canada, Australia, France) the noise ratios are much larger, indicating substantial deviations from the hypothesis.

The EHTS's implication of only one common stochastic trend does not necessarily imply that the term structure is totally driven by a single factor. It only implies that the *non-stationary* part of the term structure is driven by a single factor. There can be several other factors driving the stationary part of interest rates. Related to this issue is the question of how the EHTS fits into the single- and multi-factor equilibrium (arbitrage-free) models of e.g. the Cox *et al.* (1985) type. In these models there is a direct relationship between the level and conditional volatility of interest rates, and when interest rates are I(1), this has the consequence that interest rate *spreads* are also I(1), i.e. there is no cointegration in the way the EHTS predicts (see Pagan *et al.* (1996) and Taulbjerg (2000) for a detailed investigation of the cointegration properties implied by various arbitrage-free term structure models).

5.3. *Exchange rates*

Just like for stock prices and interest rates, simple linear rational expectations models have also been used in an attempt to explain currency exchange rates, although generally not with much success. The prototype *Monetary Model of Exchange Rates* (MMER) is one which builds on stable money demand functions, exogenous money supply, uncovered interest rate parity, and instantaneous purchasing power parity. The lead to the following present value model for the log exchange rate, e_t, between two countries

$$S_t \equiv e_t - (m_t - \gamma y) = \sum_{i=1}^{\infty} \left(\frac{\lambda}{1+\lambda} \right)^i E_t \Delta(m_{t+i} - \lambda y_{t+i})$$

written in a form equivalent to (10). m_t and y_t are nominal money and income differentials (in logs) between the two countries, respectively, and γ and λ denote the income- and interest rate elasticities of money demand. Thus, when e_t, m_t, and y_t are I(1) processes, which they typically are found to be, S_t should be stationary such that exchange rates cointegrate with money- and income differentials. Some studies in the literature, using data from the post Bretton Woods area, find this cointegration property to be fulfilled, although it seems to be inconsistent with the many studies that find the *real* exchange rate to be I(1) over the same period. Non-stationary real exchange rates imply non-stationary deviations from *purchasing power parity* (PPP), and thereby a breakdown of the MMER.

However, *given* that S_t is I(0), the MMER can be tested and evaluated directly using the methods of Sections 4.1–4.2. MacDonald and Taylor (1993, 1994) carry out such an analysis using dollar exchange rates, and they find absolutely no support for the model. An obvious explanation is the assumption of instantaneous PPP underlying the analysis. Engsted (1996c) examines the MMER using data from the German 1921–1923 hyperinflation (see Section 5.6 below), a period in which deviations from PPP are much more likely to be negligible, and he finds strong support for the model. The VAR cross-equation restrictions are not rejected statistically, and the noise ratio is only 2%, see Table 5.

Another explanation for the failure of the MMER to explain Post Bretton Woods exchange rate movements is that uncovered interest rate parity (UIP) does not hold. Konuki (1999) estimates noise ratio's, using the Durlauf-Hall methodology, for the UIP relationship, and finds that for five dollar exchange rates the noise ratio lies between 12% and 26%.

5.4. *Consumption, saving, and the balance of payments*

Risk-averse consumers will attempt to smooth consumption over time in response to changes in their income; save (accumulate assets) in periods of relatively high income, and dissave in periods of relatively low income. This implies that consumption, and thereby savings, become related to the expected movements in future income. This is the basic content of the *Permanent Income-* and *Life Cycle* hypotheses. Under certain simplifying assumptions, these hypotheses can be shown to result in the following expression for savings, S_t

$$S_t = -\sum_{i=1}^{\infty} \left(\frac{1}{1+r} \right)^i E_t \Delta Y_{t+i}$$

According to the closed-economy version of this model (Campbell, 1987), S_t is private savings defined as total disposable income less consumption, Y_t is disposable *labour* income, and r is the constant real interest rate. The open-economy version of the model (e.g. Sheffrin and Woo, 1990), leads to the same equation, but now S_t is *national* savings, i.e. the current account surplus, and Y_t is *net aggregate output* of the economy, defined as GDP less investment and government purchases. The model implies that consumers will 'save for a rainy day', i.e. when they expect their future labour income to fall. Equivalently, in an open-economy setting, a country will run a current account surplus when it expects its net output to fall in the future.

The model implies that when labour income or net output are non-stationary, I(1), private savings or the current account should be stationary. Given these restrictions, the methods of Sections 4.1–4.2 can be directly applied to examine the empirical content of the model. As seen from Table 5, the results for the closed-economy version suggest that the model fits Canadian (and to a lesser extent Danish) data quite well, and UK data quite poorly. The results for the US are ambiguous. Campbell's (1987) results, based on the Campbell-Shiller VAR methodology, in general imply quite high noise ratios (except for a low-order VAR model), while Kim (1996), based on the Durlauf-Hall approach, report quite *low* noise ratios (see, however, Engsted (2000) for a critique of the analyses in Kim (1996)).

For the open-economy version of the model, noise ratios are high for Canada, Germany, and the UK, and low for Denmark, France, Japan, Sweden, the US, and a number of developing countries. Bergin and Sheffrin (2000) find that allowing for variation in interest rates and exchange rates greatly improves the fit of this model.

5.5. *Tax-smoothing*

A model essentially similar to the one in the previous section can be imposed on the *government's* behaviour regarding setting taxes. If tax collections are distorting, a policy of minimizing the present value of tax collection costs for a given expected present value of tax revenues, leads to an optimal rule in which the government smoothes tax rates over time (just like consumers smooth consumption over time). This implies a relationship between the current budget surplus and expected future changes in government expenditures and aggregate output. The government runs a budget surplus when it expects future government spending to fall and/or aggregate output to increase.

Huang and Lin (1993) examine this model using US data and the methodology from Section 4.1. They find the empirical content of the model to be quite high; the noise ratio is only 9%. Ghosh (1995b) conducts a similar analysis using US and Canadian data, and he also reports quite favourable results, especially for the US.

5.6. *Hyperinflation*

The applications surveyed in Sections 5.1 to 5.5 are mostly based on different versions of equations (10) and (15). As we have seen, these expressions are useful when the underlying variables are I(1) processes. In some cases, however, the data to be used in the empirical analysis are second-order integrated, I(2), instead of I(1), i.e. they need to be differenced twice in order to be stationary. In almost all analyses of hyperinflation, money and prices are modelled as being I(2). Engsted (1993b) generalizes the Campbell-Shiller methodology such that it can handle I(2) variables, and he uses the extended methodology to analyze the *Cagan-model*'s ability to explain the famous German 1920–23 hyperinflation.

According to the Cagan-model, the demand for real balances is a function of expected future inflation, $m_t - p_t = -\beta E_t(p_{t+1} - p_t)$, where m_t and p_t are logs to nominal money and prices, respectively. Solving this model for p_t, and rewriting it such that it only contains stationary variables, give the following expression

$$S_t \equiv (m_t - p_t) + \beta \Delta m_t = -(1 + \beta) \sum_{i=1}^{\infty} \left(\frac{\beta}{1 + \beta} \right)^i E_t \Delta^2 m_{t+i}$$

which shows that, according to the model, real balances should cointegrate with money growth, such that S_t is I(0). Given this restriction, the model can be tested and evaluated in a VAR for the two stationary variables S_t and $\Delta^2 m_t$, using the methods from Section 4.1.

On data from various hyperinflation episodes it is generally found that there is empirical content to the simple Cagan-model, but also that there are significant deviations from the model. Noise ratios are typically found to be around 50%, see Table 5. These deviations are often interpreted as *money demand shocks*. An interesting exception occurs when, in the German case, exchange rates are used instead of prices. In that case the noise ratio reduces to 2%, c.f. Engsted (1996c). This could indicate severe measurement errors in the price-indexes used in hyperinflation studies, errors that are not present in exchange rate data.

Durlauf and Hooker (1994) and Hooker (1996) use the Durlauf-Hall approach to evaluate the Cagan-model. However, they measure noise in a version of the model which includes money demand shocks as part of fundamentals. This is problematic because these shocks are unobservable to the econometrician. Thus, we face an identification problem when trying to interpret the noise measures they report, see Engsted (1998c) for details on this, and for an alternative application of the Durlauf-Hall approach in the context of the Cagan-model.

5.7. *Linear quadratic adjustment cost models*

Many dynamic models in macroeconomics imply a present value relationship like (5), but extended such that it allows for costs of adjusting the target variable. Examples include labour demand, money demand, and inventory investments. For example, firms long-run demand for labour may depend on real wages and output. But if there are costs associated with hiring and firing labour, then in case of changes in the expected future levels of real wages and output, it will in general be inoptimal for the firm to adjust immediately to these new levels. Instead the firm should adjust labour *gradually* over time. The speed of adjustment will then depend on the magnitude of adjustment costs relative to the costs of deviating from the long-run optimal level.

In the literature the *Linear Quadratic Adjustment Cost* (LQAC) model is a simple model that captures the above features. It is based on minimizing the intertemporal loss function $L = \sum_{i=0}^{\infty} \beta^i [\theta(y_{t+i} - y_{t+i}^*)^2 + (\Delta y_{t+i})^2]$, where y_t is the target variable (e.g. labour demand), and y_t^* is the optimal long-run level of y_t (typically a linear function of some *forcing* variables, e.g. real wages and output). θ is a parameter that describes the magnitude of adjustment costs relative to the costs of deviating from y_t^*. From the first-order condition to this minimization problem, the following expression can be derived,

$$S_t \equiv \Delta y_t - (\lambda - 1)[y_{t-1} - y_{t-1}^*] - (1 - \lambda)\Delta y_t^* = (1 - \lambda) \sum_{i=1}^{\infty} (\lambda\beta)^i E_t \Delta y_{t+i}^*$$

where λ is a positive parameter less than one (a non-linear function of β and θ). As seen this expression is basically of the same form as (10), but generalized in order to account for the adjustment costs. When the underlying variables are I(1), the model implies cointegration between y_t and the variables determining y_t^*, i.e. $(y_t - y_t^*)$ is I(0), such that S_t is stationary. Thus, the LQAC model can be tested and evaluated in a VAR for S_t and first-differences of the variables determining y_t^*, using the methods in Section 4.1.

In an application for Danish labour demand, Engsted and Haldrup (1994) strongly reject the LQAC model, and they find that noise (i.e. deviations from the model) accounts for almost all the variability in the data. Amano and Wirjanto (1997) conduct a similar analysis on Canadian labour demand, and they conclude that the LQAC model provides a valid description of their data. However, by calculating a noise ratio from their reported results, it is found that noise accounts for 62% which is substantial. Strong rejections and high noise ratios are also found when applying the LQAC model in explaining money demand. The exception is Cuthbertson and Taylor (1990), but the way they construct the *theoretical spread* makes their analysis biased towards accepting the LQAC model, see Engsted and Haldrup (1997, 1999). Finally, Durlauf and Maccini (1995) use the Durlauf-Hall approach to evaluate the LQAC model's ability to explain US inventory investments. They find substantial noise in the pure *production smoothing model* of inventories, but once allowance is made for buffer stock and stockout avoidance motives, and for observable cost shocks, the noise ratios become quite low.

5.8. *Summarizing the empirical results*

The results reported in Section 4.3 for Danish stock prices indicate that a simple constant discount rate present value model captures the movements over time in the dividend-price ratio quite well, although not perfectly. On the other hand, the Hansen-Jagannathan volatility bound in Section 4.4.2 shows that the standard deviation of the discount factor must be at least close to 20% in order to be consistent with the data, which requires investors to be somewhat risk-averse, and the Hansen-Jagannathan specification error measure indicates that pricing errors associated with the C-CAPM/CRRA model never get below 15% (Engsted and Tanggaard (2001) and Engsted *et al.* (2000) analyze the Danish data in much more detail). The results reported in Section 5.1 suggest that for German and Swedish stock prices there is also an element of truth to the simple constant discount rate present value model, while this does not seem to be the case for the US and the UK.

Regarding the other applications of simple rational expectations models reported in Sections 5.2 to 5.7, it appears that in many cases such models are able to explain a substantial part of the movements in the term structure of interest rates, private savings and the current account, the government's budget surplus/deficit, and money demand during hyperinflation. However, when it comes to explaining the dynamics of foreign exchange rates, labour demand, and money demand, simple linear rational expectations models have not been very successful.

6. Concluding remarks

Simple rational expectations models based on optimizing behaviour are, like all models, literally false. Researchers are becoming increasingly aware that this trivial fact has important implications for how to empirically evaluate such models. In particular, the usual statistical approach of formal testing of overidentifying restrictions may not be as appealing as traditionally thought. One response to this is to dismiss the optimizing/rational expectations approach to economic modelling, and instead use a more data-based approach with less emphasis on economic theory. The problem with this approach is that *economic* interpretation of the models generated this way often becomes very difficult. Another response is to remain within the optimizing framework, and then develop alternative methods of empirical evaluation of economic models that do not have as a basic premise that the models represent the *true* nature of the world.

In this survey I have described and illustrated a number of such alternative methods that have been developed in the rational expectations literature, and I have given an overview of the many recent empirical studies that have applied these alternative methods.

A valid criticism that can be raised against these alternative measures is that we lack an *objective* criterion to make a judgement about them. How do we know that a noise ratio of 0.21 (meaning that the variability of noise amounts to 21% of the variability of S_t), is an economically important deviation? Similarly, how do we know that a HJ distance measure of 0.153 (meaning that pricing errors amount to 15.3% of the observed asset prices), is economically important? As they stand, it is fully up to the individual researcher to decide whether these measures represent economically important deviations.

The advantage of using *statistical* testing procedures to evaluate economic models is that they provide an objective criterion upon which we can judge the model. The drawback, however, is that this objective criterion may not be particularly relevant economically. For example, as we have seen, the *J*-test from

GMM is not directly related to the magnitude of deviations from the model. In an asset pricing framework, the model with the highest (lowest) J-test value does not necessarily produce the largest (smallest) pricing errors. Similarly, the J-test cannot be used to compare different models. This makes *economic* interpretation of the test results quite difficult. The alternative measures of fit do not have this drawback.

The Campbell-Shiller and Durlauf-Hall methodologies are designed for simple single-equation linear rational expectations models. The extension of such models in terms of multivariate non-linear general equilibrium models of the Real Business Cycle (RBC) variety is at present a very active research area. In the RBC literature it is explicitly acknowledged that the models are inherently misspecified (false), so instead of using traditional statistical evaluation techniques, researchers instead use calibration/simulation techniques in trying to match the first- and second moments of the actual data. However, the usual calibration exercises in RBC studies have been criticized for being ad hoc and with no firm statistical foundation. As a response, researchers have recently developed explicit goodness-of-fit measures and statistical inference procedures for *inherently misspecified* general equilibrium models, see e.g. Watson (1993) and Diebold *et al.* (1998). Similarly, extensions of the Hansen-Jagannathan methodology in various directions are beginning to show up. With no doubt the development of methods for evaluating dynamic rational expectations models will continue in the years to come.

Acknowledgements

I have benefitted from numerous discussions with many colleagues on the topics in this paper. In particular, I would like to thank the anonymous referee of this journal for very detailed and insightful comments. Of course, the usual disclaimer applies.

Notes

1. This is the reason why economists belonging to the *Real Business Cycle* school use *calibration* instead of statistical tests in evaluating their models, c.f. Kydland and Prescott (1996).
2. In addition, Pagan (1996) gives a very detailed survey of the many econometric techniques used in empirical financial modelling.
3. The critical quotations in the introduction from Summers (1991) do not imply that Summers in general rejects the optimizing/rational expectations approach to economic modelling. What he rejects is the way these models traditionally have been evaluated *econometrically*. In fact, as an example of work that he likes, he explicitly mentions Mehra and Prescott's (1985) informal evaluation, using calibration methods, of the equity premium puzzle based on an asset pricing model very similar to the model described in Section 2.2 below. I will return to the equity premium puzzle in Section 4.4.1.
4. The consumption based model *per se* does not require the assumption of a representative agent. This assumption is made in order to be able to use *aggregate* consumption data when empirically evaluating the model.

5. The literature on speculative bubbles in asset prices is too large to be surveyed here. See e.g. *Journal of Economic Perspectives* 4(2), 1990, which is a special issue devoted to bubbles.

6. I do not provide a detailed description of the GMM methodology. Excellent GMM surveys already exist, e.g. Hall (1993) and Ogaki (1993). The purpose of this section is only to provide the necessary background for understanding the criticism of traditional RE econometrics, that has led to the development of the alternative measures of fit described in Section 4.

7. Under the null that the C-CAPM/CRRA model is true, $h(x_{t+1}, b) \otimes z_t$ will be serially uncorrelated. However, time-aggregation, durability of consumption, and time-overlapping data (in case that returns are multi-period) will induce serial correlation and, in addition, the model does not preclude heteroscedasticity. Thus, the Newey-West estimator is typically applied in estimating S.

8. There is a large literature investigating the small-sample properties of GMM, including size and power properties of the J-test, but no clearcut and unambiguous results emerge from this literature, see e.g. the 1996 special issue of *Journal of Business and Economic Statistics* devoted to GMM estimation.

9. A related problem with the J-test is that it cannot be used to compare different models. I return to this in Section 4.4. Furthermore, as noted by e.g. Hall (1993), the J-test should not be considered an 'omnibus' specification test, since certain types of misspecification may not cause the orthogonality conditions to be violated. This implies that, ideally, many different tests in addition to the J-test should be computed in evaluating the statistical adequacy of the model. For example, Hoffman and Pagan (1989) and Ghysels and Hall (1990) develop tests for parameter constancy within the GMM framework (see Lund and Engsted (1996) for an application of such tests).

10. I emphasize that the analyses in this section, and in the subsequent Sections 4.3 and 4.4.2, should only be regarded illustrative and, hence, do not *per se* provide solid and robust evidence on the Danish stock market. Engsted and Tanggaard (2001) and Engsted *et al.* (2000) contain much more detailed analyses of the Danish data.

11. Unless, of course, the cointegrating property is found *not* to be supported by the data. For a more detailed analysis of the role of cointegration in evaluating economic models, see Søderlind and Vredin (1996).

12. Numerous methods exist for conducting the cointegration analysis. The simple OLS procedure of Engle and Granger (1987), and the full information maximum likelihood procedure of Johansen (1991), are among the most widely used.

13. Note that due to the super-consistency property of $\hat{\beta}$, it can be regarded as known when estimating the VAR model. For simplicity a VAR with only one lag is considered. However, the generalization to the case with more than one lag is straightforward using the socalled *companion form*, see Campbell and Shiller (1987) for details.

14. If the market's information set includes only current and lagged dividends, then there is no Granger causality, i.e. a_3 will be equal to zero. Note that the second equation of the VAR model (11) is an *error-correction* equation for dividends, where S_{t-1} serves as the error-correction term. Thus, another interesting implication which follows from the optimal prediction property of S_t when agents in forecasting future dividends use more information than just current and lagged dividends, is, that error-correction is *not* the result of adjustment in dividends in response to a temporary disequilibrium between prices and dividends. This disequilibrium interpretation of error-correction models is the one usually made in the literature, but in the present context error-correction is not the result of adjustment towards equilibrium because under the present value model the market is *always* in equilibrium. Instead, error-correction is the result of one economic

variable, S_t, being a rational predictor of another economic variable, ΔD_{t+i}, (see Campbell and Shiller (1988a) for a full elaboration of this point). Another thing to note is that it is possible to rewrite the traditional error-correction model for P_t and D_t, that is implied by cointegration, into the VAR model (11), see Campbell and Shiller (1988a). The VAR is particularly useful in relation with the present value model, since it allows straightforward calculation of conditional expectations (see, however, Johansen and Swensen (1999) for tests of present value models conducted within the vector ECM approach of Johansen, 1991).

15. The Wald test is computed as follows. Denote by θ the vector of VAR parameters, and $V(\hat{\theta})$ the corresponding covariance matrix. Further, let $f(\theta)$ denote the non-linear restrictions, and $(\partial f(\hat{\theta})/\partial \theta)$ the matrix of derivatives of $f(\theta)$ with respect to each element of θ, evaluated at the unrestricted estimates. Then the Wald test statistic is $f(\hat{\theta})'[(\partial f(\hat{\theta})/\partial \theta')V(\hat{\theta})(\partial f(\hat{\theta})/\partial \theta)]^{-1}f(\hat{\theta})$, which has an asymptotic χ^2 distribution with degrees of freedom equal to the number of restrictions.

16. The present value model also restricts the mean of S_t in terms of the mean of ΔD_t. To take this restriction into account, the two variables should not be measured as deviations from their means, and constant terms should then be included in the VAR. This leads to an extra restriction in addition to the dynamic restrictions in (13). Usually, however, empirical studies only test the dynamic restrictions.

17. In a more general setup, instead of collecting Δc_t and Δd_t into the composite variable $(\alpha \Delta c_t - \Delta d_t)$, one could specify separate equations for Δc_t and Δd_t, so that the VAR model would contain three variables $(\delta_t, \Delta c_t$ and $\Delta d_t)$, and then estimate α instead of prefixing it at some value. This is what Lund and Engsted (1996) do in their analysis, but the resulting estimates of α turn out to be mostly implausible and with very large standard errors.

18. To my knowledge the papers by Durlauf and Hall have remained unpublished despite the fact that they have become widely cited, and their methodology has been used to a great extent in recent literature, c.f. Section 5. In addition, the published paper by Durlauf and Maccini (1995) is fully based on the Durlauf-Hall methodology.

19. The approach is readily applicable in evaluating the present value model with a time-varying discount factor using either the present value relation that can be derived from (7), or the log-linearized model from Section 4.1.2.

20. Note that η_t is equal to $E_t \zeta_{t+1}$ from Section 4.1.1.

21. Recently the Campbell-Shiller approach has been generalized to allow for regime-changes using Hamilton's (1989) Markov switching methodology, see Blix (1997), Evans (1998), and Engsted and Nyholm (2000).

22. Analyses of the small-sample properties of VAR models similar to Campbell and Shiller's can also be found in Mattey and Meese (1986) and Hodrick (1992). None of these studies, however, consider the correlation-coefficient and standard-deviation ratio of S_t and S_t'.

23. In the finance literature the ratio of mean excess return to its standard deviation is called the *Sharpe ratio*. This ratio measures the price of one unit of risk.

24. The time-series for the risk-free rate is composed of the Danish Central Bank discount rate up to 1975, spliced together with a 1-month discount yield for the period thereafter (for 1976–1991 taken from the appendix in Engsted and Tanggaard (1994b), and for the years 1992–1996 I use the official 1-month 'Copenhagen InterBank Offered Rate'). In Denmark a reasonable liquid market for short-term claims only existed from the middle of the 1970s. Up till then the Central Bank discount rate seems to be the best proxy for the short-term interest rate.

25. In the agricultural economics literature the constant discount rate present value model has also been used to a great extent in explaining farmland prices. However, the results in Falk (1991, 1992) and Engsted (1998b) indicate that the model is a complete failure in this respect, see Table 5.

References

Agenor, P. R., Bismut, C., Cashin, P., and McDermott, C. J. (1999) Consumption smoothing and the current account: Evidence for France, 1970–1996. *Journal of International Money and Finance*, 18, 1–12.

Amano, R. A. and Wirjanto, T. S. (1997) An empirical study of dynamic labor demand with integrated forcing processes. *Journal of Macroeconomics*, 19, 697–715.

Andersen, T. M. (1994) *Price Rigidity: Causes and Macroeconomic Implications*. Clarendon Press, Oxford.

Baillie, R. T. (1989) Econometric tests of rationality and market efficiency. *Econometric Reviews*, 8, 151–186.

Bekaert, G. and Liu, J. (1999) Conditioning information and variance bounds on pricing kernels. *NBER Working Paper 6880*, Massachusetts, Cambridge.

Bergin, P. R. and Sheffrin, S. M. (2000) Interest rates, exchange rates and present value models of the current account. *Economic Journal*, 110, 535–558.

Bekaert, G., Hodrick, R. J. and Marshall, D. A. (1997) On biases in tests of the expectations hypothesis of the term structure of interest rates. *Journal of Financial Economics*, 44, 309–348.

Blix, M. (1997) *Rational Expectations and Regime Shifts in Macroeconometrics*. PhD Dissertation, Institute for International Economic Studies, Stockholm University.

Braun, P. A., Constantinides, G. M. and Ferson, W. A. (1993) Time-nonseparability in aggregate consumption: International evidence. *European Economic Review*, 37, 897–920.

Brealey, R. A. and Myers, S. C. (1996) *Principles of Corporate Finance*. 5'th edition, McGraw-Hill.

Burnside, C. (1994) Hansen-Jagannathan bounds as classical tests of asset-pricing models. *Journal of Business and Economic Statistics*, 12, 57–79.

Campbell, J. Y. (1987) Does saving anticipate declining labour income? An alternative test of the permanent income hypothesis. *Econometrica*, 55, 1249–1273.

Campbell, J. Y. and Clarida, R. H. (1988) Saving and permanent income in Canada and the United Kingdom. In E. Helpman, A. Razin and E. Sadka (eds), *Economic Effects of the Government Budget*. The MIT Press, Cambridge, MA.

Campbell, J. Y. and Hamao, Y. (1993) The interest rate process and the term structure of interest rates in Japan. In K. J. Singleton (eds), *Japanese Monetary Policy*. The University of Chicago Press.

Campbell, J. Y. and Shiller, R. J. (1987) Cointegration and test of present value models. *Journal of Political Economy*, 95, 1062–1088.

Campbell, J. Y. and Shiller, R. J. (1988a) Interpreting cointegrated models. *Journal of Economic Dynamics and Control*, 12, 505–522.

Campbell, J. Y. and Shiller, R. J. (1988b) The dividend-price ratio and expectations of future dividends and discount factors. *Review of Financial Studies*, 1, 195–228.

Campbell, J. Y. and Shiller, R. J. (1989) The dividend ratio model and small sample bias: A Monte Carlo study. *Economics Letters*, 29, 325–331.

Campbell, J. Y. and Shiller, R. J. (1991) Yield spreads and interest rate movements: A bird's eye view. *Review of Economic Studies*, 58, 495–514.

Campbell, J. Y., Lo, A. W. and MacKinlay, A. C. (1997) *The Econometrics of Financial Markets*. Princeton University Press, New Jersey.

Cecchetti, S. G., Lam, P. S. and Mark, N. C. (1994) Testing volatility restrictions on intertemporal marginal rates of substitution implied by Euler equations and asset returns. *Journal of Finance*, 49, 123–152.

Cochrane, J. H. (2001) *Asset Pricing*. Princeton University Press, New Jersey.

Cochrane, J. H. and Hansen, L. P. (1992) Asset pricing explorations for macroeconomics. *NBER Macroeconomics Annual*, 115–165.

Cox, J. C., Ingersoll, J. E. and Ross, S. A. (1985) A theory of the term structure of interest rates. *Econometrica*, 53, 385–408.

Cuthbertson, K. (1990) Modelling expectations: A review of limited information estimation methods. *Bulletin of Economic Research*, 42, 1–34.

Cuthbertson, K. (1996) The expectations hypothesis of the term structure: The UK interbank market. *Economic Journal*, 106, 578–592.

Cuthbertson, K. and Hayes, S. (1994) The behaviour of UK stock prices and returns: Is the market efficient? *Mimeo*, Department of Economics, University of Newcastle upon Tyne.

Cuthbertson, K. and Taylor, M. P. (1990) Money demand, expectations, and the forward-looking model. *Journal of Policy Modeling*, 12, 289–315.

Cuthbertson, K., Hayes, S. and Nitzsche, D. (1996) The behaviour of certificates of deposit rates in the UK. *Oxford Economic Papers*, 48, 397–414.

Cuthbertson, K., Hayes, S. and Nitzsche, D. (1997) The behaviour of UK stock prices and returns: Is the market efficient? *Economic Journal*, 107, 986–1008.

Cuthbertson, K., Hayes, S. and Nitzsche, D. (1999) Market segmentation and stock price behaviour. *Oxford Bulletin of Economics and Statistics*, 61, 217–235.

Cuthbertson, K., Hayes, S. and Nitzsche, D. (2000) Are German money market rates well behaved? *Journal of Economic Dynamics and Control*, 24, 347–360.

Diebold, F. X., Ohanian, L. E. and Berkowitz, J. (1998) Dynamic equilibrium economies: A framework for comparing models and data. *Review of Economic Studies*, 65, 433–451.

Dolado, J., Galbraith, J. W. and Banerjee, A. (1991) Estimating intertemporal quadratic adjustment cost models with integrated series. *International Economic Review*, 32, 919–936.

Durlauf, S. N. and Hall, R. E. (1989a) Bounds on the variances of specification errors in models with expectations. *NBER Working Paper 2936*, Massachusetts, Cambridge.

Durlauf, S. N. and Hall, R. E. (1989b) Measuring noise in stock prices. *Mimeo*, Department of Economics, Stanford University.

Durlauf, S. N. and Hall, R. E. (1989c) A signal extraction approach to recovering noise in expectations based models. *Mimeo*, Department of Economics, Stanford University.

Durlauf, S. N. and Hall, R. E. (1994) Quantifying specification error in models with expectations. *Mimeo*, Department of Economics, Stanford University.

Durlauf, S. N. and Hooker, M. A. (1994) Misspecification versus bubbles in the Cagan hyperinflation model. In C. Hargreaves (eds), *Non-Stationary Time-Series Analysis and Cointegration*. Oxford University Press.

Durlauf, S. N. and Maccini, L. J. (1995) Measuring noise in inventory models. *Journal of Monetary Economics*, 36, 36–90.

Engle, R. F. and Granger, C. W. J. (1987) Co-integration and error-correction: Representation, estimation, and testing. *Econometrica*, 55, 251–276.

Engsted, T. (1992) Consumption in Denmark: A counter-example to excess smoothness. *Mimeo*, Aarhus School of Business.

Engsted, T. (1993a) The term structure of interest rates in Denmark 1982–89: Testing the rational expectations/constant liquidity premium theory. *Bulletin of Economic Research*, 45, 19–38.

Engsted, T. (1993b) Cointegration and Cagan's model of hyperinflation under rational expectations. *Journal of Money, Credit, and Banking*, 25, 350–360.

Engsted, T. (1994) The classic european hyperinflations revisited: Testing the Cagan model using a cointegrated VAR approach. *Economica*, 61, 331–344.

Engsted, T. (1995) Does the long term interest rate predict future inflation? A multi-country analysis. *Review of Economics and Statistics*, 77, 42–54.

Engsted, T. (1996a) The predictive power of the money market term structure. *International Journal of Forecasting*, 12, 289–295.

Engsted, T. (1996b) Non-stationarity and tax effects in the long-term Fisher hypothesis. *Applied Economics*, 28, 883–887.

Engsted, T. (1996c) The monetary model of the exchange rate under hyperinflation: New encouraging evidence. *Economics Letters*, 51, 37–44.

Engsted, T. (1998a) Evaluating the consumption capital asset pricing model using Hansen-Jagannathan bounds: Evidence from the UK. *International Journal of Finance and Economics*, 3, 291–302.

Engsted, T. (1998b) Do farmland prices reflect rationally expected future rents? *Applied Economics Letters*, 5, 75–79.

Engsted, T. (1998c) Money demand during hyperinflation: Cointegration, rational expectations, and the importance of money demand shocks. *Journal of Macro-economics*, 20, 533–552.

Engsted, T. (2000) Measuring noise in the Permanent Income Hypothesis. *Mimeo*, The Aarhus School of Business. (forthcoming in Journal of Macroeconomics).

Engsted, T. and Haldrup, N. (1994) The linear quadratic adjustment cost model and the demand for labour. *Journal of Applied Econometrics*, 9 (supplement), S145–S159.

Engsted, T. and Haldrup, N. (1997) Money demand, adjustment costs, and forward-looking behaviour. *Journal of Policy Modeling*, 19, 153–174.

Engsted, T. and Haldrup, N. (1999) Estimating the LQAC model with I(2) variables. *Journal of Applied Econometrics*, 14, 155–170.

Engsted, T. and Nyholm, K. (2000) Regime shifts in the Danish term structure of interest rates. *Empirical Economics*, 25, 1–13.

Engsted, T. and Tanggaard, C. (1994a) Cointegration and the US term structure. *Journal of Banking and Finance*, 18, 167–181.

Engsted, T. and Tanggaard, C. (1994b) A cointegration analysis of Danish zero-coupon bond yields. *Applied Financial Economics*, 4, 265–278.

Engsted, T. and Tanggaard, C. (1995) The predictive power of yield spreads for future interest rates: Evidence from the Danish term structure. *Scandinavian Journal of Economics*, 97, 145–159.

Engsted, T. and Tanggaard, C. (2001) The Danish stock and bond markets: Comovement, return predictability and variance decomposition. *Journal of Empirical Finance*, 8, 243–271.

Engsted, T., Mammen, E. and Tanggaard, C. (2000) Evaluating the C-CAPM and the equity premium puzzle at short and long horizons: A markovian bootstrap approach. *Mimeo*, The Aarhus School of Business.

Evans, M. D. D. (1998) Dividend variability and stock market swings. *Review of Economic Studies*, 65, 711–740.

Falk, B. (1991) Formally testing the present value model of farmland prices. *American Journal of Agricultural Economics*, 73, 1–10.

Falk, B. (1992) Predictable excess returns in real estate markets: A study of Iowa farmland values. *Journal of Housing Economics*, 2, 84–105.

Ferson, W. E. and Harvey, C. R. (1992) Seasonality and consumption-based asset pricing. *Journal of Finance*, 47, 511–552.

Gallant, A. R., Hansen, L. P. and Tauchen, G. (1990) Using conditional moments of asset payoffs to infer the volatility of intertemporal marginal rates of substitution. *Journal of Econometrics*, 45, 141–179.

Garcia, M. G. P. (1993) The Fisher effect in a signal extraction framework: The recent Brazilian experience. *Journal of Development Economics*, 41, 71–93.

Ghosh, A. R. (1995a) International capital mobility amongst the major industrialized countries: Too little or too much. *Economic Journal*, 105, 107–128.

Ghosh, A. R. (1995b) Intertemporal tax smoothing and the government budget surplus: Canada and the United States. *Journal of Money, Credit, and Banking*, 27, 1033–1045.

Ghosh, A. R. and Ostry, J. D. (1995) The current account in developing countries: A perspective from the consumption-smoothing approach. *The World Bank Economic Review*, 9, 305–333.

Ghysels, E. and Hall, A. (1990) A test for structural stability of Euler conditions parameters estimated via the generalized method of moments estimator. *International Economic Review*, 31, 355–364.

Gregory, A. W. and Veall, M. R. (1985) On formulating Wald tests for nonlinear restrictions. *Econometrica*, 53, 1465–1468.

Haldrup, N. (1998) An econometric analysis of I(2) variables. *Journal of Economic Surveys*, 12, 595–650.

Hall, A. (1993) Some aspects of generalized method of moments estimation. In G. S. Maddala, C. R. Rao and H. D. Vinod (eds), *Handbook of Statistics*, Vol. 11. Elsevier Science Publishers.

Hall, R. E. (1978) Stochastic implications of the life cycle-permanent income hypothesis: Theory and evidence: *Journal of Political Economy*, 86, 971–987.

Hall, A. D., Anderson, H. M. and Granger, C. W. J. (1992) A cointegration analysis of Treasury bills. *Review of Economics and Statistics*, 74, 116–126.

Hamilton, J. D. (1989) A new approach to the economic analysis of nonstationary time series and the business cycle. *Econometrica*, 57, 357–384.

Hansen, L. P. (1992) Large sample properties of generalized method of moments estimators. *Econometrica*, 50, 1029–1054.

Hansen, L. P., Heaton, J. and Luttmer, E. (1995) Econometric evaluation of asset pricing models. *Review of Financial Studies*, 8, 237–274.

Hansen, L. P. and Jagannathan, R. (1991) Implications of security market data for models of dynamic economies. *Journal of Political Economy*, 99, 225–262.

Hansen, L. P. and Jagannathan, R. (1997) Assessing specification errors in stochastic discount factor models. *Journal of Finance*, 52, 557–590.

Hansen, L. P. and Sargent, T. J. (1980) Formulating and estimating dynamic linear rational expectations models. *Journal of Economic Dynamics and Control*, 2, 7–46.

Hansen, L. P. and Sargent, T. J. (1991) Exact linear rational expectations models: Specification and estimation. In L. P. Hansen and T. J. Sargent (eds), *Rational Expectations Econometrics*. Westview Press.

Hansen, L. P. and Singleton, K. J. (1982) Generalized instrumental variables estimation of nonlinear rational expectations models. *Econometrica*, 50, 1269–1286.

Hardouvelis, G. A. (1994) The term structure spread and future changes in long and short rates in the G7 countries: Is there a puzzle? *Journal of Monetary Economics*, 33, 255–283.

Hendry, D. F. (1995) *Dynamic Econometrics*. Oxford University Press.

Hoffman, D. and Pagan, A. R. (1989) Post-sample prediction tests for generalized method of moments estimators. *Oxford Bulletin of Economics and Statistics*, 51, 333–343.

Hodrick, R. (1992) Dividend yields and expected stock returns: Alternative procedures for inference and measurement. *Review of Financial Studies*, 5, 357–386.

Hooker, M. A. (1996) Misspecification versus bubbles in hyperinflation data: Monte Carlo and interwar European evidence. *Mimeo*, Dartmouth College.

Hoover, K. D. (1995) Facts and artifacts: Calibration and the empirical assessment of Real-Business-Cycle models. *Oxford Economic Papers*, 47, 24–44.

Huang, C. H. and Lin, K. S. (1993) Deficits, government expenditures, and tax-smoothing in the United States. *Journal of Monetary Economics*, 31, 317–339.

Hurn, A. S., Moody, T. and Muscatelli, V. A. (1995) The term structure of interbank rates in the London interbank market. *Oxford Economic Papers*, 47, 418–436.

Johansen, S. (1991) Estimation and hypothesis testing of cointegration vectors in gaussian vector autoregressive models. *Econometrica*, 59, 1551–1580.

Johansen, S. and Swensen, A. R. (1999) Testing exact rational expectations in cointegrated vector autoregressive models. *Journal of Econometrics*, 93, 73–91.

Johnson, P. A. (1994) Estimation of the specification error in the Fisher equation. *Applied Economics*, 26, 519–526.

Johnson, P. A. (1997) Estimation of the specification error in the expectations theory of the term structure. *Applied Economics*, 29, 1239–1247.

Kim, C. (1996) Measuring deviations from the permanent income hypothesis. *International Economic Review*, 37, 205–225.

Kim, K. and Pagan, A. R. (1995) The econometric analysis of calibrated macroeconomic models. In M. H. Pesaran and M. Wickens (eds), *Handbook of Applied Econometrics: Macroeconomics*, Basil Blackwell.

Kocherlakota, N. R. (1996) The equity premium: It's still a puzzle. *Journal of Economic Literature*, 34, 42–71.

Konuki, T. (1999) Measuring noise in exchange rate models. *Journal of International Economics*, 48, 255–270.

Kydland, F. E. and Prescott, E. C. (1996) The computational experiment: An econometric tool. *Journal of Economic Perspectives*, 10, 69–86.

Lazear, E. P. (2000) Economic imperialism. *Quarterly Journal of Economics*, February 2000, 99–

Lucas, R. E. (1976) Econometric policy evaluation: A critique. In K. Brunner and A. H. Meltzer (eds), *The Phillips Curve and Labor Markets*. North-Holland.

Lucas, R. E. (1978) Asset prices in an exchange economy. *Econometrica*, 46, 1429–1446.

Lucas, R. E. and Sargent, T. J. (1981) *Rational Expectations and Econometric Practice*. Minneapolis, University of Minnesota Press.

Lund, J. and Engsted, T. (1996) GMM and present value tests of the C-CAPM: Evidence from the Danish, German, Swedish, and UK stock markets. *Journal of International Money and Finance*, 15, 497–521.

Luttmer, E. G. J. (1996) Asset pricing in Economies with frictions. *Econometrica*, 64, 1439–1468.

MacDonald, R. and Speight, A. E. H. (1991) The term structure of interest rates under rational expectations: Some international evidence. *Applied Financial Economics*, 1, 211–221.

MacDonald, R. and Taylor, M. P. (1993) The monetary approach to the exchange rate. Rational expectations, long-run equilibrium, and forecasting. *IMF Staff Papers*, 40, 89–107.

MacDonald, R. and Taylor, M. P. (1994) Reexamining the monetary approach to the exchange rate: The Dollar-Franc 1976–90. *Applied Financial Economics*, 4, 423–429.

MacKinnon, J. G. (1991) Critical values for cointegration tests. In R. F. Engle and C. W. J. Granger (eds), *Long-run Economic Relationships*. Oxford University Press.

Mattey, J. and Meese, R. (1986) Empirical assessment of present value relations. *Econometric Reviews*, 5, 171–234.

Mehra, R. and Prescott, E. C. (1985) The equity premium: A puzzle? *Journal of Monetary Economics*, 15, 145–161.

Mills, T. C. (1991) The term structure of UK interest rates: Tests of the expectations hypothesis. *Applied Economics*, 23, 599–606.

Mills, T. C. (1993) Testing the present value model of equity prices for the UK stock market. *Journal of Business Finance & Accounting*, 20, 803–813.

Newey, W. K. and West, K. D. (1987) A simple positive semi-definite, heteroscedasticity and autocorrelation consistent covariance matrix. *Econometrica*, 55, 703–708.

Obstfeld, M. and Rogoff, K. (1996) *Foundations of International Macroeconomics*. The MIT Press, Cambridge, Massachusetts.

Ogaki, M. (1993) Generalized method of moments: Econometric applications. In G. S. Maddala, C. R. Rao and H. D. Vinod (eds), *Handbook of Statistics*, Vol. 11. Elsevier Science Publishers.

Otrok, C., Ravikumar, B. and Whiteman, C. H. (1999) Evaluating asset-pricing models using the Hansen-Jagannathan bound: A Monte Carlo investigation. *Working Paper*, University of Iowa.

Otto, G. (1992) Testing a present value model of the current account: Evidence from US and Canadian time series. *Journal of International Money and Finance*, 11, 414–430.

Pagan, A. R. (1996) The econometrics of financial markets. *Journal of Empirical Finance*, 3, 15–102.

Pagan, A. R., Hall, A. D. and Martin, V. (1996) Modelling the term structure. In G. S. Maddala and C. R. Rao (eds), *Handbook of Statistics*, Vol. 14, Elsevier Science Publishers.

Pesaran, H. M. (1987) *The Limits to Rational Expectations*. Basil Blackwell, Oxford.

Petrovic, P. and Vujocevic, Z. (1996) The monetary dynamics in the Yugoslav hyperinflation of 1991–1993: The Cagan money demand. *European Journal of Political Economy*, 12, 467–483.

Petursson, T. G. (1996) Are prices forward looking? Evidence from Iceland. *Mimeo*, Department of Economics, University of Iceland.

Sargan, J. D. (1958) The estimation of economic relationships using instrumental variables. *Econometrica*, 26, 393–415.

Shea, G. S. (1992) Benchmarking the expectations hypothesis of the interest-rate term structure: An analysis of cointegration vectors. *Journal of Business and Economic Statistics*, 10, 347–366.

Sheffrin, S. and Woo, W. T. (1990) Present value tests of an intertemporal model of the current account. *Journal of International Economics*, 29, 237–253.

Shiller, R. J. (1981) Do stock prices move too much to be justified by subsequent changes in dividends? *American Economic Review*, 71, 421–436.

Stock, J. H. (1987) Asymptotic properties of least squares estimators of cointegrating vectors. *Econometrica*, 55, 1035–1056.

Summers, L. H. (1991) The scientific illusion in empirical macroeconomics. *Scandinavian Journal of Economics*, 93, 129–148.

Søderlind, P. and Vredin, A. (1996) Applied cointegration analysis in the mirror of macroeconomic theory. *Journal of Applied Econometrics*, 11.

Taulbjerg, J. (2000) Cointegration and exponential affine models of the term structure. *Working Paper*, The Aarhus School of Business, Denmark.

Taylor, M. P. (1992) Modelling the yield curve. *Economic Journal*, 102, 524–537.

Warne, A. (1990) *Vector Autoregressions and Common Trends in Macro and Financial Economics*. PhD Dissertation. The Economic Research Institute, Stockholm School of Economics.

Watson, M. (1993) Measures of fit for calibrated models. *Journal of Political Economy*, 101, 1011–1041.

Weil, P. (1989) The equity premium puzzle and the risk-free rate puzzle. *Journal of Monetary Economics*, 24, 401–421.

Wickens, M. (1993) Rational expectations and integrated variables. In P. C. B. Phillips (eds), *Models, Methods, and Applications in Econometrics*. Basil Blackwell, Oxford.

Appendix

The data series, Denmark 1922–1996.

	P	D	C	RF
1922	85.17887563884	6.1216114139693	—	—
1923	103.69934791702	5.5897809568163	1.1411571678523	1.0507349703641
1924	93.17604435385	4.8328722615385	0.9638069097648	0.9720538461538
1925	88.10331900324	4.8280028687196	0.9442426319594	1.1219611021070
1926	94.89187533271	4.0232644517338	1.0143960223538	1.2166522961575
1927	111.41230830357	4.5580578670635	1.0426014374866	1.1114583333333
1928	96.14724697698	4.8326130830831	1.0401782635021	1.0594594594595
1929	95.45084600000	5.0019093000000	1.0368126838896	1.0499490000000
1930	93.84067030601	5.7591483497268	1.0555902633438	1.1387978142077
1931	76.38750609670	5.6822663679245	1.0173912635699	1.1243278301887
1932	88.48214880723	3.8213183373494	0.9821194404902	1.0676626506024
1933	105.94128671694	4.7813084106729	1.0357255157822	0.9936890951276
1934	109.02581308360	4.8925745494028	1.0007333510313	0.9593376764387
1935	114.68614005187	4.8533789419087	0.9766570366774	0.9821452282158
1936	123.43170305359	5.1328609807887	1.0438425605775	1.0098119312437
1937	109.45004694417	5.4254351126347	1.0128847949759	1.0074045053869
1938	104.10411625483	5.7269269305019	1.0168763616756	1.0249420849421
1939	94.39961470480	5.4754410055351	1.0144488549428	0.9949040590406
1940	71.85662411201	3.4039394473102	0.7943730341247	0.8371643330877
1941	74.10379748568	2.0240326543603	0.9697564759957	0.8983322724379
1942	71.47863643953	1.8363200184162	1.0937751556128	1.0029711479435
1943	84.91921712304	1.8182555367913	0.9933193738527	1.0218094089264
1944	80.23400906587	1.9492980359281	1.0505878516707	1.0325269461078
1945	78.18262376408	2.4401671902786	1.1550753099511	1.0295198577356
1946	80.61339944511	3.1290349582339	1.1843275303728	1.0417929594272
1947	64.95877361538	2.8901433025641	0.8590661384554	0.8895692307692
1948	55.73625444716	2.7159311692759	0.9785223074402	0.9874021526419
1949	57.34626285920	2.6628365086207	1.0438313434134	1.0131896551724
1950	54.68429161594	2.6701313921218	1.0691952619503	0.9729668755595
1951	50.75287483912	2.5893791363251	0.9988442354057	0.9930990685859
1952	50.32000321298	2.7804890020284	0.9804129103736	1.0061257606491
1953	51.49170636907	3.0312359465923	1.0166528740248	1.0306038262256
1954	55.95186115699	3.0512534008570	1.0412325915301	1.0262758083366
1955	62.06835631913	3.0896150074738	0.9956249108224	1.0120272795217
1956	72.45416933881	3.0144753752680	1.0062913089826	1.0089992852037
1957	75.51394725302	3.3679397619048	1.0142774330493	1.0490014214641
1958	71.67540411887	3.0310230200415	1.0167329893177	1.0209744298549
1959	81.19708023833	3.1271216219795	1.0277554810304	1.0020271433300
1960	79.53489775196	3.1873559424084	1.0560844564898	1.0429172120419
1961	79.61206032700	3.3519898598567	1.0516745765322	1.0097838679539
1962	71.04092814973	3.2918478935383	1.0190783547298	0.9734457728437
1963	79.34733745152	3.2093687562327	1.0197531595913	1.0344373961219
1964	79.11305134425	3.1079198439938	1.0448471085194	0.9958944357774
1965	76.67074524260	3.1695175934013	1.0155957946095	0.9936899563319
1966	68.48696778777	2.9204932711331	1.0213515987197	0.9869446942446
1967	57.98781444540	3.0671941884368	1.0372555400403	1.0143725910064

(*continued*)

The data series, Denmark 1922–1996. (*continued*)

	P	D	C	RF
1968	66.06509171324	2.9840020130532	1.0326865327136	1.0162941056496
1969	59.91717444316	3.0936270494973	1.0489708409154	1.0247762954370
1970	51.97577480323	2.9315722946990	1.0168556963930	1.0130242587601
1971	49.44822578756	2.9328547072406	0.9769942369773	0.9894557149926
1972	98.24396643216	2.9596082731841	1.0094825804179	0.9906500685244
1973	70.92533506192	2.7608835759494	1.0505603471144	0.9713160429279
1974	52.90305463725	2.8185008741675	0.9611540059364	0.9499919124643
1975	60.18103280141	2.5108102046690	1.0186151923697	0.9697746508901
1976	51.60009960685	2.4545054067731	1.0790295630212	1.0244607045543
1977	41.25889286377	2.2749532003214	1.0225325514952	1.0549366184610
1978	32.97177590935	2.0193077190096	1.0109873483952	1.0341370897425
1979	25.66773434535	2.1164554079696	1.0305026013589	1.0286621328273
1980	31.94698562683	1.7618445568273	0.9338061282679	1.0024151583710
1981	37.09897530864	1.7272716049383	1.0156023852060	1.0661531111111
1982	40.29829735144	1.3866737146673	1.0089587046429	1.0623926107278
1983	64.99195462115	1.3325301831807	1.0250523237035	1.0649831598668
1984	44.56822521902	1.2184319322768	1.0405069650881	1.0611453883256
1985	49.30336908756	1.3279733497141	1.0511082237109	1.0604953362000
1986	44.66959705273	1.4061063780797	1.0584792066520	1.0620970481234
1987	44.99809025507	1.4579071288424	0.9744013012452	1.0438538260301
1988	66.90096286107	1.4313867700388	0.9830556241975	1.0405880330124
1989	74.54880733945	1.4659832469087	0.9935157873797	1.0494028958915
1990	70.80184410352	1.7339377033938	0.9964842206309	1.0770232062607
1991	72.73641181777	1.4447526687716	1.0031555440324	1.0670589986468
1992	62.33585189534	1.3947671645077	1.0112120883363	1.1027807566695
1993	86.48550377468	1.1334458478513	1.0113049654621	1.1100391006098
1994	72.87233145063	1.1764924572818	1.0664906270351	1.0459792664617
1995	80.42154839615	1.2671123745350	1.0174270847692	1.0425209026462
1996	109.15667571188	1.5225431937622	1.0197399115519	1.0176917940439

P: Real stock prices (end of period)
D: Real dividends
C: Real per capita gross consumption growth rate
RF: Real gross risk-free rate

Chapter 5

SOME RECENT DEVELOPMENTS IN FUTURES HEDGING

Donald Lien

University of Texas at San Antonio

Y. K. Tse

Singapore Management University

1. Introduction

A forward or futures contract is a promise (and obligation) to deliver a specific amount of a commodity (or asset) at a future time. Forward contracts usually contain detailed specifications of the underlying commodity (or asset) and the delivery process. Thus, the grade (or quality) of the commodity, the delivery date, and the delivery location are specified. Futures contracts, on the other hand, assume a standard form with some allowance for flexibility. There are usually choices of deliverable grades and delivery locations. The delivery dates may also be allowed to vary within a month or so. The standardization facilitates futures to be traded on organized exchanges. Due to the benefits and costs of specificity versus flexibility, individuals choose between forward and futures contracts when both are available. In general, one engages in forward contracts with the expectation of delivering and receiving the commodity. On the other hand, futures positions are often offset prior to expiration. An individual assumes a short position if he sells futures contracts and a long position if he purchases futures contracts.

While futures contracts are popular among investors as a class of speculative assets, they are important in the financial markets due to their use as a hedging instrument. The latter role of futures has been the focus of much research, especially on the formulation of an optimal hedge strategy and the implementation of the strategy. Recently, much progress has seen made in the theoretical and empirical aspects of futures hedging. At the theoretical level, an optimal hedge strategy is traditionally based on the expected-utility maximization paradigm. A simplification of this paradigm leads to the minimum-variance criterion. Although this paradigm is quite well accepted, alternative approaches have been sought. Firstly, the use of variance as a measure of risk is questioned. It is argued that as far as hedging is concerned, a one-sided measure such as the downside risk is more relevant. Secondly, the application of the theories of stochastic dominance has resolved some of the restrictions in the expected-utility maximization framework. Developments in the stochastic dominance literature, such as the mean-Gini approach, facilitates the implementation of a hedge strategy.

At the empirical level, research on futures hedging has benefited from the recent developments in the econometrics literature. Much research has been done on improving the estimation of the optimal hedge ratio. As more is known about the statistical properties of financial time series, more sophisticated estimation methods are proposed. Firstly, the classical regression method, which assumes a time-invariant hedge ratio, has been replaced by time-varying estimates. Secondly, the cointegration literature suggests that futures and spot prices are cointegrated and better estimates are obtainable by exploring this relationship. Thirdly, the conditional volatility literature has provided many models, whether univariate or multivariate, that capture the time-varying variance and covariance of the spot and futures. Fourthly, the use of nonparametric methods has freed researchers from making assumptions (such as normality for asset returns) that may not be justifiable.

In this survey we review some recent developments in the literature of futures hedging. Our approach is to delineate the theoretical underpinning of various methods, and then discuss the econometric implementation of the methods. It is noted that alternative instruments are available for hedging. The most important alternative is perhaps option. While we shall make some comparisons between futures and option, we shall leave out works that are specifically targeted on option hedging. Also, we shall discuss futures hedging in general. While empirical results on specific futures contracts are covered, no efforts will be made to distinguish between hedging for specific assets such as bonds, equities, commodities or currencies. Finally, we shall assume that the hedger is faced with a given spot position to hedge. The problem of hedging quantity uncertainty will not be discussed. We should note that the rationale for excluding these topics is to narrow the scope of this survey to a manageable scale. It is not a reflection of the (lack of) importance of these issues.

In Section 2 we discuss the conventional hedging framework of expected-utility maximization and minimization of portfolio variance. Section 3 extends the traditional framework to time-varying hedge ratios. Various estimation methods are discussed, including the stochastic volatility models and the conditional heteroscedasticity models. In Section 4 we review some issues in the implementation of the traditional approach. We discuss the extended mean-Gini approach in Section 5. The lower-partial-moment criterion is introduced in Section 6. In Section 7 we review the problems with rollover hedge in futures. Finally, the paper is concluded in Section 8.

2. Conventional hedging analysis

Conventional wisdom suggests that to hedge a unit of a spot position one should assume a unit of the opposite position in the futures market. Thus, the optimal hedge ratio, that is, the amount of the futures position divided by the amount of the spot position, is 1 for both long (long in futures and short in spot) and short (short in futures and long in spot) hedgers. This hedging strategy is incorporated into the Commodity Futures Trading Commissions (CFTC) guidelines which define a *bona fide hedger* as a hedger who has equal but opposite spot and futures positions. Recognizing that the spot and futures prices have parallel but not exactly identical movements, Johnson (1960) and Stein (1961) adopted a portfolio approach to determine the optimal hedge strategy via expected-utility maximization. Mean-variance analysis then follows as a special case. Ederington (1979) applied the method to the stock index futures markets and proposed a measure for hedging effectiveness. In this section we shall focus on this conventional approach and some extensions of it in the time-invariant context. Time-varying hedging strategies will be discussed in Section 3.

Note that we only consider exchange-traded futures contracts. Therefore, futures price data are publicly available at discrete time intervals. The prices for over-the-counter derivatives, on the other hand, are quoted by offering institutes. Usually continuous-time stochastic processes are applied to determine the pricing and hedging strategies. When the underlying asset is storable, the cost-of-carry argument implies an arbitrage relationship that determines the price of the futures contract. For a non-storable asset, the arbitrage relationship cannot be applied. In this case, different pricing and hedging strategies are required. This issue, while interesting, will not be pursued in this paper.

2.1. *The analytical framework*

We illustrate hedging decisions with a one-period model. At the beginning of the period, that is, $t = 0$, an individual is committed to a given spot position, Q, on a specific asset.[1] A futures market for the security is available with different maturities. To reduce the risk exposure, the individual may choose to go short in the futures market. Due to liquidity and other concerns, we assume that he trades only in the 'nearby' futures contract (that is, the contract the maturity of which is closest to the current date). With the futures trading, the individual becomes a short hedger. Let X denote the futures position. At the end of the period, say,

$t = 1$, the hedger's return, r, is calculated as follows:

$$r = (r_p Q - r_f X)/Q, \tag{1}$$

where r_p is the return of the spot position and r_f is the return of the futures position.[2] As both spot and futures returns are unknown at $t = 0$, r is a random variable. The hedger will choose X to minimize the risk (or uncertainty) associated with the random return.

In the finance literature, the risk of a random variable is usually measured by the variance (or standard deviation) conditional on the available information. Let Φ denote the information set at $t = 0$. Then the hedger's risk is summarized by the conditional variance of r, $\text{Var}(r \mid \Phi)$. From equation (1),

$$\text{Var}(r \mid \Phi) = [\text{Var}(r_p \mid \Phi)Q^2 - 2\text{Cov}(r_p, r_f \mid \Phi)XQ + \text{Var}(r_f \mid \Phi)X^2]/Q^2. \tag{2}$$

The optimal futures position X^* is chosen to minimize $\text{Var}(r \mid \Phi)$. Thus,

$$X^* = [\text{Cov}(r_p, r_f \mid \Phi)/\text{Var}(r_f \mid \Phi)]Q = hQ, \tag{3}$$

where $h = \text{Cov}(r_p, r_f \mid \Phi)/\text{Var}(r_f \mid \Phi)$ is the minimum-variance hedge ratio.

A more general approach to the hedging problem relies upon the expected-utility framework. Suppose that the hedger is endowed with a von-Neumann Morgenstern utility function $U(.)$ such that $U'(.) > 0$ and $U''(.) < 0$. Let $E\{.\}$ denote the expectation operator with respect to the joint distribution of r_p and r_f. The optimal futures position, X^e, is chosen to maximize the (conditional) expected utility $E\{U(r \mid \Phi)\}$. That is, X^e must satisfy the following condition:

$$E\left\{ U'\left(\frac{r_p Q - r_f X^e}{Q}\right) \frac{r_f}{Q} \,\middle|\, \Phi \right\} = 0, \tag{4}$$

or alternatively,

$$\text{Cov}\left(U'\left(\frac{r_p Q - r_f X^e}{Q}\right), \frac{r_f}{Q} \,\middle|\, \Phi \right) + E\left\{ U'\left(\frac{r_p Q - r_f X^e}{Q}\right) \,\middle|\, \Phi \right\} E\left\{ \frac{r_f}{Q} \,\middle|\, \Phi \right\} = 0. \tag{5}$$

Assume that $r_p = \alpha(\Phi) + \beta(\Phi)r_f + \varepsilon$, where r_f and ε are stochastically independent.[3] Now suppose that $E\{r_f \mid \Phi\} = 0$ (that is, the futures price is unbiased), the second term on the left-hand-side of the above equation vanishes. Moreover, when $X^e = \beta(\Phi)Q$ we have $r_p Q - r_f X^e = \alpha(\Phi)Q + \varepsilon Q$, which is stochastically independent of r_f. Thus, the first term on the left-hand-side of the equation is also zero. In other words, the optimal solution is $X^e = \beta(\Phi)Q$, which is in turn equal to $\text{Cov}(r_p, r_f \mid \Phi)Q/\text{Var}(r_f \mid \Phi)$. Therefore, the optimal hedge ratio as defined by X^e/Q and derived from a general utility function is equal to the minimum-variance hedge ratio. This result was first discussed in Benninga, Eldor and Zilcha (1983) and later extended by Lence (1995a) and Rao (2000). Lien (2000a) validated the result under Knightian uncertainty.

If the futures price is biased such that $E\{r_f \mid \Phi\} \neq 0$ (due to transaction cost, for example), then the optimal hedge ratio diverges from the minimum-variance hedge ratio. In this case, however, there is a speculative motivation to trade so as to take advantage of the bias in the futures market. Consequently, X^e contains both hedging and speculative components. The former is characterized by the condition $E\{r_f \mid \Phi\} = 0$. Thus, the hedging component of the optimal futures position is equal to the minimum-variance futures position. Assuming the hedger has a mean-variance utility function given by $E\{r \mid \Phi\} - (A/2)\mathrm{Var}(r \mid \Phi)$, where $(A/2)$ is the Arrow-Pratt risk aversion coefficient, the optimal futures position X^* is $E\{-r_f \mid \Phi\}/A + [\mathrm{Cov}(r_p, r_f \mid \Phi)/\mathrm{Var}(r_f \mid \Phi)]Q$. The first component represents the speculative trading whereas the second is the usual optimal hedge position.

Note that in the above derivation both minimum-variance and optimal hedge ratios are functions of the information set Φ. As Φ changes, both hedge ratios change. Typical information sets include the historical spot and futures returns, the contract maturity and the hedge horizon. Whenever the spot and futures return distributions depend on the information variables, both optimal hedge and minimum-variance hedge strategies depend on the time-varying dynamic hedge ratios. We now turn to the issue of estimating the minimum-variance hedge ratio in this conventional framework.

2.2. *Estimating hedge ratio by regression method*

To estimate the minimum-variance hedge ratio, a conventional method involves estimating the following linear regression model:

$$r_{pt} = \alpha + \beta r_{ft} + \varepsilon_t, \tag{6}$$

where r_{pt} and r_{ft} are the spot and futures returns for period t. The ordinary least squares (OLS) estimator of β provides an estimate for the minimum-variance hedge ratio. This approach has been extensively applied in the literature.

A major problem with the OLS hedge ratio is its dependence on the unconditional second moments, whereas the (true) minimum-variance hedge ratio is based on conditional second moments. Bell and Krasker (1986) argued that the correct regression model should allow the regression coefficients to be functions of the information available, that is,

$$r_{pt} = \alpha(\Phi) + \beta(\Phi)r_{ft} + \varepsilon_t. \tag{7}$$

Note the similarity between the above equation and the pre-condition for the minimum-variance hedge ratio to be optimal.[4] Unfortunately, in empirical works the functional forms of $\alpha(\Phi)$ and $\beta(\Phi)$ are unknown and researchers have to decide on the model specification. Cita and Lien (1992) applied this method to the wheat futures market allowing both the intercept and the slope to be linear functions of the historical spot and futures returns. They found that the modified regression model outperforms the conventional method in describing the spot price behavior. The Cita-Lien specification prescribes the minimum-variance hedge ratio to be a function of the conditioning information, and hence is time-varying. We will return to this issue in the next section. Upon allowing the intercept to be a linear function of the conditioning information variables while retaining a constant slope, Myers and Thompson (1989) proposed a generalized hedge ratio via a regression model with a large number of lagged price changes as information variables. Specifically, they assumed that the spot and futures returns can be described by the following equations:

$$r_{pt} = Z'_t \theta_p + \varepsilon_{pt}, \tag{8}$$

$$r_{ft} = Z'_t \theta_f + \varepsilon_{ft}, \tag{9}$$

where Z_t is a (column) vector of (exogenous) information variables. Then the minimum-variance hedge ratio can be calculated as an estimate of β from the following regression:

$$r_{pt} = \beta r_{ft} + Z'_t \theta_p + \varepsilon_{pt}. \tag{10}$$

Myers and Thompson (1989) suggested that Z_t should consist of a large number of lagged spot and futures returns. Fama and French (1987), however, argued that the basis (defined as the difference between the futures and spot prices) has predictive power for the spot returns. They specified the intercept term as a linear function of the lagged basis while the slope term remains constant. Let p_t and f_t denote the spot and futures prices (in logarithms), respectively, at time t. The regression equation for the estimation of the hedge ratio is given by:

$$r_{pt} = \beta r_{ft} + \delta_p(f_{t-1} - p_{t-1}) + \varepsilon_{pt}. \tag{11}$$

Viswanath (1993) adopted the above approach with a different rationale. Specifically, it was argued that, due to the convergence between the spot and futures prices at the maturity date, the spot returns would adjust to the basis. Moreover, different regressions were run for different durations and different timing when the hedge is lifted. This approach can be seen as a reduced form of the Garbade and Silber (1983) equations:

$$r_{pt} = \alpha_p + \beta_p(f_{t-1} - p_{t-1} - c_{t-1}) + \varepsilon_{pt}, \tag{12}$$

$$r_{ft} = \alpha_f + \beta_f(f_{t-1} - p_{t-1} - c_{t-1}) + \varepsilon_{ft}, \tag{13}$$

where c_t is the carrying cost from time t to contract maturity. Using a market microstructure approach, Garbade and Silber (1983) derived a restriction on the coefficients, namely, $\beta_p + \beta_f = 1$. Castelino (1992) assumed that the futures price follows a random walk whereas the spot price adjusts to the lagged basis so that

$$p_t = p_{t-1} + (1/\tau_t)(f_{t-1} - p_{t-1}) + \varepsilon_{pt}, \tag{14}$$

where τ_t is the time to maturity. The minimum-variance hedge ratio is again the ratio of the (conditional) second moments. Because of the specific adjustment coefficient specification, $1/\tau_t$, the hedge ratio is a function of τ_t.

2.3. *The cointegration approach*

While Fama and French (1987), Castelino (1992) and Viswanath (1993) argued that the basis reflects the cash-futures price convergence and, therefore, is an important information variable, this approach turns out to be fully justified by the recent statistical findings in the cointegration literature. Specifically, it is now well known that spot and futures price series typically contain a unit root. Thus, random-walk type of price behavior is prevalent. The unit-root property leads to the possible existence of a cointegration relationship (Engle and Granger, 1987). In spite of some skepticism (Quan, 1992; Brenner and Kroner, 1995), the cointegration relationship plays an important role in the statistical modelling of many spot and futures prices (Lien and Luo, 1993; Ghosh, 1993; Wahab and Lashgari, 1993; Tse, 1995).

Let Δ denote the difference operator such that $\Delta p_t = p_t - p_{t-1}$ and $\Delta f_t = f_t - f_{t-1}$. Thus, Δp_t and Δf_t are, respectively, the continuously compounded return (or log return) of the spot and futures.[5] Suppose that both (logarithmic) price series contain a unit root and are, furthermore, cointegrated. Then we have the following Engle-Granger specification for an error-correction (EC) model:

$$\Delta p_t = \alpha_p + \sum_{i=1}^{m} \beta_{pi}\Delta p_{t-i} + \sum_{j=1}^{n} \gamma_{pj}\Delta f_{t-j} + \theta_p z_{t-1} + \varepsilon_{pt}, \qquad (15)$$

$$\Delta f_t = \alpha_f + \sum_{i=1}^{m'} \beta_{fi}\Delta p_{t-i} + \sum_{j=1}^{n'} \gamma_{fj}\Delta f_{t-j} + \theta_f z_{t-1} + \varepsilon_{ft}, \qquad (16)$$

where z_t is a stationary linear combination of p_t and f_t. The Engle-Granger representation specifies that at least one of θ_p or θ_f is nonzero. In many empirical studies, it is found that z_t can be well approximated by the basis $f_t - p_t$. On the other hand, the no-arbitrage principle concludes that there is a cost-of-carry relationship between the spot and futures prices depending on the time to maturity. Thus, z_t should assume the following form: $z_t = f_t - p_t - k\tau_t$, where k is the per-period cost of carry. As mentioned above, Garbade and Silber (1983) adopted this specification. However, each futures contract is usually active for only three months or so (when its maturity is the closest to the current date). Furthermore, the price series during the delivery month tend to be noisy and unreliable. To construct a long time series for a meaningful time-series study, a futures price series corresponding to the 'nearby' contract is usually constructed. The differences in the time to maturity across data points in the 'nearby' futures price series are rather small (usually ranging from two or three weeks to less than four months). Thus, the time-varying nature of the cointegration relationship is usually not identifiable from the data set (see Tse, 1995).

Following Myers and Thompson (1989), we consider the following regression model:

$$\Delta p_t = \alpha_p + \lambda\Delta f_t + \sum_{i=1}^{m} \beta_{pi}\Delta p_{t-i} + \sum_{j=1}^{n} \gamma_{pj}\Delta f_{t-j} + \theta_p z_{t-1} + \varepsilon_{pt}. \qquad (17)$$

The OLS estimate of λ is the estimated minimum-variance hedge ratio. Chou, Denis and Lee (1996) applied this approach to the Hang Seng Index and found that the hedging performance improved over the conventional OLS method. Lien and Luo (1993), Ghosh (1993), and Wahab and Lashgari (1993) all demonstrated the superior hedging performance when the hedge ratio was estimated taking into account the cointegration relationship. Lien (1996) provided a theoretical analysis to characterize the effects of the cointegration relationship on the minimum-variance hedge ratio and the hedging effectiveness.

2.4. *Fractional and threshold cointegration*

The above approach relies upon the assumption that z_t is integrated of order zero. In admitting the broader framework of fractional difference order for z_t, Sowell (1992), Cheung and Lai (1993) and Dueker and Startz (1998) considered fractional cointegration relationships between two variables of the same integration order. Lien and Tse (1999) applied this approach to determine the minimum-variance hedge ratio. Suppose that both p_t and f_t are integrated of order one whereas z_t is integrated of order $d < 1$. Let B denote the backshifting operator such that $Bz_t = z_{t-1}$. Then z_t follows a fractionally integrated autoregressive moving average (ARFIMA) model if it is generated from the following equation:

$$\Phi(B)(1 - B)^d z_t = \Theta(B)\varepsilon_t, \tag{18}$$

where $\Phi(B)$ and $\Theta(B)$ are finite-order polynomials in B and ε_t is a white noise. Here the differencing operation on z_t is given by $\Delta^d = (1 - B)^d$ with

$$(1 - B)^d = \sum_{k=0}^{\infty} \frac{\Gamma(k - d)B^k}{\Gamma(-d)\Gamma(k + 1)} \tag{19}$$

where $\Gamma(.)$ is the gamma function. We assume that all roots of $\Phi(B) = 0$ and $\Theta(B) = 0$ are outside the unit circle. If $-0.5 < d < 0.5$, z_t is stationary. When $0 < d < 0.5$, z_t exhibits long-memory characteristics.

Given the above assumptions, a fractional cointegration relationship is established between the spot and futures prices. Following Granger (1986), we have the following fractionally integrated error-correction (FIEC) model:

$$\Delta p_t = \omega_p + \sum_{i=1}^{m} \omega_{pi}\Delta p_{t-i} + \sum_{j=1}^{n} \tau_{pj}\Delta f_{t-j} + \delta_p[(1 - B)^d - (1 - B)]z_t + \varepsilon_{pt}, \tag{20}$$

$$\Delta f_t = \omega_f + \sum_{i=1}^{m'} \omega_{fi}\Delta p_{t-i} + \sum_{j=1}^{n'} \tau_{fj}\Delta f_{t-j} + \delta_f[(1 - B)^d - (1 - B)]z_t + \varepsilon_{ft}. \tag{21}$$

The minimum-variance hedge ratio can be estimated based on estimates of $\mathrm{Cov}(\varepsilon_{pt}, \varepsilon_{ft})/\mathrm{Var}(\varepsilon_{ft})$ calculated from the residuals of the two equations. Lien and Tse (1999) estimated the minimum-variance hedge ratios for the Nikkei Stock

Average (NSA) futures contract under the alternative assumptions of error correction and fractionally integrated error correction. It was found that while fractional cointegration is supported by the data, it does not lead to any improvement in the hedging performance.

To generalize the above analysis further, we may allow the spot and futures prices to be of different (fractional) integration order. Vinod (1997) demonstrated that in this case there will be no fractional cointegration. He proposed a new concept, the so-called *tie integration*, to examine the relationship among these variables. Because the spot and futures prices are expected to have similar statistical properties, tie cointegration may not be useful in futures hedging analysis.

Several recent papers addressed the possible non-linear effects of the basis on the spot and futures prices. Balke and Fomby (1997) considered a threshold-cointegration model in which the spot and futures prices follow different regimes depending upon whether the basis exceeds or falls below a threshold level. While cointegration is driven by the cost-of-carry considerations, the existence of transaction costs (in any form) validates the prevalence of threshold cointegration. Indeed, Dwyer, Locke and Yu (1996) found that the basis of the S&P 500 can be well described by a threshold autoregressive model. Gao and Wang (1999) established a similar result for the S&P 500 futures price. While the literature on threshold cointegration has grown in the last few years, the implications of threshold cointegration on the minimum-variance hedge ratio and on the hedging performance have not been investigated. Based upon the transaction-cost interpretation, we expect spot and futures prices to lie within the threshold most of the time. Any data points lying outside the threshold reflect temporary imbalance and should be short lived. Thus, threshold cointegration is only useful for high-frequency data. On the other hand, many authors found threshold in daily data. It is difficult to apply transaction-cost arguments to validate the results. One possible interpretation is that, the model simply captures parts of the underlying non-linearity contained in the data.

Broll, Chow and Wong (2000) introduced a quadratic futures term into the cointegration equation and derived the optimal hedge strategy therefrom. The results were applied to six currency markets: Australian dollar, British pound, Canadian dollar, Deutsche mark, French franc and Japanese yen. They found empirical support in every market except the Australian dollar.

3. Time-varying hedge ratios

The above section assumes that the minimum-variance hedge ratio is constant over time. Bera, Garcia and Roh (1997) considered the hedge ratio to be time-varying and, more specifically, following a random walk. They adopted a random coefficient (RC) regression model in which

$$\Delta p_t = \alpha + \beta_t \Delta f_t + \varepsilon_t, \tag{22}$$

$$\beta_t = \beta_{t-1} + u_t, \tag{23}$$

where $\{\varepsilon_t, u_t\}$ is a bivariate white noise. However, they found that the hedge strategy obtained from this method failed to improve the hedging performance. As the minimum-variance hedge ratio depends on the conditional moments of the spot and futures returns, when the conditional moments vary over time so does the hedge ratio. Recent empirical works strongly support that time-varying volatility prevails in many economic and financial time series. While deterministic volatility functions are sometimes considered (see Dumas, Fleming and Whaley, 1998), most researchers adopt the Generalized Autoregressive Conditional Heteroscedasticity (GARCH) framework. Specifically, the bivariate GARCH models are widely adopted to examine the behavior of the spot and futures prices and the dynamic hedge strategy (Baillie and Myers (1991); Myers (1991); Lien and Luo (1994); Pirrong (1997)).

3.1. *The GARCH framework*

Consider the error-correction model described by equations (15) and (16). Let σ^2_{pt} denote $\mathrm{Var}(\varepsilon_{pt})$, σ^2_{ft} denote $\mathrm{Var}(\varepsilon_{ft})$ and σ_{pft} denote $\mathrm{Cov}(\varepsilon_{pt}, \varepsilon_{ft})$. The general VECH-GARCH model suggested by Bollerslev, Engle and Wooldridge (1988) consists of the following conditional second-moment equation:[6]

$$\begin{bmatrix} \sigma^2_{pt} \\ \sigma_{pft} \\ \sigma^2_{ft} \end{bmatrix} = A + \sum_{j=1}^{m} B_j \begin{bmatrix} \sigma^2_{p,t-j} \\ \sigma_{pf,t-j} \\ \sigma^2_{f,t-j} \end{bmatrix} + \sum_{k=1}^{n} C_k \begin{bmatrix} \varepsilon^2_{p,t-k} \\ \varepsilon_{p,t-k}\varepsilon_{f,t-k} \\ \varepsilon^2_{f,t-k} \end{bmatrix}, \quad (24)$$

where A is a 3×1 column vector, and B_j and C_k are 3×3 matrices. The model contains $3 + 9m + 9n$ parameters and renders some estimation problems. To achieve parsimony, a diagonal version is sometimes considered. This model assumes that all B_j and C_k matrices are diagonal. In other words, the conditional variance of the spot returns are affected by its own history and the history of the squared innovations in the spot returns. Similar structures apply to the conditional variance of the futures returns and the conditional covariance between the spot and futures returns. While very general, the VECH-GARCH model (or the diagonal version) fails to ensure the conditional variance-covariance matrix of the spot and futures returns to be positive semi-definite. Indeed, Lien and Luo (1994) applied the model to the foreign currency markets and found in their empirical estimation that the positive semi-definiteness condition failed frequently. To overcome this difficulty, Engle and Kroner (1995) suggested the so-called BEKK specification (named after Baba, Engle, Kraft and Kroner). Bera, Garcia and Roh (1997), however, showed that this specification produced the worst hedging performance when compared to the OLS and the RC hedge ratios.

The constant-correlation GARCH (CC-GARCH) model suggested by Bollerslev (1990) is an alternative specification to resolve the problem of a possible non-positive semi-definite conditional variance-covariance matrix. In this model the conditional second-moment equations are specified as follows:

$$\sigma^2_{pt} = \gamma_p + \sum_{j=1}^{m} \alpha_{pj}\sigma^2_{p,t-j} + \sum_{k=1}^{n} \beta_{pk}\varepsilon^2_{p,t-k}; \tag{25}$$

$$\sigma^2_{ft} = \gamma_f + \sum_{j=1}^{m'} \alpha_{fj}\sigma^2_{f,t-j} + \sum_{k=1}^{n'} \beta_{fk}\varepsilon^2_{f,t-k}; \tag{26}$$

$$\sigma_{pft} = \rho\sigma_{pt}\sigma_{ft}. \tag{27}$$

Note that equations (25) and (26) maintain the assumptions of a diagonal GARCH model, while equation (27) states that the conditional correlation coefficient between the spot and futures returns, ρ, is time invariant. Thus, a CC-GARCH model imposes restrictions on the general vector GARCH (VGARCH) model to achieve parameter parsimony while maintaining the positive semi-definiteness property. Kroner and Sultan (1993) applied this model to obtain the minimum-variance hedge ratios of currency futures. Park and Switzer (1995) adopted it to estimate the minimum-variance hedge ratios of stock index futures.

Empirical results concerning the performance of GARCH hedge ratios are generally mixed. Within-sample comparisons show that, in some cases, dynamic hedging generates much better performance in terms of risk reduction but in others the benefits seem too minimal to warrant the efforts. Post-sample comparisons are mostly in favor of the conventional hedge strategy. However, these studies usually do not revise the second-moment forecasting equations (as new data arrived). Lien, Tse, and Tsui (1999) applied the CC-GARCH models to a variety of commodity, financial, and currency markets. They updated the forecasting models as new data arrived to construct the dynamic hedge ratios. The results indicate that conventional hedge strategies perform as well as or better than the GARCH strategies.

3.2. Stochastic volatility analysis

Stochastic volatility (SV) model is an alternative specification to capture time-varying second moments. The model is akin to the mixture-distribution hypothesis and is congruent with the concept that price changes are driven by information arrival (Andersen, 1996). Andersen and Sorensen (1996) provided rationales for an alternative specification to the GARCH models to be sought after. Based upon Bayesian model selection criteria, Geweke (1994) chose a stochastic volatility model over a GARCH specification for the dollar/pound exchange rates. Heynen and Kat (1994) found that the stochastic volatility model has better forecasting performance for the stock indices than either the GARCH or the exponential GARCH (EGARCH) models. For the foreign exchange markets, the EGARCH model outperforms the stochastic volatility model marginally. Andersen and Bollerslev (1998) suggested that both models should perform well for high frequency data. Andersen (1994) provided a general framework that incorporates both models as special cases.

To obtain the hedge ratio, a multivariate stochastic volatility model as suggested by Harvey, Ruiz, and Shephard (1994) is required. Danielsson (1998) reported an empirical study on the comparison between the multivariate stochastic volatility model and some VGARCH models. Uhlig (1997) provided a Bayesian analysis for the multivariate stochastic volatility models. Consider again the error-correction model of equations (15) and (16). The stochastic volatility model describes the variances of p_t and f_t and their covariance as follows:

$$\varepsilon_{it} = \exp(h_{it})u_{it}, \qquad i = p, f, \tag{28}$$

$$h_{it} = a_i + b_i h_{i, t-1} + v_{it}, \qquad i = p, f, \tag{29}$$

where both u_{pt} and u_{ft} are standard normal random variables and the correlation between them is ρ. In addition, $\{v_{pt}, v_{ft}\}$ is a bivariate normal vector, independent of $\{u_{pt}, u_{ft}\}$, such that $E\{v_{it}\} = 0$ and $Cov(v_{it}, v_{jt}) = \theta_{ij}$, for $i, j = p, f$. Equations (28) and (29) imply that the variance of ε_{it} and the covariance of ε_{pt} and ε_{ft} are all random variables. A general specification would allow h_{pt} (or h_{ft}) to be a function of $h_{p, t-1}$ and $h_{f, t-1}$. The simplifying assumption adopted in equation (29) is similar to that for the diagonal VECH-GARCH models. Indeed, the stochastic volatility model is similar to the EGARCH model, with the latter containing a conditional-variance equation of the following form:

$$h_{it} = a_i + b_i h_{i, t-1} + c_i \varepsilon_{i, t-1}^2, \qquad i = p, f. \tag{30}$$

That is, the random term in equation (29), v_{it}, is replaced by a lagged ε_{it}^2 term.

Lien (1999a) provided a theoretical analysis of the minimum-variance hedge strategy based upon the stochastic volatility model. He found that the mean of the stochastic-volatility minimum-variance hedge ratio tends to be larger than the conventional hedge ratio. Using the Ederington (1979) hedging effectiveness measure, he concluded that the stochastic volatility hedge strategy is most beneficial when the conditional variances of the spot and futures prices are highly volatile and nearly uncorrelated. Otherwise, the conventional hedge ratios will do fine even if the true data generation process follows a multivariate stochastic volatility model. Lien and Wilson (2000) provided empirical results on stochastic volatility hedge strategy.

4. Implementation of the minimum-variance hedge

In the empirical implementation of the minimum-variance hedge strategy the hedge ratio must be estimated based on some statistical models. As the hedge ratios are determined by the second moments of the spot and futures prices, we may conclude that different statistical models will give rise to different hedge ratios to the extent that they produce different estimated second moments. Obviously, the differences in the estimates of the second moments with respect to different hedge horizons have impacts on the estimated hedge ratios. In general, as the hedge horizon increases, the trading noises are smoothed out, resulting in a larger hedge ratio.

Lien and Tse (2000c) pointed out that under certain model specifications, the theoretical minimum-variance hedge ratios are stable under aggregation. That is, the same theoretical hedge ratio is applicable irrespective of the hedge horizon. In general, to estimate the optimal hedge ratio it is natural to use a statistical model in which the sampling interval coincides with the hedge horizon. However, if the stable-under-aggregation property holds, it may be desirable to use a shorter sampling interval for a more effective use of the sample data.[7] Thus, the choice of the sampling interval depends upon the tradeoff between accepting possibly some model specification errors (when the hedge ratios are in fact not stable under aggregation) versus improving the estimation efficiency through more effective use of the sample data. It is possible that, in terms of out-of-sample hedging effectiveness, the hedge ratio estimated from 1-day return data outperforms the hedge ratio estimated from 5-day return data, even when the hedge horizon is 5 days.

Lence and Hayes (1994a, 1994b) criticised the usual practice of substituting the estimated hedge ratio for the unknown optimal hedge ratio (Lence and Hayes called this the Parameter Certainty Equivalent (PCE) strategy) in implementing the hedge strategy. They argued that this decision rule ignores the estimation risk and is not commensurate with the expected-utility maximisation paradigm. In other words, when estimation risk exists, the sample estimate of the minimum-variance hedge ratio may not lead to the optimal decision. They advocated a decision rule based on Bayes' criterion. Thus, the optimal hedge strategy is selected by maximising the expected utiltiy based on the posterior probability density of the random hedged portfolio return.

Let $\mathbf{Y}$ denote the sample observations (historical futures and spot returns) based on which the parameter vector θ of the probability density function of the hedged portfolio return $f(r \mid \theta)$ is estimated. Denoting D as the feasible decision set, Bayes' optimal hedge ratio h_B is given by:[8]

$$h_B = \max_{h \in D} \ E_\theta\{E_{r \mid \theta}\{U(r)\}\}.$$ (31)

Applying Bayes' theorem to evaluate the expectation, Lence and Hayes (1994b) obtained the result:

$$h_B = \max_{h \in D} \int_{\mathbf{R}} U(r)f(r \mid \mathbf{Y}) \, dr,$$ (32)

where $\mathbf{R}$ is the domain of r and $f(r \mid \mathbf{Y})$ is the predictive probability density function of r given $\mathbf{Y}$. To implement Bayes' strategy, the researcher has to specify the utility function of the hedger and the prior probability density function of θ. Assuming $U(r) = -\text{Var}(r \mid \Phi)$, Lence and Hayes (1994a) derived an algorithm to compute h_B. In their numerical application to the soybean data, Lence and Hayes (1994a) showed that there are substantial differences between the the PCE and the Bayesian hedge ratios. They also reported that slight changes in the data may induce major impacts on the PCE hedge ratio.

A main attraction of the minimum-variance hedge strategy is that, under certain conditions, it is consistent with the expected-utility paradigm regardless of the utility function chosen. Such is the case if (i) the hedger is not allowed to borrow or lend, (ii) there are no transaction costs such as trading fees and margin accounts, and (iii) current futures prices are unbiased for future futures prices. While much has been done to improve the statistical estimation of the minimum-variance hedge ratio, not much attention has been paid to the impacts of the above restrictions on the performance of the hedge strategy. Lence (1995b) argued that the benefits of sophisticated estimation techniques of the hedge ratio is small. He advocated that hedgers may do better by focusing on simpler and more intuitive hedge models. His concerns appear to be supported by some empirical studies (see, for example, Lien, Tse and Tsui, 2001).

5. Hedging in the mean-Gini framework

It is well-known that the mean-variance portfolio theory is based on the assumptions that either the asset returns are normally distributed or the utility functions of decision makers are quadratic.[9] While the first assumption has often been refuted empirically, the second assumption leads to the implausible conclusion that decision makers exhibit increasing absolute risk aversion. Based on the weak assumptions of nonsatiability and risk aversion, stochastic-dominance rules in investment decision making are not subject to these faults of the mean-variance theory. The mean-Gini approach as developed by Yitzhaki (1982, 1983) and Shalit and Yitzhaki (1984) provides a method of implementing investment decisions that are coherent with the stochastic-dominance theories. Although consistent with the principle of maximizing expected utility, the stochastic-dominance approach is difficult to implement in practice. The mean-Gini approach provides a method of constructing portfolios that are efficient in the stochastic-dominance framework.

5.1. *Gini's mean difference and the extended Gini coefficients*

Gini's mean difference measures the variability of a random variable. We shall discuss the concept of Gini's mean difference and describe its applications to futures hedging. Deviating slightly from the notation used in Sections 2 and 4, we denote R as the random return of a portfolio. We assume R falls inside the range $[a, b]$, such that $F(a) = 0$ and $F(b) = 1$, where $F(.)$ is the distribution function of R. Denoting the density function of R by $f(.)$, Gini's mean difference Γ is defined as:

$$\Gamma = \frac{1}{2} \mathrm{E}\{|\,R_1 - R_2\,|\}$$

$$= \frac{1}{2} \int_a^b \int_a^b |\,r_1 - r_2\,| f(r_1) f(r_2)\ dr_1 dr_2, \tag{33}$$

where R_1 and R_2 are independent and have the same distribution as R. In practice, Γ can be evaluated using the following formula:

$$\Gamma = \int_a^b [1 - F(r)] \, dr - \int_a^b [1 - F(r)]^2 \, dr. \tag{34}$$

In the special case when a is finite,[10] the formula can be rewritten as:

$$\Gamma = \mu - a - \int_a^b [1 - F(r)]^2 \, dr, \tag{35}$$

where $\mu = E\{R\}$. Alternatively, Γ can be calculated as:

$$\Gamma = 2 \int_a^b \left[F(r) - \frac{1}{2} \right] f(r) \, dr. \tag{36}$$

It is noted that the variance σ^2 of R can be defined as:

$$\Gamma = \frac{1}{2} E[(R_1 - R_2)^2]$$

$$= \frac{1}{2} \int_a^b \int_a^b (r_1 - r_2)^2 f(r_1) f(r_2) \, dr_1 dr_2, \tag{37}$$

so that the similarity between Γ and σ^2 is obvious.

As a measure of income inequality, the Gini index is often defined as $E\{|R_1 - R_2|\}/(2E\{R\})$ (here R represents the wealth or income). The higher the Gini index is, the more uneven wealth is distributed. In equation (33) above, we follow the definition given by Shalit and Yitzhaki (1984), which has been adopted in the literature of options and futures hedging.

Shalit and Yitzhaki (1984) extended Gini's mean difference to a family of coefficients of variability differing from each other in a parameter denoted by ν, where $1 \leqslant \nu < \infty$. The extended Gini coefficients $\Gamma(\nu)$ are defined as:

$$\Gamma(\nu) = \int_a^b [1 - F(r)] \, dr - \int_a^b [1 - F(r)]^\nu \, dr, \tag{38}$$

which is reduced to:

$$\Gamma(\nu) = \mu - a - \int_a^b [1 - F(r)]^\nu \, dr \tag{39}$$

when a is finite. Shalit and Yitzhaki (1984) pointed out that $\Gamma(\nu)$ is nonnegative, bounded from above and nondecreasing in ν. Furthermore, it can be viewed as the risk premium that should be subtracted from the expected value of the portfolio. The case of $\nu = 1$ represents a risk-neutral investor as $\Gamma(1) = 0$. On the other hand,

$\Gamma(\nu) \rightarrow \mu - a$ as $\nu \rightarrow \infty$. In this case the risk-adjusted return is the minimum value of the return distribution. Thus, $\Gamma(\nu)$ can be used as a representative measure of risk, assuming the role of the variance in the mean-variance analysis. The decision maker may vary the criterion of measuring the *risk* of a portfolio by changing the value of ν. A more risk-averse decision maker will choose a larger value of ν. Gini's mean difference is a special member of the family of extended Gini coefficients with $\nu = 2$, that is, $\Gamma = \Gamma(2)$. The approach of formulating a hedging strategy based on the extended Gini coefficients is called the extended mean-Gini (EMG) approach.

It is not easy to evaluate $\Gamma(\nu)$ using equation (33). However, Shalit and Yitzhaki (1984) proved the following alternative formula:

$$\Gamma(\nu) = -\nu \, \text{Cov}(R, [1 - F(R)]^{\nu - 1}), \tag{40}$$

which provides a convenient method of calculating the extended Gini coefficients. This formula has been adopted in the literature for the practical implementation of the extended mean-Gini hedging strategy. We now proceed to discuss how the mean-Gini framework can be applied to futures hedging.

5.2. *Hedging using the extended mean-Gini approach*

We consider two portfolios A and B, and let the distribution functions of the return of these portfolios be denoted by $F(.)$ and $G(.)$, respectively. A decision maker may use the decision rules based on the stochastic-dominance theories to construct the set of efficient portfolios. Thus, A remains in the efficient set until a portfolio can be found to dominate A stochastically. Now, consider λ_n defined as follows:

$$\lambda_n = \int_a^b [1 - F(r)]^n \, dr - \int_a^b [1 - G(r)]^n \, dr, \qquad n = 1, 2, 3 \ldots \tag{41}$$

The following result was proved by Yitzhaki (1982): The condition $\lambda_n \geqslant 0$ for $n = 1, 2, \ldots,$ is necessary for A to dominate B under the first-degree stochastic dominance (FSD) and the second-degree stochastic dominance (SSD).

The above result can be used to derive necessary conditions for stochastic dominance based on the extended Gini coefficients. Using integration by part, we have:

$$\lambda_1 = \int_a^b [1 - F(r)] \, dr - \int_a^b [1 - G(r)] \, dr$$

$$= \mu_A - \mu_B, \tag{42}$$

where μ_A and μ_B denote the mean return of portfolios A and B, respectively. Denoting $\Gamma_i(\nu)$ as the extended Gini coefficients for $i = A, B$, we have:

$$\lambda_2 = \int_a^b [1 - F(r)]^2 \, dr - \int_a^b [1 - G(r)]^2 \, dr$$

$$= (\mu_A - \Gamma_A(2)) - (\mu_B - \Gamma_B(2)). \tag{43}$$

Thus, the following are necessary conditions for A to FSD/SSD B:

$$\mu_A \geqslant \mu_B \tag{44}$$

and

$$\mu_A - \Gamma_A(2) \geqslant \mu_B - \Gamma_B(2). \tag{45}$$

Note that these conditions form only a subset of the conditions $\lambda_n \geqslant 0$. Additional conditions will require:

$$\mu_A - \Gamma_A(\nu) \geqslant \mu_B - \Gamma_B(\nu), \qquad \nu = 3, 4, \ldots \tag{46}$$

Because $\Gamma(1) = 0$, equation (46) represents a sequence of necessary conditions with $\nu = 1, 2, \ldots$, for FSD and SSD. There are two notions as to how the extended Gini coefficients can be applied to select hedging strategies. First, the hedger can obtain an *efficient* set based on each value of ν. The efficient set is progressively reduced when the hedger performs the EMG analyses for different values of ν and retains only the intersection of the efficient sets. Second, $\Gamma(\nu)$ can be used as a representative measure of risk. It is in this context that ν is interpreted as the risk-aversion parameter. Conditional on ν, an optimal hedging strategy can be obtained by minimizing $\Gamma(\nu)$. This is analogous to the minimum-variance strategy obtained by minimizing the variance. We shall come back to these points when we discuss the empirical applications below.

5.3. *Empirical applications of the extended mean-Gini approach*

Cheung, Kwan and Yip (1990) presented the first empirical application of the mean-Gini approach to hedging. They considered hedging Japanese yen using futures and options. Portfolios consisting of spot and option as well as spot and futures were formed. Conditional on a desired portfolio return they calculated the required hedge ratios of the spot-option and spot-futures portfolios that would give rise to the preset return target. Subsequently, they compared the option and futures strategies based on the variance σ^2 and Gini's mean difference Γ of these portfolios. At each preset level of return, equation (43) is satisfied when the spot-option and spot-futures portfolios are compared. Also, the portfolio with a positive λ_2 has a smaller Γ. Thus, an efficient set that is consistent with FSD and SSD can be obtained by retaining the portfolio with the smaller Γ. On the other hand, the portfolio based on minimizing the variance need not be efficient under the stochastic dominance theory. The two risk criteria would be consistent with each other if the differences in the risk measures (whether σ^2 or Γ) between the hedged portfolios involving option and futures agree in sign. However, Cheung *et al.* found that the mean-variance criterion favours the use of futures as a hedging instrument, whereas the mean-Gini approach supports the use of option.

Kolb and Okunev (1992) extended the work of Cheung *et al.* and considered the hedging strategies based on the EMG approach. Instead of tracing the frontier of the extended Gini coefficients corresponding to various portfolio returns, Kolb and Okunev treated the extended Gini coefficients as measures of risk with different risk-aversion parameters and examined the hedging strategies that minimize these risks. To implement this procedure a sample estimate of $\Gamma(\nu)$ based on equation (40) was used. Denoting r_{pi} and r_{di} as the return of the spot and the derivative (option or futures), respectively, and r_i as the return of the portfolio consisting of the spot and derivative, we have:

$$r_i = r_{pi} - hr_{di}, \qquad i = 1, 2, ..., N, \qquad (47)$$

where h is the hedge ratio and N is the sample size. Suppose $F(.)$ is estimated by the empirical distribution function $\hat{F}(.)$, then $\Gamma(\nu)$ can be estimated by:[11]

$$\hat{\Gamma}(\nu) = -\frac{\nu}{N} \left\{ \sum_{i=1}^{N} r_i (1 - \hat{F}(r_i))^{\nu-1} - \left(\sum_{i=1}^{N} \frac{r_i}{N} \right) \left(\sum_{i=1}^{N} (1 - \hat{F}(r_i))^{\nu-1} \right) \right\}. \qquad (48)$$

The optimal hedge ratio is obtained by minimizing $\hat{\Gamma}(\nu)$ with respect to h. As $\hat{\Gamma}(\nu)$ is a rather complicated function of h, evaluating the derivative of $\hat{\Gamma}(\nu)$ with respect to h is difficult. Kolb and Okunev (1992) adopted the search method for finding the minimum. This method was applied to five spot-futures series (one stock index, one currency and three commodities). They found that the optimal hedge ratios based on the EMG approach (the EMG hedge ratios) for low level of risk aversion (that is, ν from 2 to 5) are similar to the MV hedge ratios. For higher levels of risk aversion, however, the EMG hedge ratios generally differ from the MV hedge ratio, with no regularity in their relative size. They also found that the EMG hedge ratios follow a step function. Thus, investors with similar values of ν may still have significantly different optimal futures positions. Furthermore, changes in the hedge ratio sometimes lead to significant changes in the return of the hedged portfolio.

In addition to the static analysis in which the optimal hedge ratios are assumed to be constant, Kolb and Okunev (1992) considered the situation when investors vary their positions based on recent information. Using moving windows of 50 most recent trading days, they estimated the hedge ratios. It was found that the MV hedge ratios are quite stable through time. In contrast, for moderately risk-averse ($\nu = 5$) or highly risk-averse ($\nu = 50, 100$) investors, the EMG hedge ratios are very volatile. Thus, a strongly risk-averse investor who follows a hedge-and-forget strategy would run the risk of being significantly mishedged through the contract's life.

Lien and Luo (1993) argued that the Kolb-Okunev findings were due to an inherent numerical instability in their search method for the optimal hedge ratio. One defect of this approach is that the distribution function is estimated by the empirical distribution function, which is a step function. Consequently, the estimated extended Gini coefficient is not differentiable, rendering the conventional first-order condition inapplicable. As a remedy for this, the smooth kernel method was suggested. Lien and Luo (1993) found that generally the estimated Gini coefficient has two local minima. When one local minimum overtakes the other, the resulting shift in the hedge ratio is sharp. Their analyses also showed that the hedge ratio is a smooth and monotonic function of the risk-aversion parameter. Indeed, the monotonicity of the hedge ratio could be found in Kolb and Okunev (1992), although this point had not been explicitly pointed out.

While Kolb and Okunev (1992) examined the use of the strategy of globally minimizing the extended Gini coefficients, it would be interesting to see how this strategy compares against one of maximizing the expected utility. Using the extended Gini coefficients as a measure of risk, Kolb and Okunev (1993) defined a class of utility functions in terms of the return and the extended Gini coefficients.[12] The hedging strategies corresponding to utility maximization and risk minimization were then compared. Specifically, the expected utility $E\{U[R]\}$ is assumed to be given by:

$$E\{U[R]\} = \mu - \Gamma(\nu).$$ (49)

Expected utility is maximized at the point when

$$\frac{\partial E\{U[R]\}}{\partial h} = \frac{\partial \mu}{\partial h} - \frac{\partial \Gamma(\nu)}{\partial h} = 0,$$ (50)

which implies

$$\frac{\partial \mu}{\partial \Gamma(\nu)} = 1.$$ (51)

Thus, the utility-maximizing hedge ratio corresponds to the point where the derivative in the mean-Gini coefficient space is 1.

Equation (46) can be compared to the quadratic utility function:

$$E\{U[R]\} = \mu - m\sigma^2,$$ (52)

where m is the risk-aversion parameter. Hedge ratios that minimize the expected utility in the mean-variance space correspond to different points on the mean-variance efficient frontier. The utility-maximizing portfolio moves along the mean-variance efficient frontier as m varies. The optimal hedged portfolio moves toward the global minimum-variance portfolio as m tends to infinity.

Kolb and Okunev (1993) examined the hedging strategies of four cocoa-producing countries. Various scenarios of risk aversion were considered, and both utility-maximization and risk-minimization strategies were examined. They concluded that for strongly risk-averse investors, risk-minimizing and utility-maximizing hedge ratios are generally similar. For weakly risk-averse investors, however, these hedge ratios differ significantly.

Shalit (1995) argued that the EMG hedge ratio based on risk minimization cannot be compared with the MV hedge ratio unless an explicit form of the EMG hedge ratio is available. He suggested an instrumental-variable method for an explicit formula of the estimate of the EMG hedge ratio. Suppose f_0 and f_1 denote the futures prices at time 0 (initialization of the hedge) and time 1 (close of the hedge), respectively. Similarly, let p_1 denote the spot price at time 1. The time-1 value W of the hedged portfolio (based on a unit spot position) is:

$$W = p_1 + h(f_0 - f_1). \tag{53}$$

Shalit (1995) showed that the optimal EMG hedge ratio h^* is given by:

$$h^* = \frac{\text{Cov}(s_1, [1 - H(W)]^{\nu - 1})}{\text{Cov}(f_1, [1 - H(W)]^{\nu - 1})}, \tag{54}$$

where $H(.)$ is the distribution function of W. To obtain an explicit estimate for h^*, Shalit assumed that the distribution function of f_1 is similar to that of W in the sense that the empirical rankings of the two variables are the same. Thus, in equation (50) $H(W)$ is replaced by the distribution function of f_1. This results in the following estimate of h^*:

$$\hat{h}^* = \frac{\sum_{i=1}^{N} (p_{1i} - \bar{p}_1)(y_i - \bar{y})}{\sum_{i=1}^{N} (f_{1i} - \bar{f}_1)(y_i - \bar{y})}, \tag{55}$$

where p_{1i} and f_{1i} denote the sample values of p_1 and f_1, respectively, for $i = 1, ..., N$ and

$$y_i = [1 - \hat{H}(f_{1i})]^{\nu - 1}, \tag{56}$$

with $\hat{H}(.)$ being the empirical distribution function of f_1.

In addition to providing an analytic formula for the estimate of the optimal EMG hedge ratio, Shalit (1995) suggested a method for testing the statistical significance of the difference between the EMG and the MV hedge ratios using Hausman's specification test. The validity of Shalit's approach, however, critically depends on the assumption that at the close of the hedge the rankings of the futures prices are the same as the rankings of the hedged portfolio values. Lien and Shaffer (1999) pointed out that a necessary condition for this assumption to hold is that the hedge ratio is less than one. Indeed, their empirical study showed that Shalit's hedge ratios performed inconsistently, both economically and statistically, as estimates of the true EMG hedge ratios. Following Lien and Luo (1993), Lien and Shaffer (1999) adopted a smooth kernel estimate to calculate the extended Gini coefficient. They examined six stock indexes and concluded that Shalit's instrumental-variable method does not provide a reliable estimate of the EMG hedge ratio.

6. The lower-partial-moment approach

Under the mean-variance asset pricing framework risk is measured in a two-sided notion. The survey by Adams and Montesi (1995), however, suggested that corporate managers are mostly concerned with one-sided risk, in which case only shortfall of a target is regarded as *risk*.[13] The notion that people treat gains and losses differently is commensurate with the prospect theory proposed by Kahneman and Tversky (1979) and Tversky and Kahneman (1992) in which utility is defined over gains and losses rather than levels of wealth. Benartzi and Thaler (1995) argued that, based on the psychology of decision making, individuals are more sensitive to reductions in their levels of wealth than to increases. They proposed the myopic loss aversion theory as an explanation for the equity premium puzzle pointed out by Mehra and Prescott (1985). Thus, the behaviour of loss aversion plays a central role in investment decisions.

Under the notion of loss aversion, risk may be more appropriately measured asymmetrically. Lien (2000b) analyzed the effect of loss aversion on optimal futures hedging. Previously, Kang, Brorsen, and Adam (1996) suggested a similar concept to evaluate futures hedging programs. Bawa (1975, 1978) proposed the lower partial moment as a measure of risk. Bawa and Lindenberg (1977) developed a capital asset pricing model using a mean-lower partial moment framework and showed that many of the results in the mean-variance framework can be carried over. Fishburn (1977) developed a mean-risk analysis independently, where risk is only associated with a below-target return. He proposed the α-t model and showed how different values of α are related to the efficient sets resulting from the first-, second- and third-order stochastic dominance.[14]

A similar concept to loss aversion is disappointment aversion. Grant, Kajii, and Polak (2001) compared three different notions of disappointment aversion. Lien (2001) applied the notion of Gul (1991) to determine the optimal hedging strategy.

6.1. *The lower partial moment*

Consider an individual with a given portfolio that generates a random return R. If $F(.)$ denotes the distribution function of R, the nth order lower partial moment of R (n is a nonnegative integer) is defined as follows:

$$\text{LPM}_n(c; F) = \int_{-\infty}^{c} (c - r)^n \, dF(r), \tag{57}$$

where c is the target rate of return.[15] Thus, only returns of an amount lower than c contribute to the integral, which is regarded as the relevant risk measure. Note that this measure is the same as Fishburn's risk measure, which, however, allows n to be a non-integer positive number. The parameter n is supposed to reflect the decision maker's assessment about the consequences of falling short of the target c. If the size of the shortfall is of no serious concern, a small value of n is appropriate. On the other hand, if large shortfalls are of serious concern, a large value of n is applicable. The following results, given by Bawa (1978), relate the lower partial moment criteria to the stochastic-dominance theories:

1. F is preferred to G for all strictly increasing utility functions if and only if $\text{LPM}_0(c; F) \leqslant \text{LPM}_0(c; G)$ for all c, with strict inequality for some c.[16]

2. F is preferred to G for all strictly increasing concave utility functions if and only if $\text{LPM}_1(c;\ F) \leqslant \text{LPM}_1(c;\ G)$ for all c, with strict inequality for some c.
3. F is preferred to G for all strictly increasing concave utility functions with positive third derivatives if and only if $\mu_F \geqslant \mu_G$ and $\text{LPM}_2(c;\ F) \leqslant \text{LPM}_2(c;\ G)$ for all c, with strict inequality for some c, where μ_F and μ_G are the means of the distributions F and G, respectively.

Note that when $n = 0$, the LPM is equal to the probability of shortfall. For $n = 1$, the LPM is the expected shortfall. Bigman (1996) considered the criterion $\text{LPM}_1(c)$.[17] Setting $c = 0$ and $n = 2$, we obtain $\text{LPM}_2(0)$, which is the semivariance.

6.2. *The optimal lower-partial-moment hedge ratio*

Bawa's (1978) result states that for stochastic dominance to occur there has to be a consistent relationship between the lower partial moments of two return distributions for an infinite set of target returns. The existence of a dominant strategy is, of course, not guaranteed. Given a safety-first target c, however, a hedging strategy can be formulated by minimizing the lower partial moment. This strategy is commensurate with the one-sided risk measure.[18] We shall call this strategy the minimum LPM strategy (conditional on a given c) and the corresponding hedge ratio the minimum LPM hedge ratio.

Consider a hedger with wealth W_0 and a given nontradable spot position Q at time 0. To reduce the risk exposure, the hedger establishes hQ futures positions. Let Δp and Δf denote the changes in the spot and futures prices from time 0 to time 1, respectively, The end-of-period wealth is then given by:

$$W_1 = W_0 + (\Delta p - h\Delta f)Q$$
$$= W_0 + (r_p + \theta r_f)p_0 Q, \tag{58}$$

where p_0 and f_0 are, respectively, the spot and futures prices at time 0, and $r_p = \Delta p/p_0$ and $r_f = \Delta f/f_0$ are, respectively, the returns from the spot and futures positions. Here $-\theta = hf_0/p_0$ is the *adjusted* hedge ratio.[19] We shall denote $r = r_p + \theta r_f$, which is the rate of return of the hedged portfolio.

The minimum LPM hedge ratio minimizes the nth order LPM of the portfolio return. When $n \geqslant 1$, we may rewrite $\text{LPM}_n(c)$ as $\text{E}\{(\max\{0,\ c - r\})^n\}$.[20] We denote the optimal hedge ratio under the LPM criterion, which is a function of c and n, to be $-\theta^* = -\theta^*(c, n)$. Thus, θ^* satisfies the following first order condition:

$$-n\text{E}\{(\max\{0,\ c - r_p - \theta^* r_f\})^{n-1} r_f\} = 0, \tag{59}$$

while the second order condition that θ^* maximizes $\text{LPM}_n(c)$ can be easily shown to be always satisfied. To examine the variation of θ^* with respect to n and c under the LPM criterion we revert to some comparative static analysis. From equation (55), we obtain:

$$\frac{d\theta^*}{dn} = \frac{\text{E}\{(\max\{0,\ c - r_p - \theta^* r_f\})^{n-1} \log(\max\{0,\ c - r_p - \theta^* r_f\} r_f)\}}{\text{E}\{(\max\{0,\ c - r_p - \theta^* r_f\})^{n-2} r_f^2\}}. \tag{60}$$

While the denominator is positive, the sign of the numerator is undetermined. This shows that when the order of the LPM increases, the optimal hedge ratio may increase or decrease.

To evaluate the effect of the target return on the optimal hedge ratio, we consider the following derivative:

$$\frac{d\theta^*}{dc} = \frac{E\{(\max\{0, c - r_p - \theta^* r_f\})^{n-2} r_f\}}{E\{(\max\{0, c - r_p - \theta^* r_f\})^{n-2} r_f^2\}}. \tag{61}$$

As the sign of this derivative is again ambiguous, the optimal hedge ratio may increase or decrease with respect to the target return c.

It would be interesting to compare the optimal hedge ratio under the criteria of minimum variance and minimum LPM. To reduce the scope of comparison we consider the semivariance in the latter family. Thus, we assume $n = 2$ and $c = 0$. From equation (58), the first-order condition for θ^* is:

$$\int_{-\infty}^{\infty} \int_{-\infty}^{-\theta^* r_f} (r_p + \theta^* r_f) r_f \, dF(r_p, r_f) = 0, \tag{62}$$

where, as stated before, the second order condition:

$$\int_{-\infty}^{\infty} \int_{-\infty}^{-\theta^* r_f} r_f^2 \, dF(r_p, r_f) > 0 \tag{63}$$

is always satisfied.

We denote the minimum-variance hedge ratio by $\tilde{\theta}$ and substitute θ^* in the left hand side of equation (62) by $\tilde{\theta}$. If this results in a negative number, then $\tilde{\theta} < \theta^*$. Otherwise, $\tilde{\theta} > \theta^*$. In other words, the sign of $\tilde{\theta} - \theta^*$ is the same as that of D defined as:

$$D = \int_{-\infty}^{\infty} \int_{-\infty}^{-\tilde{\theta} r_f} r_p r_f \, dF(r_p, r_f) + \int_{-\infty}^{\infty} \int_{-\infty}^{-\tilde{\theta} r_f} \tilde{\theta} r_f^2 \, dF(r_p, r_f)$$

$$= E\{(r_p + \tilde{\theta} r_f) r_f \mid r_p + \tilde{\theta} r_f \leqslant 0\}$$

$$= E\{\tilde{r} r_f \mid \tilde{r} \leqslant 0\} \tag{64}$$

where $\tilde{r} = r_p + \tilde{\theta} r_f$ is the portfolio return for the minimum-variance hedged portfolio. A further decomposition of the above leads to:

$$D = \text{Cov}(\tilde{r}, r_f \mid \tilde{r} \leqslant 0) + E\{\tilde{r} \mid \tilde{r} \leqslant 0\} E\{r_f \mid \tilde{r} \leqslant 0\}. \tag{65}$$

Now suppose both the spot and futures markets are unbiased, that is, $E\{r_p\} = E\{r_f\} = 0$. If r_f is mean independent of $\tilde{r}$, it can be easily shown that $D = 0$, so that $\tilde{\theta} = \theta^*$.[21] Thus, when the portfolio return provides no information about the mean of the futures return, the optimal hedging strategy that minimizes the downside risk coincides with that which minimizes the variance.

A special case of mean independence between the portfolio and futures returns under the assumption of unbiased spot and futures markets is the case when r_p and r_f are jointly symmetrically distributed. That is, the joint density function $f(r_p, r_f)$ of r_p and r_f satisfies $f(r_p, r_f) = f(-r_p, r_f) = f(r_p, -r_f) = f(-r_p, -r_f)$. In this case, $\tilde{r}$ and r_f are also symmetrically distributed, implying mean independence. Note that the mean independence condition is stronger than the condition of no correlation, but weaker than the condition of stochastic independence. It follows that if the portfolio return and the futures return are stochastically independent, the minimum-variance hedge ratio is the same as the minimum-semivariance hedge ratio.

6.3. *Nonparametric time-invariant hedge ratio*

Unlike the mean-variance criterion, there is no explicit analytic solution for the hedge ratio that minimizes the LPM. Lien and Tse (2000a) proposed a nonparametric method for the calculation of the optimal LPM hedge ratio. This method is summarized below. For a given θ, we calculate the sample of portfolio returns denoted by $r_1, r_2, ..., r_N$, where $r_i = r_{pi} + \theta r_{fi}$. The density function of r is then estimated by the kernel method given by:

$$\hat{f}(r) = \frac{1}{Nb} \sum_{i=1}^{N} g\left(\frac{r - r_i}{b}\right), \tag{66}$$

where b (>0) is the bandwidth and $g(.)$ is the kernel function.[22] Substituting $\hat{f}(.)$ for the unknown density function in equation (53) we obtain an estimate of $\text{LPM}_n(c)$. Thus, $\text{LPM}_n(c)$ can be estimated by:

$$\hat{l}_n(c) = \int_{\infty}^{c} (c - r)^n \left(\frac{1}{Nb}\right) \sum_{i=1}^{N} g\left(\frac{r - r_i}{b}\right) dr, \tag{67}$$

which, after a change of variable, can be written as:

$$\hat{l}_n(c) = \frac{1}{N} \sum_{i=1}^{N} Q_n(c, r_i), \tag{68}$$

with

$$Q_n(c, r_i) = \int_{-\infty}^{(c - r_i)/h} (c - bz - r_i)^n g(z) \, dz. \tag{69}$$

The evaluation of Q_n can be facilitated using recursive formulas.[23] To estimate the optimal band width Lien and Tse (2000a) followed the data-driven cross validation method as given in Silverman (1986).

Apart from the kernel estimation method, Lien and Tse (2000a) also considered the empirical distribution function method. Using the empirical distribution function method, the LPM is estimated by:

$$\tilde{l}_n(c) = \sum_{r_i < c} \frac{1}{N} (c - r_i)^n.$$ (70)

It should be noted that when the bandwidth b is very small, the kernel estimation method is similar to the empirical distribution function method. Thus, the kernel method encompasses the empirical distribution function method as a special case.

The above methods provide algorithms for the calculation of the LPM. The optimal minimum-LPM hedge ratios can be estimated by minimizing $\hat{l}_n(c)$ (or $\tilde{l}_n(c)$) as a function of θ. Lien and Tse (2000a) reported some results on comparing the minimum-LPM hedge strategy versus the minimum-variance hedge strategy using the Nikkei Stock Average futures traded on the Singapore International Monetary Exchange (SIMEX). The data set consists of weekly prices from January 1988 through August 1996. Lien and Tse (2000a) considered $n = 1, 2$ and 3, and c ranging from -1.5% to 1.5%. The following results were found. First, when $n = 3$, the minimum-variance strategy overhedges against the minimum-LPM strategy. Second, for $n = 1$ or 2, both overhedging or underhedging are possible. However, for $c = 0$, the optimal hedge ratios under the two strategies are about the same. This result agrees with the analysis above as the spot and futures returns were found to be approximately symmetrically distributed. Third, the minimum-variance hedge strategy incurs significantly more downside risk than the minimum-LPM strategy when the target return c is small and the order of the LPM n is large. Overall, a hedger who is willing to absorb small losses but otherwise extremely cautious about large losses, the optimal hedge strategy that minimizes the LPM may be sharply different from the minimum-variance hedge strategy. Thus, if a hedger cares for the downside risk only, the conventional minimum-variance hedge strategy is inappropriate.

6.4. Parametric time-varying hedge ratio

The nonparametric estimation methods for the LPM assume that the returns are independently and identically distributed across time. This assumption results in a constant optimal hedge ratio. As asset prices are often found to have time-varying volatility, the optimal hedge ratio ought to be time-varying as well. under the time-varying framework, nonparametric estimation appears to be infeasible. Lien and Tse (1998) examined the consequences of time-varying conditional heteroscedasticity on the optimal hedge ratios. For analytical tractability they assumed that the conditional distribution of the spot and futures returns follow a bivariate normal distribution. Conditional heteroscedasticity models were then fitted to historical data. The time-varying minimum-LPM hedge ratios were then estimated from the parameters of the fitted model.

Suppose r_p and r_f follow a bivariate normal distribution with $E\{r_i\} = \mu_i$ for $i = p, f$, and with variance and covariance given by $Cov(r_i, r_j) = \sigma_{ij}$ for $i, j = p, f$.

The first-order condition for θ^* to be the minimum-LPM hedge ratio is:

$$\int_{-\infty}^{\infty} \int_{-\infty}^{c-\theta^* r_f} (c - r_p - \theta^* r_f)^{n-1} r_f \, dF(r_p, r_f) = 0. \tag{71}$$

Let $\mu = (\mu_p + \theta^* \mu_f - c)\gamma$ where $\gamma = (\theta^{*2} \sigma_{ff} + 2\theta^* \sigma_{pf} + \sigma_{pp})^{-2}$, Lien and Tse (1998) showed that the condition above can be written as:

$$\int_{\mu}^{\infty} \gamma^{-1}(w - \mu)^n (\theta^* \sigma_{ff} + \sigma_{pf}) \exp\left(-\frac{w^2}{2}\right) dw$$

$$= \int_{\mu}^{\infty} (w - \mu)^{n-1}[(c - \mu_p)(\theta^* \sigma_{ff} + \sigma_{pf}) + \mu_f(\theta^* \sigma_{pf} + \sigma_{pp})]\exp\left(-\frac{w^2}{2}\right) dw.$$

$$\tag{72}$$

Thus, when $\mu_f = 0$, the minimum-LPM hedge ratio is given by $-\theta^* = \sigma_{pf}/\sigma_{ff}$, which is the minimum-variance hedge ratio.

To compute the LPM, Lien and Tse (1998) showed that the following equation can be established:

$$\text{LPM}_n(c, n) = \int_{\mu}^{\infty} \gamma^{-n}(w - \mu)^n \phi(w) \, dw. \tag{73}$$

This equation involves the evaluation of:

$$I_n(\mu) = \int_{\mu}^{\infty} w^n \phi(w) \, dw, \tag{74}$$

which can be calculated using the recursive formulas given in Patel and Read (1982).

Lien and Tse (1998) fitted a bivariate conditional heteroscedasticity model to the Nikkei Stock Average futures. The model is one with conditional correlation, but the individual conditional-variance equations are postulated to follow the asymmetric power GARCH (APARCH) model suggested by Ding, Granger and Engle (1993). This model allows for the leverage effect commonly found in the equity market.[24] Furthermore, the conditional variance is allowed to enter into the conditional-mean equation so that it forms a system with APARCH in mean. It was found that the conditional mean of the futures return μ_f is nonzero, which implies the minimum-LPM hedge ratio differs from that of the minimum-variance hedge ratio.

Lien and Tse (1998) examined the cases of $n = 1, 2, 3$ and 4, with c varying from -1.5% to 1.5%. When $c = -1.5\%$ or -1.0%, the optimal LPM hedge ratios are on average smaller than the minimum-variance hedge ratios, regardless of the order n. Also, the difference is larger for larger values of n. For larger values of c, the LPM hedge ratios are on average larger than the minimum-variance hedge ratios, and the gap shrinks as n increases. Thus, the largest difference between the LPM and the MV hedge strategies occurs when the LPM order n is large and the target return c is negative with a large absolute value.

6.5. *Options versus futures*

Because options (call or put) can eliminate downside risk associated with certain (in particular, negative) target returns, it is often argued that option would be a better derivative to use as a hedging instrument compared to futures. This conjecture was, however, rejected by Ahmadi, Sharp and Walther (1986). Using data from the Philadelphia Stock Exchange, Ahmadi *et al.* showed that for a nontradable spot position, futures provide significantly more effective hedging than options for the British pound, the Deutschemark and the Japanese yen when the target return is zero. Based upon simulations from hypothetical distributions, Korsvold (1994) demonstrated that the incorporation of the quantity risk, that is, the uncertainty in the spot position, leads to the dominance of options over futures. This result is, however, not convincing as it is based upon hypothetical distributions and simulated data. On the other hand, Adams and Montesi (1995) found that corporate managers prefer to hedge the downside risk using futures rather than options, citing the large transaction costs in options trading as the main reason.

An alternative argument that favours options hedging stems from the case of contingent exposures. Ware and Winter (1988), however, challenged this conventional wisdom. Moreover, within an analytical framework, Steil (1993) rejected this argument. Both papers concluded that options play no role in the hedging of transaction risk exposures, although Ware and Winter (1988) supported the role of options in hedging economic risk exposures. Recently, Battermann, Braulke, Broll and Schimmelpfennig (2000) showed that, based on expected-utility maximization within the production and hedging framework, futures is a better instrument than option. Given a general utility function, Bowden (1994) compared option spreads (combining calls and puts) to futures and found that there exist parameter ranges such that one dominates the other. After correcting a mistake in Bowden's analysis, Lien (1997) showed that option spreads always outperform futures.

Empirical results are mostly in favour of futures. Based upon the mean-variance type of criteria, Chang and Shanker (1986) concluded that currency futures are better hedging instruments than currency options. Hancock and Weise (1994) showed that the optimal hedge positions for the S&P 500 index options (and spreads) and that for the S&P 500 futures lead to similar mean returns. They argued that other factors are responsible for the choice of the instruments. Benet and Luft (1995) extended the earlier work of Chang and Shanker (1986) to stock index instruments. They showed that the S&P 500 futures outperform the S&P 500 options in variance reduction. Moreover, without taking into account the transaction costs, options lead to a larger excess return per unit risk than futures.

Transaction costs reverse the above conclusion, however. With the exceptions of Ahmadi, Sharp and Walther (1986) and Korsvold (1994), the comparisons are always based upon mean and variance, which requires restrictive assumptions.

We now consider how the lower-partial-moment criterion may be applied to option hedging. Suppose a hedger purchases qQ ($q \geqslant 0$) units of put options, the strike price of which is K, at a premium d. The end-of-period wealth becomes:

$$W_1 = W_0 + \{\Delta p + q[\max(K - p_1, 0)] - qd\}Q. \tag{75}$$

The market profit π is given by $\Delta p + q[\max(K - p_1, 0)] - qd$. If a unit hedge ratio is adopted (that is, $q = 1$), then $\pi \geqslant K - p_0 - d$. There will be no downside risk if the target 'profit' is below the lower bound. Otherwise, downside risk exists. Because $K - p_0 - d$ is usually a negative number, downside risk occurs when the target return is set to zero. For any other hedge ratio, π remains a function of p_1 and, therefore, downside risk exists. To determine the optimal hedge ratio (when the target profit is larger than $K - p_0 - d$), the methods discussed above can be applied.

A similar analysis applies to call options. Suppose the hedger sells q^*Q ($q^* \geqslant 0$) units of call options with strike price K at a premium d^*. The end-of-period wealth is then given by:

$$W_1 = W_0 + \{\Delta p + q^*[\min(K - p_1, 0)] + q^*d^*\}Q. \tag{76}$$

Let π_c denote the market profit $\Delta p + q^*[\min(K - p_1, 0)] + q^*c$. Then $\pi_c \leqslant K - p_0 + dq^*$. Clearly call options do not eliminate downside risk for the hedger.

The above analysis assumes the options are held until expiry. If a call option is held over a fixed hedging period, the end-of-period wealth is:

$$W_1 = W_0 + (r_p + \theta r_c)p_0 Q, \tag{77}$$

where r_c is the return of the call option and $-\theta = -q^*d^*/p_0$. The analysis is similar to the case of futures hedging.

Lien and Tse (2000b) examined the hedging effectiveness of the futures and options for three major currencies, namely, the British pound, the Deutschemark and the Japanese yen. They considered a hedging horizon of one week. Two estimation methods were applied to estimate the optimal LPM hedge ratio: the empirical distribution function method and the kernel density estimation method. They considered various values of target returns c and degree of risk aversion n. The results showed that the currency futures are almost always a better hedging instrument than the currency options. The only situation in which options outperform futures occurs when the hedger is optimistic (c is large) and not too concerned about large losses (n is small).

7. Multi-period hedging and rollover hedging

So far our analysis has assumed that the hedger faces a one-period decision problem. Alternatively, we may consider the problem when the hedger holds the same futures position within a multi-period framework. Because a futures position is marked to the market on a daily basis (i.e. the losses or gains from a futures position are calculated and accounted for daily), a multi-period consideration seems appropriate. Let $t = 0$ denote the current time. Suppose a futures position will be held in each period until the final period T. At any time t such that $0 \leqslant t < T$ a futures position X_t is assumed. This will be lifted at $t + 1$. For the most general case, the hedger chooses the optimal sequence of futures positions to maximize his end-of-period expected utility, $E\{U(W_T)\}$ subject to the constraints:

$$W_t = W_{t-1} + (\Delta p_t)Q - (\Delta f_t)X_{t-1}, \quad 1 \leqslant t \leqslant T. \tag{78}$$

Dynamic programming can be applied to solve the maximization problem. Specifically, at the final decision point $t = T - 1$ the hedger chooses the optimal futures position, X_{T-1}^*, by the following condition:

$$E\{U'(W_{T-1} + (\Delta p_T)Q - (\Delta f_T)X_{t-1}^*)\Delta f_T\} = 0. \tag{79}$$

Clearly X_{T-1}^* depends upon the utility function and the joint density function of Δp_T and Δf_T. Given X_{T-1}^*, at $t = T - 2$ the hedger perceives the end-of-period wealth as follows:

$$W_T = W_{T-2} + (\Delta p_{T-1})Q - (\Delta f_{T-1})X_{T-2} + (\Delta p_T)Q - (\Delta f_T)X_{T-1}^*. \tag{80}$$

The optimal futures position X_{T-2}^* satisfies the equation

$$E\{U'(W_{T-2} + (\Delta p_{T-1})Q - (\Delta f_{T-1})X_{T-2}^* + (\Delta p_T)Q - (\Delta f_T)X_{T-1}^*)\Delta f_{T-1}\} = 0. \tag{81}$$

Consequently, X_{T-2}^* depends upon the utility function and the joint density function of Δp_T, Δf_T, Δp_{T-1}, and Δf_{T-1}. Similar procedures can be applied to derive X_t^* for $0 \leqslant t \leqslant T - 3$.

To proceed further, assumptions for the utility function or the joint density function of $\{\Delta p_t, \Delta f_t\}$ for $t = 1, ..., T$, must be imposed. Suppose that $\Delta p_t = \beta_t \Delta f_t + \varepsilon_t$ such that Δf_s and ε_t are stochastically independent for any t and s. Then the optimal futures position is $X_t^* = \beta_t Q$. This is the simplest case in which the multi-period hedge ratio is identical to the one-period hedge ratio. Myers and Hanson (1996) provided similar results under alternative and less restrictive assumptions. Within a two-period model, Anderson and Danthine (1983) adopted a mean-variance utility function to derive the optimal futures positions. Arguing that a hedger should be concerned only with risk, Howard and D'Antonio (1991), Mathews and Holthausen (1991), and Lien (1992) assumed the hedger attempts to minimize the variance of the end-of-period wealth. Under this assumption, X_{T-1}^* is chosen to minimize $\text{Var}(W_T)$, where $W_T = W_{T-1} + (\Delta p_T)Q - (\Delta f_T)X_{t-1}$. Thus, $X_{T-1}^* = Q[\text{Cov}(\Delta p_T, \Delta f_T)/\text{Var}(\Delta f_T)]$, which is the one-period solution. At time $t = k$, the hedger chooses X_k^* to minimize

$$\text{Var}(W_T) = \text{Var}\left[(\Delta p_{k+1})Q - (\Delta f_{k+1})X_k + \sum_{t=k+1}^{T-1}(\Delta p_{t+1})Q - (\Delta f_{t+1})X_t^*\right]. \tag{82}$$

Note that the hedger knows $X_t^*, k+1 \leqslant t \leqslant T-1$ at $t=k$. Upon taking the partial derivative with respect to X_k, the following recursive relationship can be derived:

$$B_k^* = \frac{\text{Cov}(\Delta p_{k+1}, \Delta f_{k+1})}{\text{Var}(\Delta f_{k+1})} + \sum_{t=k+1}^{T-1} \frac{\text{Cov}(\Delta f_{k+1}, \Delta p_{t+1} + \Delta f_{t+1} B_t^*)}{\text{Var}(\Delta f_{k+1})}, \quad (83)$$

where $B_k^* = X_k^*/Q$. Imputing the second moments of $\{\Delta p_t, \Delta f_t\}$ for $t = 1, ..., T$, helps solving for B_k^*.

Lien (1992) considered the following simple cointegration model:

$$\Delta p_t = \alpha(f_{t-1} - p_{t-1}) + \varepsilon_{pt},$$
$$\Delta f_t = -\beta(f_{t-1} - p_{t-1}) + \varepsilon_{ft}, \quad (84)$$

where $\{\varepsilon_{pt}, \varepsilon_{ft}\}$ are independently and identically distributed over time. To simplify the notation let σ denote $\text{Cov}(\varepsilon_{pt}, \varepsilon_{ft})/\text{Var}(\varepsilon_{ft})$. It can be shown that

$$B_k^* = \sigma + \sum_{j=1}^{T-k-1} (1 - \alpha - \beta\sigma)^{j-1}(\alpha + \beta\sigma)(1 - \sigma) \quad (85)$$

provided $\alpha + \beta\sigma \neq 1$. Otherwise, $B_k^* = 1$. Consequently the optimal multi-period hedge ratios collapse to the one-period hedge ratio if and only if $\alpha + \beta\sigma = 0$ or $\sigma = 1$. Following Garbade and Silber (1983), $0 < \alpha, -\beta < 1$. It can be shown that B_k^* is a decreasing function of k (provided $\alpha + \beta\sigma \neq 1$). That is, the hedger begins with a large hedge ratio at $t = 0$ and gradually reduces the hedge ratio until the final decision point $t = T - 1$ when the hedge ratio is set at σ. A similar result was established by Howard and D'Antonio (1991).

In Lien and Luo (1993), lagged spot and futures prices are added into the cointegration equations:

$$\Delta p_t = \alpha_1(f_{t-1} - p_{t-1}) + \beta_1\Delta p_{t-1} + \gamma_1\Delta f_{t-1} + \varepsilon_{pt}, \quad (86)$$

$$\Delta f_t = \alpha_2(f_{t-1} - p_{t-1}) + \beta_2\Delta p_{t-1} + \gamma_2\Delta f_{t-1} + \varepsilon_{ft}. \quad (87)$$

Let $\varepsilon_t = (\varepsilon_{pt}, \varepsilon_{ft}, \varepsilon_{pt} - \varepsilon_{ft})'$ and let

$$A = \begin{bmatrix} \beta_1 & \gamma_1 & \alpha_1 \\ \beta_2 & \gamma_2 & \alpha_2 \\ \beta_2 - \beta_1 & \gamma_2 - \gamma_1 & 1 + \alpha_2 - \alpha_1 \end{bmatrix} \quad (88)$$

Then

$$B_k^* = \sigma + \sum_{t=k+1}^{T-1} (0, 1, 0)\text{Var}(\varepsilon_t)(A')^{t-k}(1, B_t^*, 0)'[\text{Var}(\varepsilon_{2t})]^{-1}. \quad (89)$$

Lien and Luo (1993) applied the above methods to five currency markets and three stock index markets. They found that the optimal hedge ratios first increases and then decreases as the maturity date becomes closer. Recall that the hedge ratio always decreases when the lagged price terms are not incorporated into the model.

The problem becomes much more complicated once conditional heteroscedasticity is incorporated into the cointegration system. To illustrate, consider a three-date ($t = 1, 2, 3$) two-period model. As usual, $B_2^* = \text{Cov}(\varepsilon_{p3}, \varepsilon_{f3})/\text{Var}(\varepsilon_{f3})$. Let $\delta_1(X) = X - E_1\{X\}$, where E_1 denotes the expectation taken at time 1. Lien and Luo (1994) adopted the decomposition of Bohrnstedt and Goldberger (1969) to derive the following formula for B_1^*:

$$B_1^* = \sigma + B_{11} + B_{12} + B_{13}, \tag{90}$$

where

$$B_{11} = \alpha_1 + \gamma_1 + (\beta_1 - \alpha_1)[\text{Var}_1(\varepsilon_{f2})]^{-1}\text{Cov}_1(\varepsilon_{p2}, \varepsilon_{f2}), \tag{91}$$

$$B_{12} = E_1\{B_2^*\}[\alpha_2 + \gamma_2 + (\beta_2 - \alpha_2)[\text{Var}_1(\varepsilon_{f2})]^{-1}\text{Cov}_1(\varepsilon_{p2}, \varepsilon_{f2})], \tag{92}$$

$$B_{13} = [\text{Var}_1(\varepsilon_{f2})]^{-1}[(\alpha_2 + \gamma_2)E_1\{\delta_1(B_2^*)\varepsilon_{f2}^2\} + (\beta_2 - \alpha_2)E_1\{\delta_1(B_2^*)\varepsilon_{p2}\varepsilon_{f2}\}]. \tag{93}$$

When examining five currency markets (British pound, Canadian dollar, Deutsche mark, Japanese yen and Swiss franc), they found that B_1^* was far different from B_2^* in the British pound and the Swiss franc markets. Nonetheless, the improvement in hedging effectiveness is minimal.

Multi-period hedge ratios for the above problem arise from the consideration of rebalancing (due to mark-to-market). The hedger changes positions on a given futures contract periodically. An alternative multi-period problem occurs when the long-term futures markets are missing. For example, a hedger may want to hedge a spot position that will be lifted two years from now. However, there is no futures trading available for two-year maturity. The hedger therefore continuously trades on the nearby futures contracts and upon its maturity rollover the position to the next nearby futures contract. Thus, we have a 'rollover hedging' problem. In fact, even if the long-term contract is available for trading, the market may be thin such that the hedger is better off adopting a rollover hedge strategy.

Let $f_{i,j}$ denote the price of a futures contract with maturity i at time j. Suppose there are k futures contracts with maturity t_n, for $n = 1, ..., k$, such that $1 < t_1 < \cdots < t_{k-1} < T \leqslant t_k$. Adopting rollover hedge on the nearby futures contracts, the end-of-period wealth is:

$$W_T = (p_{t_1} - p_1)Q - (f_{t_1, t_1} - f_{t_1, 1})X_1 + (p_T - p_{t_{k-1}})Q - (f_{t_k, T} - f_{t_k, t_{k-1}})X_{t_{k-1}}$$

$$+ \sum_{n=1}^{k-2} (p_{t_{n+1}} - p_{t_n})Q - (f_{t_{n+1}, t_{n+1}} - f_{t_{n+1}, t_n})X_{t_n}, \tag{94}$$

where X_j is the position on the nearby futures contract at time j. Assume the hedger is an expected-utility maximizer. Applying dynamic programming technique, the optimal futures position, $X_{t_{k-1}}^*$, is found to satisfy the following equation:

$$E\{U'(W_T)(f_{t_k, T} - f_{t_k, t_{k-1}})\} = 0. \tag{95}$$

Also, the optimal futures position, $X_{t_n}^*$, can be solved from the following equation:

$$E\{U'(W_T)(f_{t_{n+1}, t_{n+1}} - f_{t_{n+1}, t_n})\} = 0. \tag{96}$$

These equations are similar to (and more complicated than) the case of multi-period hedging discussed above. Additional structure on the utility function and the data generation processes must be imposed to obtain explicit solutions.

Earlier studies on rollover hedging include Baesel and Grant (1982), McCabe and Franckle (1983), Grant (1984), and Gardner (1989). In these studies, the mean-variance approach is adopted. Moreover, to eliminate speculative motivation, it is assumed that the hedger attempts to minimize $Var(W_T)$. Thus,

$$B_{t_{k-1}}^* = Cov(p_T - p_{t_{k-1}}, f_{t_k, T} - f_{t_k, t_{k-1}})/Var(f_{t_k, T} - f_{t_k, t_{k-1}}). \tag{97}$$

where $B_{t_{k-1}}^* = X_{t_{k-1}}^*/Q$. Moreover, at t_{k-2},

$$B_{t_{k-2}}^* = \frac{Cov(p_{t_{k-1}} - p_{t_{k-2}}, f_{t_{k-1}, t_{k-1}} - f_{t_{k-1}, t_{k-2}})}{Var(f_{t_{k-1}, t_{k-1}} - f_{t_{k-1}, t_{k-2}})}$$

$$+ \frac{Cov((p_T - p_{t_{k-1}})Q - (f_{t_k, T} - f_{t_k, t_{k-1}})B_{t_{k-1}}^*, f_{t_{k-1}, t_{k-1}} - f_{t_{k-1}, t_{k-2}})}{Var(f_{t_{k-1}, t_{k-1}} - f_{t_{k-1}, t_{k-2}})}. \tag{98}$$

The first term is the usual one-period hedge ratio whereas the second term is due to multi-period considerations. Upon repeating the procedure, a general recursive relationship for $B_{t_n}^*$ can be derived. It is similar to that applied to the multi-period hedging problem. Using empirical data, numerical values for the optimal rollover hedge ratios can be estimated and the hedging effectiveness can be assessed. Indeed, Gardner (1989) found that rollover hedging is a good substitute for (missing) long-term commodity futures contracts.

The case of Metallgesellschaft (MG) and its controversial rollover hedging strategy has increased academic scrutiny of using rollover strategies.[25] Specifically, MG adopted a hedge ratio of near 1. Culp and Miller (1994, 1995a, 1995b) defended the program as conceptually sound but faulted supervisory board members for abandoning the program when prices moved against MG. Mello and Parsons (1995) and Pirrong (1997) suggested the strategy as conceptually flawed. Edwards and Canter (1995) highlighted the potential risks and benefits of the program but were reserved in their judgement. Within the continuous-time framework, Hilliard (1997) and Brennan and Crew (1997) derived the optimal hedging strategy assuming different underlying stochastic process. Ross (1997) adopted a mean-reverting process for the spot price and derived an optimal hedge ratio that is robust to model misspecifications. All the previous works restrict the hedger to a stack strategy, that is, the hedger holds a position only on a given contract (i.e. the nearby contract). Neuberger (1995) considered the possibility of multiple futures contracts. The optimal futures positions were derived under a 'linear spanning' condition for futures prices. Using crude oil data, it was shown that the so-called strip strategy outperforms the stack strategy. However, the strategy requires a transaction volume and therefore a large transaction cost. While validating Neuberger's results in crude oil, Lien and Shaffer (2000) also found contrasting results in heating oil and unleaded gasoline. Lence and Hayenga (2000) considered multi-year rollover hedge-to-arrive contracts. They demonstrated that it is theoretically infeasible to lock in high current prices.

8. Conclusions

The importance of risk management in the financial markets cannot be overemphasized. As a widely used instrument in hedging, futures plays a significant role in risk management. Recent research has made significant contributions to the understanding of futures hedging, both in terms of the theoretical underpinning and the implementation of the strategies. In this survey we have reviewed some of the recent findings. There are, of course, many more questions that remain to be answered. For example, although nonlinearity in spot and futures returns has been incorporated in recent works, most researchers continue to adopt linear processes to model the second moments. It is likely that nonlinear processes may perform better for hedging purposes. Also, the effects of taxes on futures hedging requires a different modelling strategy. Pirrong (1995), Lien (1999b) and Lien and Metz (2000) provided some preliminary results on this issue. Assessment of hedging performance that explicitly incorporates these factors will provide better understanding of hedging price risks.

Acknowledgement

We have benefited from many individuals in preparing this manuscript. In particular, we wish to acknowledge the comments and suggestions from Wade Brorsen, Carolyn Chang, Jack Chang, Carl Chen, Thomas Chiang, Sergio Lence, Raymond Leuthold, John Sequeira, George Wang, Bob Webb and Keith Wong. Of course, we are solely responsible for any omissions and commissions.

Notes

1. The assumption that the spot position is fixed will be maintained throughout this survey. For the case where the spot position is uncertain, see Rolfo (1980), Honda (1983), Paroush and Wolf (1980) and Lapan, Moschini and Hanson (1991).
2. Except for the initial margin and subsequent margin calls, no investment is required for a futures position. Thus, the term *return of the futures position* should not be interpreted in the conventional sense. Notwithstanding this difficulty, however, we shall continue to use this term for convenience.
3. This assumption is satisfied when r_p and r_f are jointly normally distributed conditional on the information set Φ.
4. The information set Φ here includes information up to but not including t.
5. See Campbell, Lo, and MacKinlay (1997) for this terminology and Footnote 2 for the interpretation for futures return.
6. Note that the GARCH models assume that the conditional variance and covariance depend only on the past conditional second moments and residuals. Extraneous

information is ignored. The conditional moments can be specified more generally using transfer function models as in Chiang and Chiang (1996).

7. Lien and Tse (2000c) pointed out that the stable-under-aggregation property holds for both the regression and the vector autoregression models. In contrast, the error-correction model and the GARCH models do not satisfy the stability property.

8. Note that the hedged portfolio return is a function of the hedge ratio h.

9. The normality assumption may be relaxed to allow the returns to be elliptically distributed. See Ingersoll (1987) for the details.

10. Note that a is finite when there is limited liability. But the results in this section, unless otherwise stated, do not assume a is finite.

11. This presentation follows Lien and Luo (1993).

12. Kolb and Okunev (1993) considered the utility function as a function of wealth rather than return. For a given spot position the assumptions based on wealth and return are equivalent. To follow the notations used in this paper, we present our discussions in terms of returns.

13. An earlier survey by Petty and Scott (1981) also found that many managers identified risk as returns falling below a certain target.

14. In Fishburn's model, α corresponds to n (the order) and t corresponds to c (the target) of the lower partial moment.

15. Note that c may be regarded as a desired or critical Roy (1952) safety-first target rate of return.

16. We say 'F is preferred to G' to mean that the portfolio with return distribution given by F is preferred to the one with return distribution given by G.

17. We shall drop the argument representing the distribution function when it is generic.

18. The existence of a dominant strategy can then be checked over a wide range of target returns.

19. We shall use the term hedge ratio for both $-\theta$ and h. Whether it refers to the adjusted or unadjusted ratio should be clear from the context.

20. Strictly speaking, the LPM requires the parameter n to be an integer. Here we adopt an approach closer to Fishburn's measure and allow n to be any positive number.

21. r_f is said to be mean independent of $\tilde{r}$ if $E\{r_f \mid \tilde{r}\} = E\{r_f\}$. Chew and Herk (1990) showed that if r_f is mean independent of $\tilde{r}$, $E\{q(\tilde{r})r_f\} = E\{q(\tilde{r})\}E\{r_f\}$ for any measurable function $q(\tilde{r})$. The fact that $D = 0$ can be proved by defining $q(\tilde{r}) = \tilde{r}$ when $\tilde{r} \leqslant 0$, and zero otherwise.

22. A commonly used kernel function is the density function of the standard normal variate $\phi(x) = (1/\sqrt{2\pi})\exp(-x^2/2)$.

23. See Patel and Read (1982) for the details.

24. The leverage effect refers to the empirical finding that negative shock causes a bigger change in future volatilities compared to a positive shock of the same magnitude.

25. In the early 90s MG sold a huge volume of five- to ten-year heating oil and gasoline fixed price contracts. It hedged its exposure with long positions in futures contracts that were rolled over. It turned out that the price of oil fell and there were margin calls. As a result, MG closed out all the hedge positions and suffered a loss of $1.33 billion.

References

Adams, J. and Montesi, C. J. (1995) *Major Issues Related to Hedge Accounts*. Financial Accounting Standard Board: Newark, Connecticut.

Ahmadi, H. Z., Sharp, P. A. and Walther, C. H. (1986) The Effects of Futures and Options in Hedging Currency Risk. *Advances in Futures and Options Research*, 1, 171–191.

Andersen, T. G. (1994) Stochastic Autoregressive Volatility: A Framework for Volatility Modeling. *Mathematical Finance*, 4, 75–102.

Andersen, T. G. (1996) Return Volatility and Trading Volume: An Informational Flow Interpretation of Stochastic Volatility. *Journal of Finance*, 51, 169–204.

Andersen, T. G. and Bollerslev, T. (1998) Answering the Skeptics: Yes, Standard Volatility Models Do Provide Accurate Forecasts. *International Economic Review*, 39, 885–905.

Andersen, T. G. and Sorensen, B. E. (1996) GMM Estimation of a Stochastic Volatility Model: A Monte Carlo Study. *Journal of Business and Economic Statistics*, 14, 328–352.

Anderson, R. W. and Danthine, P.-J. (1983) The Time Pattern of Hedging and the Volatility of Futures Prices. *Review of Economic Studies*, 50, 249–266.

Baesel, J. and Grant, D. (1982) Optimal Sequential Futures Hedging. *Journal of Financial and Quantitative Analysis*, 17, 683–695.

Baillie, R. T. and Myers, R. J. (1991) Bivariate GARCH Estimation of the Optimal Commodity Futures Hedge. *Journal of Applied Econometrics*, 6, 109–124.

Balke, N. S. and Fomby, T. B. (1997) Threshold Cointegration. *International Economic Review*, 38, 627–645.

Battermann, H. L., Braulke, M., Broll, U. and Schimmelpfennig, J. (2000) The Preferred Hedge Instrument. *Economics Letters*, 66, 85–91.

Bawa, V. S. (1975) Optimal Rules for Ordering Uncertain Prospects. *Journal of Financial Economics*, 2, 95–121.

Bawa, V. S. (1978) Safety-First, Stochastic Dominance and Optimal Portfolio Choice. *Journal of Financial and Quantitative Analysis*, 33, 255–271.

Bawa, V. S. and Lindenberg, E. B. (1977) Capital Market Equilibrium in a Mean-Lower Partial Moment Framework. *Journal of Financial Economics*, 5, 189–200.

Bell, D. E. and Krasker, W. S. (1986) Estimating Hegde Ratios. *Finacial Management*, 15, 34–39.

Benartzi, S. and Thaler, R. H. (1995) Myopic Loss Aversion and the Equity Premium Puzzle. *Quarterly Journal of Economics*, 110, 75–92.

Benet, B. A. and Luft, C. F. (1995) Hedging Performance of SPX Index Options and S&P 500 Futures. *Journal of Futures Markets*, 15, 691–717.

Benninga, S., Eldor, R. and Zilcha, I. (1983) Optimal Hedging in the Futures Market under Price Uncertainty. *Economics Letters*, 13, 141–145.

Bera, A. K., Garcia, P. and Roh, J. S. (1997) Estimation of Time-Varying Hedging Ratios for Corn and Soybeans: BGARCH and Random Coefficient Approaches. *Sankhya*, 59, 346–368.

Bigman, D. (1996) Safety-First Criterion and Their Measures of Risk. *American Journal of Agricultural Economics*, 78, 225–235.

Bohrnstedt, G. W. and Goldberger, A. S. (1969) On the Exact Covariance of Products of Random Variables. *Journal of American Statistical Association*, 64, 1439–1442.

Bollerslev, T. (1990) Modelling the Coherence in Short-Run Nominal Exchange Rates: A Multivariate Generalized ARCH Model. *Review of Economics and Statistics*, 72, 498–505.

Bollerslev, T., Engle, R. and Wooldridge, J. M. (1988) A Capital Asset Pricing Model with Time Varying Covariances. *Journal of Political Economy*, 96, 116–131.

Bowden, R. J. (1994) Forwards or Options? Nesting Procedures for Fire and Forget' Commodity Hedging. *Journal of Futures Markets*, 6, 289–305.

Brennan, M. J. and Crew, N. I. (1997) Hedging Long Maturity Commodity Commitments with Short-Dated Futures Contracts. In: M. M. H. Dempster and S. R. Pliska, (eds), *Mathematics of Derivative Securities*, Cambridge University Press: Cambridge.

Brenner, R. J. and Kroner, K. F. (1995) Arbitrage, Cointegration, and Testing the

Unbiasedness in Financial Markets. *Journal of Financial and Quantitative Analysis*, 30, 23–42.

Broll, U., Chow, K. W. and Wong, K. P. (2000) Hedging and Nonlinear Risk Exposure. *Oxford Economic Papers*, forthcoming.

Campbell, J. Y., Lo, A. W. and MacKinlay, A. C. (1997) *The Econometrics of Financial Markets*. Princeton University Press: Princeton, NJ.

Castelino, M. G. (1992) Hedge Effectiveness: Basis Risk and Minimum-Variance Hedging. *Journal of Futures Markets*, 12, 187–201.

Chang, J. S. K. and Shanker, L. (1986) Hedging Effectiveness of Currency Options and Currency Futures. *Journal of Futures Markets*, 6, 289–305.

Cheung, C. S., Kwan, C. C. Y. and Yip, P. C. Y. (1990) The Hedging Effectiveness of Options and Futures: A Mean-Gini Approach. *Journal of Futures Markets*, 10, 61–73.

Cheung, Y. W. and Lai, K. S. (1993) A Fractional Cointegration Analysis of Purchasing Power Parity. *Journal of Business and Economic Statistics*, 7, 297–305.

Chew, S. H. and Herk, L. F. (1990) Mean Independence and Uncorrelatedness. *mimeo*.

Chiang, T. C. and Chiang, J. J. (1996) Dynamic Analysis of Stock Return Volatility in an Integrated International Capital Market. *Review of Quantitative Finance and Accounting*, 6, 5–17.

Chou, W. L., Denis, K. K. F. and Lee, C. F. (1996) Hedging with the Nikkei Index Futures: The Conventional versus the Error Correction Model. *Quarterly Review of Economics and Finance*, 36, 495–505.

Cita, J. and Lien, D. (1992) A Note on Constructing Spot Price Indices to Approximate Futures Prices. *Journal of Futures Markets*, 12, 447–457.

Culp, C. L. and Miller, M. H. (1994) Hedging a Flow of Commodity Deliveries with Futures: Lessons from Metallgesellschaft. *Derivative Quarterly*, 1, 7–15.

Culp, C. L. and Miller, M. H. (1995a) Metallgesellschaft and the Economics of Synthetic Storage. *Journal of Applied Corporate Finance*, 7, 62–76.

Culp, C. L. and Miller, M. H. (1995b) Hedging and the Theory of Corporate Finance: A Reply to Our Critics. *Journal of Applied Corporate Finance*, 8, 121–127.

Danielsson, J. (1998) Multivariate Stochastic Volatility Models: Estimation and a Comparison with VGARCH Models. *Journal of Empirical Finance*, 5, 155–173.

Ding, Z., Granger, C. W. J. and Engle, R. F. (1993) A Long Memory Property of Stock Market Returns and a New Model. *Journal of Empirical Finance*, 1, 83–106.

Dueker, M. and Startz, R. (1998) Maximum-Likelihood Estimation of Fractional Cointegration with an Application to US and Canadian Bond Rates. *Review of Economics and Statistics*, 80, 420–426.

Dumas, B., Fleming, J. and Whaley, R. E. (1998) Implied Volatility Functions: Empirical Tests. *Journal of Finance*, 53, 2059–2106.

Dwyer, G. P., Locke, P. and Yu, W. (1996) Index Arbitrage and Nonlinear Dynamics between the S&P 500 Futures and Cash. *Review of Financial Studies*, 9, 301–332.

Ederington, L. H. (1979) The Hedging Performance of the New Futures Markets. *Journal of Finance*, 34, 157–170.

Edwards, F. R. and Canter, M. S. (1995) The Collapse of Metallgesellschaft: Unhedgeable Risks, Poor Hedging Strategy, or Just Bad Luck? *Journal of Applied Corporate Finance*, 8, 86–105.

Engle, R. F. and Granger, C. W. J. (1987) Cointegration and Error Correction: Representation, Estimation and Testing. *Econometrica*, 55, 251–276.

Engle, R. F. and Kroner, K. F. (1995) Multivariate Simultaneous Generalized ARCH. *Econometric Theory*, 11, 122–150.

Fama, E. and French, K. (1987) Commodity Futures Prices: Some Evidence on the Forecast Power, Premiums and the Theory of Storage. *Journal of Business*, 60, 55–73.

Fishburn, P. J. (1977) Mean-Risk Analysis with Risk Associated with Below-Target Returns. *American Economic Review*, 67, 116–126.

Gao, A. H. and Wang, G. H. K. (1999) Modeling Nonlinear Dynamics of Daily Futures Price Changes. *Journal of Futures Markets*, 19, 325–351.

Garbade, K. D. and Silber, W. L. (1983) Price Movements and Price Discovery in Futures and Cash Markets. *Review of Economics and Statistics*, 65, 289–297.

Gardner, B. (1989) Rollover Hedging and Missing Long-Term Futures Markets. *American Journal of Agricultural Economics*, 71, 311–318.

Geweke, J. (1994) Bayesian Comparison of Econometric Models. *Working Paper* No. 532, Research Department, Federal Reserve Bank at Minneapolis.

Ghosh, A. (1993) Hedging with Stock Index Futures: Estimation and Forecasting with Error Correction Model. *Journal of Futures Markets*, 13, 743–752.

Granger, C. W. J. (1986) Developments in the Study of Cointegrated Economic Variables. *Oxford Bulletin of Economics and Statistics*, 48, 213–228.

Grant, D. (1984) Rolling the Hedge Forward: An Extension. *Financial Management*, 13, 26–28.

Grant, S., Kajii, A. and Polak, B. (2001) Different Notions of Disappointment Aversion. *Economics Letters*, 70, 203–208.

Gul, F. (1991) A Theory of Disappointment Aversion. *Econometrica*, 59, 667–686.

Hancock, G. D. and Weise, P. D. (1994) Competing Derivative Equity Instruments: Empirical Evidence on Hedged Portfolio Performance. *Journal of Futures Markets*, 14, 421–436.

Harvey, A. C., Ruiz, E. and Shephard, N. (1994) Multivariate Stochastic Variance Models. *Review of Economic Studies*, 61, 247–264.

Heynen, R. C. and Kat, H. M. (1994) Volatility Prediction: A Comparison of the Stochastic Volatility, GARCH (1,1), and EGARCH (1,1) Models. *Journal of Derivatives*, 2, 50–65.

Hilliard, J. E. (1997) Analytics Underlying the Metallgesellschaft Hedge: Short Term Futures in a Multi-Period Environment. *mimeo*. University of Georgia.

Honda, Y. (1983) Production Uncertainty and the Input Decision of the Competitive Firm Facing the Futures Market. *Economics Letters*, 11, 87–92.

Howard, C. T. and D'Antonio, L. J. (1991) Multiperiod Hedging Using Futures: A Risk Minimization Approach in the Presence of Autocorrelation. *Journal of Futures Markets*, 11, 697–710.

Ingersoll, J. (1987) *Theory of Financial Decision Making*. Rowman & Littlefield: Totowa, NJ.

Johnson, L. (1960) The Theory of Hedging and Speculation in Commodity Futures. *Review of Economic Studies*, 27, 139–151.

Kahneman, D. and Tversky, A. (1979) Prospect Theory: An Analysis of Decision Under Risk. *Econometrica*, 47, 263–291.

Kang, T., Brorsen, B. W. and Adam, B. D. (1996) A New Efficiency Criterion: The Mean-Separated Target Deviation Risk Model. *Journal of Economics and Business*, 48, 47–66.

Kolb, R. W. and Okunev, J. (1992) An Empirical Evaluation of the Extended Mean-Gini Coefficient for Futures Hedging. *Journal of Futures Markets*, 12, 177–186.

Kolb, R. W. and Okunev, J. (1993) Utility Maximizing Hedge Ratios in the Extended Mean-Gini Framework. *Journal of Futures Markets*, 13, 597–609.

Korsvold. P. E. (1994) Hedging Efficiency of Forward and Option Currency Contracts. Working Papers in Economics, No. 195, Department of Economics, University of Sydney.

Kroner, K. F. and Sultan, J. (1993) Time Varying Distribution and Dynamic Hedging with Foreign Currency Futures. *Journal of Financial and Quantitative Analysis*, 28, 535–551.

Lapan, H., Moschini, G. and Hanson, S. D. (1991) Production, Hedging, and Speculative Decisions with Options and Futures Markets. *American Journal of Agricultural Economics*, 73, 66–74.

Lence, S. H. (1995a) On the Optimal Hedge under Unbiased Futures Prices. *Economics Letters*, 47, 385–388.

Lence, S. H. (1995b) The Economic Value of Minimum-Variance Hedges. *American Journal of Agricultural Economics*, 77, 353–364.

Lence, S. H. and Hayenga, M. L. (2000) On the Pitfalls of Multi-Year Rollover Hedges: The Case of Hedge-To-Arrive Contracts. *American Journal of Agricultural Economics*, forthcoming.

Lence, S. H. and Hayes, D. J. (1994a) The Empirical Minimum-Variance Hedge. *American Journal of Agricultural Economics*, 76, 94–104.

Lence, S. H. and Hayes, D. J. (1994b) Parameter-Based Decision Making Under Estimation Risks: An Application in Futures Trading. *Journal of Finance*, 49, 345–357.

Lien, D. (1992) Optimal Hedging and Spreading in Cointegrated Markets. *Economics Letters*, 40, 91–95.

Lien, D. (1996) The Effect of the Cointegration Relationship on Futures Hedging: A Note. *Journal of Futures Markets*, 16, 773–780.

Lien, D. (1997) Forwards or Options: A Correction. *Journal of Futures Markets*, 17, 975–978.

Lien, D. (1999a) Stochastic Volatility and Futures Hedging. *Advances in Futures and Options Research*, 10, 253–265.

Lien, D. (1999b) Uncertain Tax Rules and Futures Hedging. *Managerial and Decision Economics*, 20, 429–436.

Lien, D. (2000a) Production and Hedging under Knightian Uncertainty. *Journal of Futures Markets*, 20, 397–404.

Lien, D. (2000b) A Note on Loss Aversion and Futures Hedging. *Journal of Futures Markets*, forthcoming.

Lien, D. (2001) Futures Hedging under Disappointment Aversion. *Journal of Futures Markets*, forthcoming.

Lien, D. and Luo, X. (1993) Estimating Extended Mean-Gini Coefficient for Futures Hedging. *Journal of Futures Markets*, 13, 665–676.

Lien, D. and Luo, X. (1994) Multiperiod Hedging in the Presence of Conditional Heteroskedasticity. *Journal of Futures Markets*, 14, 927–955.

Lien, D. and Metz, M. (2000) Hedging Downside Risk under Asymmetric Taxation. *Journal of Futures Markets*, 20, 361–374.

Lien, D. and Shaffer, D. (1999) A Note on Estimating the Minimum Extended Gini Hedge Ratio. *Journal of Futures Markets*, 19, 101–113.

Lien, D. and Shaffer, D. (2000) Multiperiod Strip Hedging of Forward Commitments. *Review of Quantitative Finance and Accounting*, forthcoming.

Lien, D. and Tse, Y. K. (1998) Hedging Time-Varying Downside Risk. *Journal of Futures Markets*, 18, 705–722.

Lien, D. and Tse, Y. K. (1999) Fractional Cointegration and Futures Hedging. *Journal of Futures Markets*, 19, 457–474.

Lien, D. and Tse, Y. K. (2000a) Hedging Downside Risk with Futures Contracts. *Applied Financial Economics*, 10, 163–170.

Lien, D. and Tse, Y. K. (2000b) Hedging Downside Risk: Futures versus Options. *International Review of Economics and Finance*, forthcoming.

Lien, D. and Tse, Y. K. (2000c) A Note on the Length Effect of Futures Hedging. *Advances in Investment Analysis and Portfolio Management*, 7, 131–143.

Lien, D., Tse, Y. K. and Tsui, A. K. C. (2001) Evaluating the Hedging Performance of the Constant-Correlation GARCH Models. *Applied Financial Economics*, forthcoming.

Lien, D. and Wilson, B. (2000) Multiperiod Hedging in the Presence of Stochastic Volatility. *International Review of Financial Analysis*, forthcoming.

Mathews, K. H. and Holthausen, D. M. (1991) A Simple Multiperiod Minimum Risk Hedge Model. *American Journal of Agricultural Economics*, 73, 1020–1026.

McCabe, G. M. and Franckle, C. T. (1983) The Effectiveness of Rolling the Hedge Forward in the Treasury Bill Futures Market. *Financial Management*, 12, 21–29.

Mehra, R. and Prescott, E. C. (1985) The Equity Premium: A Puzzle. *Journal of Monetary Economics*, 15, 145–162.

Mello, A. S. and Parsons, J. E. (1995) The Maturity Structure of a Hedge Matters: Lessons from the Metallgesellschaft Debacle. *Journal of Applied Corporate Finance*, 8, 106–120.

Myers, R. J. (1991) Estimating Time-Varying Optimal Hegde Ratios on Futures Markets. *Journal of Futures Markets*, 11, 39–53.

Myers, R. J. and Hanson, S. D. (1996) Optimal Dynamic Hedging in Unbiased Futures Markets. *American Journal of Agricultural Economics*, 78, 13–20.

Myers, R. J. and Thompson, S. R. (1989) Generalized Optimal Hedge Ratio Estimation. *American Journal of Agricultural Economics*, 71, 858–868.

Neuberger, A. (1995) Hedging Long-Term Exposures with Multiple Short-Term Futures Contracts. *Review of Financial Studies*, 12, 429–459.

Park, T. H. and Switzer, L. N. (1995) Bivariate GARCH Estimation of the Optimal Hedge Ratios for Stock Index Futures. *Journal of Futures Markets*, 15, 61–67.

Paroush, J. and Wolf, A. (1986) Production and Hedging Decisions with Futures and Forward Markets. *Economics Letters*, 21, 139–143.

Patel, J. K. and Read, C. B. (1982) *Handbook of the Normal Distributions*. Marcel Dekker: New York.

Petty, J. W. and Scott, D. F. (1981) Capital Budgeting Practice in Large American Firms: A Retrospective Analysis and Update. In: G. J. Derkinderen and R. L. Cruni (eds), *Readings in Strategies for Corporate Investment*. Pitman Publishing: Boston.

Pirrong, S. C. (1995) The Welfare Cost of Arkansas Best: The Inefficiency of Asymmetric Taxation of Hedging Gains and Losses. *Journal of Futures Markets*, 15, 111–129.

Pirrong, S. C. (1997) Metallgesellschaft: A Prudent Hegder Ruined, or a Wildcatter on NYMEX? *Journal of Futures Markets*, 17, 543–578.

Quan, J. (1992) Two-Step Testing Procedure for Price Discovery Role of Futures Prices. *Journal of Futures Markets*, 12, 129–139.

Rao, V. K. (2000) Preference-Free Optimal Hedging Using Futures. *Economics Letters*, 66, 223–228.

Rolfo, J. (1980) Optimal Hedging under Price and Quantity Uncertainty: The Case of a Cocoa Producer. *Journal of Political Economy*, 88, 100–116.

Ross, S. A. (1997) Hedging Long Run Commitments: Exercises in Incomplete Market Pricing. *Economic Notes*, 26, 385–419.

Roy, A. D. (1952) Safety First and the Holding of Assets. *Econometrica*, 20, 431–449.

Shalit, H. (1995) Mean-Gini Hedging in Futures Markets. *Journal of Futures Markets*, 15, 617–635.

Shalit, H. and Yitzhaki, S. (1984) Mean-Gini, Portfolio Theory and the Pricing of Risky Assets. *Journal of Finance*, 38, 1449–1468.

Silverman, B. W. (1986) *Density Estimation for Statistics and Data Analysis*. Chapman and Hall: New York.

Sowell, F. (1992) Maximum Likelihood Estimation of Stationary Univariate Fractionally Integrated Time Series Models. *Journal of Econometrics*, 53, 165–188.

Steil, B. (1993) Currency Options and the Optimal Hedging of Contingent Foreign Exchange Exposure. *Economica*, 60, 413–431.

Stein, J. (1961) The Simultaneous Determination of Spot and Futures Prices. *American Economic Review*, 51, 1012–1025.

Tse, Y. K. (1995) Lead–Lag Relationship between Spot and Futures Prices of the Nikkei Stock Average. *Journal of Forecasting*, 14, 553–563..

Tversky, A. and Kahneman, D. (1992) Advances in Prospect Theory: Cumulative Representation of Uncertainty. *Journal of Risk and Uncertainty*, 5, 297–323.

Uhlig, H. (1997) Bayesian Vector Autoregressions with Stochastic Volatility. *Econometrica*, 65, 59–73.

Vinod, H. D. (1997) A Looser Cointegration Concept Using Fractional Integration Parameters and Quantification of Market Responsiveness. *Journal of Statistical Planning and Inference*, forthcoming.

Viswanath, P. V. (1993) Efficient Use of Information, Convergence Adjustments, and Regression Estimates of Hedge Ratios. *Journal of Futures Markets*, 13, 43–53.

Wahab, M. and Lashgari, M. (1993) Price Dynamics and Error Correction in Stock Index and Stock Index Futures Markets: A Cointegration Approach. *Journal of Futures Markets*, 13, 711–742.

Ware, R. and Winter (1988) Forward Markets, Currency Options and Hedging of Foreign Exchange Risk. *Journal of International Economics*, 25, 291–302.

Yitzhaki, S. (1982) Stochastic Dominance, Mean Variance, and Gini's Mean Difference. *American Economic Review*, 72, 178–185.

Yitzhaki, S. (1983) On an Extension of the Gini Inequality Index. *International Economic Review*, 24, 617–628.

Chapter 6

ASSET PRICING WITH OBSERVABLE
STOCHASTIC DISCOUNT FACTORS

Peter Smith and Michael Wickens

University of York

1. Introduction

The stochastic discount factor (SDF) model is rapidly emerging as the most general and convenient way to price assets. Most existing asset pricing methods can be shown to be particular versions of the SDF model. This includes the capital asset pricing model (CAPM) of Sharpe (1964), Lintner (1965) and Black (1972), the general equilibrium consumption-based inter-temporal capital asset pricing model (CCAPM) of Rubinstein (1976) and Lucas (1978), and even the Black-Scholes theorem for pricing options. A detailed analysis of the SDF model may be found in the book by Cochrane (2000), and in the surveys by Ferson (1995) and Campbell (1999).

Cochrane argues that there are two polar approaches to asset pricing: absolute and relative asset pricing. Absolute pricing involves pricing each asset with reference to its exposure to fundamental sources of macroeoconomic risk. This provides a positive theory of asset prices and is the typical academic approach. Relative asset pricing is less ambitious. It aims to price an asset with reference to the prices of other assets. CAPM (i.e. the 'beta' model) and the Black-Scholes theorem are examples of this. And bonds are commonly priced off the short rate. The SDF model can be used for both approaches. This survey focuses mainly on the absolute approach to asset pricing.

Another way to classify asset pricing models is whether they involve the use of observable or latent factors. Most of the research that has made explicit use of the SDF model has used latent factors. Sometimes an attempt is then made to give an economic interpretation to the estimated latent factors. Many studies that have implicitly used the SDF model (such as CAPM and CCAPM) have used observable factors. In this survey we seek to promote the explicit use of the SDF model with observable macroeconomic factors. The attraction of this approach is that it identifies the sources of risk, enables an assessment of their significance and offers the possibility of tilting portfolios to provide a hedge against these risks.

This approach is not without its problems. In the SDF model risk is measured by the conditional covariance of returns with the factors. For risk premia to be time-varying the factors must exhibit conditional heteroskedasticity. The drawback with using observable macroeconomic factors is that they do not display much heteroskedasticity, especially when the data are quarterly, or of lower frequency. There is more evidence of heteroskedasticity at higher frequencies, but there is not much data on macroeconomic variables at monthly or higher frequencies. Related problems are that the statistical models tend to be highly parameterised, and there is a lack of heteroskedasticity in macroeconomic variables. Together they make it difficult to obtain statistically well-determined models.

The SDF model is not the only factor model of asset pricing. The well-known arbitrage pricing theory (APT) of Ross (1976, 1977) is an example of a factor pricing model. A key feature, not possessed by other factor pricing models, is that in the SDF model the factors are linear functions of the conditional covariances between the factors and the excess return on the risky asset. This is not true, for example, of the APT.

In the past much econometric work on asset pricing and tests of market efficiency made use of a vector autoregressive (VAR) model, see for example, Campbell and Shiller (1987, 1988) and Campbell, Lo and MacKinlay (1997). If the excess return is one of the variables in the VAR, then implicitly the risk premium is the right-hand side, i.e. the lag structure. Such a model can also be interpreted as a linear factor model in which the lagged variables are the factors. Usually no attempt is made to restrict the VAR to satisfy the no-arbitrage condition. It is not clear therefore what value this approach has except to test the joint hypothesis of market efficiency *and risk neutrality*, i.e. the expectations hypothesis. The null hypothesis is that the right-hand side variables are jointly insignificant. An exception to this, discussed later, occurs when certain affine factor models are used.

The paper is set out as follows. In Section 2 we discuss the SDF asset pricing model in general terms, setting out the theory and then relating this to specific implementations such as CCAPM, CAPM, affine factor models and APT. We then explain the implications of this for empirical finance. In Section 3 we discuss the econometric methodology commonly used in estimating SDF models. We include a discussion of VAR models, multivariate conditional heteroskedasticity models, simulation methods using the efficient method of moments and the generalised method of moments. We then consider applications of the SDF approach to the term structure (Section 4), the foreign exchange market (Section 5) and equity (Section 6). We review the use of unobservable and observable SDF models, and we suggest new ways to implement the observable SDF model using the multivariate generalised autoregressive conditional heteroskedasticity (GARCH)-in-mean specification. We report our conclusions in Section 7.

2. The SDF asset pricing model

The SDF model is based on a very simple proposition. The price of an asset in period t is the expected discounted value of the asset's pay-off in period $t + s$ based on information available in period t

$$P_t = E_t[M_{t+s}X_{t+s}] \qquad (1)$$

where P_t = the price of the asset in period t, X_{t+s} = the pay-off of the asset in period $t + s$, M_{t+s} = the discount factor for period $t + s$ ($0 \leqslant M_{t+s} \leqslant 1$), and E_t = the expectation taken with respect to information available in period t. Thus P_t is the current value of the period $t + s$ income X_{t+s}. In general this income will not be known in period t and will be a random variable. The discount factor is sometimes called the pricing kernel and will be a stochastic variable. For convenience, unless explicitly changed, hereafter we will assume that $s = 1$.

Equation (1) can also be written in terms of the asset's gross return $R_{t+1} = X_{t+1}/P_t = 1 + r_{t+1}$

$$1 = E_t\left[M_{t+1}\frac{X_{t+1}}{P_t}\right] = E_t[M_{t+1}R_{t+1}] \qquad (2)$$

Gross returns can be defined either in nominal or real terms; correspondingly, the discount factor must then also be expressed in nominal or real terms.

Examples of assets that can be priced in this way together with their pay-offs are:

1. A stock that pays a dividend of D_{t+1} and has a re-sale value of P_{t+1} at $t + 1$ has the pay-off $X_{t+1} = P_{t+1} + D_{t+1}$.
2. A T-bill that pays one unit of the consumption good regardless of the state of nature next period has $X_{t+1} = 1$.
3. A bond that has a constant coupon payment of C and can be sold for P_{t+1} next period has $X_{t+1} = P_{t+1} + C$.
4. A bank deposit that pays the risk-free rate of return r_t^f between t and $t + 1$ has $X_{t+1} = 1 + r_t^f$.

5. A call option costing P_t that gives the holder the right to purchase a stock at the exercise price K at date T has $X_{t+1} = \max[S_T - K, 0]$.

As

$$E_t(M_{t+1}R_{t+1}) = E_t(M_{t+1})E_t(R_{t+1}) + Cov_t(M_{t+1}R_{t+1}),   \quad (3)$$

the expected return on the asset is given by

$$E_t(R_{t+1}) = \frac{1 - Cov_t(M_{t+1}, R_{t+1})}{E_t(M_{t+1})}. \quad (4)$$

The conditional covariance between M_{t+1} and R_{t+1} can be estimated as the covariance of the error terms in the joint model of M_{t+1} and R_{t+1}, and possibly other variables.

Equation (4) holds whether the asset is risky or risk free. If it is risk free, then its pay-off in period $t + 1$ is known with certainty. Without loss of generality, this can be assumed to be 1. As a result, R_{t+1} will be known in period t and can be written as $R_{t+1} = 1 + r_t^f$, where r_t^f is the risk-free rate of return. Equation (2) can then be written as

$$1 = E_t[M_{t+1}(1 + r_t^f)] = (1 + r_t^f)E_t(M_{t+1}) \quad (5)$$

Thus $E_t(M_{t+1}) = 1/(1 + r_t^f)$. This carries the implication that the discount factor is the random variable $M_{t+1} = 1/(1 + r_t^f) + \xi_{t+1}$ where the random variable ξ_{t+1} has zero conditional mean, i.e. $E_t\xi_{t+1} = 0$.

The excess return over the risk-free rate is obtained by substituting equation (5) into (4) and using $R_{t+1} = 1 + r_{t+1}$ to give

$$E_t r_{t+1} - r_t^f = -(1 + r_t^f)Cov_t(M_{t+1}, R_{t+1})$$
$$= -(1 + r_t^f)Cov_t(M_{t+1}, r_{t+1} - r_t^f) \quad (6)$$

This is the no-arbitrage condition that all correctly priced assets must satisfy. The term on the right-hand side is the risk premium. It is the extra return over the risk-free rate that is required to compensate investors for holding the risky asset.

2.1. Risk

Since risk-averse investors require compensation for taking on risk, the risk premium must be non-negative. This implies that $Cov_t(M_{t+1}, R_{t+1}) \leqslant 0$. The source of the risk is that when the discount factor is in a high state, the return on the asset is in a low state. A risk-neutral investor is indifferent to such considerations and does not require a risk premium.

Another way to write (6), the no-arbitrage equation, is

$$\{E_t[r_{t+1} + (1 + r_t^f)Cov_t(M_{t+1}, R_{t+1})]\} - r_t^f = 0$$

The first term (in braces) is the expected return on a risky asset after adjusting for risk. It is also known as the expected return on the risky asset where expectations are taken with respect to the risk-neutral distribution, i.e. using E_t^N instead of E_t. In effect, to obtain the risk-neutral distribution, the true distribution is shifted to the left by subtracting the risk premium from $r_t + 1$. The risk-neutral distribution is used in pricing derivative assets such as options. Thus

$$E_t^N(r_{t+1}) = E_t[r_{t+1} + (1 + r_t^f)Cov_t(M_{t+1}, R_{t+1})] = r_t^f$$

Consequently, a self-financing portfolio consisting of borrowing at the risk-free rate and investing the proceeds in the risky asset will have zero expected return when the expected return on the risky asset is evaluated using its risk-neutral distribution.

The price and quantity of risk are concepts sometimes used in relation to the risk premium. They are analogous to the notion of total expenditure being equal to price multiplied by quantity. Thus

$$\text{risk premium} = \text{price of risk} \times \text{quantity of risk}$$

$$= -(1 + r_t^f)Cov_t(M_{t+1}, r_{t+1} - r_t^f)$$

$$= \beta_t \lambda_t$$

$$\beta_t = \text{price of risk} = -(1 + r_t^f) \frac{Cov_t(M_{t+1}, r_{t+1} - r_t^f)}{SD_t(r_{t+1} - r_t^f)}$$

$$\lambda_t = \text{quantity of risk} = SD_t(r_{t+1} - r_t^f)$$

where SD_t means the conditional standard deviation. The price of risk can also be written as

$$\beta_t = Cov_t \left[\frac{M_{t+1}}{E_t(M_{t+1})}, \frac{r_{t+1} - r_t^f}{SD_t(r_{t+1} - r_t^f)} \right].$$

This is also the conditional correlation coefficient, and the regression coefficient of $M_{t+1}/E_t(M_{t+1})$ on $(r_{t+1} - r_t^f)/SD_t(r_{t+1} - r_t^f)$ (or vice-versa). It measures the effect on the stochastic discount factor (scaled to be unit-free) of a unit change in the standardised excess return (also scale free), etc. The quantity of risk is just due to variability in the excess return.

We have not yet discussed how to specify the discount factor or, when it is unknown, what properties we expect it to possess. We can, however, derive bounds for both the risk premium and the discount factor. As they are free from any additional behavioural assumptions, these bounds might be useful when looking for suitable proxy variables for M_{t+1}.

If $\rho_t(M_{t+1}, r_{t+1})$ is denoted as the correlation coefficient of the joint conditional distribution of M_{t+1} and r_{t+1}, and $V_t(M_{t+1})$ and $V_t(R_{t+1})$ are their conditional variances, then

$$Cov_t(M_{t+1}, r_{t+1})^2 = \rho_t^2(M_{t+1}, r_{t+1})V_t(M_{t+1})V_t(r_{t+1})$$

$$\leqslant V_t(M_{t+1})V_t(r_{t+1}),$$

as $-1 \leqslant \rho_t(M_{t+1}, r_{t+1}) \leqslant 1$, this provides upper and lower bounds for the risk premium. As the risk premium must be non-negative, these are

$$0 \leqslant E_t(r_{t+1} - r_t^f) \leqslant (1 + r_t^f)SD_t(M_{t+1})SD_t(r_{t+1})$$

This provides a lower bound for $V_t(M_{t+1})$ that can be calculated from just knowledge of the returns and the conditioning information:

$$V_t(M_{t+1}) \geqslant \left[\frac{E_t(r_{t+1} - r_t^f)}{1 + r_t^f} \right]^2 \frac{1}{V_t(r_{t+1})}. \tag{7}$$

A widely used assumption, due partly to its convenience and because it is a reasonably good approximation, is that the stochastic discount factor and the gross return are jointly distributed as lognormal. If $\ln x$ is $N(\mu, \sigma^2)$ then $E(x) = \exp(\mu + \sigma^2/2)$ and hence $\ln E(x) = \mu + \sigma^2/2$. If $m_{t+1} = \ln M_{t+1}$ and $r_{t+1} = \ln R_{t+1}$ are jointly normally distributed then

$$1 = E_t[M_{t+1}R_{t+1}] = \exp\{E_t[\ln(M_{t+1}R_{t+1})] + V_t[\ln(M_{t+1}R_{t+1})]/2\}.$$

Taking logarithms yields

$$\ln E_t[M_{t+1}R_{t+1}] = E_t[\ln(M_{t+1}R_{t+1})] + V_t[\ln(M_{t+1}R_{t+1})]/2$$

$$= E_t(m_{t+1}) + E_t(r_{t+1}) + V_t(m_{t+1})/2 + V_t(r_{t+1})/2$$

$$+ cov_t(m_{t+1}, r_{t+1}) = 0. \tag{8}$$

When $r_{t+1} = r_t^f$, the risk-free rate, equation (8), becomes

$$E_t(m_{t+1}) + r_t^f + \tfrac{1}{2}V_t(m_{t+1}) = 0 \tag{9}$$

as $E_t(r_t^f) = r_t^f$ and $V_t(r_t^f) = 0$. Subtracting (9) from (8) produces the key no-arbitrage condition under log-normality:

$$E_t(r_{t+1} - r_t^f) + \tfrac{1}{2}V_t(r_{t+1}) = -Cov_t(m_{t+1}, r_{t+1}). \tag{10}$$

Comparing equations (10) and (6), apart from the switch to logarithms, (10) involves an additional term on the left-hand side, namely, half the conditional variance of returns. This is called the Jensen effect. It arises because expectations are being taken of a non-linear function, and $E[f(x)] \neq f[E(x)]$ unless $f(x)$ is linear. The right-hand side of (10) is the risk premium.

2.2. How to choose M_{t+1}?

The various asset pricing models differ primarily due to their choice of discount factor. This can be either an implicit or an explicit choice. Further, we can either use observable or unobservable (latent variable) factors. First we consider the two leading examples of implicit observable factor models, the consumption-based inter-temporal capital asset pricing model (CCAPM) and the capital asset pricing model (CAPM).

2.2.1. CCAPM

This is a general equilibrium model. All investments are evaluated in terms of $\mathcal{U}_t$, the investor's expected present value of current and future utility, where $U(C_t)$ is utility in period t and C_t is real consumption of goods and services. The investor's problem in period t is to choose consumption C_{t+s}, and the real stock of financial assets W_{t+s+1}, for all $s \geqslant 0$, subject to the investor's budget constraint. Assuming time-separable utility, the problem can be solved using stochastic dynamic programming. It can be written:

$$\max_{C_t} \{\mathcal{U}_t = U(C_t) + \beta E_t(\mathcal{U}_{t+1})\} \tag{11}$$

subject to the budget constraint

$$C_t + W_{t+1} = Y_t + W_t R_t \tag{12}$$

where Y_t is real income, R_t is the real gross return on equity, $0 \leqslant \beta = 1/(1+\theta) \leqslant 1$ is the discount factor for preferences and θ the corresponding rate of discount. The solution is the Euler equation

$$E_t\left[\frac{\beta U'(C_{t+1})}{U'(C_t)} R_{t+1}\right] = 1. \tag{13}$$

Comparing this with equation (2), we can see that CCAPM has implicitly defined the SDF (or pricing kernel) as

$$M_{t+1} = \frac{\beta U'(C_{t+1})}{U'(c_t)} \simeq \beta(1 - \sigma_t \Delta \ln C_{t+1}) \tag{14}$$

where $\sigma_t = -C_t U''_t / U'_t > 0$ is the coefficient of relative risk aversion. Hence, the no-arbitrage condition for the real rate of return on a risky asset is

$$E_t(r_{t+1} - r_t^f) = \beta(1 + r_t^f)\sigma_t Cov_t(\Delta \ln C_{t+1}, r_{t+1}) \tag{15}$$

If we assume that $\Delta \ln C_{t+1}$ and r_{t+1} are jointly lognormal then, using $m_{t+1} \simeq -(\theta + \sigma_t \Delta \ln C_{t+1})$, we obtain the no-arbitrage condition

$$E_t(r_{t+1} - r_t^f) + \tfrac{1}{2}V_t(r_{t+1}) = \sigma_t Cov_t(\Delta \ln C_{t+1}, r_{t+1}). \tag{16}$$

Equations (15) and (16) both imply that the greater the correlation between consumption growth and the risky return, the higher the risk premium, i.e. lower future returns are associated with lower future consumption growth, a common feature of the business cycle.

For the special case of the widely-used power utility function

$$U(C_t) = \frac{C_t^{1-\sigma} - 1}{1 - \sigma} \tag{17}$$

which has constant coefficient of relative risk aversion σ,

$$M_{t+1} = \beta \left(\frac{C_{t+1}}{C_t} \right)^{-\sigma} \simeq \beta(1 - \sigma\Delta \ln C_{t+1}) \tag{18}$$

In applications to equity pricing it was found that CCAPM produced a risk premium that is too low. This result is known as the equity premium puzzle, see Mehra and Prescott (1985). The failure of CCAPM has been attributed to a lack of sufficient volatility in the stochastic discount factor to match that of equity returns. Inspection of equation (16) shows that this failure could be due either to too low volatility in the consumption growth rate, or to a too low a coefficient of relative risk aversion, σ_t, or to both. As shown by Mehra and Prescott, implausibly large values of σ_t are required to eliminate the equity premium puzzle. This led to a search for utility functions that produce a larger risk premium. Attention focused on the assumption of time separable utility.

An example of the alternative of time non-separable utility is the habit persistence model where $U_t = U(C_t, X_t)$ and X_t is the habitual level of consumption. Constantinides (1990) proposed the form

$$U_t = \frac{(C_t - \lambda X_t)^{1-\sigma} - 1}{1 - \sigma}$$

The stochastic discount factor implied by this is $M_{t+1} = \beta((C_{t+1} - \lambda X_{t+1})/(C_t - \lambda X_t))^{-\sigma}$. By a suitable choice of λ and X_t it is possible to produce a discount factor that displays greater volatility and hence a larger risk premium. Later, we shall consider habit persistence models in more detail together with other versions of the habit persistence model, and also their implementation.

A second example of time non-separable utility has been proposed by Kreps-Porteus (1978). Their general formulation is

$$\mathcal{U}_t = \mathcal{U}[C_t, E_t(\mathcal{U}_{t+1})]$$

Epstein-Zin (1989, 1990, 1991) have implemented a special case of this based on the constant elasticity of substitution (CES) function. This is

$$\mathcal{U}_t = [(1 - \beta)C_t^{1 - 1/\gamma} + \beta(E_t(\mathcal{U}_{t+1}^{1-\sigma}))^{(1 - 1/\gamma)/(1 - \sigma)}]^{1/(1 - 1/\gamma)}$$

where β = the discount factor, σ = the coefficient of relative risk aversion and γ = the elasticity of inter-temporal substitution. Thus, whereas the additively separable inter-temporal utility function restricts the coefficient of relative risk aversion and the elasticity of inter-temporal substitution to be identical, the time non-separable model allows them to be different. Epstein and Zin show that maximising $\mathcal{U}_t$ subject to the slightly different budget constraint $W_{t+1} = R^m_{t+1}(W_t - C_t)$, where $r^m_{t+1} = R^m_{t+1} - 1$ is the return on the portfolio of invested wealth, gives the following asset pricing equation for any individual asset:

$$E_t\left\{\left[\left[\beta\left(\frac{C_{t+1}}{C_t}\right)^{-1/\gamma}\right]^{(1-\sigma)/(1-1/\gamma)}(R^m_{t+1})^{1-(1-\sigma)/(1-1/\gamma)}R_{t+1}\right\} = 1. \quad (19)$$

Thus the stochastic discount factor is

$$M_{t+1} = \left[\beta\left(\frac{C_{t+1}}{C_t}\right)^{-1/\gamma}\right]^{(1-\sigma)/(1-1/\gamma)}(R^m_{t+1})^{1-(1-\sigma)/(1-1/\gamma)} \quad (20)$$

Compared with time separable utility, this has two additional degrees of freedom which can boost the size of the risk premium. First, the power index is no longer the coefficient of relative risk aversion, and is therefore free to take on large values. Second, M_{t+1} now varies with the return on the portfolio. Assuming log-normality, Campbell, Lo and MacKinlay (1997) have rewritten the no-arbitrage condition equation (19) as

$$E_t(r_{t+1} - r^f_t) + \tfrac{1}{2}V_t(r_{t+1}) = \frac{1-\sigma}{1-\gamma}Cov_t(\Delta \ln C_{t+1}, r_{t+1})$$

$$+ \left(1 + \frac{\gamma(1-\sigma)}{1-\gamma}\right)Cov_t(r^m_{t+1}, r_{t+1}) \quad (21)$$

Thus, this more general class of inter-temporal utility functions is also an SDF model with observable factors. Equation (21) has two factors, consumption growth and the portfolio (or market) return. The last term in equation (21) is a potential additional source of risk. We examine evidence on the Epstein-Zin model below. A footnote presents an alternative derivation of the Euler equation.[1]

2.2.2. CAPM

Static CAPM relates the expected excess return on the risky asset over the risk-free rate to the excess return of the market portfolio, r^m_{t+1} which is given by $(1 + r^m_{t+1}) = (W_{t+1})/W_t$, where W_t is wealth. The key results are:

$$E_t(r_{t+1} - r^f_t) = \beta_t E_t(r^m_{t+1} - r^f_t),$$

$$\beta_t = \frac{Cov_t(r^m_{t+1}, r_{t+1})}{V_t(r^m_{t+1})} \quad (22)$$

$$E_t(r^m_{t+1} - r^f_t) = \sigma_t V_t(r^m_{t+1}).$$

Thus the risk premium depends in part on the market return. But we can also write equation (22) as

$$E_t(r_{t+1} - r_t^f) = \sigma_t Cov_t(r_{t+1}^m, r_{t+1}) = \sigma_t Cov_t\left(\frac{\Delta W_{t+1}}{W_t}, r_{t+1}\right).$$

This shows that the risk premium arises from the conditional covariance of the asset's return with the market return or, equivalently, the rate of growth of wealth. We conclude therefore that, in effect, CAPM is an SDF model in which the discount factor is $\sigma_t(1 + r_{t+1}^m)$ or $\sigma_t \Delta W_{t+1}/W_t$. In implementing CAPM there is some disagreement about which assets should be included in wealth. In principle all assets should be included, but in practice it is common to use only financial wealth.

Comparing CCAPM — and in particular equation (15) — with CAPM, we observe that CCAPM uses the covariance of consumption growth with the risky asset to measure risk while CAPM uses the covariance of the growth rate of wealth with the risky asset. If consumption is proportional to wealth, then the determination of the risk premia in CAPM and CCAPM are identical. Apart from CAPM and CCAPM the problem of how to implement the stochastic discount factor model remains. How might we model the discount factor (or pricing kernel) M_{t+1} without making either of these assumptions?

2.3. Multi-factor models

CAPM and CCAPM under time separability are examples of single-factor models. CAPM assumes that the stochastic discount factor is $M_{t+1} = \sigma_t \times (1 + r_{t+1}^m)$, time-separable CCAPM assumes that it is $M_{t+1} = \beta U_{t+1}'/U_t' \simeq \beta[1 - \sigma_t \Delta \ln C_{t+1}]$. In each case, for $\sigma_t = \sigma$, a constant, we can write

$$M_{t+1} = a + bz_{t+1}$$

or, assuming log-normality,

$$\ln M_{t+1} = m_{t+1} = a + bz_{t+1}$$

where z_{t+1} is r_{t+1}^m or $\Delta \ln C_{t+1}$. Multi-factor generalisations are:

$$M_{t+1} = \alpha + \sum_i b_i z_{i,t+1},$$

$$\ln M_{t+1} = m_{t+1} = a + \sum_i b_i z_{i,t+1}.$$

Because these are linear models, they are also called *affine* factor models (meaning linear).

The implication for asset pricing is that

$$E_t(r_{t+1} - r_t^f) = -(1 + r_t^f)Cov_t(M_{t+1}, r_{t+1})$$

$$= -(1 + r_t^f) \sum_i b_i Cov_t(z_{i,t+1}, r_{t+1}) = \sum_i \beta_i f_{it}, \qquad (23)$$

or, assuming log-normality,

$$E_t(r_{t+1} - r_t^f) + \tfrac{1}{2}V_t(r_{t+1}) = -Cov_t(m_{t+1}, r_{t+1})$$

$$= -\sum_i b_i Cov_t(z_{i,t+1}, r_{t+1}) = \sum_i \beta_i f_{it},$$

where the f_{it} are known as *common factors*. Time non-separable CCAPM and CAPM are respectively examples of factor SDF models where the factors are in $\Delta \ln C_{t+1}$ and r_{r+1}^m. If returns are nominal and not real then CCAPM has two factors: $\Delta \ln C_{t+1}$ and π_{t+1}, the inflation rate.

2.4. *Latent variable affine factor models*

We now consider explicit but unobservable factor models. The most widely-used are the latent variable affine factor models of Vasicek (1977) and Cox, Ingersoll and Ross (1985). Both assume that the logarithm of the stochastic discount factor m_{t+1} can be expressed as a linear function of one or more random variables each of which follows a mean-reverting first-order autoregressive process. Moreover, instead of m_{t+1} being an exact linear function of the factors as above, allowance is made for an additional random error. We illustrate these models using the single factor z_{t+1}.

2.4.1. *Vasicek model*

In the Vasicek model it is assumed that

$$m_{t+1} = \alpha + \beta z_{t+1} + \lambda \sigma \varepsilon_{t+1}$$
$$z_{t+1} - \mu = \theta(z_t - \mu) + \sigma \varepsilon_{t+1}, \qquad 0 \leqslant |\theta| < 1 \qquad (24)$$

where $e_{t+1} \sim iid(0, 1)$. These assumptions imply that m_{t+1} is the ARMA(1, 1):

$$m_{t+1} = (\alpha + \beta\mu)(1 - \theta) + \theta m_t + (\lambda + \beta)\sigma\varepsilon_{t+1} - \theta\lambda\sigma\varepsilon_t.$$

Using the log-normal version of the asset pricing model, the no-arbitrage equation becomes

$$E_t(r_{t+1} - r_t^f) + \tfrac{1}{2}V_t(r_{t+1}) = -Cov_t(m_{t+1}, r_{t+1})$$
$$= -(\lambda + \beta)\sigma Cov_t(\varepsilon_{t+1}, r_{t+1}).$$

2.4.2. Cox, Ingersoll and Ross (CIR) model

In this model it is assumed that

$$m_{t+1} = \alpha + \beta z_{t+1} + \lambda \sigma \sqrt{z_t} \varepsilon_{t+1}$$

$$z_{t+1} - \mu = \theta(z_t - \mu) + \sigma \sqrt{z_t} \varepsilon_{t+1}.$$

The attraction of the CIR model is that the return on the asset is bounded at, or above, zero. In the Vasicek model it can become negative. In the CIR model $V_t(z_{t+1}) = \sigma^2 z_t$, hence $\lim_{z_t \to 0} V_t(z_{t+1}) = 0$, i.e. as the factor approaches zero, its variance also converges to zero. The no-arbitrage equation is

$$E_t(r_{t+1} - r_t^f) + \tfrac{1}{2}V_t(r_{t+1}) = -(\lambda + \beta)\sigma\sqrt{z_t}Cov_t(\varepsilon_{t+1}, r_{t+1}).$$

The CIR model can be generalised to,

$$m_{t+1} = \alpha + \beta z_{t+1} + \lambda(z_t)\varepsilon_{t+1}$$

$$\Delta z_{t+1} = \mu(z_t) + \sigma(z_t)\varepsilon_{t+1}$$

A common version of this is to choose $\sigma(z_t) = \sqrt{\phi + \omega z_t}$ and $\lambda(z_t) = \lambda\sigma(z_t)$, see Dai and Singleton (2000). Later we show how this can be implemented for the term structure.

2.5. Multi-asset multi-factor models

The pricing equations derived so far refer to a single asset. The form of the pricing equation for every asset will be the same. If the return on the *jth* asset is $r_{j,t+1}$ then its no-arbitrage equation is

$$E_t(r_{j,t+1} - r_t^f) = -(1 + r_t^f)\sum_i b_{ij}Cov_t(z_{i,t+1}, r_{j,t+1}) \qquad (25)$$

The equivalent equation under log-normality is

$$E_t(r_{j,t+1} - r_t^f) + \tfrac{1}{2}V_t(r_{j,t+1}) = -\sum_i b_{ij}Cov_t(z_{i,t+1}, r_{j,t+1}) \qquad (26)$$

In matrix terms, equations (25) and (26) can be written

$$E_t(\mathbf{r}_{t+1} - r_t^f\ell) = -(1 + r_t^f)\mathscr{C}_t$$

$$E_t(\mathbf{r}_{t+1} - r_t^f\ell) + \tfrac{1}{2}\nu_t = -(1 + r_t^f)\mathscr{C}_t$$

where $\mathbf{r}_{t+1}$ is vector of returns, $\mathscr{C}_t$ is a column vector formed from the diagonal elements of $\mathbf{BV}_t$, where $\mathbf{B} = \{b_{ij}\}$ and $\mathbf{V}_t = \{Cov_t(z_{i,t+1}, r_{j,t+1})\}$, ν_t is column vector formed from the diagonal elements of $\mathbf{V}_t$ and ℓ is a vector of ones.

2.6. *Other types of factor models*

Some asset pricing models involve the use of factors but are not examples of SDF models — even implicitly. The best known example is APT. This satisfies the condition of no-arbitrage. Another widely used model in empirical finance, especially for testing market efficiency, is a VAR model in which the excess return on the risky assets is one of the variables. In general a VAR is neither an SDF model, nor does it satisfy the no-arbitrage condition. This calls into question such uses of a VAR in finance.

2.6.1. *Arbitrage Pricing Theorem (APT)*

This is one of the best-known multi-factor models of asset pricing. For a survey of APT see Connors and Korajczyk (1995). The basic idea underlying the APT is to avoid the formality of CAPM or CCAPM and simply model the return on any asset j as the sum of k common factors plus an idiosyncratic component that is uncorrelated with the common factors. These factors are sometimes assumed to be obtainable from the principal components of the returns on a vector of assets.

The return on the jth asset is

$$r_j = a_j + \sum_{i}^{k} b_{ij} f_i + \varepsilon_j, \qquad j = 1, ..., n, \tag{27}$$

where $E(\varepsilon_j) = 0$, and $E(\varepsilon_j, f_i) = 0$. In this expression, f_i are some variables useful for forecasting r_j, e.g. f_i are returns on other assets. Equation (27) therefore has the same form as (23). The difference lies primarily in the choice of factors, f_i and whether a risk-free asset exists.

The aim is to 'diversify away' the risk in asset j arising from the idiosyncratic component ε_j by forming no-arbitrage portfolios. A portfolio $r^P = \sum_{j+1}^{n} w_j r_j$ is a no-arbitrage portfolio if $r^P = 0$, with some $w_j < 0$. Hence, $0 = r^P = \sum_j w_j a_j + \sum_i^k (\sum_j^n w_j b_{ij}) f_i + \sum_j w_j \varepsilon_j$, where $w_n = 1 - \sum_{j=1}^{n-1} w_j$. In general therefore, each of the terms $\sum_j w_j a_j$, $\sum_j^n w_j b_{ij}$ and $\sum_j w_j \varepsilon_j$ will be zero. If one of the assets the nth (say) is risk-free, then $f_k = r_n = r^f$. The return on the no-arbitrage portfolio can then be written as

$$r^P + \sum_{j}^{n-1} w_j r_j + \left(1 - \sum_{j}^{n-1} w_j\right) r^f = \sum_{j}^{n-1} w_j (r_j - r^f) + r^f = 0$$

Hence, for any single asset, the excess return is

$$r_l - r^f = \sum_{i \neq j}^{n-1} \frac{w_j}{w_i} (r_j - r^f) = - \sum_{i \neq j}^{n-1} \frac{w_j}{w_i} \left\{ \left[a_j + \sum_{i}^{k-1} b_{ij} f_i + b_{kj} r^f + \varepsilon_j \right] - r^f \right\}$$

$$= \sum_{i}^{k-1} \beta_i f_i + \beta_f r^f$$

Thus the APT has factors f_i and r^f. Since f_i need not be a conditional covariance, the APT is not in general an SDF model.

2.7. *The implications of the SDF model for empirical finance*

So far the main broad conclusions to emerge for empirical finance are that, unless it is explicitly assumed that investors are risk neutral, a risk premium should be included in the model. The SDF approach shows that this is a (possibly linear) function of the conditional covariance between the factors and the excess return. This implies that in general in empirical finance the model must be multivariate, not univariate, as the joint distribution of the excess return and the factors is required to model the risk premium. Further, it is not sufficient simply to specify the model with a time-varying conditional covariance matrix. The model must also have the conditional covariances in the conditional mean of the excess return equation in order for this equation to satisfy the no-arbitrage condition. Very few of the models that have been used in empirical finance (to study, for example, equity, bonds or foreign exchange) satisfy these requirements.

Two qualifications may be made to these strictures, both of which are examined in more detail later. First, there is a special case where it is not necessary to explicitly include conditional covariances in the mean of an SDF model in order to satisfy the condition of no arbitrage, as the conditional covariances are included implicitly. In this case not all of the strictures above apply. This happens where, due to the assumed structure for the stochastic discount factor, the conditional covariances are functions of the variables themselves. An example is the CIR latent variable model of the term structure. It can be shown that, in the case of a single-factor model, the conditional covariance between the factor and the excess return on a long bond (and hence its risk premium) is a linear function of the short rate and hence, in effect, is an observable factor. If there is more than one factor, then the risk premium is a linear function of short and long rates. In these cases it would be possible to model the term structure using a VAR. We examine this idea further below. The no-arbitrage condition would imply restrictions on the coefficients of the VAR.

Second, it is often possible to estimate the parameters and to carry out statistical tests using the Euler equation itself. Solving the Euler equation to obtain an expression for the risky return would not then be necessary. An example of this approach is direct generalised method of moments (GMM) estimation of the Euler equation. The GMM estimator exploits the lack of correlation between the discounted pay-off and the information set used in conditioning. The null hypothesis is that

$$E[(M_{t+1}(\theta)(R_{t+1} - 1)I_t] = 0 \qquad (28)$$

or

$$E[(M_{t+1}(\theta)(r_{t+1} - r_t^f)I_t] = 0$$

where I_t is the information set and θ is the set of parameters to be estimated. The implication is that I_t contains no information about $M_{t+1}(\theta)(r_{t+1} - r_t^f)$, the discounted excess return in period $t + 1$. Nevertheless, the results above suggest that unless the information set has time varying volatility, it will be unlikely to prove suitable. Surprisingly perhaps, in practice, this has not usually been a consideration. If an estimate of the risk premium is required, GMM estimation of the Euler equation would not be appropriate. We now turn to a more detailed consideration of econometric methods.

3. Econometric Methods

To a large extent the choice of econometric methodology will be dictated by the SDF model being used. We discuss four different methods: the use of a VAR, multivariate conditional heteroskedasticity models, the efficient method of moments (a simulation estimator), and GMM. This is a large subject in its own right. To make it manageable, we focus on their application to observed factor models. Another estimation method commonly used for latent variable affine factor pricing models is the Kalman filter as this does not require data on the factors.

3.1. *VAR models*

There is a vast literature on the use of VAR models in empirical finance, see for example the surveys of Campbell, Lo and MacKinlay (1997) and Cuthbertson (1996). The VAR is typically specified in terms of the excess return and other variables appropriate to the underlying theory, or in terms of the returns themselves together with any other variables. When a vector of returns is used the coefficient matrix of the VAR is restricted to satisfy the no-arbitrage condition.

Despite its popularity it is our contention that, in general, using a VAR is not a valid way to estimate asset pricing models, or to test market efficiency. This is because for risk averse investors the no-arbitrage condition of asset pricing will require a risk premium and this involves conditional covariance terms. As a VAR does not include conditional covariances, in general, it is not an appropriate model to use.

There are two main exceptions to this for which a VAR may be appropriate. One is where risk neutrality is assumed, and so on the null hypothesis there is no risk premium. This is the assumption underlying the expectations or unbiasedness hypothesis. For a survey, see Bekaert and Hodrick (2001). Under the null hypothesis of unbiasedness none of the lags of the VAR should be non-zero in the equation for the excess return. When a vector of returns is used the unbiasedness hypothesis implies that the coefficient matrix of the VAR is restricted. The aim is then to test these restrictions.

It is not clear what can be inferred from a failure to reject the null hypothesis. It does not necessarily imply a lack of market efficiency, since if investors are risk averse, the model should have included a well-specified risk premium, or a suitable proxy for the risk premium. For an example of this, see Tzavalis and Wickens (1997) who show that rejection of the rational expectations hypothesis of the term structure (REHTS) is probably due to omitting the term premium. When the term premium is appropriately proxied in the VAR the REHTS is no longer rejected. The power of a test is likely to depend on whether a model is well specified on the alternative hypothesis. The absence of conditional covariance terms in these tests implies that the model is well not specified against the alternative hypothesis of risk aversion, and so may have low power.

Implicitly, the lagged variables in the VAR are acting as proxies for the risk premium. The second exception we mention, therefore, is where the right-hand side of the VAR is a suitable proxy for the risk premium. Without a careful consideration of how good a proxy the VAR provides, it should be assumed that it is not appropriate. Tzavalis and Wickens (1997) illustrate how this might be achieved in tests of the REHTS. Another exception is where the risk premium can be shown to be a linear function of the variables in the VAR. Although hardly ever exploited in the literature, it is shown below that the Vasicek and CIR affine factor models of the term structure have this implication. In the Vasicek model the risk premium is constant over time. In the CIR model it is a linear function of the yields.

3.2. *Multivariate conditional heteroskedasticity models*

Two important implications follow from equations (6) and (10). First, in general, econometric models that satisfy the no-arbitrage condition must have (time-varying) conditional covariance terms in the mean. Second, since covariance is a multi-variate concept, the econometric model will need to be multivariate and not univariate, and the conditional covariance will need to be modelled at the same time as everything else. These requirements eliminate much of the literature on financial econometrics from further consideration.

An obvious econometric model that does satisfy these requirements is the multivariate GARCH in-mean model, but not of course the multivariate GARCH model.[2] GARCH is preferred to ARCH on the grounds of its greater flexibility, and on the basis of previous empirical findings. We illustrate the use of the multivariate GARCH-in-mean (MGM) model under the assumption of log-normality. It is also possible to use other distributions such as the t-distribution, see Wickens and Smith (2001).

Many practical problems arise in using the MGM model. One is the computational problem of achieving numerical convergence due to the large number of parameters that need to be estimated. As a result, a trade-off arises between choosing a model that has sufficient flexibility, and one that is sufficiently parsimonious to be estimable. A second problem, is the availability of suitable observable factors. We would like to be able to identify the fundamental sources of risk, and for the most part these will be macroeconomic. The problem is that a time-varying risk premium requires conditional heteroskedasticity both in the excess return and the macroeconomic factors.

Even for returns, conditional heteroskedasticity tends to be observable only at frequencies of a month or higher (e.g. stock returns). There is very little macroeconomic data at frequencies higher than quarterly. The main macro-economic series likely to prove useful for our purposes that are available monthly are industrial production, retail sales, consumer price inflation and the money supply.

In principle, a multivariate stochastic volatility model could be used instead of the MGM model. The advantage of this would be the greater flexibility it offers in modelling volatility. When volatility is fluctuating violently — as it can over short periods — the coefficients of the GARCH process describing volatility struggle to capture these fluctuations. As a result, the GARCH process often displays a unit root in the variance. The advantage of a stochastic volatility model is that it includes a disturbance in the volatility process. This can be used to absorb extreme fluctuations in volatility, which should be of help computationally. The conceptual value of this is perhaps less clear. A practical problem is that, to our knowledge, to date no multivariate stochastic volatility model which includes the conditional second moments in the mean has been proposed in the literature.[3]

For a single asset, the MGM model must be capable of satisfying the no-arbitrage condition, equations (25) or (26), where the factors z_{it} are assumed to be observable. It follows that we require an MGM in the vector $\mathbf{x}_{t+1} = (r_{t+1} - r_t^f, z_{1,t+1}, z_{2,t+1}, ...)'$. We now require the conditional distribution of $\mathbf{x}_{t+1}$. This is obtained from the joint distribution of $\mathbf{x}_{t+1}$ and any variables required in the information set that are not simply past values of $\mathbf{x}_{t+1}$. This will ensure that the conditional distribution of $\mathbf{x}_{t+1}$ (including the conditional covariance terms) is well specified. The MGM model can be written

$$\mathbf{x}_{t+1} = \boldsymbol{\alpha} + \boldsymbol{\Gamma}\mathbf{x}_t + \boldsymbol{\Phi}\mathbf{g}_t + \varepsilon_{t+1} \tag{29}$$

where the distribution of ε_{t+1} conditional on I_t, information available at time t, is

$$\varepsilon_{t+1} \mid I_t \sim N[0, \mathbf{H}_{t+1}] \tag{30}$$

$$\mathbf{g}_t = vech\{\mathbf{H}_{t+1}\} \tag{31}$$

The *vech* operator converts the the lower triangle of a symmetric matrix into a vector. A key feature of this approach is that the first equation of (29) must be restricted so that it satisfies the condition of no arbitrage. Thus the first row of $\boldsymbol{\Gamma}$ is zero and the first row of $\boldsymbol{\Phi}$ is $(-\frac{1}{2}, -b_{11}, -b_{12}, -b_{13}, ...)$. Contrasting the MGM model with a VAR, we note that in a VAR $\boldsymbol{\Phi}$ is implicitly zero and $\mathbf{H}_{t+1}$ is assumed to be homoskedastic.[4]

The remaining specification issue is how to choose $\mathbf{H}_{t+1}$. There have been several good surveys of these issues, see for example Bollerslev (2001). A model with considerable generality is the BEKK model described and generalized in Engle and Kroner (1995). This can be formulated as

$$vech(\mathbf{H}_{t+1}) = \boldsymbol{\Lambda} + \sum_{i=0}^{p-1} \boldsymbol{\Phi}_i vech(\mathbf{H}_{t-i}) + \sum_{j=0}^{q-1} \boldsymbol{\Theta}_j vech(\varepsilon_{t-j}\varepsilon'_{t-j}) \tag{32}$$

where the matrices $\mathbf{\Lambda}$, $\mathbf{\Phi}$ and $\mathbf{\Theta}$ may be unrestricted. If there are $n-1$ factors z_{it} then $\mathbf{\Phi}$ and $\mathbf{\Theta}$ are both square matrices of size $n(n+1)/2$ and $\mathbf{\Lambda}$ is a size $n(n+1)/2$ vector.

A variant of the BEKK model that ensures the time-varying covariance matrices are symmetric and positive definite, and involves far fewer coefficients, is to specify the conditional covariance matrix as an error correction model (ECM)

$$\mathbf{H}_{t+1} = \mathbf{V}'\mathbf{V} + \mathbf{A}'(\mathbf{H}_t - \mathbf{V}'\mathbf{V})\mathbf{A} + \mathbf{B}'(\varepsilon_t\varepsilon_t' - \mathbf{V}'\mathbf{V})\mathbf{B}. \tag{33}$$

The first term on the right-hand side of equation (33) is the long-run, or unconditional, covariance matrix. The other two terms capture the short-run deviation from the long run. This formulation enables us to see more easily how volatility in the short run differs from that in the long run. To reduce the number of parameters further, we can specify $\mathbf{V}$ to be lower triangular and $\mathbf{A}$ and $\mathbf{B}$ to be symmetric matrices.

A specification that involves even fewer parameters is the constant correlation model. This has been found by Ding and Engle (1994) to give a fairly good performance in comparison with the more general BEKK model. It can be written

$$\mathbf{h}_{ij,t+1} = \rho_{ij}[\mathbf{h}_{ii,t+1} \times \mathbf{h}_{jj,t+1}]^{1/2} \tag{34}$$

$$\mathbf{h}_{ii,t+1} = v_i + a_i\mathbf{h}_{ii,t} + b_i\varepsilon_{it}^2 \tag{35}$$

where ρ_{ij} is the (constant) correlation between $\varepsilon_i(t+1)$ and $\varepsilon_j(t+1)$. The conditional variances $\mathbf{h}_{ii}(t+1)$ each have a GARCH(1,1) structure.

It is instructive to compare the number of parameters involved in each of these formulations. If $n=3$ and $p=q=1$, then we find that BEKK $= n(n+1)/2 + (p+q)n^2(n+1)^2/4 = 78$, ECM unrestricted $= 3n^2 = 27$, ECM restricted $= 3n(n+1)/2 = 18$, and constant correlation $= 3n + n(n-1)/2 = 12$. Ideally, we would choose the most general model, but it is clear that this involves estimating a very large number of parameters. The ECM may be a useful compromise. But sometimes the constant correlation model may be the best that one can achieve. Further variants of these models can, of course, be considered.

3.3. *Efficient Method of Moments (EMM)*

The EMM estimator is an alternative way to estimate equations with unobservable variables. It is particularly suitable for more general affine models than the Vasicek model, for non-Gaussian distributions and where dependencies in the processes for the (unobserved) state variables make evaluation of the likelihood function impossible. Estimation of the CIR affine model is such a case. Simulation-based method of moments estimators have been developed to analyse dynamic highly non-linear models such as these. Variants of these methods were originally proposed by Gallant and Tauchen (1996) (EMM), Duffie and Singleton (1993) and Ingram and Lee (1991) (Simulated Method of Moments) and Smith A. (1993) and Gourieroux, Monfort and Renault (1993) (Indirect Inference).

The EMM method proceeds in two stages. In the first stage, an auxiliary model to the theoretical (or structural) model is chosen whose variables are observable and whose likelihood can be evaluated. The score of the likelihood for this model can then be evaluated using a GMM criterion where data for the dependent variables of interest (here the returns) is generated by simulation of the dynamic non-linear structural model. If the auxiliary model is a 'good' approximation of the structural model, Gallant and Long (1997) show that the EMM estimator will be asymptotically efficient. If the structural model is close to the true model, the GMM criterion will be close to zero.

Using the affine models above as an example, let $f(y_t, \Omega)$ be the auxiliary model where the returns y_t are determined by past values of returns $x_{t-1} = (y_{t-1}, y_{t-2}, \ldots y_{t-j})$ with parameter Ω. This could be thought of as a reduced-form equation. The score of the maximised likelihood function for this model can be evaluated for two sets of data for current and past values of the returns. First, for the actual data we know that the average of the scores must be zero i.e.

$$\frac{1}{T} \sum_{t=1}^{T} \frac{\partial}{\partial \Omega} \ln f(y_t \mid x_{t-1}, \Omega) = 0 \tag{36}$$

as these are the first-order conditions for a maximum. The EMM proceeds by replacing both y_t and x_{t-1} with values $\bar{y}_t$ and $\bar{x}_{t-1}$ generated by simulation of the structural model $g(y_t, x_{t-1}, \beta)$ for a particular set of parameters β. The resulting scores are then

$$S(\beta, \tilde{\Omega}) = \frac{1}{T} \sum_{t=1}^{T} \frac{\partial}{\partial \Omega} \ln f(\bar{y}_t \mid \bar{x}_{t-1}, \tilde{\Omega}) \tag{37}$$

EMM then proceeds by choosing estimates of structural parameters β that minimise the GMM criterion

$$S'(\beta, \tilde{\Omega}). \, W.S(\beta, \tilde{\Omega}) \tag{38}$$

for a weighting matrix W.

Recent research reviewed by Gallant and Tauchen (2001) shows that the choice of auxiliary function $f(y_t \mid x_{t-1}, \Omega)$ is crucial to the performance of the EMM estimator. On the one hand it needs to be computationally simple enough to make repeated solution not excessively burdensome. On the other hand it needs to be close to the theoretical model to deliver maximum likelihood estimates — were they to exist. Gallant and Tauchen (1996, 2001) propose the use of a semi-non parametric (SNP) auxiliary function. Others have concentrated on choosing a function which matches characteristics of the data. In evaluating various affine models of the term structure Dai and Singleton (2000) choose an SNP function they describe as a 'non-Gaussian, VAR(1), ARCH(2), Homogenous-Innovation' function. This attempts to capture the non-Gaussian dependencies in bond returns.

The evaluation of models estimated by EMM can be more intuitive than for a likelihood-based method in that elements of the score can be examined along with the t-statistics associated with them. The testing of individual components of the score allows particular areas of model weakness to be identified. Following a similar logic, van der Sluis (1998) presents various tests of structural stability for the EMM estimator.

The computational burden of simulating the full structural model for each candidate set of structural parameters has limited the scale of the models which have been evaluated using this technique. A closely associated, more limited information, estimation method is direct estimation by GMM but evaluating a limited set of moments.

3.4. *Generalised Method of Moments (GMM)*

GMM is a non-linear instrumental variables estimator originally proposed by Hansen (1982) and widely employed in estimating affine and other non-linear asset pricing models. It is particularly suited to the direct estimation of the Euler equation and avoids the need to solve for the risky rate of return. The robustness of GMM to heteroskedasticity has encouraged its use with financial data. Comprehensive presentations of GMM are available in Hall (1992) and Hamilton (1994).

In implementing the estimation of equation (39) by GMM, the information set I_t consists of a set of instruments h_t. We define the set of moments that are being set equal to zero as $E[f_t(\theta)]$. Hence,

$$E[f_t(\theta)] = E[M_{t+1}(\theta)(R_{t+1} - 1) \otimes h_t] = 0 \qquad (39)$$

where $\otimes$ is the Kronecker product. The model and the errors have the property that there exists a true set of parameters θ_0 for which the error vector is orthogonal to the set of instruments h_t. Defining the sample average of $f_t(\theta)$ as $g_T(\theta) = T^{-1} \sum_{t=1}^{t} f_t(\theta)$, the GMM estimator minimises $Q_T(\theta) \equiv g_T(\theta)'.W_T.g_T(\theta)$ where $W_T = 1/T \sum f_t(y_t, \tilde{\theta}).f_t(y_t, \tilde{\theta})'$ is a weighting matrix and $\tilde{\theta}$ is a consistent estimate of θ. The first-order conditions are $D_T(\hat{\theta}_T)'.W_T.g_T(\hat{\theta}) = 0$ where $D_T(\theta_T) = \partial g_T(\theta)/\partial \theta$. The variance of the estimator of θ is $\Omega = ((D_T(\hat{\theta}_T)'.W_T.D_T(\hat{\theta}_T))^{-1}$.

Given that W_T must itself be estimated, asymptotically efficient estimates can be obtained in two steps. First an arbitrary weighting matrix W can be used to obtain an initial set of consistent estimates $\tilde{\theta}$. Second, these estimates can be used to construct a second weighting matrix W_T and thence efficient estimates. It has been shown that in large-scale systems the finite sample performance of GMM can be improved by further iterations (see Ferson and Foerster (1994)). A further attractive feature of GMM is that the error ε_t can be heteroskedastic and autocorrelated. In the case of autocorrelation, the adjustment to the weighting matrix W_T proposed by Newey and West (1987) is commonly employed, although other weighting schemes have been proposed, and are canvassed by Hamilton (1994).

The leading specification test for models estimated by GMM is the J-test of over-identifying restrictions proposed by Hansen (1982). This can be constructed when the number of orthogonality conditions exceeds the number of estimated parameters. Further hypothesis tests based on the evaluation of individual orthogonality conditions can also be constructed. For example, structural parameter stability can be assessed in a similar way to EMM. Examples of applications of this approach to latent variable models are Gibbons and Ferson (1985) to equity markets, Campbell (1987) to stock returns and the term structure, and Smith P. (1993) to FOREX and the term structure.

In applications such as the latent variable model, the lack of guidance from theory on the number and type of instruments may potentially lead to lack of power of the J-test in rejecting the model restrictions when wrong. A price sometimes paid for the robustness is bias in the estimates and in the test statistics arising from a version of the 'weak instruments' problem, see Staiger and Stock (1997).

4. SDF models of the term structure

The SDF model has been used in the most part to price bonds, and to model the term structure. Of the different versions of the SDF model mentioned earlier, the Vasicek and CIR models are usually used. There is a vast literature on this that has been surveyed by Shiller (1990), Marsh (1995) and Cochrane (2001). The present discussion will focus mainly on the use of latent variable affine factor models as there seems to be little in the literature on the use of observable factors models at present. We suggest how observable factor models might be used.

First, we specialise the previous discussion to the pricing of zero-coupon bonds. A bond with a coupon can be converted to one without. Given the paucity of bonds of different maturities available at any time, data on zero-coupon bond yields are usually a constructed series based on coupon bonds, and the use of interpolation methods to fill in missing maturities.

We define the following variables: $P_{n,t}$ = nominal price of a zero-coupon n-period bond at t (i.e. has n periods to maturity), $P_{0,t} = 1$ (i.e. the pay-off at maturity is 1), $R_{n,t}$ = yield to maturity on an n-period bond, $R_{1,t} = s_t$ (i.e. one period rate — the risk free rate), $h_{n,t+1}$ = return to holding an n-period bond for one period (i.e. from t to $t+1$). $R_{n,t}$ is defined as $P_{n,t} = 1/[1+R_{n,t}]^n$ and $h_{n,t+1}$ is defined as $1 + h_{n,t+1} = P_{n-1,t+1}/P_{n,t}$. Using the logarithmic approximation $\ln(1+x) \simeq x$ for small x, $\ln P_{n,t} = -n \ln(1+R_{n,t}) \simeq -nR_{n,t}$, and $h_{n,t} \simeq p_{n-1,t+1} - p_{n,t} = nR_{n,t} - (n-1)R_{n-1,t+1}$, where $p_{n,t} = \ln P_{n,t}$.

From the SDF model, $P_{n,t}$ the price of an n-period zero-coupon bond in period t, is the discounted value of $P_{n-1,t+1}$, the price of the bond in $t+1$ when it has $n-1$ periods to maturity: $P_{nt} = E_t[M_{t+1}P_{n-1,t+1}]$. Thus

$$E_t[M_{t+1}(1 + h_{n,t+1})] = 1$$

When $n = 1$ the bond is risk free and

$$(1 + s_t)E_t[M_{t+1}] = 1$$

Assuming that $P_{n,t}$ and M_{t+1} are jointly log-normal with $m_{t+l} = \ln M_{t+1}$,

$$p_{nt} = E_t(m_{t+1} + p_{n-1,t+1}) + \tfrac{1}{2}V_t(m_{t+1} + p_{n-1,t+1}) \tag{40}$$

$$= E_t(m_{t+1}) + E_t(p_{n-1,t+1}) + \tfrac{1}{2}V_t(m_{t+1}) + \tfrac{1}{2}V_t(P_{n-1,t+1})$$

$$+ Cov_t(m_{t+1}, p_{n-1,t+1}) \tag{41}$$

Similarly, as $p_{o,t} = 0$,

$$p_{1,t} = E_t(m_{t+1}) + \tfrac{1}{2}V_t(m_{t+1}) \tag{42}$$

Subtracting (42) from (41) and re-arranging gives the no-arbitrage equation

$$E_t(p_{n-1,t+1}) - p_{n.t} + p_{1,t} + \tfrac{1}{2}V_t(p_{n-1,t+1}) = -Cov_t(m_{t+1}, p_{n-1,t+1}) \tag{43}$$

This can be re-written in terms of yields as

$$-(n-1)E_t(R_{n-1,t+1}) + nR_{n,t} - s_t + \frac{(n-1)^2}{2}V_t(R_{n-1,t+1})$$

$$= (n-1)Cov_t(m_{t+1}, R_{n-1,t+1})$$

and, since $h_{n,t} \simeq -(n-1)R_{n-1,t+1} + nR_{n,t}$, as

$$E_t(h_{n,t+1} - s_t) + \tfrac{1}{2}V_t(h_{n,t+1}) = -Cov_t(m_{t+1}, h_{n,t+1}) \tag{44}$$

This is the fundamental no-arbitrage condition for an n-period bond. The term on the right-hand side is the term premium.

Each point on the yield curve must satisfy this no-arbitrage condition. As $V_t(h_{n,t+1}) = V_t(h_{n,t+1} - s_t) = (n-1)^2 V_t(R_{n-1,t+1})$ and $Cov_t(m_{t+1}, h_{n,t+1}) = Cov_t(m_{t+1}, h_{n,t+1} - s_t) = -(n-1)Cov_t(m_{t+1}, R_{n-1,t+1})$, the term spread (the slope of the yield curve) for an n-period bond must comply with

$$R_{n,t} - s_t = \frac{n-1}{n}E_t(R_{n-1,t+1} - s_{t+1}) + \frac{n-1}{n}E_t\Delta s_{t+1}$$

$$-\frac{1}{2}\frac{(n-1)^2}{n}V_t(R_{n-1,t+1}) - \frac{n-1}{n}Cov_t(m_{t+1,t+1}) \tag{45}$$

The yield itself can be expressed as

$$R_{n,t} = \frac{1}{n}\sum_{i=0}^{n-1}E_t s_{t+i} - \frac{1}{2n}\sum_{i=0}^{n-1}(n-i-1)^2 V_t(R_{n-i-1,t+i+1})$$

$$-\frac{1}{n}\sum_{i=0}^{n-1}(n-i-1)Cov_t(m_{t+i+1}, R_{n-i-1,t+i+1})$$

This is a modification of the usual result that under risk neutrality the yield is the average of current and expected future short rates. From the Fisher equation

$s_t = r_t + E_t \pi_{t+1}$, where r_t is the real return and π_{t+1} is the inflation rate, the shape of the yield curve is determined by average future value of real returns, the inflation rate and the risk premia on that bond until maturity.

4.1. *Affine models of the term structure*

4.1.1. *The single factor affine model*

In a single factor affine model we write $p_{n,t}$ as a linear function of the factor z_t:

$$p_{n,t} = -[A_n + B_n z_t]$$

The coefficients differ for each maturity but are related in such a way that there are no arbitrage opportunities across maturities. Below, we derive the restrictions implied by this. The yield to maturity is

$$R_{n,t} = -\frac{1}{n} p_{n,t} = \frac{A_n}{n} + \frac{B_n}{n} z_t$$

and the one-period risk-free rate is

$$s_t = -p_{1,t} = A_1 + B_1 z_t$$

In order to derive the restrictions on A_n and B_n we need to introduce an assumption about the process generating z_t. We consider first the CIR model.

The Cox-Ingersoll-Ross model (CIR).   The CIR model assumes that

$$-m_{t+1} = z_t + \lambda e_{t+1} \tag{46}$$

$$z_{t+1} - \mu = \theta(z_t - \mu) + e_{t+1}. \tag{47}$$

where $e_{t+1} = \sigma \sqrt{z_t} \varepsilon_{t+1}$ and $\varepsilon_{t+1} \sim iid(0,1)$. Thus $V_t(e_{t+1}) = \sigma^2 z_t$. We now evaluate equation (43) using these assumptions. We note that

$$E_t[m_{t+1} + p_{n-1,t+1}] = -[z_t + A_{n-1} + B_{n-1} E_t z_{t+1}]$$

$$= -[z_t + A_{n-1} + B_{n-1}(\mu(1-\phi) + \phi z_t)]$$

and

$$V_t[m_{t+1} + p_{n-1,t+1}] = V_t[\lambda e_{t+1} + B_{n-1} e_{t+1}] = (\lambda + B_{n-1})^2 V_t(e_{t+1})$$

$$= (\lambda + B_{n-1})^2 \sigma^2 z_t$$

hence equation (40) becomes

$$-[A_n + B_n z_t] = -[(1 + \phi B_{n-1})z_t + A_{n-1} + B_{n-1}\mu(1-\phi)] + \tfrac{1}{2}(\lambda + B_{n-1})^2 \sigma^2 z_t$$

$$= -[A_{n-1} + B_{n-1}\mu(1-\phi)] - [1 + \phi B_{n-1} - \tfrac{1}{2}(\lambda + B_{n-1})^2 \sigma^2)]z_t$$

Equating terms on the left-hand and right-hand sides (i.e. the intercepts and the coefficients on z_t) gives the recursive formulae

$$A_n = A_{n-1} + B_{n-1}\mu(1-\phi)$$

$$B_n = 1 + \phi B_{n-1} - \tfrac{1}{2}(\lambda + B_{n-1})^2\sigma^2$$

Using $P_{0,t} = 1$ implies $p_{0,t} = 0$ and $A_0 = 0$, $B_0 = 0$. This enables us to use the two formulae to solve recursively for all A_n, B_n. For $n = 1$, $B_1 = 1 - \tfrac{1}{2}\lambda^2\sigma^2$ and $A_1 = 0$. Hence

$$s_t = -p_{1,t} = A_1 + B_1 z_t$$

$$= (1 - \tfrac{1}{2}\lambda^2\sigma^2)z_t \tag{48}$$

The no-arbitrage condition, equation (43), is therefore

$$E_t[p_{n-1,t+1}] - p_{nt} + p_{1,t} = E_t[h_{n,t+1} - s_t] = \tfrac{1}{2}B_{n-1}^2\sigma^2 z_t + \lambda B_{n-1}\sigma^2 z_t$$

The first term is the Jensen effect and the second is the risk premium. Thus

$$\text{risk premium} = -Cov_t(m_{t+1}, p_{n-1,t+1}) = \lambda B_{n-1}\sigma^2 z_t$$

Both are linear functions of z_t. We note that if $\lambda = 0$ (i.e. if $m_{t+1} = -z_t$ and non-stochastic) then the risk premium is zero.

So far z_t has been treated as a latent variable and assumed to be unobservable. However, equation (48) shows z_t that it is a linear function of s_t which is observable. This implies that we can replace z_t everywhere by s_t. As a result $p_{n,t}$, $R_{n,t}$ and the risk premium can all be shown to be linear functions of s_t and the model becomes an SDF model with observable factors. Thus

$$p_{n,t} = -[A_n + B_n z_t] = -\left[A_n + \frac{B_n}{1 - \tfrac{1}{2}\lambda^2\sigma^2}s_t\right]$$

$$R_{n,t} = \frac{1}{n}[A_n + B_n z_t] = \frac{A_n}{n} + \frac{B_n}{n(1 - \tfrac{1}{2}\lambda^2\sigma^2)}s_t$$

$$\text{risk premium} = \lambda B_{n-1}\sigma^2 z_t = \frac{\lambda B_{n-1}\sigma^2}{1 - \tfrac{1}{2}\lambda^2\sigma^2}s_t$$

This implies that over time the shape of the yield curve is constant and the curve shifts up and down due to movements in the short rate. Since the shape of the yield curve actually varies over time, this single-factor CIR model is clearly not an appropriate model of the term structure.

The Vasicek model.   The Vasicek model is also based on equations (46) and (47), but it assumes that $e_t = \sigma\varepsilon_{t+1}$, i.e. e_t is homoskedastic. The analysis proceeds as for the CIR model. It can be shown that

$$V_t[m_{t+1} + p_{n-1,t+1}] = (\lambda + B_{n-1})^2\sigma^2$$

and equation (40) is

$$-[A_n + B_n z_t] + -[A_{n-1} + B_{n-1}\mu(1 - \phi) + \tfrac{1}{2}(\lambda + B_{n-1})^2\sigma^2)] - [1 + \phi B_{n-1}]z_t$$

Thus $A_n = A_{n-1} + B_{n-1}\mu(1 - \phi) + \tfrac{1}{2}(\lambda + B_{n-1})^2\sigma^2)$ and $B_n = 1 + \phi B_{n-1}$. Using $p_{0,t} = A_0 = B_0 = 0$ we obtain $B_1 = 1$ and $A_1 = \tfrac{1}{2}\lambda^2\sigma^2$. Thus

$$s_t = -p_{1,t} = A_1 + B_1 z_t = \tfrac{1}{2}\lambda^2\sigma^2 + z_t$$

Once again we can therefore re-write the yields as a linear function of s_t:

$$p_{n,t} = -[A_n + B_n z_t] = -[A_n - \tfrac{1}{2}\lambda^2\sigma^2 B_n] - B_n s_t$$

$$R_{n,t} = \frac{1}{n}[A_n + B_n z_t] = \frac{1}{n}[A_n - \tfrac{1}{2}\lambda^2\sigma^2 B_n] + \frac{B_n}{n} s_t$$

From equation (43), and as $B_n = (1 - \phi^n)/(1 - \phi)$,

$$E_t[p_{n-1,t+1}] - p_{nt} + p_{1,t} = E_t[h_{n,t+1} - s_t]$$

$$= \tfrac{1}{2}B_{n-1}^2\sigma^2 + \lambda B_{n-1}\sigma^2$$

$$= \frac{1}{2}\left(\frac{1 - \phi^n}{1 - \phi}\right)^2\sigma^2 + \frac{\lambda(1 - \phi^{n-1})\sigma^2}{1 - \phi}$$

$$\text{risk premium} = \frac{\lambda(1 - \phi^{n-1})\sigma^2}{1 - \phi}.$$

Thus, like the CIR model, yields are linear functions of the short rate, the shape of the yield curve is constant through time and shifts due to changes in the short rate. But unlike the CIR model, the risk premium depends only on the time to maturity and not on time itself. The Vasicek model is, therefore, an even more unsatisfactory way to model the term structure than the single-factor CIR approach. Clearly, both specifications should be rejected *a priori*.

4.1.2. *Multi-factor affine models*

One of the problems with these CIR and Vasicek models is that they are single factor models. A multi-factor affine CIR model may be better able to capture both changes in the shape of the yield curve over time and shifts. A two-factor CIR model of the term structure has been used by Gong and Remolona (1997) and by Remolona, Wickens and Gong (1998). Dai and Singleton (2000) have used a three-factor continuous-time CIR model. The evidence suggests that although two factors capture most of the behaviour of the yield curve, a third may still prove to be significant.

The multi-factor CIR model of the term structure proposed by Dai and Singleton can be written in discrete time as:

$$p_{n,t} = -[A_n + \mathbf{B}'_n \mathbf{z}_t] \tag{49}$$

where $\mathbf{z}_t$ is a vector of factors. The stochastic discount factor is

$$-m_{t+1} = \ell' \mathbf{z}_t + \boldsymbol{\lambda}' \mathbf{e}_{t+1}$$

$$\mathbf{z}_{t+1} - \boldsymbol{\mu} = \boldsymbol{\theta}(\mathbf{z}_t - \boldsymbol{\mu}) + \mathbf{e}_{t+1}$$

$$\mathbf{e}_{t+1} = \sum \sqrt{\mathbf{S}_t}\varepsilon_{t+1}$$

$$\mathbf{S}_{ii,t} = \nu_i + \Phi'_i \mathbf{a}_t$$

where ℓ is a vector of ones, $\mathbf{S}_t$ is a diagonal matrix, ε_{t+1} is $i.i.d(0, I)$, and θ and $\sum$ are both square matrices. Gong and Remolona and Remolona, Wickens and Gong use particular versions of this.

To illustrate, we consider the case where the factors are independent so that $\boldsymbol{\theta}$ and $\sum$ are diagonal matrices. Also, we set $\mathbf{S}_{ii,t} = z_{it}$. The whole model is therefore additive. As result, it can be shown that

$$E_t[p_{n-1,t+1}] - p_{nt} + p_{1,t} = \frac{1}{2} \sum_i B^2_{i,n-1} \sigma^2_i z_{it} + \sum_i \lambda_i B_{i,n-1} \sigma^2_i z_{it}$$

$$\text{risk premium} = \sum_i \lambda_i B_{i,n-1} \sigma^2_i z_{it}$$

Hence the risk premium is the sum of the risk effects associated with each factor. Further, the short rate is a linear function of both factors

$$s_t = -p_{1,t} = \frac{1}{2} \sum_i (\lambda^2_i \sigma^2_i + z_{it})$$

which implies that the yields and the term premia can no longer be written as a linear function of the short rate. Since every yield is a linear function of the factors, if there are n factors, it would require the short rate plus $n-1$ further yields to represent the factors. If there are more than n yields (including the short rate) then the factors would not be a unique linear function of the yields. A way would then be needed to project the yields onto the lower dimension factor space. A possibility is principal components. If there were less than n yields no observable representation of the factors would be possible, and the model could not be re-interpreted as an observable factor model. If each yield is a linear function of two or more reference yields then the shape of the yield curve can now change over time, although only with limited additional flexibility.

We may summarise our findings as far as the term structure is concerned in the following way. The SDF model commonly used is the affine term structure model factor. This requires at least two factors to adequately represent the yield curve.

But having more factors than yields implies that the model cannot necessarily be interpreted as an observable factor model.

4.2. Empirical Evidence on Affine Models

4.2.1. Vasicek models

Estimation of the Vasicek model is typically carried out by Kalman filter methods in order to obtain maximum likelihood estimates. Hamilton (1994) presents a comprehensive treatment of these recursive methods which rely on assumption of Gaussian errors and are therefore not suitable for estimation of the more general CIR-type models. Jegadeesh and Pennacchi (1996) employ the Kalman filter to estimate the parameters of single and two-factor Vasicek models. The single factor model is given in (46) and (47) with $e_t = \sigma \varepsilon_t$, whilst the two factor model is a restricted version of (49). The motivation for the second factor in Jegadeesh and Pennacchi (1996) is as a time-varying mean, or 'target', for the short-term interest rate, the observable single factor of the Vasicek model. The structure of the model for the state variables is therefore:

$$z_{1t+1} = (1 - \theta_1)\mu_1 + \theta_1 z_{1t} + \sigma_1 \varepsilon_{1t+1} \tag{50}$$

$$z_{2t+1} = (1 - \theta_2)z_{1t} + \theta_2 z_{2t} + \sigma_2 \varepsilon_{2t+1} \tag{51}$$

where the short-term interest rate is z_{2t} and the 'target' or 'central tendency' is z_{1t}. The data set employed is monthly sampled three-month Eurodollar futures prices based on the 90-day LIBOR for contracts of four different maturities from 1992 to 1995 (i.e. n = 1, ... 4.). The maturities are concentrated at the short end but extend up to five years. This is an actively traded market and, the authors argue, less susceptible to the consequences of thin trading seen in some of the bond markets which have been used to construct term structure data. Whilst many of the parameters of the single factor model are significantly different from zero, the steady-state level of the state variable, the short interest rate is not. The point estimate is also counter-intuitively negative. The single state variable is found to mean-revert at a very slow rate. The estimate of 0.934 implies a half-life of 10.5 years. This implied borderline unit-root behaviour of interest rates seems counter-intuitive. The estimate of the price of risk is positive and close to one. The implication is that the risk premium, which is constant over time, is positive and increases with maturity, and the yield curve is upward sloping.

In the two factor model, the coefficient is positive. A likelihood ratio test of $\theta_2 = \infty$, the restriction implied by the single factor Vasicek model, is rejected at less than 1% significance. Mean reversion in the short rate is somewhat closer to that found elsewhere in the literature, with a half-life closer to four years. The short rate reverts somewhat faster to its central tendency according to these estimates. Given these adjustment speeds, any interpretation of these factors as reflecting the conduct of monetary policy seem unreliable — contrary to the claims of Jegadeesh and Pennacchi. The estimate of the mean interest rate to which these state variables converge is positive but, as for the single-factor model, not well determined. This, taken together with the theoretical drawbacks of the Vasicek model discussed above, suggests that a more general specification may further improve the model.

4.2.2. *General affine models with unobservable factors*

As noted, the empirical literature has gravitated to the conclusion that three factor models probably contain enough flexibility to fit the yield curve to most term structure data sets. Heteroskedasticity in the term structure, along with the theoretical considerations discussed above, have motivated the analysis of multi-factor CIR models. Dai and Singleton (2000) provide the most complete statistical comparison of various three factor models. They provide tests of models with both one and two sources of conditional volatility amongst the three affine factors. Here we focus on the single source case, that preferred by Dai and Singleton. To be compatible with our earlier discussion, we present discrete-time versions of their models. The preferred structure of the model of the three state variables is

$$z_{1t+1} = (1 - \theta_1)\mu_1 + \theta_1 z_{1t} + \sigma_1 \sqrt{z_{1t}} \varepsilon_{1t+1} \tag{52}$$

$$z_{2t+1} = (1 - \theta_2)\mu_2 + \theta_2 z_{2t} + \sqrt{\nu_2 + z_{1t}} \varepsilon_{2t+1} + \sigma_{23} \sqrt{z_{1t}} \varepsilon_{3t+1} \tag{53}$$

$$z_{3t+1} = (1 - \theta_3)z_{2t} + \theta_3 z_{3t} + \sqrt{z_{1t}} \varepsilon_{3t+1} + \sigma_{31}\sigma_1 \sqrt{z_{1t}} \varepsilon_{1t+1} + \sigma_{32}\nu_2 \varepsilon_{2t+1} \tag{54}$$

where the short-term interest rate is z_{3t}, the 'central tendency' is z_{2t}, and the 'volatility' factor z_{1t} is the sole source of conditional volatility. A similar three-factor model is proposed by Balduzzi *et al.* (1996) with the restrictions $\sigma_{23} = \sigma_{32} = 0$ (i.e. the conditional correlation between the short rate and the 'central tendency' is zero). This structure can be incorporated into the stochastic discount factor through equation (49).

Dai and Singleton (2000) estimate the three-factor model on a dataset of yields on plain-vanilla, fixed-for-variable rate US dollar swap contracts. The data are weekly from April 1987–August 1996 on three yields; 6 month LIBOR and 2 and 10-year fixed-for-variable rate swaps. The continuity of swap yield data makes them preferable to treasury rates. The estimation method employed is EMM. To capture the non-Gaussian dependencies in bond returns, Dai and Singleton choose a semi-non-parametric function as the auxiliary model. Interestingly, this includes forms of heteroscedasticity, such as ARCH, that are more general than those assumed in the structural affine model being estimated. Whether a more general specification not constrained to be affine would be preferable is still an open question.

4.2.3. *Vasicek Model with Observable Macro Factors*

Ang and Piazzesi (2000) use a modification of the multi-factor Vasicek model discussed above with additional observable macroeconomic factors, but with

Gaussian errors.The structure of the model is

$$-m_{t+1} = \ell'\boldsymbol{\lambda}'\mathbf{z}_t + \boldsymbol{\lambda}'\mathbf{e}_{t+1}$$

$$\mathbf{z}_{t+1} - \boldsymbol{\mu} = \boldsymbol{\theta}(\mathbf{z}_t - \boldsymbol{\mu}) + \mathbf{e}_{t+1}$$

$$\mathbf{e}_{t+1} = \sum \varepsilon_{t+1}$$

$$s_t = \boldsymbol{\delta}'\mathbf{z}_t$$

where $\mathbf{z}_t = (z_t^o, z_t^u)'$ includes observable factors z_t^o and unobservable factors z_t^u, and the short interest rate is assumed to be a linear function of the factors. Ang and Piazzesi choose a specification with two observable macroeconomic and three unobservable factors. The macroeconomic factors are inflation and real activity factors created as principal components from a larger set of macroeconomic data. The factors are assumed to follow ARMA processes, the parameterisation of which is dealt with in the construction of the θ matrix.

Ang and Piazzesi estimate a restricted version of the model in which the price of risk is zero. The model is estimated in two steps. The coefficients on the observed factors are first estimated by GMM. Those for the unobserved factors are estimated by maximum likelihood in a manner similar to that for the Vasicek models discussed above. Their term structure data are bond yields for maturities 1, 6, 12, 36 and 60 months. In order to identify the three unobservable factors, they assume that the 1, 12 and 60 month yields are measured without error.

The macroeconomic factors account for about 30% of the forecast variance at the mid-range of the term structure, but somewhat less at the longer end. The estimates of the processes generating the state variable show strong persistence in two of the three unobservable state variables. These three factors are assumed to be independent of each other as well as of the two macroeconomic variables which by construction are independent of each other. Ang and Piazzesi report that the persistence in the two most persistent unobservables in a standard multi-factor Vasicek model is not significantly affected by adding the macroeconomic factors. But the third factor becomes more persistent. Both macroeconomic factors and all three unobservable factors are found to have a significant impact on the short interest rate and hence the term structure. They are not independent of the unobservable factors. There is a clear statistical relationship between the two most persistent of the unobservable factors from the Vasicek model and the macroeconomic factors of the full model suggesting that the macroeconomic factors are picking up part of the behaviour of the unobservable factors.

The incorporation into affine term structure models of observable macroeconomic factors in addition to the short interest rate is a clear step forward. However, the restrictions implied by the Vasicek model — even one that is multivariate with independent factors — limit the credibility of the results.

4.3. *Nominal and real term structures and inflation risk*

In some countries data exist on indexed as well as on nominal yields. The UK has the longest data set of indexed yields and the few studies available on indexed bonds

have used these data. An additional interest in these data is that, when combined
with nominal yields, it is possible, from financial data alone, to extract an estimate
of future inflation, and of the inflation risk premium. Evans (1998) and Remolona,
Wickens and Gong (1998) have estimated SDF models of the real term structure. In
the UK, indexation occurs with a lag of eight months, so indexed yields are not
exactly the same as real yields. We illustrate the methodology by describing the
approach of Remolona, Wickens and Gong (RWG). Evans takes a very different
approach and does not use affine factor models.

RWG assume a two-factor CIR model for nominal yields and a one-factor CIR
model for indexed yields. Thus, for the logarithm of nominal bond prices,

$$p_{n,t}^N = -[A_n^N + B_{1,n}^N z_{1t} + B_{2,n}^N z_{2t}]$$

and for the logarithm of indexed prices

$$p_{n,t}^r + -[A_n^r + B_n^r z_{1t}]$$

The pricing kernel for indexed bonds is

$$-m_{t+1}^r = z_{1t} + \lambda_1 e_{1,t+1}$$

and that for nominal bonds is

$$-m_{t+1}^N = -m_{t+1}^r + z_{2t} + \lambda_2 e_{2,t+1}$$

RWG assume that e_{1t} and e_{2t} are uncorrelated. The model is therefore additively
separable. The model for the nominal yields is that for the indexed yields plus an
independent factor that can be interpreted as an inflation factor. The factors are
assumed to be generated by generalised CIR models

$$z_{i,t+1} - \mu_i = \theta_i(z_{it} - \mu_i) + e_{i,t+1}.$$

$e_{i,t+1} = \sigma_i \sqrt{1 + \nu_i z_{it}} \varepsilon_{i,t+1}$ and $\varepsilon_{i,t+1} \sim iid(0, 1)$ for $i = \{1, 2\}$. Recursive relations
can be derived for the coefficients of the price equations, and expressions for the
risk premia can be obtained as above. The risk premium for nominal yields is the
sum of the risk premia for indexed yields and inflation. The pricing equations can
be combined into a multi-variate model where the vector of nominal and indexed
yields are linear functions of the two factors. As the factors are unobservable, this
model together with the equations for the two factors, was estimated using the
Kalman filter.

Information about inflation can be extracted from this model by noting that the
nominal and indexed yields to maturity satisfy

$$R_{n,t} = \frac{1}{2} \sum_{i=0}^{n-1} E_t R_{1,t+i} + \frac{1}{2} \sum_{i=0}^{n-1} E_t \varphi_{1,t+i}^N$$

$$r_{n,t} = \frac{1}{2} \sum_{i=0}^{n-1} E_r r_{1,t+i} + \frac{1}{2} \sum_{i=0}^{n-1} E_t \varphi_{1,t+i}^r$$

where $R_{n,t}$ and $r_{n,t}$ are the yields on n-period nominal and indexed bonds, $\varphi^N_{n,t}$ and $\varphi^r_{n,t}$ are their combined risk premia and Jensen effects. Using the Fisher equation $R_{1,t} = r_{1,t} + E_t\pi_{t+1}$, where π_{t+1} is the inflation rate, and noting that if $\varphi^\pi_{n,t}$ is the sum of the Jensen effect and inflation risk premium, then $\varphi^\pi_{n,t} = \varphi^N_{n,t} - \varphi^r_{n,t}$, and hence the average expected inflation over the next n periods is

$$\frac{1}{2}\sum_{i=0}^{n-1} E_t\pi_{t+i} = R_{nt} - r_{nt} - \frac{1}{2}\sum_{i=0}^{n-1} E_t\varphi^\pi_{1,t+i} \tag{55}$$

To estimate future inflation, it is necessary to subtract the average expected value of the inflation risk premium plus the Jensen effect from the difference between the nominal and indexed yields, rather than use the difference itself. The inflation risk premium varies over time and is estimated to be around 1% for the UK in the 1990's.

Evans (1998) proceeds very differently. He estimates equation (55) directly using as the dependent variable data on inflation over the next n-periods. The yields on n-period nominal and indexed bonds are the explanatory variables and the inflation risk premium is not taken into account. A variant is based on using the VAR approach to proxy the risk premia in which the risk premium is taken into account. The VAR is defined in terms of all of these variables. Thus Evans does not specify the stochastic discount factors explicitly. From the results above, however, it may be noted that if the factors were specified and the CIR model used, then the risk premia would in fact be a linear function of nominal and indexed yields.

4.4. Observable factors using the MGM model

We complete our discussion of SDF models of the term structure by considering how one might go about using the approach based on observable factors and the MGM model. We have shown that the no-arbitrage condition for bond yields is equation (44) or equivalently, equation (45). If we also assume that the log discount factor is generated by

$$m_{t+1} = a + \sum_i b_i z_{i,t+1}.$$

then the no-arbitrage condition for bond yields can be written as

$$E_t(h_{n,t+1} - s_t) + \tfrac{1}{2}V_t(h_{n,t+1}) = -\sum_i b_i Cov_t(z_{i,t+1}, h_{n,t+1})$$

or as

$$R_{n,t} - s_t = \frac{n-1}{n} E_t(R_{n-1,t+1} - s_{t+1}) + \frac{n-1}{n} E_t\Delta s_{t+1}$$

$$-\frac{1}{2}\frac{(n-1)^2}{n} V_t(R_{n-1,t+1}) - \frac{n-1}{n} \sum_i b_i Cov_t(z_{i,t+1}, R_{n-1,t+1})$$

This suggests that we model the joint distribution of $\mathbf{x}_{t+1} = (h_{n_1,t+1} - s_t,$ $h_{n_2,t+1} - s_t, ..., z_{1,t+1}, z_{2,t+1}, ...)'$ as an MGM model defined by equations (29), (30) and (31), where we include the maturities n_1, n_2 ... in the model.

As yields are nominal, using CCAPM with power utility would give the log discount factor

$$m_{t+1} = \theta - \sigma\Delta \ln C_{t+1} - \pi_{t+1}$$

Thus the factors would consist of just consumption growth and inflation. There is also an argument for including Δs_{t+1} as one of the factors, as this is an independent source of variation. Other possible factors are output, money growth, the exchange rate, and for countries other than the US, perhaps the change in the US short rate. We are currently pursuing this approach.

5. SDF models of the foreign exchange rate risk premium

5.1. *The forward premium puzzle*

The SDF approach has only recently been applied to modelling FOREX. Surveys of the FOREX market have been written by Lewis (1995) and Engel (1996) following earlier coverage of futures as well as forward markets by Hodrick (1987). In this area modelling has become focused on potential solutions to what is known as the forward premium puzzle. Before analysing SDF models, we first outline the nature of the puzzle.

Consider two countries (domestic and foreign) each of which issues a one-period bond that is risk-free in terms of its own currency. Let R_{t+1} denote the excess return to domestic investors from investing at time t in the foreign bond. Thus

$$R_{t+1} = i_t^* + \Delta s_{t+1} - i_t \tag{56}$$

where i_t and i_t^* are the domestic and foreign one-period nominal interest rates, respectively and s_t is the logarithm of the domestic price of foreign exchange. If investors are risk neutral and rational then the expectation of R_{t+1} conditional on information at time t is $E_t[R_{t+1}] = 0$, the uncovered interest parity condition. But if investors are risk averse then $E_t[R_{t+1}] = \phi_t$, where, for the moment, ϕ_t will be given the interpretation of a risk premium. If only domestic investors are exposed to exchange risk (i.e. foreign investors hold only their own bond) then $\phi_t \geqslant 0$. The sign is reversed if only foreign investors are exposed to exchange risk. More generally, ϕ_t can be positive or negative depending on the relative magnitudes of these portfolio composition effects.

If the logarithm of the forward rate is denoted by $f_t = s_t + i_t - i_t^*$ then the excess return can be written

$$R_{t+1} = s_{t+1} - f_t = \Delta s_{t+1} - [f_t - s_t] \tag{57}$$

where $f_t - s_t$ is the forward premium. If the rational expectations innovation is defined as $\varepsilon_{t+1} = R_{t+1} - E_t[R_{t+1}]$, then equation (57) can be expressed as

$$R_{t+1} = \alpha + \beta[f_t - s_t] + e_{t+1} \tag{58}$$

where $e_{t+1} = \phi_{t+1}$.

Equation (58) — or more commonly a variant in which R_{t+1} is replaced by Δs_{t+1} — is the basis of most tests of the efficiency of the foreign exchange market. Efficiency implies that $\alpha = \beta = 0$ and rationality implies that $E_t[\varepsilon_{t+1}] = 0$. If, in addition, investors are risk neutral then $\phi_t = 0$, and so $E_t[e_{t+1}] = 0$. When all these assumptions hold the OLS estimators of α and β will be consistent.[5] Equation (58) – or more commonly a variant in which R_t is replaced by Δs_{t+1} – is used as the alternative hypothesis in most tests of the efficiency of the FOREX market.

Estimates of (58) based on the assumption of risk neutrality uniformly reject the parameter restrictions required for market efficiency. In particular, many studies find estimates of β which are negative. Although theory predicts that the dollar will depreciate if the forward premium is positive, the implication of a negative value of β is that it will appreciate. Thus, instead of the interest differential $i - i^*$ compensating investors for an expected future exchange rate depreciation, this evidence implies that it is accompanied by an exchange rate appreciation. Or, put differently, the greater the interest differential of the foreign over the domestic bond $i^* - i$, the larger will be the excess return. This is the forward premium puzzle. In general, therefore, the appropriate investment strategy would be to hold the bond with the higher interest rate; the subsequent exchange change will usually reinforce this advantage. In practice, this would be bound to lead to destabilizing FOREX speculation; investing in the bond with the higher domestic currency return is therefore a one-way bet.

The implausibility of the presence of such an arbitrage opportunity suggests that there must be another explanation for the puzzle. One explanation is that the estimate of β is biased downwards due to the presence of the risk premium in the error term of the regression. This is also consistent with the finding of significant serial correlation and heteroskedasticity in the residuals. Assuming that the FOREX market is efficient and investors are rational, using the standard formula for omitted variable bias, Fama (1984) has shown that the bias in β can be expressed as

$$bias = cov[f_t - s_t, \phi_t] / var[f_t - s_t]$$

$$= \rho \left[\frac{var[\phi_t]}{var[f_t - s_t]} \right]^{1/2} \tag{59}$$

where ρ is the correlation between $f_t - s_t$ and ϕ_t, (i.e. between the forward and risk premia). Negative bias implies, therefore, that $\rho < 0$. This can be interpreted as meaning that for US investors, the greater the expected depreciation of domestic currency, the lower is the required risk premium for holding foreign assets. Furthermore, the size of the bias (about -2 in many studies) implies that the variance of the risk premium must be greater than four times the variance of the forward premium.

It may be noted that when the test is carried using a regression of s_{t+1} on f_t, the slope coefficient is close to its theoretical value of unity even though a risk premium is still being omitted. The probable explanation for the different outcome is that whereas s_{t+1} and f_t are non-stationary processes, the risk premium is stationary. Hence super-consistent estimates are obtained even when the risk premium is omitted. This test can therefore tell us nothing about whether there should be a risk premium, although it does suggest that $\beta = 0$ in (58).

5.2. SDF FOREX Models

We consider how to obtain an expression for the foreign exchange risk premium using the stochastic discount model. These factors are jointly distributed with the excess return on foreign exchange, the only asset we consider. The SDF model in this case can be expressed as

$$1 = E_t[M_{t+1}(1 + i_t^* + \Delta s_{t+1})] \tag{60}$$

Here, M_{t+1} is the discount factor required to make the present value of the total income $1 + i_t^*$ from holding a foreign bond and converted to domestic currency equal to one unit of domestic currency. The only source of uncertainty here is the one-period ahead spot exchange rate as both i_t and i_t^* are known at time t. Taking logarithms of equation (60) and assuming log-normality gives

$$E_t[m_{t+1} + i_t^* + \Delta s_{t+1}] + \tfrac{1}{2}V_t[m_{t+1} + i_t^* + \Delta s_{t+1}] = 0 \tag{61}$$

Replacing R_{t+1} in equations (60) and (61) by the risk free rate i_t gives

$$E_t[m_{t+1} + i_t] + \tfrac{1}{2}V_t[m_{t+1}] = 0 \tag{62}$$

Subtracting equation (62) from equation (61) gives

$$E_t[R_{t+1}] + \tfrac{1}{2}V_t[R_{t+1}] = -Cov_t[m_{t+1}, R_{t+1}] \tag{63}$$

The last term on the left hand-side of equation (63) is the Jensen effect. The term of the right hand-side is the FOREX risk premium for the US investor. Comparing equation (63) with our previous result that $E_t[R_{t+1}] = \phi_t$ implies that ϕ_t is not in fact just the risk premium but is

$$\phi_t = -\tfrac{1}{2}V_t[R_{t+1}] - Cov_t[m_{t+1}, R_{t+1}] \tag{64}$$

This implies that ϕ_t will have a higher variance than the FOREX risk premium which will be of some assistance in helping to generate the additional variability required in ϕ_t.[6]

Because equation (63) involves conditional expectations, and given equation (57), it can be expressed in other ways, for example, as[7]

$$E_t[R_{t+1}] + \tfrac{1}{2}V_t[\Delta s_{t+1}] = -Cov_t[m_{t+1}, \Delta s_{t+1}] \tag{65}$$

This shows explicitly that uncertainty about the future spot exchange rate is a necessary element in the risk premium. The larger the predicted covariance between the rate of appreciation of domestic currency and the discount rate, the smaller the risk premium of domestic investors holding foreign denominated assets. Although these domestic investors only suffer a loss when domestic currency appreciates, the larger the discount rate, the less this loss is.

It has been implicitly assumed that the risk is being borne by domestic investors through their holding of foreign bonds. This would imply that the discount factor is that appropriate for domestic investors. In practice, of course, foreign investors are exposed to the same FOREX risk in reverse.[8] Measuring returns and the discount factor in foreign currency would give

$$E_t[R^*_{t+1}] + \tfrac{1}{2}V_t[R^*_{t+1}] = -Cov_t[m^*_{t+1}, R^*_{t+1}] \tag{66}$$

where $-m^*$ is the foreign investor's discount rate and is measured in foreign currency, and $R^* = -R$. This implies that for the UK investor the expected excess return is determined by

$$E_t[-R_{t+1}] + \tfrac{1}{2}V_t[R_{t+1}] = Cov_t[m^*_{t+1}, R_{t+1}] \tag{67}$$

where $Cov_t[m^*_{t+1}, R_{t+1}]$ is the risk premium. Subtracting equation (67) from (63) gives

$$E_t[R_{t+1}] = -Cov_t[\tfrac{1}{2}(m_{t+1} + m^*_{t+1}), R_{t+1}] \tag{68}$$

Thus the Jensen effect disappears. The combined risk premium is the difference between the individual investor risk premia and is due to covariation between the average of the discount factors of the domestic and foreign investors and the excess return defined for the domestic investor (or, equivalently, Δs_{t+1}). Adding equations (68) and (63) gives

$$V_t[R_{t+1}] = Cov_t[m^*_{t+1}, \Delta s_{t+1}] - Cov_t[m_{t+1}, \Delta s_{t+1}] \tag{69}$$

This implies that $\Delta s_{t+1} = m^*_{t+1} - m_{t+1} + \eta_{t+1}$ with $Cov_t[\Delta s_{t+1}, \eta_{t+1}] = 0$. Equation (69) reveals that there is a linear relation between $V_t[\Delta s_{t+1}]$, $Cov_t[m^*_{t+1}, \Delta s_{t+1}]$ and $Cov_t[m_{t+1}, \Delta s_{t+1}]$ and only two terms are required, as in equation (68). There is an important proviso to this result. If, as is likely, there is measurement error in the proxy for the discount factor, then it will not hold in practice in the data. This is not a weakness of SDF theory *per se*, but an indication of the likely effects of modelling the discount factor incorrectly.

In the case of complete markets the two discount factors are identical when measured in the same currency, see Backus, Foresi and Telmer (2001). Hence $m^*_{t+1} = m_{t+1} + \Delta s_{t+1}$. This would imply that equations (65) and (67) are then identical.

5.3. *Affine Models of FOREX*

The affine models of the term structure discussed above can be applied to the FOREX problem. Backus *et al.* (2001) assess the ability of two affine models to

match the properties of the risk premium set out by Fama (1984). The first model
they consider is a two factor CIR model where the factors are assumed to be
independent and country-specific. As we have seen, this is a model that was
rejected by Dai and Singleton (2000) as a good description of the term structure.
However, it can be used to make the issues with multi-country affine models clear.
Using the notation employed earlier, the structure of the affine models of the SDF
for each country and the processes for the unobservable state variables are

$$-m_{t+1} = z_{1t} + \lambda_1 \sigma_1 \sqrt{z_{1t}} \varepsilon_{1t+1}$$

$$-m^*_{t+1} = z_{2t} + \lambda_2 \sigma_2 \sqrt{z_{2t}} \varepsilon_{2t+1}$$

$$z_{1,t+1} - \mu = \theta(z_{1t} - \mu) + \sigma_1 \sqrt{z_{1t}} \varepsilon_{1t+1}.$$

$$z_{2,t+1} - \mu = \theta(z_{2t} - \mu) + \sigma_2 \sqrt{z_{2t}} \varepsilon_{2t+1}$$

It can be shown that the independent state variables, the short interest rate for
each country, are proportional to the country-specific state variable

$$r_t = (1 - \tfrac{1}{2}\lambda_1^2 \sigma_1^2) z_{1t} \tag{70}$$

$$r^*_t = (1 - \tfrac{1}{2}\lambda_2^2 \sigma_2^2) z_{2t} \tag{71}$$

Backus *et al.* work in a complete markets environment. This gives the forward
premium

$$f_t - s_t = (1 - \tfrac{1}{2}\lambda^2 \sigma^2)(z_{1,t} - z_{2,t}) \tag{72}$$

for the simplified case where the prices of risk and unconditional variances are
symmetric $\lambda_1 = \lambda_2 = \lambda$ and $\sigma_1 = \sigma_2 = \sigma$. The expected rate of depreciation of the
spot rate is

$$E_t \Delta s_{t+1} = z_{1,t} - z_{2,t} \tag{73}$$

and the implied risk premium is

$$rp_t = -\tfrac{1}{2}\lambda^2 \sigma^2 (z_{1,t} - z_{2,t}) \tag{74}$$

In this case the first of Fama's requirements is satisfied, namely, the risk premium
and the expected rate of depreciation are negatively correlated. The implied slope
coefficient in a regression of the expected rate of depreciation on the forward
premium is $1/(1 - \tfrac{1}{2}\lambda^2\sigma^2)$ which will be positive and greater than one for plausible
calibrations. Hence this fails to provide an explanation for the empirical results
discussed above. Backus *et al.* show that this slope coefficient can be negative if a
common independent factor is added to the model. However, in this case there is a
finite probability that interest rates could be counter-factually negative.

Backus *et al.* also use a version of the two-factor affine model that is closer to
that preferred by Dai and Singleton (2000), namely a two-factor model with
interdependent factors. Again, in theory, this model is capable of matching both
the negative correlation between the risk premium and the expected rate of
depreciation, and the negative regression slope. But this only happens if the home

country factor has a larger impact on the interest rate in the foreign country, and vice versa.

Backus *et al.* also present GMM estimates of the parameters of the unobserved state variable processes based on matching the first two moments and the autocorrelation coefficient of the home currency short rate, the variance and autocorrelation of the forward premium, the variance of the depreciation rate and the slope parameter of the forward premium regression. Using monthly data on the US dollar — sterling exchange rate from July 1974–November 1994, their estimates imply extreme distributional properties for the unobserved factors and the forward premium for both the CIR independent factors and for the interdependent factor models. In particular, if these factors were interpreted in the term structure context, interdependent factors imply high prices of risk and counterfactually steep term structure slopes. Backus *et al.* therefore conclude that whilst the more general model with interdependent factors can in theory be consistent with the features of the risk premium that were laid out by Fama, the estimates suggest the model has severe shortcomings. A more direct comparison with observed factor models could be made if other moments were used in the estimation, or the direct estimation approach of Dai and Singleton were followed.

An extended version of the approach followed by Backus et al. *is* presented in Hollifield and Yaron (2001). They extend the model to allow for the risk premium to be decomposed into real and nominal components for each country, and for their interaction. Using GMM estimation, Hollifield and Yaron find that all of the predictable components in FOREX returns can be ascribed to predictable variation in real risk and none to nominal risk, or to the interaction between the two. An interesting conclusion is that the effects of monetary policy on predictable returns are not observable in inflation rates, but only in interest rate differentials.

5.4. *The SDF FOREX model with observable factors*

5.4.1. *CCAPM*

An early study of the SDF model of the FOREX market is that of Mark (1985). Based on CCAPM with power utility, assuming complete markets and taking the US as the home country, he uses GMM to estimate the Euler equation for a number of exchange rates. This can be written

$$\beta E_t \left[\beta \left(\frac{C_{t+1}}{C_t} \right)^{-\sigma} \frac{P_t}{P_{t+1}} \frac{S_{t+1}}{S_t} \frac{(1 + i_t^*)}{(1 + i_t)} \right] = 1$$

where P_t is the domestic price level and S_t *is* the domestic price of foreign exchange. Mark finds estimates of the coefficient of relative risk aversion σ which are both large and not well determined. He rejects the over-identifying restrictions implied by CCAPM. Also using GMM, Hodrick (1989) subsequently confirmed this result, but for a wider set of currencies and for additional home countries.

Although the model was not rejected for one or two configurations, the overall conclusion is negative.

Wickens and Smith (2001) compare the use of two models: CCAPM and CAPM. Both are expressed as observable stochastic discount factor models. They also note the relevance of the market structure: whether it is assumed that investors are domestic residents, foreign residents or both. They consider the sterling dollar exchange rate, where s_t is the logarithm of the number of dollars per pound. For the US domestic investor the no-arbitrage condition for the excess return is

$$E_t R_{t+1} + \tfrac{1}{2} V_t[R_{t+1}] = \sigma^{us} Cov_t[\Delta c^{us}_{t+1}, R_{t+1}] + Cov_t[\Delta p^{us}_{t+1}, R_{t+1}] \quad (75)$$

where $R_{t+1} = \Delta s_{t+1} + i_t^* - i_t$, C = nominal consumption, P = price level, $c = \ln C$ and $p = \ln P$. Thus, the larger the predicted covariation of the depreciation of domestic currency with the rate of growth of domestic consumption and with domestic inflation, the greater the risk premium for domestic investors in foreign bonds. For the UK investor the no-arbitrage condition is

$$E_t R_{t+1} + \tfrac{1}{2} V_t[R_{t+1}] = \sigma^{uk} Cov_t[\Delta c^{uk}_{t+1}, R_{t+1}] + Cov_t[\Delta p^{uk}_{t+1}, R_{t+1}] \quad (76)$$

When both investors are in the market these two equations can be added to obtain

$$R_{t+1} = \tfrac{1}{2}\{\sigma^{us} Cov_t[\Delta c^{us}_{t+1}, R_{t+1}] + Cov_t[\Delta p^{us}_{t+1}, R_{t+1}]$$

$$- \sigma^{uk} Cov_t[\Delta c^{uk}_{t+1}, R_{t+1}] - Cov_t[\Delta p^{uk}_{t+1}, R_{t+1}]\} \quad (77)$$

Under the assumption of complete markets, the US and UK discount factors are identical when expressed in the same currency. It can be shown that in this case the three equations (75), (76) and (77) are identical.

5.4.2. CAPM

The discussion in Section 2 shows that in traditional CAPM the value function is defined in terms of the mean and variance of financial wealth rather than consumption. For the two-period problem this gives

$$M_{t+1} = \sigma_t \frac{W_{t+1}}{W_t} = \sigma_t(1 + R^W_{t+1}) \quad (78)$$

where W_t is nominal financial wealth and R^W_{t+1} is the nominal return on wealth. The discount factors can be obtained from the variables that explain this portfolio return.

The relevance of CAPM to FOREX is the widespread use of mean-variance analysis in hedging FOREX risk. The uncertainty about the pay-off to the possibly partly-hedged portfolio then arises from the future return on the portfolio. In the case of FOREX this is just pure currency risk and anything correlated with this — such as tomorrow's domestic and foreign money supplies and output — could be used to help reduce it. Wickens and Smith use the monetary model of the exchange rate to generate observable factors that determine the exchange rate. In the monetary model, the exchange rate is determined by future expected relative money supplies and output levels, see for example Frenkel (1976) and Obstfeld and Rogoff (1998). This would suggest that exchange risk might be due to forecast covariation between today's exchange rate and tomorrow's domestic and foreign money supplies and output.

The index of industrial production is used as the monthly output measure, and narrow money as the measure of money. For the US investor model, only US industrial production and the US money supply are used, and for the UK investor model, only UK industrial production and the UK money supply. The combined investor model includes all four variables Wickens and Smith then use the monetary model of the exchange rate to explain this, and hence to provide the macroeconomic factors.

5.4.3. *Empirical evidence*

Wickens and Smith (2001) estimate all of the CCAPM and CAPM models using constant correlation MGM for the vector of stationary variables $x_{t+1} = \{R_{t+1}, z'_{t+1}\}'$ where the z_{t+1} is the vector of observable factors appropriate for each specification. As explained in Section 3.2, the equation for the excess return must be constrained to avoid arbitrage possibilities. For comparison purposes, a general alternative model is also estimated. This can be written

$$R_{t+1} = \gamma_1 R_t + \gamma_2[f_t - s_t] + \gamma_3 V_t[R_{t+1}] + \beta^{us\prime} z^{us}_{t+1} + \beta^{uk\prime} z^{uk}_{t+1} + \varepsilon_{1t+1}$$

where z^{us}_{t+1} and z^{uk}_{t+1} denote the macroeconomic factors associated with the US and UK investor models, respectively. ε_{1t+1} is used to refer to the error term in the excess return equation no matter which model is chosen. In practice the error terms in each model would be different.

The data used are monthly from 1975.1–1997.12. As consumption data are not available monthly, deflated retail sales data are used. The output series are the indices of industrial production. The money supply is the money base for the US and M0 for the UK. At a monthly frequency there are significant ARCH effects for all of the variables. Estimates are presented for the dollar-based investor holding sterling assets, the sterling-based investor and for both types of investor. For CCAPM, the conditional covariance terms in the two single investor models are significant at the 10% level. In the two-investor model only the conditional covariance with US consumption is significant. In the general model none of the conditional covariances is significant, but the covariance with UK consumption is significant. The implied estimate of the coefficient of relative risk aversion for the US and UK investors is −289 and −283. For the two-investor model it is −410 for US investors. All of these estimates therefore have the wrong sign and are very large. Moreover, in the general model none of the conditional covariances is significant and, as would be expected in view of this, the lagged excess return and forward premium retain their significance. In other words, the forward premium puzzle is not resolved. The broad conclusion that emerges from these results about CCAPM is similar to those of Mark and Wu (1998), Lewis (1995) and Engel (1996). Estimates based on power utility are not consistent with the theory.

The theoretical predictions for the monetary model are that the coefficient on conditional covariances should be positive for US money and negative for US output, and these signs should be reversed for the UK variables. The estimates for the UK investor have the correct sign and are significant. For the two investor model all the signs are correct, but the covariances with UK money are not significant. In the general model the output covariances are the most significant. These results therefore show considerable support for the monetary model and hence for the traditional models of currency risk. The continued significance of the lagged excess return and forward premium in the general model indicates, however, that the forward premium puzzle is not resolved even if output, and in some cases money, seem to be significant sources of FOREX risk.

6. SDF models of equity returns

A great deal of empirical evidence has been accumulated on equity returns based on the capital asset pricing model (for surveys of this see, for example, Ferson (1995) who refers to them as beta models, and Campbell, Lo and MacKinlay (1997)) and on the use of VAR models to test the present value model of equity (see, for example, the surveys of Campbell, Lo and MacKinlay (1997), Cuthbertson (1996) and Bollerslev and Hodrick (1995)). Although we have shown that CAPM can be interpreted as an SDF model, and the present value model of equity is an SDF model with a constant discount factor, for space reasons, we will not include this material in this survey. The beta versions of the CAPM as implemented in many empirical studies of portfolio returns assume that the risk premium is constant; this rules these models out *a priori*.[9] Instead, we will concentrate on the more explicit use of the SDF model to price equity.

The theory is straightforward. We can use the SDF models, equations (6) or (10) using $1 + r_{t+1} = (P_{t+1} + D_{t+1})/P_t \cdot 1/(1 + \pi_{t+1})$ as our measure of real equity returns.[10] The remaining issues are the choice of discount factor model and the method of estimation. Nearly all of the research on SDF models for pricing equity are based on CCAPM or its variants. For recent surveys see Ferson (1995) and Campbell (1999). Almost no work has been carried out using other methods. A notable exception is the explicit use of the affine factor model by Bekaert and Grenadier (1999).

6.1. *CCAPM*

The widely cited paper by Hansen and Singleton (1982) was the first to estimate the Euler equation directly. Their SDF model was CCAPM based on power utility and their method estimation was GMM. Using equations (13) and (18) their Euler equation can be written

$$E_t\left[\beta\left(\frac{C_{t+1}}{C_t}\right)^{-\sigma}(1+r_{t+1})-1\right]=0 \qquad (79)$$

This is a particular case of equation (39). The instruments used were lags of $(C_{t+1}/C_t)(1+r_{t+1})$. The estimates were found to give some, but not strong, support for the theory.

The consensus of a large number of studies, using a wide variety of usually less formal empirical methods, including calibration, is that equity returns are not well explained by CCAPM based on power utility. As noted above, the general conclusion is that equity returns are too large to be explained by the model and implausibly large values of the coefficient of relative risk aversion, σ_t, would be required to remedy this. This is the equity premium puzzle. Attention therefore turned to reformulating the utility function to produce a larger risk premium. We now examine these attempts in more detail.

6.1.1. Habit persistence

One of the most successful alternatives is the habit persistence model in which instantaneous utility is assumed to depend on current consumption and past consumption habits (or the sustainable level of consumption) X_t to give $U(C_t, X_t)$. We consider two examples. Abel (1990) assumes that the utility function can be written

$$U_t=\frac{\left(\dfrac{C_t}{X_t}\right)^{1-\sigma}-1}{1-\sigma}$$

where X_t is a function of past consumption, for example, $X_t=C_{t-1}^\delta$. The stochastic discount factor becomes

$$M_{t+1}=\beta\left(\frac{\dfrac{C_{t+1}}{X_{t+1}}}{\dfrac{C_t}{X_t}}\right)^{-\sigma}$$

and the no-arbitrage condition is

$$E_t(r_{t+1}-r_t^f)=\beta(1+r_t^f)\sigma_t Cov_t(\Delta\ln C_{t+1}-\Delta\ln X_{t+1}, r_{t+1}) \qquad (80)$$

It appears from this that there is additional flexibility in the risk premium arising from the conditional covariance between $\Delta\ln X_{t+1}$ and r_{t+1}. But if X_t is a function of past consumption then the conditional covariance is zero, and equation (80) simply reverts to (16), an unhelpful outcome.

As noted earlier, Constantinides (1990) has proposed a utility function of the form

$$U_t = \frac{(C_t - \lambda X_t)^{1-\sigma} - 1}{1 - \sigma}$$

This has been used by Campbell and Cochrane (1999) with the restriction that $\lambda = 1$. They introduce the concept of surplus consumption, defined as $S_t = (C_t - X_t)/C_t$. Maintaining the framework above, the no-arbitrage condition can be written

$$E_t(r_{t+1} - r_t^f) = \beta(1 + r_t^f)\sigma_t Cov_t(\Delta \ln C_{t+1}, r_{t+1}) + \beta(1 + r_t^f)\sigma_t Cov_t(\ln S_{t+1}, r_{t+1})$$

This has the added flexibility provided by the conditional covariance of $\ln S_{t+1}$ and r_{t+1}. Campbell and Cochrane assume that $\ln S_t$ is generated by an AR(1) process with a disturbance term whose variance depends on $\ln S_t$. They do not estimate the resulting model but, like Constantinides, use calibration methods. By calibrating the variance of the error term of the AR process suitably, it is possible to force the conditional covariance between $\ln S_{t+1}$ and r_{t+1} to be of the necessary size. By this means success is virtually guaranteed. A final judgement about habit persistence models must await the use of empirical methods based on classical statistical inference that are less biased in favour of the model.

6.1.2. *Time non-separable preferences*

Empirical work on time non-separable utility has concentrated on the Epstein-Zin utility function. This has been implemented by, for example, Epstein and Zin (1991). They estimate the Euler equation

$$E_t\left\{ \left[\beta\left(\frac{C_{t+1}}{C_t}\right)^{-1/\gamma} \right]^{(1-\sigma)/(1-1/\gamma)} (R_{t+1}^m)^{1 - (1-\sigma)/(1-1/\gamma)} R_{t+1} - 1 \right\} = 0 \quad (81)$$

by GMM using as instruments current and lagged consumption growth and R_t^m which is measured by the value-weighted index of NYSE shares. R_t is an individual share price. Using the parameter definitions above, a typical example of their estimates is $\beta = 0.997$, $\sigma = -0.94$, $\gamma = -0.97$. Since the estimates of σ and γ are negative, and not positive, this is not encouraging.

Campbell and Viceira (1999) also use the Epstein-Zin model in an examination of portfolio choice, but they calibrate the model and do not estimate it. They assume log-normality and use the no-arbitrage condition, equation (19).

6.2. Affine models of equity

Bekaert and Grenadier (1999) have proposed a class of affine factor models for pricing equity that involves observable factors. Starting with CCAPM, they argue that in equilibrium the consumption process C_t must equal the exogenous aggregate real dividend process D_t and hence, from equation (18), the log stochastic discount factor can be written

$$m_{t+1} = \ln \beta - \sigma \Delta d_{t+1}$$

where $\ln D = d$. They then assume that the dividend process is driven by real productivity shocks x_t so that

$$\Delta d_{t+1} = \frac{\sigma}{2} \sigma_d^2 + \frac{\ln \beta}{\sigma} + \frac{1}{\sigma} x_t + \sigma_d \xi_{t+1}$$

and they assume that x_t has a **CIR** process. We write this as

$$x_{t+1} - \mu = \theta(x_t - \mu) + \sigma_x \sqrt{x_t} \varepsilon_{t+1}$$

ξ_t and ε_t are assumed to be $iid(0, 1)$ processes. They do not derive the no-arbitrage equation for pricing equity that would be implied by this, but it is

$$E_t(r_{t+1} - r_t^f) + \tfrac{1}{2} V_t(r_{t+1}) = \sigma Cov_t(\Delta d_{t+1}, r_{t+1}) = 0.$$

Hence the equity risk premium is zero. If the dividend process had been written instead as

$$\Delta d_{t+1} = \frac{\sigma}{2} \sigma_d^2 + \frac{\ln \beta}{\sigma} + \frac{1}{\sigma} x_{t+1} + \sigma_d \xi_{t+1}$$

then the no-arbitrage condition would become

$$E_t(r_{t+1} - r_t^f) + \tfrac{1}{2} V_t(r_{t+1}) = \sigma_x \sqrt{x_t} Cov_t(\varepsilon_{t+1}, r_{t+1}).$$

This would be a more useful formulation.

Bekaert and Grenadier model equity and bonds together. They therefore introduce another factor, the inflation rate, which is also assumed to be generated by a CIR process. The whole model is estimated by GMM. Given the complexities involved, and the space that would be required to explain these estimates, we are unable to go into further detail.

6.3. Observable factors using the MGM model

As for the term structure, we complete our discussion of SDF models of equity by proposing a new approach using observable factors and the MGM model. This is based on a discussion paper currently in preparation, see Smith, Sorensen and Wickens (2002). A problem with the affine factor approach of Bekaert and Grenadier is the assumption that the macroeconomic variables are generated by

CIR processes. This is unlikely to be correct. Ideally, we would like to model the macroeconomic factors using appropriate macroeconomic theory and econometric models, and not necessarily models that satisfy finance conventions, however convenient this may be. On the other hand, to be useful for asset pricing, the macroeconomic variables must exhibit time-varying volatility, something very few macroeconometric models allow.

Our starting point is the assumption that the log discount factor is generated by

$$m_{t+1} = a + \sum_i b_i z_{i, t+1}.$$

and hence the no-arbitrage condition is

$$E_t(r_{t+1} - r_t^f) + \tfrac{1}{2} V_t(r_{t+1}) = - \sum_i b_i Cov_t(z_{i, t+1}, r_{t+1}) \qquad (82)$$

Instead of assuming that the factors are generated by CIR processes we suppose that the joint distribution of $\mathbf{x}_{t+1} = (r_{t+1} - r_t^f, z_{1, t+1}, z_{2, t+1}, ...)'$ is the MGM model defined by equations (29), (30) and (31). Next we must choose the factors. We could do so on the basis of any (or all) of the equity pricing models discuss in this section. The alternative hypothesis could be formulated from an inclusive choice, and the null hypothesis from any specific model. The previous discussion suggests that possible variables are the growth in consumption, output and dividends. we could also include, for example, bond yields, inflation, the exchange rate, money growth and earnings growth. It would, of course, be more satisfactory if our choice had sound theoretical underpinnings. Essentially, we are aiming to exploit any volatility contagion between equity returns and other variables. For stock markets other than the US, contagion from the US stock market is likely to be important. There may also be contagion from the domestic bond market and the foreign exchange market. There is, therefore no shortage of potential factors. The main practical problem is that the more factors we include, the larger the number of parameters to be estimated, and the more difficult it is to achieve numerical convergence. As shown above, the parameters in the unrestricted BEKK model grow at the rate n^4, and for the other models they grow at the rate n^2.

Among the models considered by Smith, Sorensen and Wickens is CCAPM with power utility. For real returns, this generates just one stochastic discount factor, the rate of growth of consumption. Although the estimate of the coefficient on the conditional covariance in mean (i.e. the coefficient of relative risk aversion) is positive and significant, it is implausibly large, like previous studies based on CCAPM. The estimate of the CRRA is reduced if additional variables are included in the MGM, although not included in the no-arbitrage condition, and if the conditional covariance with output growth is included in the no-arbitrage condition. This extra variable is also significant.

7. Conclusion

Empirical work on financial markets has recently become more conscious of using a well-specified no-arbitrage condition to price assets, rather than the more more traditional expectations hypothesis. The stochastic discount factor model provides a general way of deriving this condition that encompasses most standard asset pricing models. One of the main problems that remain is how to implement the SDF model. In this paper we have provided a selective survey of the methods that have been used in the literature, and we have shown how they been implemented in the three principal financial markets: the bond market, the foreign exchange market and the stock market.

We have outlined the main features of the SDF approach and shown why a large number of standard asset pricing methods are implicitly SDF models. A key issue in selecting an SDF model is the choice of pricing kernel, or discount factor. Both latent and observable factors have been used. In general, the SDF model is a highly nonlinear. This greatly complicates the estimation of the model. One response is to use affine factor models. Another is to find better non-linear estimators. We discuss both approaches. We have considered in some detail the implementation of latent variable and observable affine factors models, especially in the bond market. And we have described several non-linear econometric methods and their application.

In addition to surveying the literature, we have proposed a new way to formulate and estimate the SDF model using observable factors. This provides a general formulation convenient for comparing and testing different types of SDF model. We show how the model can be estimated by multivariate GARCH-in-mean and we include empirical examples of this approach based largely on our own research.

Acknowledgements

The authors would like to acknowledge the support of the ESRC for this research. Research Nos 020R00464 and 020R01266.

Notes

1. The complexity of the derivation of the Euler equation has led subsequent authors to simply quote the original result. A simpler derivation is possible for the two period case where $\mathcal{U}_t = [(1 - \beta)U(C_t)^\alpha + \beta(E_t(U(C_{t+1})^\alpha)^\theta]^{1/\alpha}$ and the budget constraint is $a_{t+1} + c_t = (1 + r_t)a_t$. It can be shown that $\partial \mathcal{U}_t/\partial C_t = 0$ implies the Euler equation $\beta\theta[E_t U(C_{t+1})^\alpha]^{\theta-1}E_t[(U(C_{t+1})/U(C_t))^{\alpha-1}U'(C_{t+1})/U'(C_t)(1 + r_{t+1})] = 1$ Subtracting the corresponding equation for the risk-free rate away from this gives the no-arbitrage condition $E_t[(U(C_{t+1})/U(C_t))^{\alpha-1}U'(C_{t+1})/U'(C_t)(r_{t+1} - r_t^f)] = 0$. For power utility $U(C_t) = C_t^{1-\sigma}/(1 - \sigma)$ this becomes $E_t[(C_{t+1}/C_t)^{\alpha(1-\sigma)-1}(r_{t+1} - r_t^f)] = 0$. Thus α is an additional parameter compared with time separable power utility.
2. A further illustration of the general lack of appreciation of the requirements is that FANPAC, a recent computer package especially designed for financial analysis and

based on GAUSS. does not contain a single program that satisfies these requirements. A similar criticism can be made about the programs discussed in this issue by Laurent and Peters.

3. Stochastic volatility models have been used for univariate models of returns. Interestingly, it can be shown that a model with an AR(1) volatility process can be transformed into an ARMA(1,1) model in the return with homoskedastic errors. If this were a valid no-arbitrage condition it would imply that the risk premium is a linear function of the past return and the past forecast error of returns.

4. It may be noted that the factors may themselves be jointly determined with other variables. It could, therefore, be argued that the joint distribution should also include these other variables, but the variables themselves should be constrained from entering the equation for the excess return.

5. A more familiar way of writing this model is in terms of $\Delta s(t+1)$ instead of $R(t+1)$ when equation (58) becomes

$$\Delta s(t+1) = \alpha + (\beta+1)[f(t) - s(t)] + e(t+1)$$

6. If logarithms are not taken, and the excess return is defined as $1 + R(t+1) = (1 + i^*(t))S(t+1)/(1 + i(t))S(t)$ then the arbitrage relation would be $E_t[R(t+1)] = -Cov_t[M(t+1), R(t+1)]$ which does not involve the Jensen effect.

7. $\Delta s(t+1)$ could be replaced in equation (65) by $s(t+1)$.

8. It is also possible for domestic investors to hold short positions. In this case the source of risk would be the same as that of foreign investors, though the discount factor would still be that of the domestic investor. We ignore this complication in our discussion. It is probable that a relatively small proportion of FOREX transactions are of this type.

9. An interesting debate has recently begun over whether more precise estimates can be obtained from estimation of factor models such as the CAPM by traditional beta methods or by treating the model as an SDF. Kan and Zhou (1999) find in favour of beta methods in a very restrictive case. Whilst Cochrane (2000) and Jagannathan and Wang (2002) show how restrictive this case is, it may be relevant in particular for linear or linearised models such as those reviewed by Campbell (1999) and thus be of more general importance.

10. It may be noted that when the discount factor M_{t+1} is the constant M, equation (1) becomes $P_t = E_t[M_{t+1}X_{t+1}] = ME_t[P_{t+1} + D_{t+1}] = \sum_{s=1}^{\infty} M^s E_t D_{t+s}$ if $\lim_{n\to\infty} \times M^s P_{t+s} = 0$, implying that the price of equity is the present value of discounted expected future dividends. And since $E_t(M_{t+1}) = M = 1/1 + r_t^f$ equation (6) becomes $E_t r_{t+1} = r_t^f = 1/M - 1$.

References

Abel, A. B. (1990) Asset prices under habit formation and catching up with the Joneses. *American Economic Review*, 80, 38–42.

Backus, D. Foresi, S. and Telmer, C. (1996) Affine models of currency pricing, NBER Working Paper No. 5623.

Backus, D. Foresi, S. and Telmer, C. (1998) Discrete-time models of bond pricing, NBER Working Paper No. 6736.

Backus, D. Foresi, S. and Telmer, C. (2001) Affine term structure models and the forward premium anomaly. *Journal of Finance*, 56, 1, 279–304.

Baillie, and Bollerslev, T. (1990) A multivariate generalized ARCH approach to modeling risk premia in forward foreign exchange rate markets. *Journal of International Money and Finance*, 9, 309–324.

Balduzzi, P. Das, Foresi, S. R. and Sundaram, R. K. (1996) A simple approach to three factor affine term structure models. *Journal of Fixed Income*, 6, 43–53.

Bekaert, G. and Grenadier, S. R. (1999) Stock and bond pricing in an affine economy, NBER Working Paper 7346.

Bekaert, G. and Hodrick, R. J. (2001) Expectations hypothesis tests. *Journal of Finance*, 56, 1357–1393.

Black, F. (1972) Capital market equilibrium with restricted borrowing. *Journal of Business*, 45, 444–454.

Bollerslev, T. (2001) Financial econometrics: past developments and future challenges. *Journal of Econometrics, 100*, 41–51.

Bollerslev, T., Engle, R. F. and Nelson D. B. (1994), ARCH models. In Engle, R. F. and McFadden, D. (eds). *Handbook of Econometrics*, vol IV, North-Holland, Amsterdam.

Bollerslev, T., Chou, R. Y. and Kroner, K. F. (1992) ARCH modeling in finance: a selective review of the theory and selective evidence. *Journal of Econometrics*, 52, 5–59.

Bollerslev, T. and Hodrick, R. J. (1995) Financial market effeciency tests. In *Handbook of Applied Econometrics*, eds Pesaran, M. H. and Wickens, M. R., Blackwell.

Campbell, J. Y. (1987) Stock returns and the term structure. *Journal of Financial Economics*, 18, 373–399.

Campbell, J. Y. (1993) Intertemporal asset pricing without consumption data. *American Economic Review*, 83, 487–512.

Campbell, J. Y. (1996) Understanding risk and return. *Journal of Political Economy*, 104, 298–345.

Campbell, J. Y. (1999) Asset pricing, consumption, and the business cycle. In *Handbook of Macroeconomics*, eds Taylor, J. B. and Woodford, M., vol. 1, Elsevier.

Campbell, J. Y. and Cochrane, J. H. (1999) By force of habit: a consumption-based explanation of aggregate stock market behaviour. *Journal of Political Economy*, 107, 205–251.

Campbell, J. Y., Lo, A. and MacKinlay, A. (1997) *The Econometrics of Financial Markets*, Princeton University Press, Princeton, New Jersey.

Campbell, J. Y. and Shiller, R. (1987) Cointegration and tests of present value models. *Journal of Political Economy*, 95, 1062–1087.

Campbell, J. Y. and Shiller, R. (1988) Stock prices, earnings and expected dividends. *Journal of Finance*, 43, 661–676.

Campbell, J. Y. and Viceira, L. M. (1999) Consumption and portfolio decisions when expected returns are time varying. *Quarterly Journal of Economics*, 114, 433–495.

Cochrane, J. H. (2000) A rehabilitation of stochastic discount factor methodology, mimeo, University of Chicago.

Chen, N. Roll, R. and Ross, S. (1986) Economic forces and the stock market. *Journal of Business*, 59, 383–404.

Chen, R. R. and Scott, L. (1993) Maximum likelihood estimation for a multi-factor equilibrium model of the term structure of interest rates. *Journal of Fixed Income*, 3, 14–31.

Cochrane, J. (2000) A resurrection of the stochastic discount factor/GMM methodology, mimeo, University of Chicago.

Cochrane, J. (2001) *Asset Pricing*, Princeton University Press, Princeton, New Jersey.

Connor, G. and Korajczyk, R. A. (1995) The arbitrage pricing theory and multifactor models of asset returns. In *Finance, Handbooks in Operational Research and Management Science, vol 9*, eds Jarrow, R. A., Maksimovic, V. and Ziemba, W. T., North-Holland, Amsterdam.

Constantinides, G. M. (1990) Habit formation: a resolution of the equity premium puzzle. *Journal of Political Economy*, 98, 519–543.

Cuthbertson, K. (1996) *Quantitative Financial Economics*, Wiley, London.

Cox, J. C., Ingersoll, J. and Ross, S. (1985) A theory of the term structure of interest rates. *Econometrica*, 53, 385–408.

Dai, Q. and Singleton, K. (2000) Specification analysis of affine term structure models. *Journal of Finance*, 55, 1943–1978.

Ding, Z. and Engle, R. F. (1994) Large scale conditional covariance matrix modelling, estimation and testing, mimeo, University of California, San Diego.

Duffie, D. and Kan, R. (1996) A yield factor model of interest rates. *Mathematical Finance* 6, 379–406.

Duffie, D. and Singleton, K. (1993) Simulated method of moments estimation of markov models of asset prices. *Econometrica*, 61, 929–952.

Duffie, D. and Singleton, K. (1997) An econometric model of the term structure of interest rate swap yields. *Journal of Finance*, 52, 1287–1321.

Engel, C. (1996) The forward discount anomaly and the risk premium: a survey of recent evidence. *Journal of Empirical Finance*, 3, 123–192.

Engle, R. F. and Kroner, K. K. (1995) Multivariate simultaneous generalised GARCH. *Econometric Theory*, 11, 122–150.

Epstein, L. G. and Zin, S. E. (1989) Substitution, risk aversion and the temporal behaviour of consumption and asset returns: a theoretical framework. *Econometrica*, 57, 937–968.

Epstein, L. G. and Zin, S. E. (1990) First order risk aversion and the equity premium puzzle. *Journal of Monetary Economics*, 26, 387–407.

Epstein, L. G. and Zin, S. E. (1991) Substitution, risk aversion and the temporal behaviour of consumption and asset returns: an empirical investigation. *Journal of Political Economy*, 99, 263–286.

Evans, M. D. D. (1998) Real rates, expected inflation and inflation risk premia. *Journal of Finance*, 53, 187–218.

Fama, E. (1984) Forward and spot exchange rates. *Journal of Monetary Economics*, 14, 319–338.

Ferson, W. E. (1995) Theory and empirical testing of asset pricing models. In *Finance, Handbooks in Operational Research and Management Science, vol 9*, eds Jarrow, R. A., Maksimovic, V. and Ziemba, W. T., North-Holland, Amsterdam.

Ferson, W. E. and Foerster, S. R. (1994) Small sample properties of the generalized method of moments in tests of conditional asset pricing. *Journal of Financial Economics*, 36, 29–36.

Flavin, T. J. and Wickens, M. R. (1998) A risk management approach to optimal asset allocation, mimeo, University of York.

Frenkel, J. A. (1976) A monetary approach to the exchange rate: doctrinal aspects and empirical evidence. *Scandanavian Journal of Economics*, 78, 169–191.

Gallant, R. and Long, J. (1997) Estimating stochastic differential equations efficiently using minimum chi-squared methods. *Biometrika*, 84, 125–141.

Gallant, R. and Tauchen, G. (1996) Which moments to match? *Econometric Theory*, 12, 657–681.

Gallant, R. and Tauchen, G. (2001) Simulated score methods and indirect inference for continuous time models, mimeo, University of North Carolina.

Gong, F. F. and Remolona, E. M. (1997) Two factors along the yield curve. *Papers in Money, Macroeconomics and Finance: The Manchester School Supplement*, 65, 1–31.

Gourieroux, C. Monfort, A. and Renault, E. (1993) Indirect inference. *Journal of Applied Econometrics*, 8, S85–S199.

Gibbons, M. R. and Ferson, W. E. (1985) Testing asset pricing models with changing expectations and an unobservable market portfolio. *Journal of Financial Economics*, 14, 217–236.

Hall, A. (1992) Some aspects of generalized method of moments estimation. In Maddala, G., Rao, C. and Vinod, H., (eds). *Handbook of Statistics, Vol. 11: Econometrics*, North-Holland, Amsterdam.

Hamilton, J. (1994) *Time Series Analysis*, Princeton University Press, Princeton, New Jersey.

Hansen, L. P. (1982) Large sample properties of the generalised method of moments estimators. *Econometrica*, 55, 587–613.

Hansen, L. and Jagannathan, R. (1991) 'Implications of security market data for models of dynamic economies'. *Journal of Political Economy*, 99, 225–262.

Hansen, L. P. and Singleton, K. (1982) Generalized instrumental variables estimation of nonlinear rational expectations models. *Econometrica*, 50, 1269–1286.

Hollifield, B. and Yaron, A. (2001) The foreign exchange risk premium: real and nominal factors, mimeo, Carnegie Mellon University.

Hodrick, R. (1987) *The Emprical Evidence on the Efficiency of the Foward and Futures Foreign Exchange Markets*, Harwood, Chur.

Hodrick, R. (1989) Risk uncertainty and exchange rates. *Journal of Monetary Economics*, 23, 433–459.

Ingram, B. F. and Lee, B. S. (1991) Simulation estimation of time series models. *Journal of Econometrics*, 47, 197–250.

Jagannathan, R. and Wang, Z. (2002) Empirical evaluation of asset pricing models: a comparison of the SDF and Beta methods. *Journal of Finance*, Oct.

Jegadeesh, N. and Pennacchi, G. (1996) The behavior of interest rates implied by the term structure of Eurodollar futures. *Journal of Money, Credit and Banking*, 28, 3, 426–446.

Kaminisky, G. and Peruga, R. (1990) Can a time varying risk premium explain excess returns in the forward market for foreign exchange? *Journal of International Economics*, 28, 47–70.

Kan, R. and Zhou, G. (1999) A critique of the stochastic discount methodology. *Journal of Finance*, 54, 1221–1248.

Kreps, D. and Porteus, E. (1978) Temporal resolution of uncertainty and dynamic choice theory. *Econometrica*, 46, 185–200.

Lewis, K. K. (1995) Puzzles in international financial markets. In Grossmand, G. and Rogoff, K., (eds). *Handbook of International Economics, Vol 3*. Ch 37, North Holland, Amsterdam.

Lintner, J. (1965) The valuation of risk assets and the selection of risky investments in stock portfolios and capital budgets. *Review of Economics and Statistics*, 47, 13–37.

Lucas, E. R. (1978) Asset prices in an exchange economy. *Econometrica*, 46, 1429–1446.

Mark, N. (1985) On time-varying risk premia in the foreign exchange market: an econometric analysis. *Journal of Monetary Economics*, 16, 3–18.

Mark, N. and Wu, Y. (1998) Rethinking deviations from uncovered interest parity: the role of covariance risk and noise. *Economic Journal*, 108, 1686–1706.

Marsh, T. A. (1995) Term structure of interest rates and the pricing of fixed income claims and bonds. In *Finance, Handbooks in Operational Research and Management Science, vol 9*, eds Jarrow, R. A., Maksimovic, V. and Ziemba, W. T., North-Holland, Amsterdam.

Mehra, R. and Prescott, E. (1985) The equity premium puzzle. *Journal of Monetary Economics*, 15, 145–161.

Newey, W. and West, K. (1987) A simple, positive definite, heteroskedasticity and autocorrelation consistent covariance matrix. *Econometrica*, 55, 703–708.

Obstfeld, M. and Rogoff, K. (1998) Risk and exchange rates, NBER Working Paper No. 6694

Pagan, A. R. (1996) The econometrics of financial markets. *Journal of Empirical Finance*, 3, 15–102.

Remolona, M. R., Wickens, E. M. and Gong, F. F. (1998) What was the market's view of UK monetary policy? Estimating inflation risk and expected inflation with indexed bonds, Federal Reserve Bank of New York Discussion Paper.

Ross, S. A. (1976) The arbitrage theory of capital asset pricing. *Journal of Economic Theory*, 13, 341–360.

Ross, S. A. (1977) Risk, return and arbitrage. In Friend, I. and Bicksler, J., (eds), *Risk and Return in Finance I*, Ballinger, Cambridge, MA.

Rubinstein, M. (1976) The valuation of uncertain income streams and the pricing of options. *Bell Journal of Economics and Managements Science*, 7, 407–425.

Sharpe, W. (1964) Capital asset prices: a theory of market equilibrium under conditions of risk. *Journal of Finance*, 19, 425–422.

Shiller, R. (1990) The term structure of interest rates. In Friedmand, B. and Hahn, F., (eds). *Handbook of Monetary Economics*, North Holland, Amsterdam.

Singleton, K. (1990) Specification and Estimation of inter-temporal Asset Pricing Models. In Friedman, B. and Hahn, F., (eds). *Handbook of Monetary Economics*, North Holland Vol. 1, Ch 12.

Smith, A. A. (1993) Estimating non-linear time series models using simulated vector autoregressions. *Journal of Applied Econometrics*, 8, S63–S84.

Smith, P. N. (1993) Modelling risk premia in international asset markets. *European Economic Review*, 37, 159–176.

Smith, P. N., Sorenson, S. and Wickens, M. R. (2002) Modelling the equity risk premium using the SDF model with observable macroeconomic factors. Mimeo, University of York.

Staiger, D. and Stock, J. (1997) Instrumental variables regression with weak instruments. *Econometrica*, 65, 557–586.

Tzavalis, E. and Wickens, M. R. (1997) Explaining the failures of term spread models of the rational expectations hypothesis of the term structure. *Journal of Money, Credit and Banking*, 29, 364–380.

van der Sluis (1998) Computationally attractive stability tests for the efficient method of moments, *Econometrics Journal*, 1, C203–C227.

Vasicek, O. (1977) An equilibrium characterization of the term structure. *Journal of Financial Economics*, 5, 177–188.

Wickens, M. R. and Smith, P. N. (2001) Macroeconomic sources of FOREX risk, mimeo University of York; http://www-users.york.ac.uk/-pns2/forex.pdf

Chapter 7

G@RCH 2.2: AN OX PACKAGE FOR ESTIMATING AND FORECASTING VARIOUS ARCH MODELS

Sébastien Laurent

CREPP, Université de Liège, CORE, Université catholique de Louvain, Belgium and Maastricht University, Netherlands

Jean-Philippe Peters

Université de Liège, Belgium.

1. Introduction

It has been recognized for a long time that the dynamic behavior of economic variables is difficult to understand. And this difficulty certainly increases with the observation frequency of the data.

Most time series of asset returns can be characterized as serially dependent. This is revealed by the presence of positive autocorrelation in the squared returns, and sometimes (to a much smaller extent) by autocorrelation in the returns. To fully account for the characteristics of high-frequency financial returns we need to specify a model in which the conditional mean and the conditional variance may be time-varying. The most widespread modelling approach to capture these properties is to specify a dynamic model for the conditional mean and the conditional variance, such as an ARMA-ARCH model or one of its various extensions (see the seminal paper of Engle, 1982). Another well established stylized fact of financial returns, at least when they are sampled at high frequencies, is that they exhibit fat tails (which corresponds to a kurtosis coefficient larger than three) and are often skewed (which corresponds to a positive or negative skewness coefficient).

The estimation of univariate GARCH models is commonly undertaken by maximizing a Gaussian likelihood function. Even if this hypothesis is unrealistic in practice, the normality assumption may be justified by the fact that the Gaussian Quasi Maximum Likelihood (QML) estimator is consistent assuming that the conditional mean and the conditional variance are specified correctly (Weiss, 1986; Bollerslev and Wooldridge, 1992). The price to pay for this property is that this method it not efficient, the degree of inefficiency increasing with the degree of departure from normality (Engle and González-Rivera, 1991). Searching for a more suitable distribution may thus be of primary importance to gain efficiency. From a practical point of view, the issue of skewness (asymmetry) and kurtosis (fat tails) is important in many respects for financial applications. Indeed, Peiró (1999) emphasizes the relevance of the modelling of higher-order features in asset pricing models,[1] portfolio selection[2] and option pricing theories[3] while Giot and Laurent (2001) show that modelling skewness and kurtosis is crucial in Value-at-Risk applications.

A researcher is thus facing the problem of the specification choice. Which model to select? And which selection criterion to use? It is not our goal to answer these questions. However, it is almost sure that this researcher is going to estimate several candidate models, with different lag orders and perhaps different log-likelihood functions.

Well known statistical packages such as Eviews, Gauss, Matlab, Microfit, PcGive, Rats, SAS, S-Plus or TSP provide various options to estimate sophisticated econometric models in very different areas such as cointegration, panel data, limited dependent model, etc.

The aim of this paper is to provide an overview of a package dedicated to the estimation and forecasting of various univariate ARCH-type models. Contrary to the software mentioned above, G@RCH 2.2 is only concerned with ARCH-type models (Engle, 1982), including some recent contributions in this field such as the GARCH (Bollerslev, 1986), EGARCH (Nelson, 1991), GJR (Glosten, Jagannathan and Runkle, 1993), APARCH (Ding, Granger and Engle, 1993), IGARCH (Engle and Bollerslev, 1986) but also FIGARCH (Baillie, Bollerslev and Mikkelsen, 1996a; Chung, 1999), HYGARCH (Davidson, 2001), FIEGARCH (Bollerslev and Mikkelsen, 1996) and FIAPARCH (Tse, 1998) specifications of the conditional variance and an AR(FI)MA specification of the conditional mean (Baillie, Chung and Tieslau, 1996; Tschernig, 1995; Teyssière, 1997; Lecourt, 2000; or Beine, Laurent and Lecourt, 2000). This package provides a number of features, including two standard errors estimation methods (Approximate ML and Approximate QML) for four distributions (normal, Student-t, GED or skewed Student-t).

Moreover, explanatory variables can enter the mean and/or the variance equations. Finally, h-step-ahead forecasts of both the conditional mean and conditional variance are available as well as many mispecification tests (Nyblom, SBT, Pearson goodness-of-fit, Box-Pierce, ...).

The package has been developed using the Ox 3.0 matrix programming language of Doornik (1999).[4] It can be used on several platforms, including Windows, Unix, Linux and Solaris. For most of the specifications, it is generally very fast and its main characteristic is its ease of use. G@RCH 2.2 may be used freely for *non-commercial* purposes and downloaded from the web site **http:// www.egss.ulg.ac.be/garch/**.

Two (complementary) versions of the program are available and called the 'Light Version' and the 'Full Version', respectively. The 'Full Version' offers a friendly dialog-oriented interface similar to PcGive and some graphical features by using OxPack, a GiveWin batch client module. This version requires a professional version of Ox and GiveWin.

The 'Light Version' is launched from a simple Ox file. It does not take advantage of the OxPack extension (no dialog-oriented interface and no graphs) and can therefore be used with a free version of Ox. This version thus simply requires any Ox executable and a text editor.

This paper is structured as follows: in Section 2, we present an overview of the package's features, with the presentation of the different specifications of the conditional mean and conditional variance. Comments on estimation procedures (parameters constraints, distributions, tests, forecasts, accuracy of the package and a comparison of its features with those of nine well-known econometric packages) are introduced in Section 3. Then a user guide is provided for both versions of G@RCH 2.2 in Section 4 with an application using the CAC40 stock index. Finally, Section 5 concludes.

2. Features of the package

This section proceeds to describe the models implemented in G@RCH 2.2 and gives some technical details. Our attention will be first devoted to review the specifications of the conditional mean equation. Then, some recent contributions in the ARCH modelling framework will be presented.

2.1. *Mean equation*

Let us consider an univariate time series y_t. If Ω_{t-1} is the information set at time $t-1$, we can define its functional form as:

$$y_t = E(y_t \mid \Omega_{t-1}) + \varepsilon_t, \tag{1}$$

where $E(.\mid.)$ denotes the conditional expectation operator and ε_t is the disturbance term (or unpredictable part), with $E(\varepsilon_t) = 0$ and $E(\varepsilon_t \varepsilon_s) = 0, \forall\, t \neq s$.

This is the mean equation which has been studied and modelled in many ways. Two of the most famous specifications are the Autoregressive (AR) and Moving

Average (MA) models. Mixing these two processes and introducing n_1 explanatory variables in the equation, we obtain this ARMAX(n, s) process,

$$\Psi(L)(y_t - \mu_t) = \Theta(L)\varepsilon_t$$

$$\mu_t = \mu + \sum_{i=1}^{n_1} \delta_i x_{i,t}, \tag{2}$$

where L is the lag operator,[5] $\Psi(L) = 1 - \sum_{i=1}^{n} \psi_i L^i$ and $\Theta(L) = 1 + \sum_{j=1}^{s} \theta_j L^j$. To start the recursion, it is convenient to set the initial conditions at $\varepsilon_t = 0$ for all $t \leqslant \max\{p, q\}$.

Several studies have shown that the dependent variable (interest rate returns, exchange rate returns, etc.) may exhibit significant autocorrelation between observations widely separated in time. In such a case, we can say that y_t displays long memory, or long-term dependence and is best modelled by a fractionally integrated ARMA process (so called ARFIMA process) initially developed in Granger (1980) and Granger and Joyeux (1980) among others.[6] The ARFIMA(n, ζ, s) is given by:

$$\Psi(L)(1 - L)^{\zeta}(y_t - \mu_t) = \Theta(L)\varepsilon_t, \tag{3}$$

where the operator $(1 - L)^{\zeta}$ accounts for the long memory of the process and is defined as:

$$(1 - L)^{\zeta} = \sum_{k=0}^{\infty} \frac{\Gamma(\zeta + 1)}{\Gamma(k + 1)\Gamma(\zeta - k + 1)} L^k$$

$$= 1 - \zeta L - \tfrac{1}{2}\zeta(1 - \zeta)L^2 - \tfrac{1}{6}\zeta(1 - \zeta)(2 - \zeta)L^3 - \cdots$$

$$= 1 - \sum_{k=1}^{\infty} c_k(\zeta)L^k, \tag{4}$$

with $0 < \zeta < 1$, $c_1(\zeta) = \zeta$, $c_2(\zeta) = \tfrac{1}{2}\zeta(1 - \zeta)$, ... and $\Gamma(.)$ denoting the Gamma function (see Baillie, 1996, for a survey on this topic). The truncation order of the infinite summation is set to $t - 1$.

It is worth noting that Doornik and Ooms (1999) recently provided an Ox package for estimating, forecasting and simulating ARFIMA models. However, in contrast to our package, they assume that the conditional variance is constant over time.

2.2. *Variance equation*

The ε_t term in Eq. (1)–(3) is the innovation of the process. Two decades ago, Engle (1982) defined as an Autoregressive Conditional Heteroscedastic (ARCH) process, all ε_t of the form:

$$\varepsilon_t = z_t \sigma_t, \tag{5}$$

where z_t is an independently and identically distributed (*i.i.d.*) process with $E(z_t) = 0$ and $Var(z_t) = 1$. By definition, ε_t is serially uncorrelated with a mean equal to zero, but its conditional variance equals σ_t^2 and, therefore, may change over time, contrary to what is assumed in the standard regression model.

The models provided by our program are all ARCH-type.[7] They differ based on the functional form of σ_t^2 but the basic principles are the same. Besides the traditional ARCH and GARCH models, we focus mainly on two kinds of models: the asymmetric models and the fractionally integrated models. The former are defined to take account of the so-called 'leverage effect' observed in many stock returns, while the latter allows for long-memory in the variance. Early evidence of the 'leverage effect' can be found in Black (1976), while persistence in volatility is a common finding of many empirical studies; see for instance Bera and Higgins (1993) and Palm (1996) for excellent surveys on ARCH models.

2.2.1. ARCH Model

The ARCH (q) model can be expressed as:

$$\varepsilon_t = z_t \sigma_t$$

$$z_t \sim i.i.d.\ D(0, 1) \tag{6}$$

$$\sigma_t^2 = \omega + \sum_{i=1}^{q} \alpha_i \varepsilon_{t-i}^2,$$

where $D(.)$ is a probability density function with mean 0 and unit variance (it will be defined in Section 3.2).

The ARCH model can describe volatility clustering. The conditional variance of ε_t is indeed an increasing function of the square of the shock that occurred in $t-1$. Consequently, if ε_{t-1} was large in absolute value, σ_t^2 and thus ε_t is expected to be large (in absolute value) as well. Notice that even if the conditional variance of an ARCH model is time-varying ($\sigma_t^2 = E(\varepsilon_t^2 \mid \psi_{t-1})$), the unconditional variance of ε_t is constant and, provided that $\omega > 0$ and $\sum_{i=1}^{q} \alpha_i < 1$, we have:

$$\sigma^2 \equiv E(\varepsilon_t^2) = \frac{\omega}{1 - \sum_{i=1}^{q} \alpha_i}. \tag{7}$$

Note also that the ARCH model can explain part of the excess kurtosis that we observe in financial time series. As shown by Engle (1982) for the ARCH(1) case under the normality assumption, the kurtosis of ε_t is equal to $3(1 - \alpha_1^2)/(1 - 3\alpha_1^2)$. The kurtosis is thus finite if $\alpha_1 < \frac{1}{3}$ and larger than 3 (the kurtosis of a standard normal distribution) if $\alpha_1 > 0$.

The computation of σ_t^2 in Eq. (6) depends on past (squared) residuals (ε_t^2), that are not observed for $t = 0, -1, \ldots, -q+1$. To initialize the process, the unobserved squared residuals have been set to their sample mean.

In the rest of the paper, ω is assumed fixed. If n_2 explanatory variables are introduced into the model, $\omega_t = \omega + \sum_{i=1}^{n_2} \omega_i x_{i,t}$ with an exception for the exponential models (EGARCH and FIEGARCH) where $\omega_t = \omega + \ln(1 + \sum_{i=1}^{n_2} \omega_i x_{i,t})$.

Finally, σ_t^2 has obviously to be positive for all t. Sufficient conditions to ensure that the conditional variance in Eq. (6) is positive are given by $\omega > 0$ and $\alpha_i \geqslant 0$. Furthermore, when explanatory variables enter the ARCH equation, these positivity constraints are not valid anymore (even if the conditional variance still has to be non-negative).

2.2.2. GARCH Model

Early empirical evidence has shown that a high ARCH order has to be selected to capture the dynamics of the conditional variance (thus involving the estimation of numerous parameters). The Generalized ARCH (GARCH) model of Bollerslev (1986) is an answer to this issue. It is based on an infinite ARCH specification and it allows a reduction in the number of estimated parameters by imposing non-linear restrictions on them. The GARCH (p, q) model can be expressed as:

$$\sigma_t^2 = \omega + \sum_{i=1}^{q} \alpha_i \varepsilon_{t-i}^2 + \sum_{j=1}^{p} \beta_j \sigma_{t-j}^2. \tag{8}$$

Using the lag or backshift operator L, the GARCH (p, q) model is:

$$\sigma_t^2 = \omega + \alpha(L)\varepsilon_t^2 + \beta(L)\sigma_t^2, \tag{9}$$

with $\alpha(L) = \alpha_1 L + \alpha_2 L^2 + \cdots + \alpha_q L^q$ and $\beta(L) = \beta_1 L + \beta_2 L^2 + \cdots + \beta_p L^p$.

If all the roots of the polynomial $|1 - \beta(L)| = 0$ lie outside the unit circle, we have:

$$\sigma_t^2 = \omega[1 - \beta(L)]^{-1} + \alpha(L)[1 - \beta(L)]^{-1}\varepsilon_t^2, \tag{10}$$

which may be seen as an ARCH(∞) process since the conditional variance linearly depends on all previous squared residuals. In this case, the conditional variance of y_t can become larger than the unconditional variance given by:

$$\sigma^2 \equiv E(\varepsilon_t^2) = \frac{\omega}{1 - \sum_{i=1}^{q} \alpha_i - \sum_{j=1}^{p} \beta_j},$$

if past realizations of ε_t^2 are larger than σ^2 (Palm, 1996).

As in the ARCH case, some restrictions are needed to ensure σ_t^2 is positive for all t. Bollerslev (1986) shows that imposing $\omega > 0$, $\alpha_i \geqslant 0$ (for $i = 1, \ldots, q$) and $\beta_j \geqslant 0$ (for $j = 1, \ldots, p$) is sufficient for the conditional variance to be positive. In practice, the GARCH parameters are often estimated without the positivity restrictions. Nelson and Cao (1992) argued that imposing all coefficients to be nonnegative is too restrictive and that some of these coefficients are found to be negative in practice while the conditional variance remains positive (by checking on a case-by-case basis). Consequently, they relaxed this constraint and gave sufficient conditions for the GARCH(1, q) and GARCH(2, q) cases based on the infinite representation given in Eq. (10). Indeed, the conditional variance is strictly positive provided $\omega[1 - \beta(1)]^{-1} > 0$ is positive and all the coefficients of the infinite polynomial $\alpha(L)[1 - \beta(L)]^{-1}$ in Eq. (10) are nonnegative. The positivity constraints proposed by Bollerslev (1986) can be imposed during the estimation (see 3.1). If not, these constraints, as well as the ones implied by the ARCH(∞) representation, will be tested *a posteriori* and reported in the output.

2.2.3. EGARCH Model

The Exponential GARCH (EGARCH) model is introduced by Nelson (1991). Bollerslev and Mikkelsen (1996) propose to re-express the EGARCH model as follows:

$$\ln \sigma_t^2 = \omega + [1 - \beta(L)]^{-1}[1 + \alpha(L)]g(z_{t-1}). \tag{11}$$

The value of $g(z_t)$ depends on several elements. Nelson (1991) notes that, '*to accommodate the asymmetric relation between stock returns and volatility changes (...) the value of $g(z_t)$ must be a function of both the magnitude and the sign of z_t*'.[8] That is why he suggests to express the function $g(.)$ as

$$g(z_t) \equiv \underbrace{\gamma_1 z_t}_{\text{sign effect}} + \underbrace{\gamma_2[|z_t| - E|z_t|]}_{\text{magnitude effect}}. \tag{12}$$

$E|z_t|$ depends on the assumption made about the unconditional density of z_t. For the normal distribution, $E(|z_t|) = \sqrt{2/\pi}$. For the skewed Student distribution,

$$E(|z_t|) = \frac{4\xi^2}{\xi + \frac{1}{\xi}} \frac{\Gamma\left(\frac{1+\upsilon}{2}\right)\sqrt{\upsilon - 2}}{\sqrt{\pi}(\upsilon - 1)\Gamma\left(\frac{\upsilon}{2}\right)},$$

where $\xi = 1$ for the symmetric Student. For the GED, we have

$$E(|z_t|) = \lambda_\upsilon 2^{1/\upsilon} \frac{\Gamma\left(\frac{2}{\upsilon}\right)}{\Gamma\left(\frac{1}{\upsilon}\right)}.$$

ξ, υ and λ_{υ} concern the shape of the non-normal densities and will be defined in Section 3.2.

Note that the use of a *ln* transformation of the conditional variance ensures that σ_t^2 is always positive.

2.2.4. *GJR Model*

This popular model is proposed by Glosten, Jagannathan and Runkle (1993). Its generalized version is given by:

$$\sigma_t^2 = \omega + \sum_{i=1}^{q} (\alpha_i \varepsilon_{t-i}^2 + \gamma_i S_{t-i}^- \varepsilon_{t-i}^2) + \sum_{j=1}^{p} \beta_j \sigma_{t-j}^2, \qquad (13)$$

where S_t^- is a dummy variable.

In this model, it is assumed that the impact of ε_t^2 on the conditional variance σ_t^2 is different when ε_t is positive or negative. The TGARCH model of Zakoian (1994) is very similar to the GJR but models the conditional standard deviation instead of the conditional variance. Finally, Ling and McAleer (2002) have proposed, among other stationarity conditions for GARCH models, the conditions of existence of the second and fourth moment of the GJR.

2.2.5. *APARCH model*

This model was introduced by Ding, Granger and Engle (1993). The APARCH (p, q) model can be expressed as:

$$\sigma_t^\delta = \omega + \sum_{i=1}^{q} \alpha_i, (| \varepsilon_{t-i} | - \gamma_i \varepsilon_{t-i})^\delta + \sum_{j=1}^{p} \beta_j \sigma_{t-j}^\delta, \qquad (14)$$

where $\delta > 0$ and $-1 < \gamma_i < 1$ $(i = 1, ..., q)$.

This model combines the flexibility of a varying exponent with the asymmetry coefficient (to take the 'leverage effect' into account). The APARCH includes seven other ARCH extensions as special cases:[9]

- The ARCH of Engle (1982) when $\delta = 2$, $\gamma_i = 0$ $(i = 1, ..., p)$ and $\beta_j = 0$ $(j = 1, ..., p)$.
- The GARCH of Bollerslev (1986) when $\delta = 2$ and $\gamma_i = 0$ $(i = 1, ..., p)$.
- Taylor (1986)/Schwert (1990)'s GARCH when $\delta = 1$, and $\gamma_i = 0$ $(i = 1, ..., p)$.
- The GJR of Glosten, Jagannathan and Runkle (1993) when $\delta = 2$.
- The TARCH of Zakoian (1994) when $\delta = 1$.
- The NARCH of Higgins and Bera (1992) when $\gamma_i = 0 (i = 1, ..., p)$ and $\beta_j = 0$ $(j = 1, ..., p)$.
- The Log-ARCH of Geweke (1986) and Pentula (1986), when $\delta \to 0$.

Following Ding, Granger and Engle (1993), if $\omega > 0$ and $\sum_{i=1}^{q} \alpha_i E(|z| - \gamma_i z)^{\delta} + \sum_{j=1}^{p} \beta_j < 1$, a stationary solution for Eq. (14) exists and is:

$$E(\sigma_t^{\delta}) = \frac{\omega}{1 - \sum_{i=1}^{q} \alpha_i E(|z| - \gamma_i z)^{\delta} - \sum_{j=1}^{p} \beta_j}.$$

Notice that if we set $\gamma = 0$, $\delta = 2$ and z_t has zero mean and unit variance, we have the usual stationarity condition of the GARCH(1, 1) model ($\alpha_1 + \beta_1 < 1$). However, if $\gamma \neq 0$ and/or $\delta \neq 2$, this condition depends on the assumption made about the innovation process.

Ding, Granger and Engle (1993) derived a closed form solution to $\kappa_i = E(|z| - \gamma_i z)^{\delta}$ in the Gaussian case. Lambert and Laurent (2001) show that for the standardized skewed Student:[10]

$$\kappa_i = \{\xi^{-(1+\delta)}(1 + \gamma_i)^{\delta} + \xi^{1+\delta}(1 - \gamma_i)^{\delta}\} \frac{\Gamma\left(\dfrac{\delta + 1}{2}\right) \Gamma\left(\dfrac{\upsilon - \delta}{2}\right) (\upsilon - 2)^{(1+\delta)/2}}{\left(\xi + \dfrac{1}{\xi}\right) \sqrt{(\upsilon - 2)\pi}\Gamma\left(\dfrac{\upsilon}{2}\right)}.$$

For the GED, we can show that:

$$\kappa_i = \frac{[(1 + \gamma_i)^{\delta} + (1 - \gamma_i)^{\delta}]2^{(\delta - \upsilon)/\upsilon}\Gamma\left(\dfrac{\delta + 1}{\upsilon}\right)\lambda_{\upsilon}^{\delta}}{\Gamma\left(\dfrac{1}{\upsilon}\right)}.$$

Note that ξ, υ and λ_{υ} concern the shape of the non-normal densities and will be defined in Section 3.2.

2.2.6. IGARCH model

In many high-frequency time-series applications, the conditional variance estimated using a GARCH(p, q) process has the following property:

$$\sum_{j=1}^{p} \beta_j + \sum_{i=1}^{q} \alpha_i \approx 1.$$

If $\sum_{j=1}^{p} \beta_j + \sum_{i=1}^{q} \alpha_i < 1$, the process (ε_t) is second order stationary, and a shock to the conditional variance σ_t^2 has a decaying impact on σ_{t+h}^2, when h increases, and is asymptotically negligible. Indeed, let us rewrite the ARCH(∞)

representation of the GARCH(p, q), given in Eq. (10), as follows:

$$\sigma_t^2 = \omega^* + \lambda(L)\varepsilon_t^2, \tag{15}$$

where $\omega^* = \omega[1 - \beta(L)]^{-1}$, $\lambda(L) = \alpha(L)[1 - \beta(L)]^{-1} = \sum_{i=1}^{\infty} \lambda_i L^i$ and λ_i are lag coefficients depending nonlinearly on α_i and β_i. For a GARCH$(1,1)$, $\lambda_i = \alpha_1 \beta_1^{i-1}$. Recall that this model is said to be second order stationary provided that $\alpha_1 + \beta_1 < 1$ since it implies that the unconditional variance exists and equals $\omega/(1 - \alpha_1 - \beta_1)$. As shown by Davidson (2001), the amplitude of the GARCH$(1,1)$ is measured by $S = \sum_{i=1}^{\infty} \lambda_i = \alpha_1/(1 - \beta_1)$, which determines 'how large the variations in the conditional variance can be' (and hence the order of the existing moments). This concept is often confused with the memory of the model that determines 'how large shocks to the volatility take to dissipate'. In this respect, the GARCH$(1,1)$ model has a geometric memory $\rho = 1/\beta_1$, where $\lambda_i = O(\rho^{-i})$.

In practice, we often find $\alpha_1 + \beta_1 = 1$. In this case, we are confronted to an Integrated GARCH (IGARCH) model.

Recall that the GARCH(p, q) model can be expressed as an ARMA process. Using the lag operator L, we can rearrange Eq. (8) as:

$$[1 - \alpha(L) - \beta(L)]\varepsilon_t^2 = \omega + [1 - \beta(L)](\varepsilon_t^2 - \sigma_t^2).$$

When the $[1 - \alpha(L) - \beta(L)]$ polynomial contains a unit root, i.e. the sum of all the α_i's and the β_j's is one, we have the IGARCH(p, q) model of Engle and Bollerslev (1986). It can then be written as:

$$\phi(L)(1 - L)\varepsilon_t^2 = \omega + [1 - \beta(L)](\varepsilon_t^2 - \sigma_t^2), \tag{16}$$

where $\phi(L) = [1 - \alpha(L) - \beta(L)](1 - L)^{-1}$ is of order $[\max\{p, q\} - 1]$.

We can rearrange Eq. (16) to express the conditional variance as a function of the squared residuals. After some manipulations, we have its ARCH(∞) representation:

$$\sigma_t^2 = \frac{\omega}{[1 - \beta(L)]} + \{1 - \phi(L)(1 - L)[1 - \beta(L)]^{-1}\}\varepsilon_t^2. \tag{17}$$

For this model, $S = 1$ and thus the second moment does not exist. However, this process is still short memory. To show this Davidson (2001) considers an IGARCH$(0, 1)$ model defined as $\varepsilon_t = \sigma_t z_t$ and $\sigma_t^2 = \varepsilon_{t-1}^2$. This process is often wrongly compared to a random walk since the long-range forecast $\sigma_{t+h}^2 = \varepsilon_t^2$, for any h. However, $\varepsilon_t = z_t |\varepsilon_{t-1}|$ meaning that the memory of a large deviation persists for only one period.

2.2.7. *Fractionally integrated models*

Volatility tends to change quite slowly over time, and, as shown in Ding, Granger and Engle (1993) among others, the effects of a shock can take a considerable time to decay.[11] Therefore, the distinction between I(0) and I(1) processes seems to be far too restrictive. Indeed, the propagation of shocks in an I(0) process occurs at an exponential rate of decay (so that it only captures the short-memory), while for an I(1) process the persistence of shocks is infinite. In the conditional mean, the ARFIMA specification has been proposed to fill the gap between short and complete persistence, so that the short-run behavior of the time-series is captured by the ARMA parameters, while the fractional differencing parameter allows for modelling the long-run dependence.[12]

To mimic the behavior of the correlogram of the observed volatility, Baillie, Bollerslev and Mikkelsen (1996) (hereafter denoted BBM) introduce the Fractionally Integrated GARCH (FIGARCH) model by replacing the first difference operator of Eq. (17) by $(1 - L)^d$.

The conditional variance of the FIGARCH (p, d, q) is given by:

$$\sigma_t^2 = \underbrace{\omega[1 - \beta(L)]^{-1}}_{\omega^*} + \underbrace{\{1 - [1 - \beta(L)]^{-1}\phi(L)(1 - L)^d\}}_{\lambda(L)} \varepsilon_t^2, \qquad (18)$$

or $\sigma_t^2 = \omega^* + \sum_{i=1}^{\infty} \lambda_i L^i \varepsilon_t^2 = \omega^* + \lambda(L)\varepsilon_t^2$, with $0 \leqslant d \leqslant 1$. It is possible to show that $\omega > 0$, $\beta_1 - d \leqslant \phi_1 \leqslant (2 - d)/2$ and $d[\phi_1 - (1 - d)/2] \leqslant \beta_1(\phi_1 - \beta_1 + d)$ are sufficient to ensure that the conditional variance of the FIGARCH $(1, d, 1)$ is positive almost surely for all t. Setting $\phi_1 = 0$ gives the condition for the FIGARCH $(1, d, 0)$.

Davidson (2001) notes the interesting and counterintuitive fact that the memory parameter of this process is $-d$, and is increasing as d approaches zero, while in the ARFIMA model the memory increases when ζ increases. According to Davidson (2001), the unexpected behavior of the FIGARCH model may be due less to any inherent paradox than to the fact that, embodying restrictions appropriate to a model in levels, it has been transplanted into a model of volatility. The main characteristic of this model is that it is not stationary when $d > 0$. Indeed,

$$(1 - L)^d = \sum_{k=0}^{\infty} \frac{\Gamma(d+1)}{\Gamma(k+1)\Gamma(d-k+1)} L^k$$

$$= 1 - dL - \tfrac{1}{2}d(1 - d)L^2 - \tfrac{1}{6}d(1 - d)(2 - d)L^3 - \cdots$$

$$= 1 - \sum_{k=1}^{\infty} c_k(d)L^k, \qquad (19)$$

where $c_1(d) = d$, $c_2(d) = \tfrac{1}{2}d(1 - d)$, etc. By construction, $\sum_{k=1}^{\infty} c_k(d) = 1$ for any value of d, and consequently, the FIGARCH belongs to the same 'knife-edge-nonstationary' class represented by the IGARCH. To test whether this nonstationarity feature holds, Davidson (2001) proposes a generalized version of the FIGARCH and calls it the HYperbolic GARCH. The HYGARCH is given by Eq. (18), when $\lambda(L)$ is replaced by $1 - [1 - \beta(L)]^{-1}\phi(L)\{1 + \alpha[(1 - L)^d - 1]\}$. Note that we report $\ln(\alpha)$ and not α. The $c_k(d)$ coefficients are thus weighted by α. Interestingly, the HYGARCH nests the FIGARCH when $\alpha = 1$ (or equivalently when $\ln(\alpha) = 0$) and if the GARCH component satisfies the usual covariance stationarity restrictions, then this process is stationary with $\alpha < 1$ (or equivalently when $\ln(\alpha) < 0$) (see Davidson, 2001 for more details).

Chung (1999) underscores some drawbacks of the BBM model: there is a structural problem in the BBM specification since the parallel with the ARFIMA framework of the conditional mean equation is not perfect, leading to difficult interpretations of the estimated parameters. Indeed the fractional differencing operator applies to the constant term in the mean equation (ARFIMA) while it does not in the variance equation (FIGARCH). Chung (1999) proposes a slightly different process:

$$\phi(L)(1-L)^d(\varepsilon_t^2 - \sigma^2) = [1 - \beta(L)](\varepsilon_t^2 - \sigma_t^2), \qquad (20)$$

where σ^2 is the unconditional variance of ε_t.

If we keep the same definition of $\lambda(L)$ as in Eq. (18), we can formulate the conditional variance as:

$$\sigma_t^2 = \sigma^2 + \{1 - [1 - \beta(L)]^{-1}\phi(L)(1-L)^d\}(\varepsilon_t^2 - \sigma^2)$$

or

$$\sigma_t^2 = \sigma^2 + \lambda(L)(\varepsilon_t^2 - \sigma^2). \qquad (21)$$

$\lambda(L)$ is an infinite summation which, in practice, has to be truncated. BBM propose to truncate $\lambda(L)$ at 1000 lags (this truncation order has been implemented as the default value in our package, but it may be changed by the user) and initialize the unobserved ε_t^2 at their unconditional moment. Contrary to BBM, Chung (1999) proposes to truncate $\lambda(L)$ at the size of the information set $(t-1)$ and to initialize the unobserved $(\varepsilon_t^2 - \sigma^2)$ at 0 (this quantity is small in absolute values and has a zero mean).[13]

The idea of fractional integration has been extended to other GARCH types of models, including the Fractionally Integrated EGARCH (FIEGARCH) of Bollerslev and Mikkelsen (1996) and the Fractionally Integrated APARCH (FIAPARCH) of Tse (1998).[14]

Similarly to the GARCH(p,q) process, the EGARCH(p,q) of Eq. (11) can be extended to account for long memory by factorizing the autoregressive polynomial $[1 - \beta(L)] = \phi(L)(1-L)^d$ where all the roots of $\phi(z)=0$ lie outside the unit circle. The FIEGARCH (p, d, q) is specified as follows:

$$\ln(\sigma_t^2) = \omega + \phi(L)^{-1}(1-L)^{-d}[1 + \alpha(L)]g(z_{t-1}). \qquad (22)$$

Finally, the FIAPARCH (p, d, q) model can be written as:[15]

$$\sigma_t^\delta = \omega + \{1 - [1 - \beta(L)]^{-1}\phi(L)(1-L)^d\}(|\varepsilon_t| - \gamma\varepsilon_t)^\delta. \qquad (23)$$

3. Estimation Methods

3.1. Parameters Constraints

When numerical optimization is used to maximize the log-likelihood function with respect to the vector of parameters Ψ, the inspected range of the parameter space is $]-\infty; \infty[$. The problem is that some parameters might have to be constrained in a smaller interval. For instance, the leverage effect parameter γ of the APARCH model must lie between -1 and 1. To impose these constraints one could estimate Ψ^* (which ranges from $-\infty$ to $+\infty$) instead of Ψ where Ψ is recovered using the non-linear function: $\Psi = x(\Psi^*)$. In our package, $x(.)$ is defined as:

$$x(\Psi^*) = Low + \frac{Up - Low}{1 + e^{-\Psi^*}}, \qquad (24)$$

where Low is the lower bound and Up the upper bound (i.e. in our example, $Low = -1$ and $Up = 1$).

Applying unconstrained optimization of the log-likelihood function with respect to Ψ is equivalent to applying constrained optimization with respect to Ψ^*. Therefore, the optimization process of the program results in $\hat{\Psi}^*$ with the covariance matrix being noted $Cov(\hat{\Psi}^*)$. The estimated covariance of the parameters of interest $\hat{\Psi}$ is:

$$Cov(\hat{\Psi}) = \left(\frac{\partial x(\hat{\Psi}^*)}{\partial \Psi^*}\right) Cov(\hat{\Psi}^*) \left(\frac{\partial x(\hat{\Psi}^*)}{\partial \Psi^*}\right)'. \qquad (25)$$

In our case, we have

$$Cov(\hat{\Psi}) = Cov(\hat{\Psi}^*) \frac{\exp(-\hat{\Psi}^*)(Up - Low)}{[1 + \exp(-\hat{\Psi}^*)]^2}.$$

Note that, in G@RCH 2.2, lower and upper bounds of the parameters can be easily modified by the user in the file *startingvalues.txt*.

3.2. *Distributions*

Four distributions are available in our program: the usual Gaussian, the Student-t, the Generalized Error Distribution (GED) and the skewed Student distribution.

The GARCH models are estimated using an approximate Maximum Likelihood (ML) approach. It is evident from Eq. (6) (and all the following equations of Section 2) that the recursive evaluation of this function is conditional on unobserved values. The ML estimation is therefore not perfectly exact. To solve the problem of unobserved values, we have set these quantities to their unconditional expected values.

If we express the mean equation as in Eq. (1) and $\varepsilon_t = z_t \sigma_t$, the log-likelihood function of the standard normal distribution is given by:

$$L_{norm} = -\frac{1}{2} \sum_{t=1}^{T} [\ln(2\pi) + \ln(\sigma_t^2) + z_t^2], \qquad (26)$$

where T is the number of observations.

For a Student-t distribution, the log-likelihood is:

$$L_{Stud} = T\left\{ \ln \Gamma\left(\frac{v+1}{2}\right) - \ln \Gamma\left(\frac{v}{2}\right) - \frac{1}{2}\ln[\pi(v-2)] \right\}$$

$$- \frac{1}{2} \sum_{t=1}^{T} \left[\ln(\sigma_t^2) + (1+v)\ln\left(1 + \frac{z_t^2}{v-2}\right) \right], \tag{27}$$

where v is the degrees of freedom, $2 < v \leqslant \infty$ and $\Gamma(.)$ is the gamma function.

The GED log-likelihood function of a normalized random variable is given by:

$$L_{GED} = \sum_{t=1}^{T} \left[\ln(v/\lambda_v) - 0.5\left|\frac{z_t}{\lambda_v}\right|^v - (1+v^{-1})\ln(2) - \ln \Gamma(1/v) - 0.5 \ln(\sigma_t^2) \right], \tag{28}$$

where $0 < v < \infty$ and

$$\lambda_v \equiv \sqrt{\frac{\Gamma\left(\frac{1}{v}\right)2^{-2/v}}{\Gamma\left(\frac{3}{v}\right)}}. \tag{29}$$

The main drawback of the last two densities is that despite accounting for fat tails, they are symmetric. Skewness and kurtosis are important in many financial applications (in asset pricing models, portfolio selection, option pricing theory or Value-at-Risk applications among others). To overcome this problem, we can rely on the skewed Student density proposed by Lambert and Laurent (2001) whose log-likelihood is:

$$L_{SkSt} = T\left\{ \ln \Gamma\left(\frac{v+1}{2}\right) - \ln \Gamma\left(\frac{v}{2}\right) - 0.5 \ln[\pi(v-2)] + \ln\left(\frac{2}{\xi + \frac{1}{\xi}}\right) + \ln(s) \right\}$$

$$- 0.5 \sum_{t=1}^{T} \left\{ \ln \sigma_t^2 + (1+v)\ln\left[1 + \frac{(sz_t + m)^2}{v-2}\xi^{-2I_t}\right] \right\}. \tag{30}$$

where

$$I_t = \begin{cases} 1 & \text{if } z_t \geqslant -\dfrac{m}{s} \\[2ex] -1 & \text{if } z_t < -\dfrac{m}{s} \end{cases},$$

ξ is the asymmetry parameter, v is the degree of freedom of the distribution,

$$m = \frac{\Gamma\left(\dfrac{v+1}{2}\right)\sqrt{v-2}}{\sqrt{\pi}\,\Gamma\left(\dfrac{v}{2}\right)} \left(\xi - \frac{1}{\xi}\right)$$

and

$$s = \sqrt{\left(\xi^2 + \frac{1}{\xi^2} - 1\right) - m^2}.$$

In principle, the gradient vector and the hessian matrix can be obtained numerically or by evaluating its analytic expressions. Due to the high number of possible models and distributions, we use numerical techniques to approximate the derivatives of the log-likelihood function with respect to the parameter vector.

3.3. *Tests*

In addition to the possibilities offered by GiveWin (ACF, PACF, QQ-plots...), several tests are provided:

- Four Information Criteria (divided by the number of observations):[16]

  — Akaike $= -2\dfrac{LogL}{n} + 2\dfrac{k}{n}$;

  — Hannan-Quinn $= -2\dfrac{LogL}{n} + 2\dfrac{k \ln[\ln(n)]}{n}$;

  — Schwartz $= -2\dfrac{LogL}{n} + 2\dfrac{\ln(k)}{n}$;

  — Shibata $= -2\dfrac{LogL}{n} + \ln\left(\dfrac{n+2k}{n}\right)$.

- The value of the skewness and the kurtosis of the standardized residuals $(\hat{z}_t)$ of the estimated model, their t-tests and p-values. The Jarque-Bera normality test (Jarque and Bera, 1987) is also reported.
- The Box-Pierce statistics at lag l^* for both standardized, i.e. $BP(l^*)$, and squared standardized, i.e. $BP^2(l^*)$, residuals. Under the null hypothesis of no autocorrelation, the statistics $BP(l^*)$ and $BP^2(l^*)$ are respectively $\chi^2(l^* - m - l)$ and $\chi^2(l^* - p - q)$ distributed (see McLeod and Li, 1983).
- The Engle LM ARCH test (Engle, 1982) to test for the presence of ARCH effects in a series.
- The diagnostic test of Engle and Ng (1993) to investigate possible misspecification of the conditional variance equation. The Sign Bias Test (SBT) examines the impact of positive and negative return shocks on volatility not predicted by the model under construction. The negative Size Bias Test (resp. positive Size Bias Test) focuses on the different effects that large and small negative (resp. positive) return shocks have on volatility, which is not predicted by the volatility model. Finally, a joint test for these three tests is also provided.
- The adjusted Pearson goodness-of-fit test. The Pearson goodness-of-fit test compares the empirical distribution of the innovations with the theoretical one. In order to carry out this testing procedure, it is necessary to first classify the residuals in cells according to their magnitude.[17] For a given number of cells denoted g, the Pearson goodness-of-fit statistics is:

$$P(g) = \sum_{i=1}^{g} \frac{(n_i - En_i)^2}{En_i}, \tag{31}$$

where n_i is the number of observations in cell i and En_i is the expected number of observations (based on the ML estimates). For i.i.d. observations, Palm and Vlaar (1997) show that under the null of a correct distribution the asymptotic distribution of $P(g)$ is bounded between a $\chi^2(g - 1)$ and a $\chi^2(g - k - 1)$ where k is the number of estimated parameters. As explained by Palm and Vlaar (1997), the choice of g is far from being obvious. For $T = 2252$, these authors set g equal to 50. According to König and Gaab (1982), the number of cells must increase at a rate equal to $T^{0.4}$.
- The Nyblom test (Nyblom, 1989; and Lee and Hansen, 1994) to check the constancy of parameters over time. See Hansen (1994) for an overview of this test.

3.4. Forecasts

When estimating a model it can be useful to try to understand the mechanism that produces the series of interest. It can also suggest a solution to an economic problem. Is it the only game in town? Certainly not. Indeed, the main purpose of building and estimating a model with financial data is to produce a forecast.

G@RCH 2.2 also provides forecasting tools. In particular, forecasts of both the conditional mean and the conditional variance are available as well as several forecast error measures.

3.4.1. *Forecasting the conditional mean*

Our first goal is to give the optimal h-step-ahead predictor of y_{t+h} given the information we have up to time t.

For instance, for the following AR(1) process,

$$y_t = \mu + \hat{\psi}_1(y_{t-1} - \mu) + \varepsilon_t. \tag{32}$$

The optimal[18] h-step-ahead predictor of y_{t+h}, i.e. $\hat{y}_{t+h|t}$, is its conditional expectation at time t (given the estimated parameters $\hat{\mu}$ and $\hat{\psi}_1$):

$$\hat{y}_{t+h|t} = \hat{\mu} + \hat{\psi}_1(\hat{y}_{t+h-1|t} - \hat{\mu}), \tag{33}$$

where $\hat{y}_{t+i|t} = y_{t+i}$ for $i \leqslant 0$.

For the AR(1), the optimal 1-step-ahead forecast equals $\hat{\mu} + \hat{\psi}_1(\hat{y}_t - \hat{\mu})$. For $h > 1$, the optimal forecast can be obtained recursively or directly as $\hat{y}_{t+h|t} = \hat{\mu} + \hat{\psi}_1^h(\hat{y}_t - \hat{\mu})$.

In the general case of an ARFIMA(n, ζ, s) as given in Eq. (3), the optimal h-step-ahead predictor of y_{t+h} is:

$$\hat{y}_{t+h|t} = \left[\hat{\mu}_{t+h|t} + \sum_{k=1}^{\infty} \hat{c}_k(\hat{y}_{t+h-k} - \hat{\mu}_{t+h|t}) \right]$$

$$+ \sum_{i=1}^{n} \hat{\psi}_i \left\{ \hat{y}_{t+h-i} - \left[\hat{\mu}_{t+h|t} + \sum_{k=1}^{\infty} \hat{c}_k(\hat{y}_{t+h-i-k} - \hat{\mu}_{t+h|t}) \right] \right\}$$

$$+ \sum_{j=1}^{s} \hat{\theta}_j(\hat{y}_{t+h-j} - \hat{y}_{t+h-j|t}). \tag{34}$$

Recall that when exogenous variables enter the conditional mean equation, μ becomes $\mu_t = \mu + \sum_{i=1}^{n_1} \delta_i x_{i,t}$ and consequently, provided that the information $x_{i,t+h}$ is available at time t (which is the case for instance if $x_{i,t}$ is a 'day-of-the-week' dummy variable), $\hat{\mu}_{t+h|t}$ is also available at time t. When there is no exogenous variable in the ARFIMA model and $n = 1$, $s = 0$ and $\zeta = 0$ ($c_k = 0$), the forecast of the AR(1) process given in Eq. (33) can be recovered.

3.4.2. *Forecasting the conditional variance*

Independently from the conditional mean, one can forecast the conditional variance. In the simple GARCH(p, q) case, the optimal h-step-ahead forecast of the conditional variance, i.e. $\hat{\sigma}^2_{t+h|t}$ is given by:

$$\sigma^2_{t+h|t} = \hat{\omega} + \sum_{i=1}^{q} \hat{\alpha}_i \varepsilon^2_{t+h-i|t} + \sum_{j=1}^{p} \hat{\beta}_j \sigma^2_{t+h-j|t}, \tag{35}$$

where $\varepsilon^2_{t+i|t} = \sigma^2_{t+i|t}$ for $i > 0$ while $\varepsilon^2_{t+i|t} = \varepsilon^2_{t+i}$ and $\sigma^2_{t+i|t} = \sigma^2_{t+i}$ for $i \leqslant 0$. Eq. (35) is usually computed recursively, even if a closed form solution of $\sigma^2_{t+h|t}$ can be obtained by recursive substitution in Eq. (35).

Similarly, one can easily obtain the h-step-ahead forecast of the conditional variance of an ARCH, IGARCH and FIGARCH model. By contrast, for threshold models, the computation of the out-of-sample forecasts is more complicated. Indeed, for the EGARCH, GJR and APARCH models (as well as for their long-memory counterparts), the assumption made on the innovation process may have an effect on the forecast (especially for $h > 1$).

For instance, for the GJR (p, q) model,

$$\hat{\sigma}^2_{t+h|t} = \hat{\omega} + \sum_{i=1}^{q} (\hat{\alpha}_i \varepsilon^2_{t-i+h|t} + \hat{\gamma}_i S^-_{t-i+h|t} \varepsilon^2_{t-i+h|t}) + \sum_{j=1}^{p} \hat{\beta}_j \sigma^2_{t-j+h|t}. \tag{36}$$

When all the γ_i parameters equal 0, one recovers the forecast of the GARCH model. Otherwise, one has to compute $S^-_{t-i+h|t}$. Note first that $S^-_{t+i|t} = S^-_{t+i}$ for $i \leqslant 0$. However, when $i > 1$, $S^-_{t+i|t}$ depends on the distribution choice of z_t. When the distribution of z_t is symmetric around 0 (for the Gaussian, Student and GED density), the probability that ε_{t+i} will be negative is $S^-_{t+i|t} = 0.5$. If z_t is (standardized) skewed Student distributed with asymmetry parameter ξ and degree of freedom v, $S^-_{t+i|t} = 1/(1 + \xi^2)$ since ξ^2 is the ratio of probability masses above and below the mode.

For the APARCH (p, q) model,

$$\hat{\sigma}^\delta_{t+h|t} = E(\sigma^\delta_{t+h} \mid \Omega_t)$$

$$= E\left(\hat{\omega} + \sum_{i=1}^{q} \hat{\alpha}_i (\mid \varepsilon_{t+h-i} \mid - \hat{\gamma}_i \varepsilon_{t+h-i})^{\hat{\delta}} + \sum_{j=1}^{p} \hat{\beta}_j \sigma^{\hat{\delta}}_{t+h-j} \mid \Omega_t \right)$$

$$= \hat{\omega} + \sum_{i=1}^{q} \hat{\alpha}_i E[(\varepsilon_{t+h-i} - \hat{\gamma}_i \varepsilon_{t+h-i})^{\hat{\delta}} \mid \Omega_t] + \sum_{j=1}^{p} \hat{\beta}_j \sigma^{\hat{\delta}}_{t+h-j|t}, \tag{37}$$

where $E[(\varepsilon_{t+k} - \hat{\gamma}_i \varepsilon_{t+k})^{\hat{\delta}} \mid \Omega_t] = \kappa_i \sigma^{\hat{\delta}}_{t+k|t}$, for $k > 1$ and $\kappa_i = E(\mid z \mid - \gamma_i z)^{\hat{\delta}}$ (see Section 3.2).

For the EGARCH (p, q) model,

$$\ln \hat{\sigma}^2_{t+h|t} = E(\ln \sigma^2_{t+h} \mid \Omega_t)$$

$$= E\{\hat{\omega} + [1 - \hat{\beta}(L)]^{-1}[1 + \hat{\alpha}(L)]\hat{g}(z_{t+h-1}) \mid \Omega_t\}$$

$$= [1 - \hat{\beta}(L)]\hat{\omega} + \hat{\beta}(L)\ln \hat{\sigma}^2_{t+h|t} + [1 + \hat{\alpha}(L)]\hat{g}(z_{t+h-1|t}), \tag{38}$$

where $\hat{g}(z_{t+k|t}) = \hat{g}(z_{t+k})$ for $k \leqslant 0$ and 0 for $k > 0$.

Finally, the h-step-ahead forecast of the FIAPARCH and FIEGARCH models are obtained in a similar way.

One of the most popular measures to check the forecasting performance of the ARCH-type models is the Mincer-Zarnowitz regression, i.e. on ex-post volatility regression:

$$\check{\sigma}_t^2 = a_0 + a_1 \hat{\sigma}_t^2 + u_t, \tag{39}$$

where $\check{\sigma}_t^2$ is the ex-post volatility, $\hat{\sigma}_t^2$ is the forecasted volatility and a_0, a_1 are parameters to be estimated. If the model for the conditional variance is correctly specified (and the parameters are known) and $E(\check{\sigma}_t^2) = \hat{\sigma}_t^2$, it follows that $a_0 = 0$ and $a_1 = 1$. The R^2 of this regression is often used as a simple measure of the degree of predictability of the ARCH-type model.

However, $\check{\sigma}_t^2$ is never observed. By default, G@RCH 2.2 uses $\check{\sigma}_t^2 = (y_t - \bar{y})^2$, where $\bar{y}$ is the sample mean of y_t. The R^2 of this regression is often lower than 5% and this could lead to the conclusion that GARCH models produce poor forecasts of the volatility (see, among others, Schwert, 1990; or Jorion, 1996). But, as described in Andersen and Bollerslev (1998), the reason of these poor results is the choice of what is considered as the 'true' volatility. G@RCH 2.2 allows selection of any series as the 'observed' volatility (Obs.-Var., see Figure 1). The user may then compute the daily realized volatility as the sum of squared intraday returns and use it as the 'true' volatility. Actually, Andersen and Bollerslev (1998) show that this measure is a more useful one than squared daily returns. Therefore, using 5-minute returns for instance, the realized volatility can be expressed as:

$$\check{\sigma}_t^2 = \sum_{k=1}^{K} y_{k,t}^2, \tag{40}$$

where $y_{k,t}$ is the return of the kth 5-minutes interval of the tth day and K is the number of 5-minutes intervals per day.

Finally, to compare the adequacy of the different distributions, G@RCH 2.2 also allows the computation of density forecasts tests developed in Diebold, Gunther and Tay (1998). The idea of density forecasts is quite simple.[19] Let $f_i(y_i \mid \Omega_i)_{i=1}^{m}$ be a sequence of m one-step-ahead density forecasts produced by a given model, where Ω_i is the conditioning information set, and $p_i(y_i \mid \Omega_i)_{i=1}^{m}$ the sequence of densities defining the Data Generating Process y_i (which is never observed). Testing whether this density is a good approximation of the true density $p(.)$ is equivalent to testing:

$$H_0 : f_i(y_i \mid \Omega_i)_{i=1}^{m} = p_i(y_i \mid \Omega_i)_{i=1}^{m} \tag{41}$$

Diebold, Gunther and Tay (1998) use the fact that, under Eq. (41), the probability integral transform $\hat{\zeta}_i = \int_{-\infty}^{y_i} f_i(t)dt$ is $i.i.d.$ $U(0,1)$, i.e. independent and identically distributed uniform. To check H_0, they propose to use a goodness-of-fit test and independence test for $i.i.d.$ $U(0,1)$. The $i.i.d.$-ness property of $\hat{\zeta}_i$ can be evaluated by plotting the correlograms of $(\zeta - \hat{\zeta})^j$, for $j = 1, 2, 3, 4, ...$, to detect potential dependence in the conditional mean, variance, skewness, kurtosis, etc. Departure from uniformity can also be evaluated by plotting an histogram of $\hat{\zeta}_i$. According to Bauwens, Giot, Grammig and Veredas (2000), *a humped shape of the ζ-histogram would indicate that the issued forecasts are too narrow and that the tails of the true density are not accounted for. On the other hand, a U-shape of the histogram would suggest that the model issues forecasts that either under- or overestimate too frequently.* Moreover, Lambert and Laurent (2001) show that an *inverted S* shape of the histogram would indicate that the errors are skewed, i.e. the true density is probably not symmetric.[20] An illustration is provided in Section 4 with some formal tests and graphical tools.

3.5. *Accuracy*

McCullough and Vinod (1999) and Brooks, Burke and Persand (2001) use the daily German mark/British pound exchange rate data of Bollerslev and Ghysels (1996) to compare the accuracy of GARCH model estimation among several econometric software packages. They choose the GARCH(1,1) model described in Fiorentini, Calzolani and Pamattani (1996) (hereafter denoted FCP) as the benchmark. In this section, we use the same methodology with the same dataset to check the accuracy of our procedures. Coefficients and standard error estimates of G@RCH 2.2 are reported in Table 1 together with the results of McCullough and Vinod (1999) (based on the FORTRAN procedure of FCP and thus entitled 'FCP' in the table).

G@RCH 2.2 gives very satisfactory results since the first four digits (at least) are the same as those of the benchmark for all but two estimations. In addition, it competes well compared to other well known econometric softwares. Table 2 presents the coefficient estimates for the 5 pieces of software.

Moreover, to investigate the accuracy of our forecasting procedures, we have run an 8-step ahead forecast of the model, similar to Brooks, Burk and Persand (2001). Table 4 in Brooks, Burke, and Persand (2001) reports the conditional

Table 1. Accuracy of the GARCH procedure

	Coefficient		Standard Errors		Robust Standard Errors	
	G@RCH	FCP	G@RCH	FCP	G@RCH	FCP
μ	−0.006184	−0.006190	0.008462	0.008462	0.009187	0.009189
ω	0.010760	0.010761	0.002851	0.002852	0.006484	0.006493
α_1	0.153407	0.153134	0.026569	0.026523	0.053595	0.053532
β_1	0.805879	0.805974	0.033542	0.033553	0.072386	0.072461

Table 2. GARCH Accuracy Comparison

	FCP	G@RCH	Eviews[21]	PcGive	TSP	S-Plus
μ	−0.00619	−0.00618	−0.00617	−0.00625	−0.00619	−0.00919
ω	0.010761	0.010760	0.010761	0.010760	0.010761	0.011696
α_1	0.153134	0.153407	0.153134	0.153397	0.153134	0.154295
β_1	0.805974	0.805879	0.805975	0.805886	0.805974	0.800276

variance forecasts given by six well-known software packages and the correct values. Contrary to E-Views, Matlab and SAS, G@RCH 2.2 hits the benchmarks for all steps to the third decimal (note that GAUSS, Microfit and Rats also do).

Finally, Lombardi and Gallo (2001) extend the work of Fiorentini, Calzolani and Pamattani (1996) to the FIGARCH model of Baillie, Bollerslev and Mikkelsen (1996) and derive analytic expressions for the second-order derivatives of this model in the Gaussian case. For the same DEM/UKP database as in the previous example, Table 3 reports the coefficient estimates and their standard errors for our package (using numerical gradients and the BFGS optimization method) and for Lombardi and Gallo (2001) (using analytical gradients and the Newton-Raphson algorithm; results correspond to the columns entitled 'LG').

Results show that G@RCH 2.2 provides accurate estimates, even for an advanced model such as the FIGARCH. As expected, it is however more time-consuming than the C code of Lombardi and Gallo (2001)[22] (163 sec. vs 43 sec. using a PIII processor with 450 Mhz).

3.6. *Features comparison*

The goal of this section is to compare more objectively the features offered by G@RCH 2.2 with respect to nine other well known econometric software packages, namely PcGive 10 (also programmed in Ox), GAUSS and its Fanpac package, Eviews 4, S-Plus 6 and its GARCH module, Rats 5.0 and its *garch.src*

Table 3. Accuracy of the FIGARCH procedure

	Coefficient		Standard Errors	
	G@RCH	LG	G@RCH	LG
μ	0.003606	0.003621	0.009985	0.009985
ω	0.015772	0.015764	0.003578	0.003581
α_1	0.198134	0.198448	0.042508	0.042444
β_1	0.675652	0.675251	0.051800	0.051693
d	0.570702	0.569951	0.075039	0.074762

Table 4. GARCH Features Comparison

	G@RCH	PcGive	Fanpac	Eviews	S-Plus	Rats	TSP	Microfit	SAS	Stata
Version	2.0	10	–	4.0	6	5.0	4.5	4	8.2	7
Conditional mean										
Explanatory variables	+	+	+	+	+	+	+	+	+	+
ARMA	+	+	+	+	+	+	+	+	+	+
ARFIMA	+	–	–	–	–	–	–	–	–	–
ARCH-in-Mean	–	+	+	+	+	+	+	–	+	+
Conditional variance										
Explanatory variables	+	+	+	+	+	+	+	+	+	+
GARCH	+	+	+	+	+	+	+	+	+	+
IGARCH	+	–	+	–	–	+	–	–	+	–
EGARCH	+	+	+	+	+	+	–	+	+	+
GJR	+	+	–	+	+	+	–	–	–	+
APARCH	+	–	–	–	+	–	–	–	–	+
C-GARCH	–	–	–	+	+	–	–	–	–	–
FIGARCH	+	–	+	–	+	–	–	–	–	–
FIEGARCH	+	–	–	–	–	–	–	–	–	–
FIAPARCH	+	–	–	–	–	–	–	–	–	–
HYGARCH	+	–	–	–	–	–	–	–	–	–
Distributions										
Normal	+	+	+	+	+	+	+	+	+	+
Student-t	+	+	+	–	+	+	–	+	+	–
GED	+	+	–	–	+	+	–	–	–	–
Skewed-t	+	–	–	–	–	–	–	–	–	–
Double Exponential	–	–	–	–	+	–	–	–	–	–
Estimation										
MLE	+	+	+	+	+	+	+	+	+	+
QMLE	+	+	+	+	–	–	–	–	–	+

A '+' (resp. '–') means that the corresponding option is (resp. is not) available for this software. C-GARCH corresponds to the Component GARCH of Engle and Lee (1999).

procedure,[23] TSP 4.5, Microfit 4, SAS 8.2 and Stata 7. It is thus not our intention to evaluate a program against another, but we will rather present an overview of what can or cannot be done with these packages.

The proposed models and options differ widely from one program to another as can be seen in Table 4. Regarding the range of different univariate models, many programs propose asymmetric models, very few (G@RCH, S-Plus with the FIGARCH and the FIEGARCH and Fanpac with the FIGARCH) offer long memory models in the variance equation and none (except G@RCH) offers a fractionally integrated specification in the mean. As for the distribution, the choice is often limited to symmetric densities (except G@RCH which provides a skewed Student likelihood). Finally, robust standard errors are proposed in 5 of the 10 packages we have compared (G@RCH, PcGive, GAUSS Fanpac, Eviews and Stata).

4. Application

4.1. *Data and methodology*

To illustrate the G@RCH 2.2 package with a concrete application, we analyze the French CAC40 stock index for the years 1995–1999 (1249 daily observations). It is computed by the exchange as a weighted measure of the prices of its components and is available in the database on an intraday basis with the price index being computed every 15 minutes. For the time period under review, the opening hours of the French stock market were 10.00 am to 5.00 pm, thus 7 hours of trading per day. This translates into 28 intraday returns used to compute the daily realized volatility. Intraday prices are the outcomes of a linear interpolation between the closest recorded prices below and above the time set in the grid. Correspondingly, all returns are computed as the first difference in the regularly time-spaced log prices of the index. Because the exchange is closed from 5.00 pm to 10.00 am the next day, the first intraday return is the first difference between the log price at 10.15 am and the log price at 5.00 pm the day before. Then, the intraday data are used to compute the daily realized volatility using Eq. (40). Finally, daily returns in percentage are defined as 100 times the first difference of the log of the closing prices.[24]

The estimation of the parameters is carried out for the 800 observations while forecasting is computed for the last observations.

4.2. *Using the 'full version'*

Once the installation process is correctly completed following the instructions of the *readme.txt* file, the user may open the database in GiveWin (in the example 'CAC15.xls'), and then select the OxPack module.

Once the package has been selected, one can launch the **Model/Formulate** menu. The list of all the variables of the database appears in the *Database* section (see Figure 1). There are four possible statuses for each variable: dependent

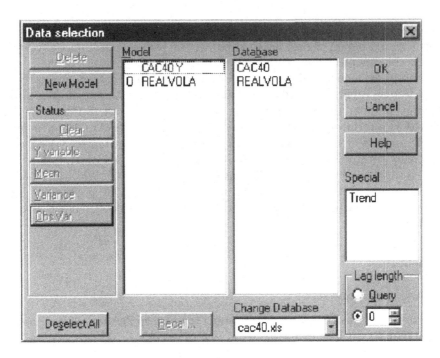

Figure 1. Selecting the variables.

variable (Y variable), regressor in the mean (Mean), regressor in the variance (Variance) or observed volatility (Obs. Var.). The program provides estimates for univariate models,[25] so only one Y variable per model is accepted. However one can include several regressors in the mean and the variance equations and the same variable can be a regressor in both equations.

Once the OK button is pressed, the **Model/Model Settings** box automatically appears. This box allows selection and specification of the model: AR(FI)MA orders for the mean equation, GARCH orders, type of GARCH model for the variance equation and the distribution (Figure 2). The default specification is an ARMA(0,0)-GARCH(1,1) with normal errors. In our application, we select an ARMA(1,0)-APARCH(1,1) specification with a skewed Student likelihood.

As explained in Section 3.1, it is possible to constrain the parameters to range between a lower and an upper bound by selecting the **Bounded Parameters** option. The defaults bounds can be changed in the *startingvalues.txt* file.

In the next window, the user is asked to make a choice regarding the starting values (Figure 3): they might (1) let the program use the predefined starting values,[26] (2) enter them manually, element by element, or (3) enter the starting values in a vector form (the required form is 'value1;value2;value3').

Then, the estimation method for standard deviations is selected: ML or QML (with a specified pseudo-likelihood) or both. In this window (see Figure 4), one may also select the sample and some maximization options (such has the number

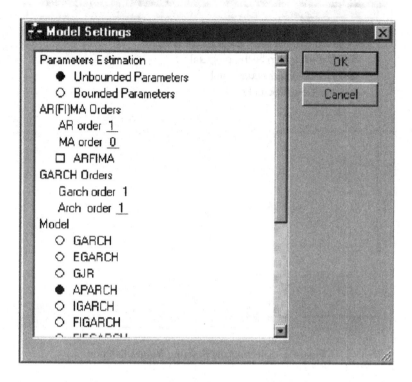

Figure 2. Model Settings.

of iterations between intermediary results printings) when clicking on the *Options* button.

The estimation procedure is then launched and the program comes back to GiveWin. Let us assume that the element-by-element method has been selected. A new window appears (see Figure 5) with all the possible parameters to be estimated. Depending on the specification, some parameters have a value, others do not. The user should replace only the former, since they correspond to the parameters to be estimated for the specified model.

Once this step is completed, the program starts the iteration process. The final output is divided by default into two main parts: first, the model specification reminder; second, the estimated values and other useful statistics of the parameters.[27] The output is given in the box 'Output 1'.

After the estimation of the model, new options are available in **OxPack: Menu/Tests, Menu/Graphic Analysis, Menu/Forecasts, Menu/Exclusion Restrictions, Menu/Linear Restrictions** and **Menu/Store**.

The **Menu/Graphic Analysis** option allows ploting using different graphics (see Figure 6 for details). Just as any other graphs in the GiveWin environment, they can be easily edited (color, size, ...) and exported in many formats (.eps, .ps, .wmf,

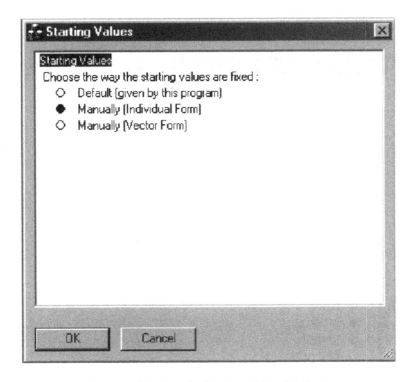

Figure 3. Selecting the Starting Values Method.

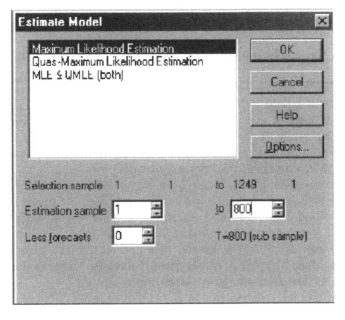

Figure 4. Standard Errors Estimation Methods.

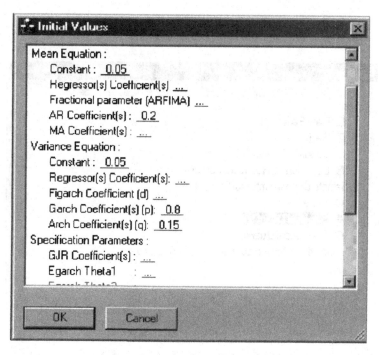

Figure 5. Entering the Starting Values.

```
**************************
* SPECIFICATIONS **
**************************
```

Mean Equation: ARMA (1, 0) model.
No regressor in the mean.
Variance Equation : APARCH (1, 1) model.
No regressor in the variance.
The distribution is a Skewed Student distribution, with a tail coefficient of 15.72 and an asymmetry coefficient of -0.08751.
Strong convergence using numerical derivatives

Maximum Likelihood Estimation

	Coefficient	Std.Error	t-value	t-prob
Cst(M)	0.065337	0.037157	1.758	0.0791
AR(1)	0.004704	0.037117	0.1267	0.8992
Cst(V)	0.017498	0.013488	1.297	0.1949
Beta1	0.947590	0.020193	46.93	0.0000
Alpha1	0.038464	0.017776	2.164	0.0308
Gamma1	0.676364	0.348702	1.940	0.0528
Delta	1.462837	0.533581	2.742	0.0063
Asymmetry	-0.087512	0.054314	-1.611	0.1075
Tail	15.718323	8.087414	1.944	0.0523

No. Observations: 800   No. Parameters: 9
Mean (Y): 0.08103   Variance (Y): 1.27405
Log Likelihood: -1190.521   Alpha[1]+Beta[1]: 0.98605

The sample mean of squared residuals was used to start recursion.
The condition for existence of $E(\sigma^\delta)$ and $E(|e^\delta|)$ is observed.
The constraint equals 0.9926 and should be < 1.
Vector of estimated parameters:
0.065337; 0.004704; 0.017498; 0.947590; 0.038464; 0.676364; 1.462837;-0.087512;15.718323

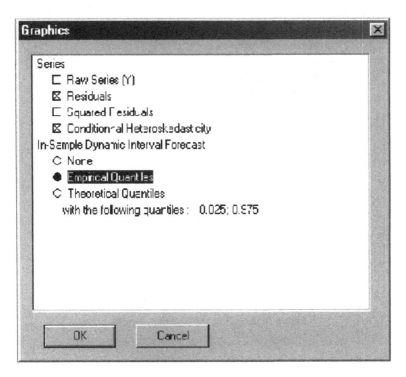

Figure 6. Graphics Menu.

.emf and .gwg). Figure 7 provides the graphs of the squared residuals and the conditional mean with a 95% confidence interval.

The **Menu/Tests** option allows different tests to be run (see Section 3.2 for further explanations). It also allows the printing of the variance-covariance matrix of the estimated parameters (Figure 8). The results of these tests are printed in GiveWin. An example of output is reported in the next box ('Output 2').

We do not intend to comment upon this application in detail. However, looking at these results, one can briefly argue that the model seems to capture the dynamics of the first and second moments of the CAC40 (see the Box-Pierce statistics). Moreover, the Sign Bias tests shows that there is no remaining leverage component in the innovations while the Nyblom stability test suggests that the estimated parameters are quite stable during the investigated period. Finally, our model specification is not rejected by the goodness-of-fit tests for various lag lengths.

To obtain the h-step-ahead forecasts, access the menu **Test/Forecast** and set the number of forecasts, pre-sample observations (to be plotted) as well as some other graphical options.

Figure 9 shows 10 pre-sample observations and the forecasts up to horizon 10 of the conditional mean. The forecasted bands are $\pm 2\hat{\sigma}_{t+h\,|\,t}$ (note that the critical value 2 can be changed).

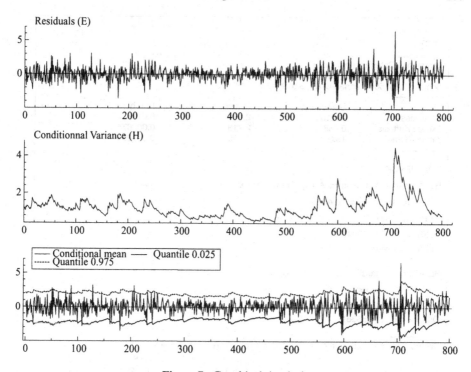

Figure 7. Graphical Analysis.

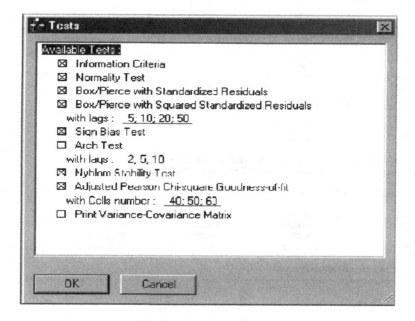

Figure 8. Tests Dialog Box.

Output 2

TESTS:
─────

Information Criterium (minimize)
Akaike 2.998802 Shibata 2.998553
Schwarz 3.051504 Hannan-Quinn 3.019048
─────

	Statistic	t-value	t-prob
Skewness	-0.2135	2.47	0.0135
Excess Kurtosis	0.4684	2.713	0.006674
Jarque-Bera	13.39	13.39	0.001235
─────

BOX-PIERCE:

H0: No serial correlation $\Rightarrow$ Accept H0 when prob. is High [Q < Chisq(lag)]

Box-Pierce Q-statistics on residuals

$\rightarrow$ P-values adjusted by 1 degree(s) of freedom

Q(10) = 14.47 [0.1064]
Q(20) = 21.67 [0.3012]

Box-Pierce Q-statistics on squared residuals

$\rightarrow$ P-values adjusted by 2 degree(s) of freedom

Q(10) = 9.887 [0.2731]
Q(20) = 16.13 [0.5838]
─────

Diagnostic test based on the news impact curve (EGARCH vs. GARCH)

	Test	Prob
Sign Bias t-Test	0.98838	0.32297
Negative Size Bias t-Test	0.14581	0.88407
Positive Size Bias t-Test	0.62400	0.53263
Joint Test for the Three Effects	5.13914	0.16189
─────

Joint Statistic of the Nyblom test of stability: 2.727
Individual Nyblom Statistics:

Cst(M)	0.72438
AR(1)	0.68524
Cst(V)	0.51505
Beta1	0.42785
Alpha1	0.46229
Gamma1	0.43489
Delta	0.54130
Asymmetry	0.21342
Tail	0.08950

Rem: Asymptotic 1% critical value for individual statistics = 0.75.
Asymptotic 5% critical value for individual statistics = 0.47.
─────

Adjusted Pearson Chi-square Goodness-of-fit test

Lags	Statistic	P-Value(lag-1)	P-Value(lag-k-1)
40	24.9000	0.961261	0.729877
50	26.7500	0.995994	0.946240
60	32.6500	0.997893	0.972622

Rem.: k = # estimated parameters

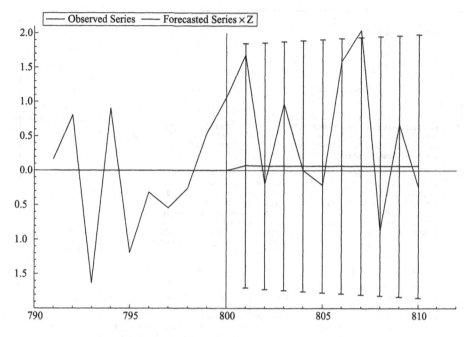

Figure 9. Forecasts from an AR(1)-APARCH(1,1).

4.3. *Using the 'light version'*

First, to specify the model you want to estimate, you have to edit *GarchEstim.ox* with any text editor. We recommend OxEdit. It is shareware that highlights Ox syntax in color (see http://www.oxedit.com for more details). An example of the *GarchEstim.ox* file is displayed below.

The **GarchEstim** file consists of five parts:

- the 'Data' part deals with the database, the sample and the variables selection;
- the 'Specification' part is related to the choice of the model, the lag orders and the shape of the distribution;
- the 'Tests & Forecasts' part allows computation of different tests and parameterisation of the forecasts. Note that **BOXPIERCE**, **ARCHLAGS** and **PEARSON** all require a vector of integers corresponding to the lags used in the computation of the statistics;
- the 'Output' part includes several options including **MLE** that refers to the computation method of the standard deviations of the estimated parameters, **TESTONLY**, which is useful when you want to run some tests on the raw series, prior to any estimation and **GRAPHS** and **FOREGRAPHS**, to print graphs for estimation and forecasting, respectively;[28]
- the 'Parameters' part consists of five procedures. **BOUNDS** to constraint several parameters to range between a lower and an upper bound (see

```
                                                                    GarchEstim.ox
#import <packages/garch/garch>
main()
{
    decl garchobj;
    garchobj = new Garch();
//*** DATA ***//
    garchobj.Load("/data/cac40.xls");
    garchobj.Info();

    garchobj.Select(Y_VAR, {"CAC40",0,0});
//  garchobj.Select(X_VAR, {"NAME",0,0});        // REGRESSOR IN THE MEAN
//  garchobj.Select(Z_VAR, {"NAME",0,0});        // REGRESSOR IN THE VARIANCE
//  garchobj.Select(O_VAR, {"REALVOLA",0,0});    // REALIZED VOLATILITY
    garchobj.SetSelSample(-1, 1, 1000, 1);

//*** SPECIFICATIONS ***//
    garchobj.CSTS(1,1);              // cst in Mean (1 or 0), cst in Variance (1 or 0)
    garchobj.DISTRI(1);             // 0 for Gauss, 1 for Student, 2 for GED, 3 for Skewed-Student
    garchobj.ARMA_ORDERS(1,0);      // AR order (p), MA order (q).
    garchobj.ARFIMA(0);             // 1 if Arfima wanted, 0 otherwise
    garchobj.GARCH_ORDERS(1,1);     // p order, q order
    garchobj.MODEL(1);              //   1:GARCH    2:EGARCH    3:GJR    4:APARCH    5:IGARCH
                                    //   6:FIGARCH(BBM) 7:FIGARCH(Chung)    8:FIEGARCH(BBM only)
                                    //   9:FIAPARCH(BBM) 10: FIAPARCH(Chung) 11: HYGARCH(BBM)

    garchobj.TRUNC(1000);           // Truncation order (only F.I. models with BBM method)

//*** TESTS & FORECASTS ***//
    garchobj.BOXPIERCE(<10;15;20>); // Lags for the Box-Pierce Q-statistics, <> otherwise
    garchobj.ARCHLAGS(<2;5;10>);    // Lags for Engle's LM ARCH test, <> otherwise
    garchobj.NYBLOM(1);             // 1 to compute the Nyblom stability test, 0 otherwise
    garchobj.PEARSON(<40;50;60>);   // Cells for the adjusted Pearson Chi-square Goodness-of-fit test
    garchobj.FORECAST(0,9,1);       // Arg.1 : 1 to launch the forecasting procedure, 0 otherwize
                                    // Arg.2 : Number of forecasts
                                    // Arg.3 : 1 to Print the forecasts, 0 otherwise

//*** OUTPUT ***//
    garchobj.MLE(1);                // 0 : both, 1 : MLE, 2 : QMLE
    garchobj.COVAR(0);              // if 1, prints variance-covariance matrix of the parameters.
    garchobj.ITER(0);               // Interval of iterations between printed intermediary results
    garchobj.TESTSONLY(0,0);        // Arg.1 : if 1, runs tests for the raw Y series, prior to ...
                                    // Arg.2 : if 1, runs tests after the estimation.
    garchobj.GRAPHS(0,0,"");        // Arg.1 : if 1, displays graphics of the estimations.
                                    // Arg.2 : if 1, saves these graphics in a EPS file
                                    // Arg.3 : Name of the saved file.
    garchobj.FOREGRAPHS(1,0,"");    // Same as GRAPHS(p,s,n) but for the graphics of the forecasts.

//*** PARAMETERS ***//
    garchobj.BOUNDS(1);             // 1 if bounded parameters wanted, 0 otherwise
    garchobj.FixParam(1);           // 1 to fix some parameters to their starting values, 0 otherwize
    garchobj.FixedParam(<0;0;0;0;0;0;1>);
                                    // 1 to fix and 0 to estimate the corresponding parameter
    garchobj.DoEstimation(<>);

// m_vPar = m_clevel | m_vbetam | m_dARFI | m_vAR | m_vMA | m_calpha0 | m_vgammav | m_dD | m_vbetav |
//          m_valphav | m_vleverage | m_vtheta1 | m_vtheta2 | m_vpsy | m_ddelta | m_cA | m_cV | m_vHY
//garchobj.DoEstimation(<0.02;0.05;0.45;0.22;0.01;0.025;0.8;0.1;-0.15;0.2;6>);

    garchobj.STORE(0,0,0,0,0,"01",0); // Arg.1,2,3,4,5 : if 1 -> stored. (Res-SqRes-CondV-...
                                    // Arg.6 : Suffix. The name of the saved series will be...
                                    // Arg.7 : if 0, saves as an Excel spreadsheet (.xls)...
    delete garchobj;
}
```

Section 3.1), **FixedParam** to fix some parameters to their starting values, **DoEstimation** that launches the estimation of the model and the **STORE** function allowing storage of some series. The arguments of the **DoEstimation** procedure are a vector containing starting values of the parameters in a specified order (but the user can also let the program choose defaults values).

Note that the 'Light Version' is more than just a replication of the 'Full Version' without the graphical interface. Indeed, G@RCH uses the object-oriented programming features of Ox and provides a new class called **Garch**. All the functions of this class can thus be used within an Ox program. To illustrate the potentiality of the package, we also provide *Forecast.ox*, an example that computes 448 one-step-ahead forecasts of the conditional mean and conditional variance (using the estimated parameters presented in the previous section), compute the Mincer-Zarnowitz regression and perform some out-of-sample density forecast tests as suggested by Diebold, Gunther and Tay (1998).

The interesting part of *Forecast.ox* is printed in the next box. This code has been used to produce Figure 10 and the outputs associated with this forecasting experiment (see page 480).

In the first four panels of Figure 10, we show the correlograms of $(\hat{\zeta} - \bar{\hat{\zeta}})^j$, for $j = 1, 2, 3, 4$. This graphical tool has been proposed by Diebold, Gunther and Tay (1998) to detect potential remaining dependence in the conditional mean, variance, skewness, kurtosis. In our example, it seems that the probability integral transform is independently distributed.

Panel 5 of Figure 10 also shows the histogram (with 30 cells) of $\hat{\zeta}$ with the 95% confidence bands. From this figure, it is clear that the AR(1)-APARCH(1,1) model

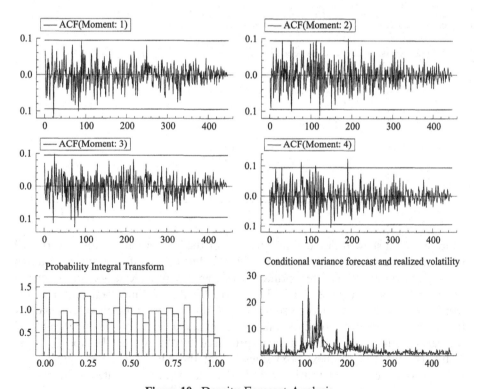

Figure 10. Density Forecast Analysis.

```
                                                                    Forecast.ox
#import <packages/garch/garch>
main()
{
    decl garchobj;
    garchobj = new Garch();

    ...

    garchobj.DoEstimation(<>);
    decl number_of_forecasts=448; // number of h_step_ahead forecasts
    decl step=1;                  // specify h (h-step-ahead forecasts)
    decl T=garchobj.GetcT();
    decl par=garchobj.PAR()[][0];
    println("!!! Please Wait while computing the forecasts !!!");
    decl forc=<>,h,yfor=<>,Hfor=<>;
    decl RV=columns(garchobj.GetGroup(O_VAR));
    decl shape=<>;
    if (garchobj.GetDistri()==1 || garchobj.GetDistri()==2)  // Except for the HYGARCH
        shape=par[rows(par)-1];
    else if (garchobj.GetDistri()==3)
        shape=par[rows(par)-2:rows(par)-1];
    for (h=0; h<number_of_forecasts; ++h)
    {
        garchobj.FORECAST(1,step,0);
        garchobj.SetSelSample(-1, 1, T+h, 1);
        garchobj.InitData();
        yfor|=garchobj.GetForcData(Y_VAR, step);
        forc|=garchobj.FORECASTING();
        if (RV==1)
            Hfor|=garchobj.GetForcData(O_VAR, step);          // If you use the realized volatility
    }
    decl cd=garchobj.CD(yfor-forc[][0],forc[][1],garchobj.GetDistri(),shape);
    println("Density Forecast Test on Standardized Forecast Errors");
    garchobj.APGT(cd,20|30,rows(par));
    garchobj.AUTO(cd, number_of_forecasts, -0.1, 0.1, 0);
    garchobj.confidence_limits_uniform(cd,30,0.95,1,4);
    if (RV==0)
    {
        DrawTitle(5, "Conditional variance forecast and absolute returns");
        Hfor = (yfor - meanc(yfor)).^2;
    }
    else
        DrawTitle(5, "Conditional variance forecast and realized volatility");
    Draw(5, (Hfor~forc[][1])');
    ShowDrawWindow();
    garchobj.MZ(Hfor, forc, number_of_forecasts);
    garchobj.FEM(forc, yfor~Hfor);

    garchobj.STORE(0,0,0,0,0,"01",0); // Arg.1,2,3,4,5 ...
                                      // Arg.6 : Suffix. ...
                                      // Arg.7 : if 0, ...
    delete garchobj;
}
```

coupled with a skewed Student distribution for the innovations performs very well with the dataset we have investigated. This conclusion is reinforced by the Pearson Chi-square goodness-of-fit test printed hereafter that provides a statistical version of the graphical test presented in Figure 10. Finally, the program performs the Mincer-Zarnowitz regression given in Eq. (39) that regresses the observed volatility (in our case the realized volatility) on a constant and a vector of 448 one-step-ahead forecasts of the conditional variance (produced by the APARCH model).[29] The results (reported in the next box) suggest that the APARCH model gives good forecasts of the conditional variance. Indeed, looking at the estimated parameters of this regression, one can hardly conclude that the APARCH model provides biases

Density Forecast Test on Standardized Forecast Errors Adjusted Pearson Chi-square Goodness-of-fit test			
Lags	Statistic	P-Value(lag-1)	P-Value(lag-k-1)
20	21.0179	0.335815	0.020969
30	26.5089	0.598181	0.149654

Rem.: k = number of estimated parameters

Mincer-Zarnowitz regression on the forecasted volatility

	Coefficient	Std.Error	t-value	t-prob
a_0	-0.225818	0.264837	-0.8527	0.3940
a_1	1.370648	0.176086	7.784	0.0000

R^2: 0.402914

Note: S.E. are Heteroskedastic Consistent (White, 80)

forecasts. Moreover, the R^2 of this regression is higher than 40% (See Andersen and Bollerslev (1998) for more details).

5. Conclusions

This paper documents the software G@RCH 2.2, an Ox package allowing to estimation and forecasting of numerous univariate ARCH-type processes including GARCH, EGARCH, GJR, APARCH, IGARCH, FIGARCH, HYGARCH, FIEGARCH and FIAPARCH specifications of the conditional variance. Several features of the program are worth noting since they are unavailable in most of the traditional econometric softwares: the asymmetric and fractionally integrated processes, four distributions (normal, Student-t, GED and skewed Student-t), (editable) parameters bounds, several mispecification tests and h-step-ahead forecasts.

G@RCH 2.2 is free of charge when used for educational or research purposes and can be downloaded at **http://www.egss.ulg.ac.be/garch/**.

Acknowledgements

While remaining responsible for any error in this paper, the authors would like to thank F. Palm, J-P. Urbain, J. Davidson and M. McAleer for useful comments and suggestions.

Notes

1. Asset pricing models are indeed incomplete unless the full conditional model is specified.
2. Chunhachinda, Dandapani, Hamid and Prakash (1997) find that the incorporation of skewness into the investor's portfolio decision causes a major change in the construction of the optimal portfolio.

3. Corrado and Su (1996) and Corrado and Su (1997) show that when skewness and kurtosis adjustment terms are added to the Black and Scholes formula, improved accuracy is obtained for pricing options.

4. For a comprehensive review of this language, see Cribari-Neto and Zarkos (2001).

5. Recall that $L^k y_t = y_{t-k}$.

6. ARFIMA models have been combined with an ARCH-type specification by Baillie, Chung and Tieslau (1996), Tschernig (1995), Teyssière (1997), Lecourt (2000) and Beine, Laurent and Lecourt (2000).

7. For stochastic volatility models, see Koopman, Shepard and Doornik (1998).

8. Note that with the EGARCH parameterization of Bollerslev and Mikkelsen (1996), it is possible to estimate an EGARCH $(p, 0)$ since $\ln \sigma_t^2$ depends on $g(z_{t-1})$, even when $q = 0$.

9. Complete developments leading to these conclusions are available in Ding, Granger and Engle (1993).

10. For the symmetric Student density, $\xi = 1$.

11. In their study of the daily S&P500 index, they find that the squared returns series has positive autocorrelations over more than 2,500 lags (or more than 10 years!).

12. See Bollerslev and Mikkelsen (1996, p. 158) for a discussion on the importance of non-integer values of integration when modelling long-run dependencies in the conditional mean of economic time series.

13. See Chung (1999) for more details.

14. Notice that the GJR has not been extended to the long-memory framework. It is however nested in the FIAPARCH class of models.

15. When using the BBM option in G@RCH for the FIEGARCH and FIAPARCH, $(1 - L)^d$ and $(1 - L)^{-d}$ are truncated at some predefined value (see above). It is also possible to truncate this polynomial at the information size at time t, i.e. $t - 1$.

16. $LogL$ = log-likelihood value, n is the number observations and k the number of estimated parameters.

17. See Palm and Vlaar (1997) for more details.

18. By optimal, we mean optimal under expected quadratic loss, or in a mean square error sense.

19. For more details about density forecasts and applications in finance, see the special issue of *Journal of Forecasting* (Timmermann, 2000).

20. Confidence intervals for the ζ-histogram can be obtained by using the properties of the histogram under the null hypothesis of uniformity.

21. Note that the default in Eviews 4 is to initialize the initial variance required for GARCH terms by using backcasting methods. To set the presample values of the variance and the squared residual to the unconditional variance (which is the case in our example), one has therefore to 'turn off' the backcasting option. Results reported as Table 2 are obtained in this way. In addition the default convergence option was changed to 1e-6. See the Eviews for more details.

22. This C code is available at **http://www.ds.unifi.it/~mjl/** in the 'software' section. Note that the only configuration available is a FIGARCH $(1, d, 1)$ with a constant in the mean and variance equations and a Gaussian likelihood.

23. This file is available at **http://www.estima.com/procindx.htm** for download.

24. By definition and using the properties of the log distribution, the sum of the intraday returns is equal to the observed daily return based on the closing prices.

25. The extension of this package to multivariate GARCH models is currently under development.

26. Note that these default values can be modified by the user as they are stored in the *startingvalues.txt* file installed with the package.
27. Recall that the estimations are based on the numerical evaluation of the gradients.
28. Graphics will only be displayed when using GiveWin as front-end.
29. The realized and one-step-ahead forecasts are plotted in the last panel of Figure 10.

References

Andersen, T. and Bollerslev, T. (1998) Answering the Skeptics: Yes, Standard Volatility Models do Provide Accurate Forecasts. *International Economic Review*, 39, 885–905.

Baillie, R. (1996) Long Memory Processes and Fractional Integration in Econometrics. *Journal of Econometrics*, 73, 5–59.

Baillie, R., Bollerslev, T. and Mikkelsen, H. (1996) Fractionally Integrated Generalized Autoregressive Conditional Heteroskedasticity. *Journal of Econometrics*, 74, 3–30.

Baillie, R., Chung, C. and Tieslau, M. (1996) Analyzing Inflation by the Fractionally Integrated ARFIMA-GARCH Model. *Journal of Applied Econometrics*, 11, 23–40.

Bauwens, L., Giot, P. Grammig, J. and Veredas, D. (2000) A Comparison of Financial Duration Models Via Density Forecasts. CORE DP 2060.

Beine, M., Laurent, S. and Lecourt, C. (2000) Accounting for Conditional Leptokurtosis and Closing Days Effects in FIGARCH Models of Daily Exchange Rates. *Forthcoming in Applied Financial Economics*.

Bera, A. and Higgins, M. (1993) ARCH Models: Properties, Estimation and Testing. *Journal of Economic Surveys*.

Black, F. (1976) Studies of Stock Market Volatility Changes. *Proceedings of the American Statistical Association, Business and Economic Statistics Section*, pp. 177–181.

Bollerslev, T. (1986) Generalized Autoregressive Condtional Heteroskedasticity. *Journal of Econometrics*, 31, 307–327.

Bollerslev, T. and Ghysels, E. (1996) Periodic Autoregressive Conditional Heteroskedasticity. *Journal of Business and Economics Statistics*, 14, 139–152.

Bollerslev, T. and Mikkelsen, H. O. (1996) Modeling and Pricing Long-Memory in Stock Market Volatility. *Journal of Econometrics*, 73, 151–184.

Bollerslev, T. and Wooldridge, J. (1992) Quasi-maximum Likelihood Estimation and Inference in Dynamic Models with Time-varying Covariances. *Econometric Reviews*, 11, 143–172.

Brooks, C., Burke, S. and Persand, G. (2001) Benchmarks and the Accuracy of GARCH Model Estimation. *International Journal of Forecasting*, 17, 45–56.

Chung, C.-F. (1999) Estimating the Fractionnally Intergrated GARCH Model. National Taïwan University working paper.

Chunhachinda, P., Dandapani, K. Hamid, S. and Prakash, A. (1997) Portfolio Selection and Skewness: Evidence from International Stock Markets. *Journal of Banking and Finance*, 21, 143–167.

Corrado, C. and Su, T. (1996) Skewness and Kurtosis in S&P 500 Index Returns Implied by Option Prices. *Journal of Financial Research*, 19, 175–192.

—— (1997) Implied Volatility Skews and Stock Return Skewness and Kurtosis Implied by Stock Option Prices. *European Journal of Finance*, 3, 73–85.

Cribari-Neto, F. and Zarkos, S. (2001) Econometric and Statistical Computing Using Ox. *Forthcoming* in Computational Economics.

Davidson, J. (2001) Moment and Memory Properties of Linear Conditional Heteroscedasticity Models. Manuscript, Cardiff University.

Diebold, F. X., Gunther, T. A. and Tay, A. S. (1998) Evaluating Density Forecasts, with Applications to Financial Risk Management. *International Economic Review*, 39, 863–883.

Ding, Z., Granger, C. W. J. and Engle, R. F. (1993) A Long Memory Property of Stock Market Returns and a New Model. *Journal of Empirical Finance* 1, 83–106.

Doornik, J. A. (1999) *An Object Oriented Matrix Programming Language*. Timberlake Consultant Ltd., third edn.

Doornik, J. A. and Ooms, M. (1999) A Package for Estimating, Forecasting and Simulating Arfima Models: Arfima package 1.0 for Ox. Discussion paper, Econometric Intitute, Erasmus University Rotterdam.

Engle, R. (1982) Autoregressive Conditional Heteroscedasticity with Estimates of the Variance of United Kingdom Inflation. *Econometrica*, 50, 987–1007.

Engle, R. and Bollerslev, T. (1986) Modeling the Persistence of Conditional Variances. *Econometric Reviews*, 5, 1–50.

Engle, R. and González-Rivera, G. (1991) Semiparametric ARCH Model. *Journal of Business and Economic Statistics*, 9, 345–360.

Engle, R. and Lee, G. (1999) *A Permanent and Transitory Component Model of Stock Return Volatility*. pp. 475–497. In R. Engle and H. White (eds), Cointegration, Causality, and Forecasting: A Festschrift in Honor of Clive W. J. Granger. Oxford University Press.

Engle, R. and Ng, V. (1993) Measuring and Testing the Impact of News on Volatility. *Journal of Finance*, 48, 1749–1778.

Fiorentini, G., Calzolari, G. and Panattoni, L. (1996) Analytic Derivatives and the Computation of GARCH Estimates. *Journal of Applied Econometrics*, 11, 399–417.

Geweke, J. (1986) Modeling the Persistece of Conditional Variances: A Comment. *Econometric Review*, 5, 57–61.

Giot, P. and Laurent, S., (2001) Valut-at-Risk for Long and Short Positions. CORE DP 2001–22, Maastricht University METEOR RM/01/005.

Glosten, L., Jagannathan, R. and Runkle, D. (1993) On the Relation Between Expected Value and the Volatility of the Nominal Excess Return on Stocks. *Journal of Finance*, 48, 1779–1801.

Granger, C. (1980) Long Memory Relationships and the Aggregation of Dynamic Models. *Journal of Econometrics*, 14, 227–238.

Granger, C. and Joyeux, R. (1980) An Introduction to Long-Memory Time Series Models and Fractional Differencing. *Journal of Time Series Analysis* 1, 15–29.

Hansen, B. (1994) Autoregressive Conditional Density Estimation. *International Economic Review*, 35, 705–730.

Higgins, M. and Bera, A. (1992) A Class of Nonlinear ARCH Models. *International Economic Review*, 33, 137–158.

Jarque, C. and Bera, A., (1987) A Test for Normality of Observations and Regression Resid-uals. *International Statistical Review*, 55, 163–172.

Jorion, P. (1996) *Risk and Turnover in the Foreign Exchange Market*. In J. A. Frankel, G. Galli, and A. Giovanni (eds), The Microstructure of Foreign Exchange Markets. Chicago: The University of Chicago Press.

König, H. and Gaab, W. (1982) *The Advanced Theory of Statistics*, vol. 2 of *Inference and Relationships*. Haffner.

Koopman, S., Shepard, N. and Doornik, J. (1998) Statistical Algorithms for Models in State Space using SsfPack 2.2. *Econometrics Journal* 1, 1–55.

Lambert, P. and Laurent, S. (2001) Modelling Financial Time Series Using GARCH-Type Models and a Skewed Student Density. Mimeo, Université de Liège.

Lecourt, C. (2000) Dépendance de Court et Long Terme des Rendements de Taux de Change. *Economie et Prévision*, 5, 127–137.

Lee, S. and Hansen, B. (1994) Asymptotic Properties of the Maximum Likelihood Estimator and Test of the Stability of Parameters of the GARCH and IGARCH Models. *Econometric Theory*, 10, 29–52.

Ling, S. and McAleer, M. (2002) Stationarity and the Existence of Moments of a Family of GARCH processes. *Journal of Econometrics*, 106, 109–117.

Lombardi, M. and Gallo, G. (2001) Analytic Hessian Matrices and the Computation of FIGARCH Estimates. Manuscript, Università degli studi di Firenze.

McCullough, B. and Vinod, H. (1999) The Numerical Reliability of Econometric Software. *Journal of Economic Literature*, 37, 633–665.

McLeod, A. and Li, W. (1983) Diagnostic Checking ARMA Time Series Models Using Squared Residuals Autocorrelations. *Journal of Time Series Analysis* 4, 269–273.

Nelson, D. (1991) Conditional Heteroskedasticity in Asset Returns: a New Approach. *Econometrica*, 59, 349–370.

Nelson, D. and Cao, C. (1992) Inequality Constraints in the Univariate GARCH Model. *Journal of Business and Economic Statistics*, 10, 229–235.

Nyblom, J. (1989) Testing for the Constancy of Parameters Over Time. *Journal of the American Statistical Association*, 84, 223–230.

Palm, F. (1996) GARCH Models of Volatility. In G. S. Maddala, C. R. Rao (eds), *Handbook of Statistics* (pp. 209–240).

Palm, F. and Vlaar, P. (1997) Simple Diagnostics Procedures for Modelling Financial Time Series. *Allgemeines Statistisches Archiv*, 81, 85–101.

Peiró, A. (1999) Skewness in Financial Returns. *Journal of Banking and Finance*, 23, 847–862.

Pentula, S. (1986) Modeling the Persistece of Conditional Variances: A Comment. *Econometric Review*, 5, 71–74.

Schwert, W. (1990) Stock Volatility and the Crash of '87. *Review of Financial Studies* 3, 77–102.

Taylor, S. (1986) *Modelling Financial Time Series* Wiley, New York.

Teyssière, G. (1997) Double Long-Memory Financial Time Series. Paper presented at the ESEM, Toulouse.

Timmermann, A. (2000) Density Forecasting in Economics and Finance. *Journal of Forecasting*, 19, 120–123.

Tschernig, R. (1995) Long Memory in Foreign Exchange Rates Revisited. *Journal of International Financial Markets, Institutions and Money*, 5, 53–78.

Tse, Y. (1998) The Conditional Heteroscedasticity of the Yen-Dollar Exchange Rate. *Journal of Applied Econometrics*, 193, 49–55.

Weiss, A. (1986) Asymptotic Theory for ARCH Models: Estimation and Testing. *Econometric Theory*, 2, 107–131.

Zakoian, J.-M. (1994) Threshold Heteroskedasticity Models. *Journal of Economic Dynamics and Control*, 15, 931–955.

INDEX